People of the Watershed

Photographs by John Macfie

Paul Seesequasis

McMichael Figure.1

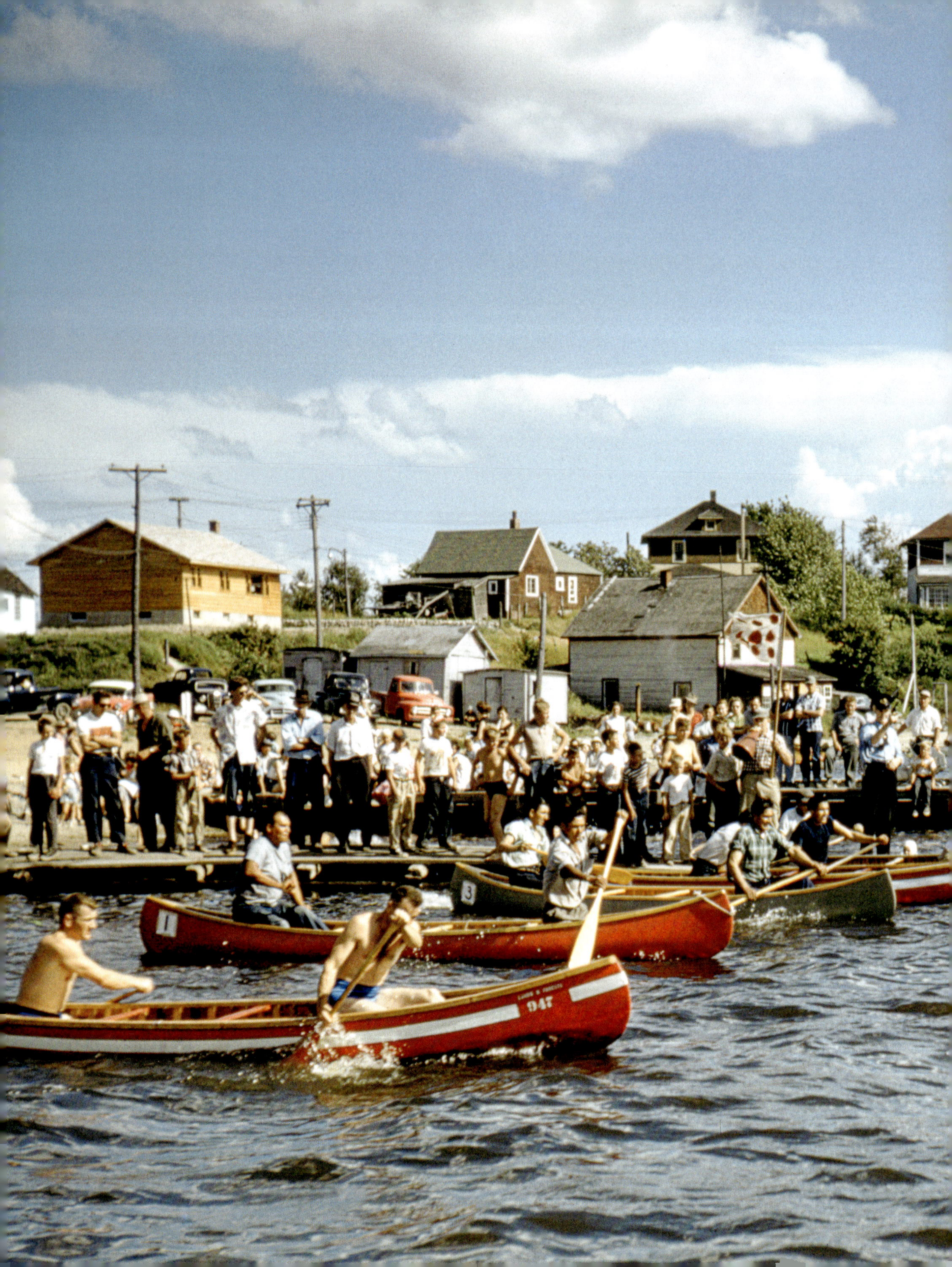

I
3
947

Publication Sponsors
Bryce and Nicki Douglas

Generously supported by
Doug and Ruth Grant
Dragonfly Ventures
Roz and Andy Heintzman
K.M. Hunter Charitable Foundation
Lynwood Foundation
Dennis and Denny Starritt

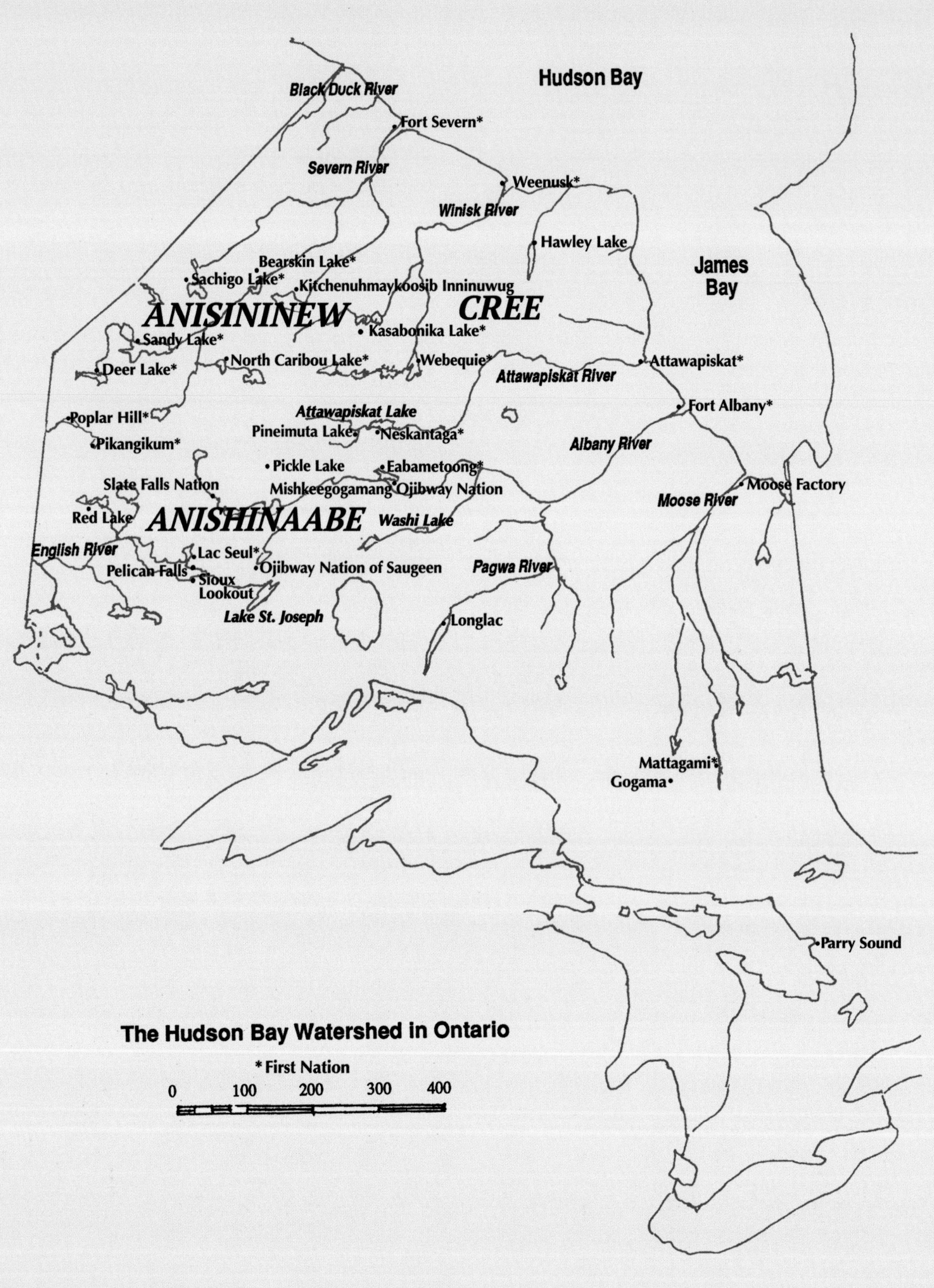

Hudson Bay
Black Duck River
Fort Severn*
Severn River
Weenusk*
Winisk River
Hawley Lake
James Bay
Bearskin Lake*
Sachigo Lake*
Kitchenuhmaykoosib Inninuwug
ANISININEW
CREE
Kasabonika Lake*
Sandy Lake*
North Caribou Lake*
Webequie*
Attawapiskat*
Deer Lake*
Attawapiskat River
Fort Albany*
Poplar Hill*
Attawapiskat Lake
Pineimuta Lake
Neskantaga*
Albany River
Pikangikum*
Pickle Lake
Eabametoong*
Slate Falls Nation
Mishkeegogamang Ojibway Nation
Moose Factory
Moose River
Red Lake
ANISHINAABE
Washi Lake
English River
Lac Seul*
Pelican Falls
Ojibway Nation of Saugeen
Pagwa River
Sioux Lookout
Lake St. Joseph
Longlac
Mattagami*
Gogama
Parry Sound
The Hudson Bay Watershed in Ontario
* First Nation
0
100
200
300
400

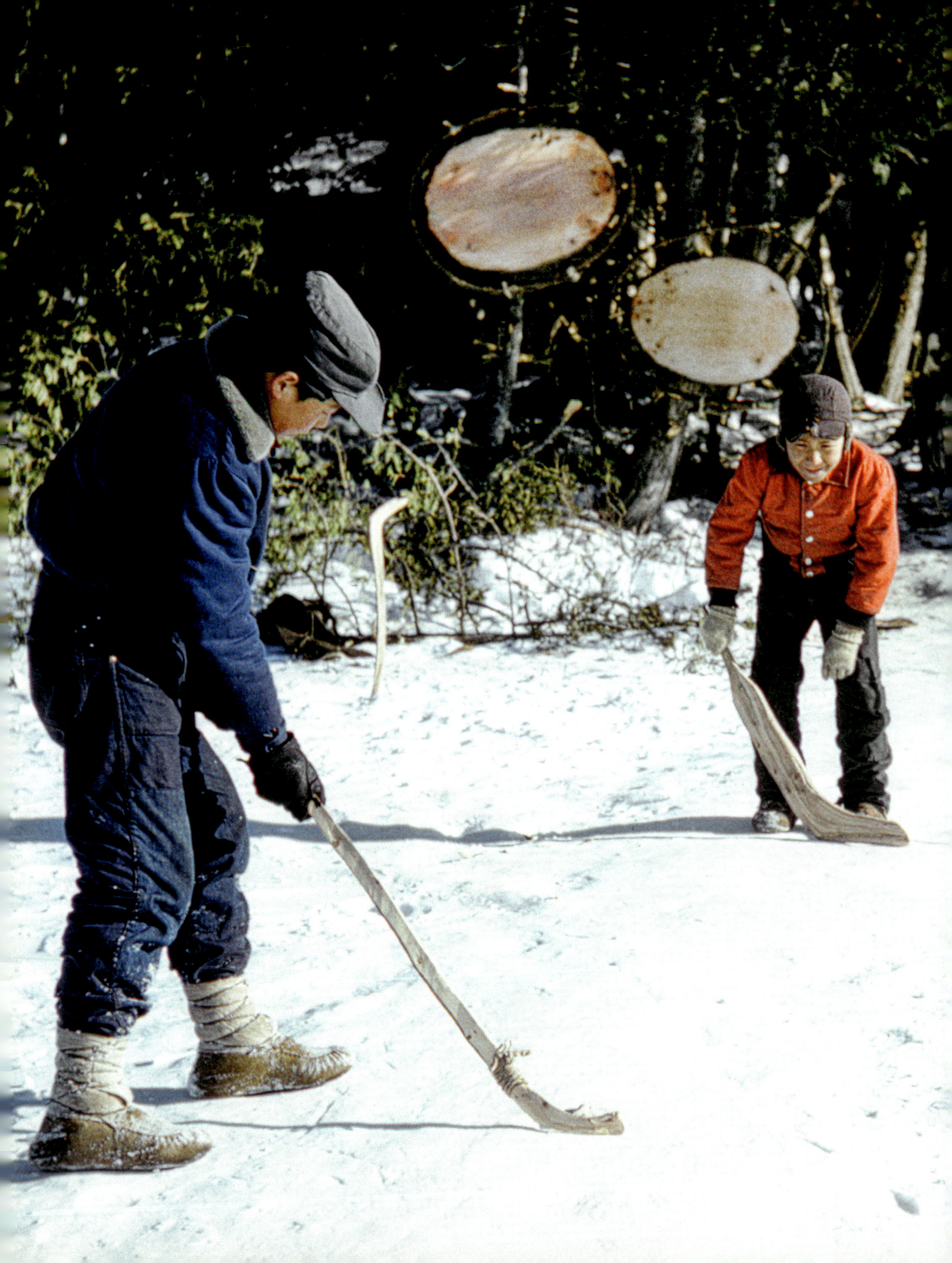

Director's Foreword

I first became aware of the work of the writer, activist, and curator Paul Seesequasis five years ago, when I came across his publication *Blanket Toss Under Midnight Sun* (2019), a photographic testament to the resilience of eight Indigenous communities across North America. Combing through archives and online sources, and examining the work of myriad photographers, Paul found images that bring those places to life.

The front cover of that book says it all: two young Inuit women chatting together and laughing, holding their babies, their clothing warm against a grey sky powdery with clouds and cold. In this photograph by Wilfred Doucette from 1951, one woman wears a tartan blanket, a trade good, while the other is clad in a traditional amauti edged with fur. It's a picture of a culture in transition. The title of the book is borrowed from an image inside. Taken by Steve McCutcheon in Alaska in 1962, it records the playing of an Iñupiat summer game in which participants, each one in turn, are flung high in the air by the snap of a blanket held tight by a circle of friends below. Looking, we too feel that sudden surge of weightlessness, and that joy. This is the magic that Paul brings, making a case for the strength of Indigenous communities: the importance of family ties and friendships, of life lived close to the land and the seasons, of belonging. There is a richness here.

With *People of the Watershed,* Paul returns to these affirming themes, honouring the record left by one photographer, a settler trapline manager named John Macfie (1925–2018), who travelled the Hudson Bay watershed for a dozen years through the 1950s to 1962, camera in hand. Macfie's images persuade us again of the integrity of Indigenous communities in the face of enormous and often traumatic social change. What we see is adaptation—loyalty to tradition but also the embrace of the new—and the ability to find pleasure and connection in ways that are wholly enviable.

My thanks to Paul for trusting us with this project, and for his sensitive and insightful essay in these pages as he walks in Macfie's footsteps, piecing together the lives these photographs record, and rooting out the connections between subjects and their stories in a devoted act of reclamation. Paul's research will no doubt continue in the years to come as he builds on this strong foundation. It has been an honour for all of us at the McMichael to support his good work.

Sarah Milroy
Executive Director and Chief Curator
McMichael Canadian Art Collection

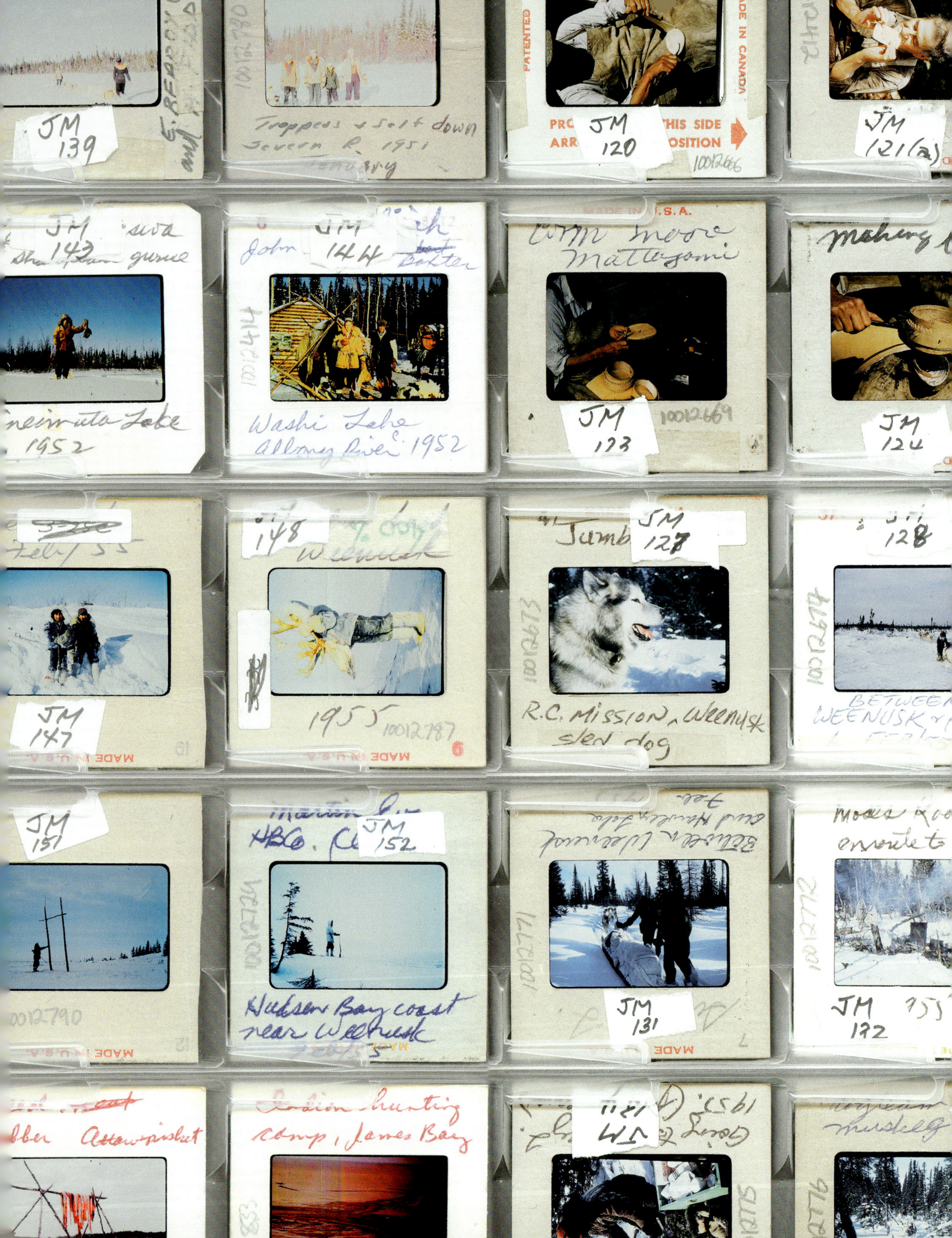

JM 139
Trappers & Sett down
Severn R. 1951
10012780
PATENTED
MADE IN CANADA
JM 120
10012666
JM 121(a)
JM 143
1952
John
JM 144
10012414
Washi Lake
Albany River 1952
Wm Moore
Mattagami
JM 123
10012669
JM 124
JM 147
MADE IN U.S.A.
148
1955
10012787
JM 127
10012673
R.C. Mission, Weenusk
sled dog
128
BETWEEN
WEENUSK
JM 151
10012790
MADE IN U.S.A.
HBC.
JM 152
10012724
Hudson Bay coast
near Weenusk
10012771
JM 131
JM 132
Indian hunting
camp, James Bay

People of the Watershed

Paul Seesequasis

In the mid-1950s, John Macfie was a young trap management officer with the Ontario Department of Lands and Forests (now the Ministry of Northern Development, Mines, Natural Resources and Forestry). It was his responsibility to meet with Indigenous trappers, collect data on harvests, introduce and explain the latest conservation practices (these changed seasonally with fluctuations in animal populations) and tally quota limits on furs such as mink, muskrat, and beaver. Macfie's work involved travelling across a vast area of Northern Ontario, meeting and photographing Indigenous trappers at their traplines and in their villages. He was also a working journalist, and he found the communities of the Hudson Bay watershed to be a rich source of stories. From 1950 to 1962, he travelled the region, camera in hand, making careful notations in his journals, and bearing witness to a time of many transitions for the various Cree, Anishinaabe, and Anisininew communities in the vast watershed area. His encounters are recorded in this volume, from Sandy Lake near the border with Manitoba, to Fort Severn on the shore of Hudson Bay, to Moose Factory near the border with Quebec, and finally as far south as Mattagami.

In the summer of 1956, five years into his time as a trapline manager, Macfie heard of an Anishinaabe woman who lived off the land and who visited the closest town, Osnaburgh (now Mishkeegogamang First Nation), only once a month to pick up supplies, such as tools and canned goods, and her old age pension. As in so many other Northern Ontario villages at the time, the Hudson's Bay Company outlet served not only as the store but also as the post office, bank, community meeting place, and medical clinic.

The story of this "woman of the land" intrigued Macfie. He packed up his Zeiss Contax camera and, timing it right, walked to Lake St. Joseph and waited. It was not too long before he saw a woman and a child paddling toward the shore in a canoe (below). Macfie waved, standing on the shoreline. The woman's name was Maria Mikenak. She was likely in her mid- to late sixties and lived a nearly self-sufficient life in the bush, sustaining herself and her family on fish, berries, manomim (wild rice), potatoes, rabbits, and birds. Travelling with her that day was her grandson. Mikenak spoke only Anishinaabe, with a sprinkling of English words, while Macfie spoke English and a bit of Cree, so they communicated mostly through hand gestures.

Macfie was impressed by her canoe. "At that time few people were making canoes out of birchbark anymore," he later explained to me. "They were mostly all replaced by commercially made canoes which the HBC sold across the North." Mikenak's birchbark canoe, on the other hand, was of her own making, as was her spruce paddle, and she did her own patchwork and repairs as needed. "I noticed one spot where she had repaired a tear with a wire nail or two and some cotton twine." In the bush, necessity is truly the mother of invention.

I came across Macfie's photographs of Maria Mikenak and her grandson more than sixty years after they were taken, while researching images of the North at the Archives of Ontario in Toronto. Macfie shot an entire roll of film of her paddling, setting up camp by the shore, and starting a fire. He also took close-ups of her canoe. The images captivated me, and I wondered about the photographer, assuming that after all this time he would be deceased. I looked him up, and to my pleasant surprise found that he was still alive, in his nineties, and retired in Parry Sound, Ontario.

Macfie was active on Facebook, so I got in touch and we began a regular correspondence. As I delved deeper into his portfolio of Northern Ontario photographs and heard his stories, I realized that there was something more here than just compelling snapshots; this was a thematically integrated oeuvre, a visual narrative chronicling a decade in the lives of the Indigenous people and

OPPOSITE
One of John Macfie's slide sheets, with his notations

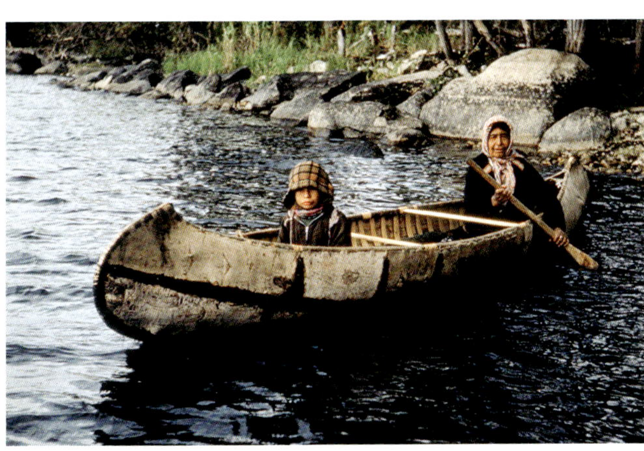

RIGHT
Maria Mikenak and her grandson in a birchbark canoe she made, Lake St. Joseph, Kenora and Thunder Bay Districts 1956

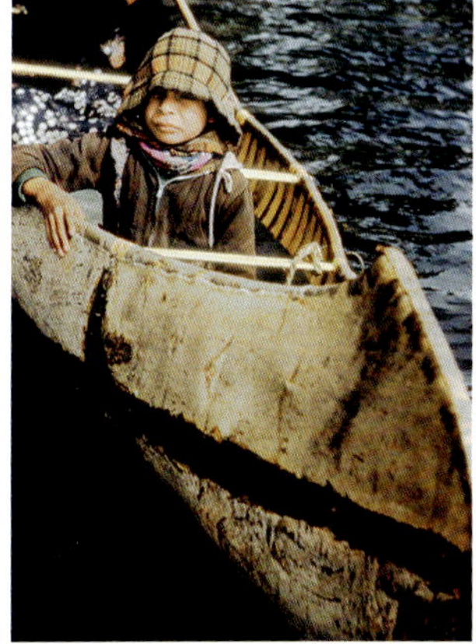

Maria Mikenak's grandson, Lake St. Joseph 1956

communities across the vast territory of the Hudson Bay watershed. As well, it is a testament to a way of life that was about to radically change.

These were the last years of snowshoes, dog teams, canoes, and sleds for travel. In the mid-1950s, snowmobiles had not yet become common, and traplines were still maintained and passed down through families as they had been for generations. The traditional, seasonally nomadic old ways were still the norm. But change was happening at every level. Even at the time these images were taken, outboard motors were increasingly used to power the square-stern canoes, and bush planes had become essential for transport. The watershed area comprises some 324,000 square kilometres—an area the size of France—covering Treaties 9, 3, and 5 and extending from the Canadian Shield to muskeg and then to tundra. For reaching the less accessible locations, the Department of Lands and Forests operated a fleet of close to fifty Otter, Beaver, and Norseman aircraft, with the central airport at Sioux Lookout and smaller bases at Red Lake, Armstrong, and Pickle Lake, Ontario.

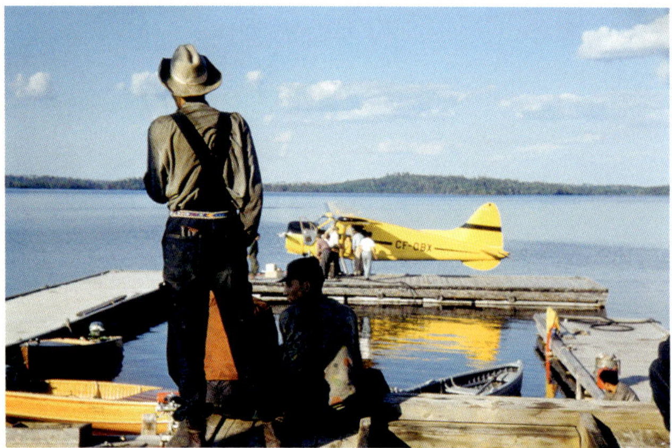

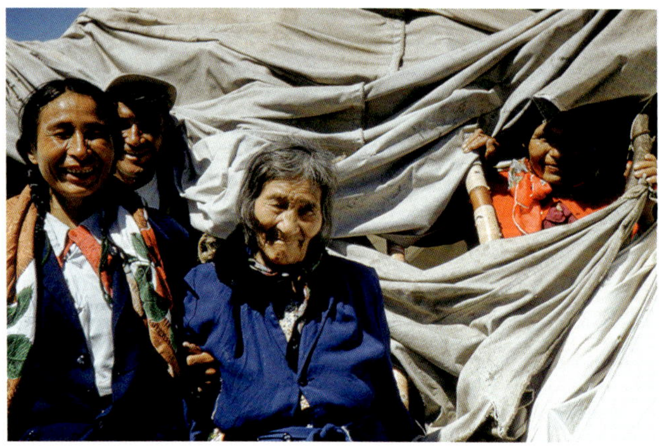

Watching distant forest fires at Red Lake, Kenora District 1956

The Suganaqueb family at Neskantaga for Treaty Time; the women are Matilda Suganaqueb, a midwife, and Nancy Suganaqueb, a medicine woman c. 1955

The path that had led John Alvin Macfie to these people and places was a circuitous one. He was born in 1925 on his family's farm in Dunchurch, Ontario, near Parry Sound, one of Edith and Roy Macfie's seven children. Options were limited for a boy growing up in rural Ontario in the 1930s, Macfie recalled. He could stay on the farm and try to make a life or "go to the bush" as a lumberjack. He would probably have been inclined to choose the latter; however, in 1939, the Second World War intervened. Macfie, by the time he reached eighteen in 1943, had decided to become a pilot and enlisted in the Royal Canadian Air Force. "I only had a Grade 10 education, putting me at a disadvantage," Macfie later commented, "which I was acutely aware of. An inferiority complex, coming from the farm, with all these slick city boys."

Macfie completed his training in Toronto and Windsor and was in western Canada, preparing to join a bomber squadron in the Pacific theatre, when Japan unconditionally surrendered and the war ended. He returned to the Parry Sound region and, at a loss to know what to do next, tried his hand at various things, including typing, which he hated—but it was a skill that would serve him well later as a writer.

In 1950, Macfie applied for and won a job competition in the Department of Lands and Forests. He became one of two trap management officers and moved to Sioux Lookout. With this change of scene, he gained a sense of vocation and new purpose. Responsible for a huge swath of territory, Macfie travelled Northwestern Ontario, working in many Indigenous communities, meeting many Indigenous trappers, and getting to know the land. On arrival in a community, he would usually unpack his bedroll and sleep at the home of the local HBC representative; there were no hotels or fishing lodges at the time. The next day, equipped with his Rolleicord for black-and-white photography, and his Zeiss Contax for 35 mm colour slides, he would set out to visit traplines across the immensity of Northwestern Ontario, travelling by boat, bush plane or dogsled, depending on the season.

In 1954, Macfie met and married Joan Ramsay, who joined him in the North, though not on his travels. The couple had three children, Robert, Elizabeth, and Ian. After leaving Sioux Lookout, the Macfie family moved, first to Gogama and then to the Parry Sound area, where their children grew up and where Macfie finished his career as Fish and Wildlife supervisor for the region.

When Macfie was growing up, his mother, who was a teacher, had enjoyed taking photographs, and that no doubt helped inspire him to take his journals and cameras with him on his travels, likely giving him the idea of creating "photo stories" of his adventures and the people he encountered. Macfie's natural curiosity about people, his unassuming attitude, and his increasing familiarity with the land came together to create a sense of closeness between camera and subject that was neither contrived nor romantic. It allowed him to frame his subjects in the viewfinder and adjust the focus only enough to bring a clarity that seems straightforward but is in fact very subtle, imbuing his photography with a casual, intimate quality.

One day at Weagamow First Nation in the District of Kenora, Macfie encountered an Anisininew girl by a smoke lodge where she had been smoking a moosehide,[1] and his photographs of her embody this sensitive approach. Macfie took both colour slides and black-and-white photographs that day, inside and outside the lodge. There is a dreamlike quality to many of these images. In one, the girl stands inside the lodge before the hanging hides, the fire crackling near her and her eyes closed as the smoke fills the lodge. Macfie was drawn to people like her, those who were immersed in ancestral knowledge and practices. Although he kept detailed records, some of his notebooks have been mislaid over the years; the Anisininew girl's name is not recorded in Macfie's surviving journals and may now be lost to history.

Not so William Moore, the subject of dozens of Macfie's photographs (upper left). Moore was Cree—originally from Moose Factory, Ontario—and later lived in Mattagami, Ontario. He was exactly what the photographer was seeking: old-timers who were still around, still active, and possessed of encyclopedic knowledge of the "old ways." Through Macfie's photographs and journals we get a picture of this self-sufficient and talented man with a lifetime of experience of the land. William Moore crafted wooden bow drills for making fires, carved spruce paddles and ladles, wove intricate birchbark baskets and, on the artistic side, did birchbark biting[2] and made games such as nabahon,[3] a challenging ring and pin game of eye and hand coordination.

One of the common effects of the outsider's gaze in photography is the disassociation of images from the subjects themselves: the framing and interpretation lie solely in the hands of the photographer. As a result, beginning in the days of the daguerreotype in the 1830s and 1840s and continuing into the 1950s and beyond, Indigenous people have often been represented as disappearing victims of manifest destiny. Inevitably, such stereotyping erases the subject's story and individuality as a human being. Macfie, however, was not a mere outsider. He had personal relationships to varying degrees with his subjects as part of his job, and he recorded their stories in his journals in a non-nostalgic manner. His engagement adds an important narrative layer to his photographs. It gives them story. It gives them context.

"I went with Moore on a material-gathering expedition one day," Macfie recalled, "collecting birchbark and assorted wood

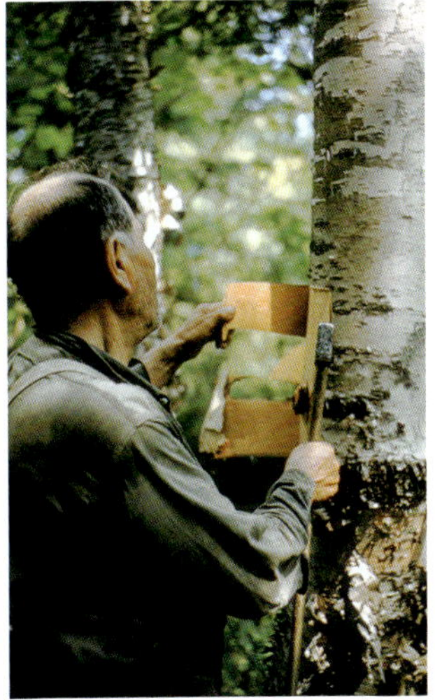

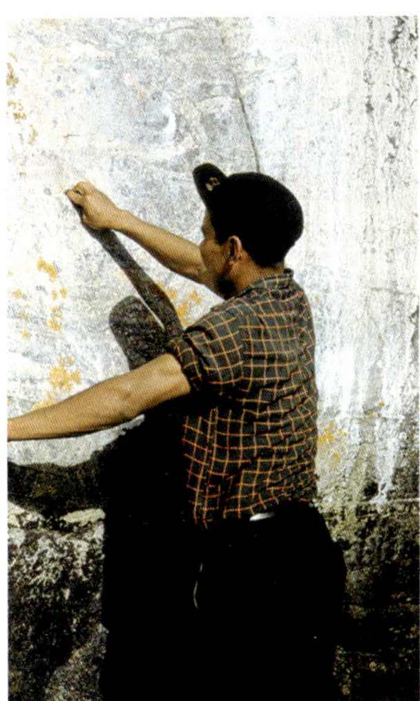

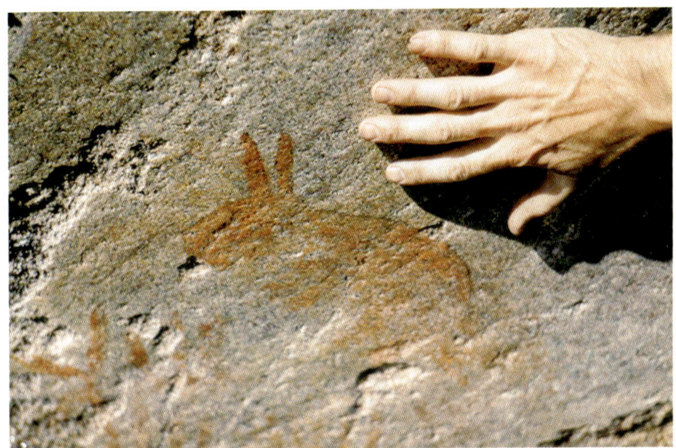

William Moore of Mattagami First Nation checking the condition of birchbark on a tree before deciding whether to harvest it 1958

Albert Carpenter offering tobacco at a pictograph site, Carling Lake, Kenora District 1954

Rabbit pictograph at Deer Lake, Kenora District June 1956

to make spoons and spruce roots to sew baskets with." Birchbark is best harvested in June, Moore told him, at the height of the tree's period of new growth, but not every tree yields usable bark. With his expert eye, honed from years of observation and trial, Moore could quickly identify which tree was exactly right for his needs. He also knew which plants were used for medicines and when to harvest them. Moore was familiar with pictograph sites; he knew their locations and the stories associated with them. He showed Macfie the caves on rock facings, "small doorways in the cliffs," as Macfie writes, "where the mischievous mamakwayseeuk, the little people, lived." Some locals would avoid these locations. Others left offerings of tobacco.

One of Macfie's early trips, in 1951, led him to what is now Deer Lake First Nation, close to the Manitoba border. There he met Chief Tom Fiddler, who in Macfie's estimation was a chief of the old school, meaning that the Indian Act and its band council system had little influence with him or his people. The church, too, held less sway there; the Mide (Midewiwin), or Grand Medicine Society,[4] and its ways were still strong. Other old beliefs persisted. Unlike other communities, here it was the chief who called the local regional trappers' meeting, not Macfie or any other department official, and it was done on "community time," not on the government's schedule. Macfie knew enough to be patient. When the regional trappers' meeting did take place at Deer Lake, the tone was set by the chief with a lengthy oration in Anisininew and, though Macfie knew Fiddler had a proficient command of English, the proceedings were always conducted through interpreters. Later, in the spring of 1952, Macfie was invited by the chief to the spring Wabano ceremony. (Waaban means "dawn," or the east, and the ceremony celebrates the year's beginning.) This was not an invitation commonly extended to outsiders.

"When I arrived on the scene at about dusk," Macfie later recalled, "the hundred or more men, women, and children had just finished eating. Chief Fiddler then took up a position before a water drum, consisting of a metal nail keg over whose open end a piece of wetted, tanned moosehide was tightly stretched. I had listened to the bewitching deep booming of this instrument the night before, from the Hudson's Bay compound a good two kilometres away." Macfie was permitted to take some pictures during the ceremony. Several show Tom Fiddler beating a drum before a decorated shrub inside the lodge; another, taken by someone else, shows Macfie respectfully placing tobacco in the stone pipe bowl of Councillor Francis Meekis (below), while smiling men queue for their turn and several young boys look on, their faces expressing a sense of excitement and anticipation about the spring to come.

The change of seasons was marked not just by the melting snows, longer days and thawing ice, but by people on the move, coming together. One such family was the Suganaqueb family from Webequie First Nation, north of Thunder Bay in the District of Kenora, whom Macfie photographed in the spring of 1956. They had just arrived, having travelled more than a hundred kilometres by canoe to join dozens of other families at Lansdowne House (now Neskantaga First Nation), on the shore of Attawapiskat Lake, for one of the biggest events of the spring: Treaty Time.[5] Government treaty representatives visited all the larger settlements in Treaty 9 territory, and families in outlying communities would journey to the treaty gatherings. White canvas tents, similar to the one behind the Suganaquebs in the photograph, popped up all around Neskantaga, creating a temporary treaty town. In Macfie's words, "a little canvas colony of people from Webequie sprang up each spring. I went there and took many pictures that day. I also did my requisite trappers' meeting for the area at the same time."

In addition to the ceremony, there were speeches by various chiefs. The Indian Agent and a Mountie in red serge also attended,

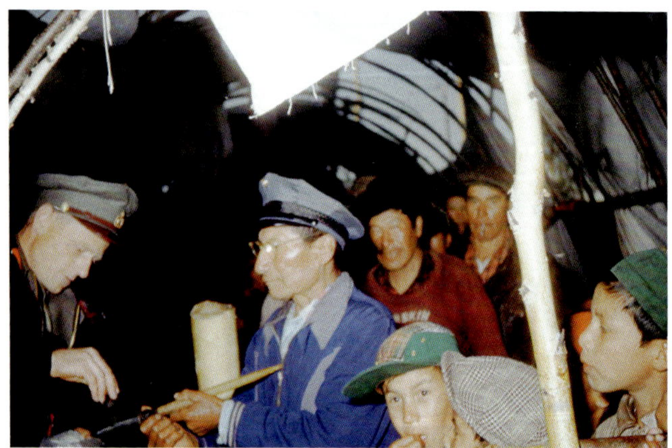

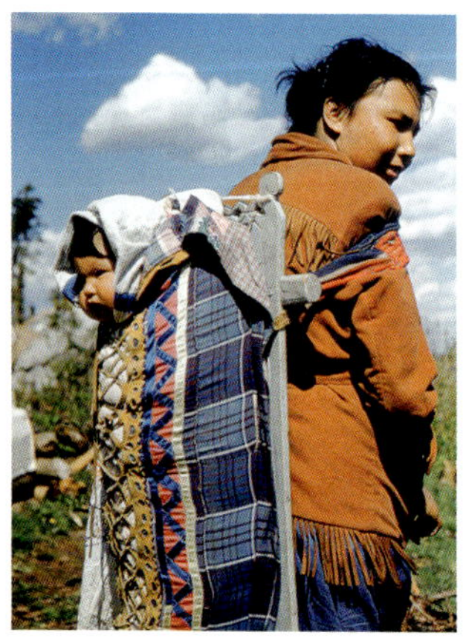

John Macfie offering tobacco for Francis Meekis's pipe 1952

A woman with her baby in a tikinagan, Sandy Lake 1956

representing the federal government; the annual treaty payment of four dollars was received by each Treaty 9 adult.[6] It was an occasion for families and friends who often hadn't seen each other since the winter freeze-up to reconnect and share stories. There was a square dance at Neskantaga, with local fiddlers and guitar players providing the Scottish-inspired music. On the more serious side, attendees could have a check-up with a doctor, and there was an X-ray machine on hand.[7]

Many of Macfie's photographs of families with their infants in tikinagans capture the celebratory essence of these days. The familiar blue Royal Canadian Air Force tartan is also evident in some photographs, the material having been purchased from the local HBC store and used in the making of skirts, shawls, and as in the picture on the opposite page, the outer wrapping of the infant's bundle. This tikinagan also sports a net made of white muslin that could be unrolled to protect the baby from deerflies, horseflies, and the ubiquitous mosquitoes.

Along the shallow, unprotected shore of Hudson Bay, the boreal forest and muskeg give way to tundra and windswept beaches. Here, both wind and tide must be respected. Macfie heard cautionary stories, passed on by travellers, of people who had perished far out in the bay at low tide when their canoes became stuck in the deep mud and could not be refloated as a storm tide rushed over them.

Philip "Swampy" Mathew was a trapper, hunter, and guide who became a travelling companion of Macfie's and a frequent subject of his photographs. Macfie recounted how Mathew had once walked the Hudson Bay shoreline on foot, all the way from Fort Severn to York Factory, to play his fiddle at the Treaty Time dances. Up there, wood was scarce and was often floated for kilometres up the Severn River. The wind-driven currents of the bay also provided rare resources; boats that had been beached or wrecked sometimes washed ashore in pieces. With some hard work, the iron could be salvaged and used to make tools such as anvils or hammers. On one trip, Macfie and Mathew came across a large white birch log, which had presumably escaped from a beaver dam far inland and floated up to the bay. In one photo Mathew stands by the birch in his waders. It would soon be added to their precious cargo, with Mathew telling Macfie it was meewasin ("good" in Cree) for making sturdy axe handles.

The ingenuity to make what you needed from what was available was not a skill confined to the tundra or the treeless subarctic. At Moose Factory, at the southern end of James Bay, Macfie photographed brothers Charlie and Norman Echum playing hockey in the winter of 1956. This was and remains a common winter pastime across Canada, but these images reveal some Moose Factory specifics: both the hockey sticks and the goalie stick are hand carved from saplings, the puck is a stone, and the goalposts are two sticks. Behind the boys, hanging from the stunted trees, a half dozen stretched beaver pelts are suspended to be cured by the wind and frost.

There has never been a factory at Moose Factory. The name of the predominantly Cree community comes from the word "factor," the term for a retail agent representing the Hudson's Bay Company during the fur trade. Established in 1673, Moose Factory is also the second oldest HBC post in what is now Canada, after Fort Rupert. The Cree were quick to recognize the opportunities the post gave them as they began to expand their monopoly along the many rivers of the watershed. But the post's success also led to its demise, when in 1686 a small contingent of French soldiers, with their Algonquin allies, captured Moose Fort and renamed it Fort St. Louis. French control was short-lived, however; in 1696 a British fleet arrived and the fort was burned to the

Philip "Swampy" Mathew 1963

Men on the steps of the Hudson's Bay Company store in Sandy Lake 1955

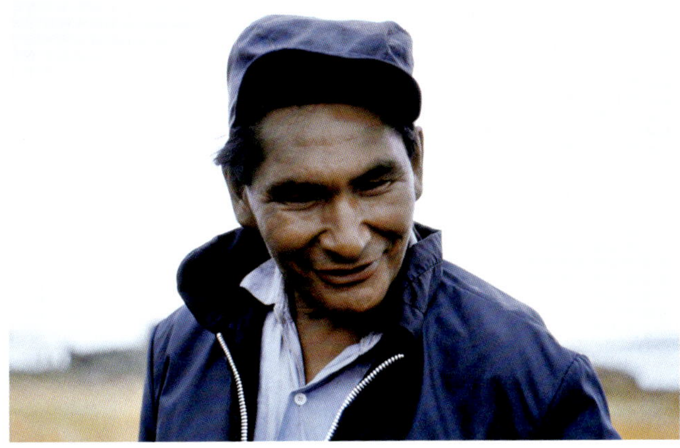

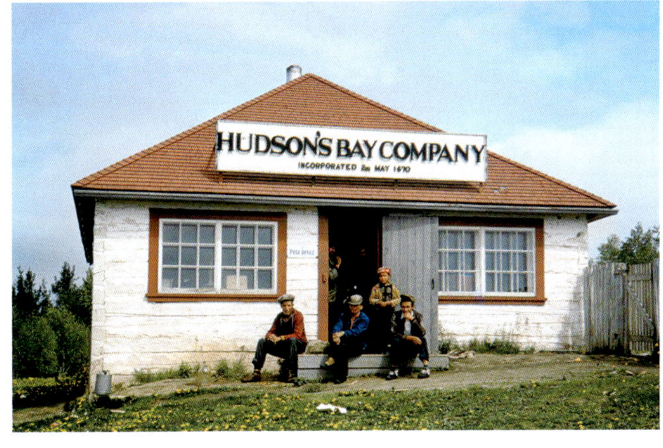

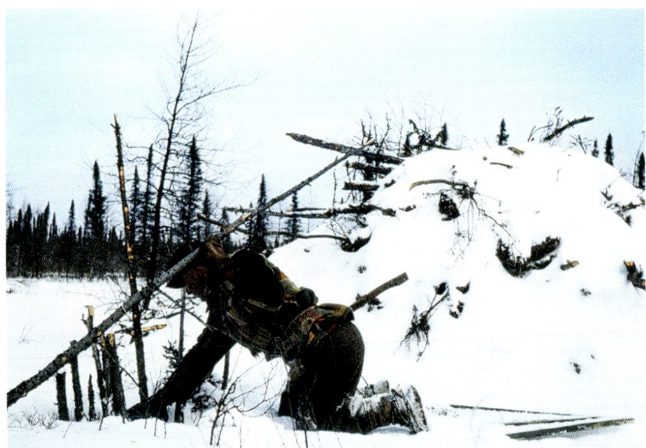

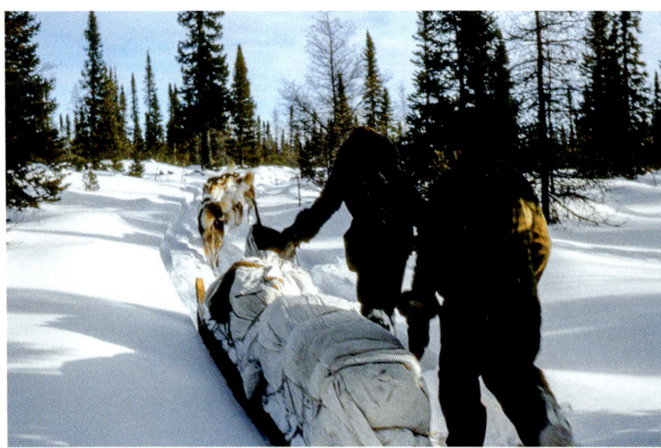

George Baxter checking a snare on his trapline at Washi Lake December 1951

Moses Koostachin and Father Gagnon travelling between Weenusk and Hawley Lake February 1955

ground. Its exact location remains unknown to this day. The HBC built a new fort at a different site nearby, and by the mid-1700s the threat of the French and Algonquins had waned, and an HBC hegemony was established that would continue for generations.

During John Macfie's decade as a field man for the department, the mainstays of the fur industry in Ontario were beaver, muskrat, mink, and otter. Lynx, fox, wolf, and marten were also trapped; they were more lucrative, but rarer. The trapping season began around the middle of November, after the first snows fell, and continued through the early winter, when mink were at their best. Beaver became prime later in the winter, while muskrat were trapped in the early spring. It was the trappers' responsibility to maintain their own lines, respect others, count and note the number and locations of beaver lodges, and follow the quotas. Macfie, as the government's agent, visited them on their traplines, travelled with them, kept records, and took photographs. He was also occasionally tasked with hearing and responding to territorial disputes between trappers. At the time of these photographs, before the rise of the animal rights movement in Europe and urban North America, the fur trade was the principal occupation for families in the vastness of the watershed. It was not simply a vocation. It was a way of life.

A photograph Macfie took of Deer Lake, near the Manitoba border, in the spring of 1953 shows a group of trappers going over the winter's tally and completing all the other paperwork that marked the end of the hunting season. The image shows most of the trappers in the then-ubiquitous flat cap (or newsboy cap) that was the fashion in town.

The land itself is both awe-inspiring and unforgiving. The knowledge that the men and women who worked the traplines depended on had been passed down from generation to generation. There was no GPS at the time these photographs were taken. There was no 911 emergency call system. If an accident occurred, or a medical condition arose, the nearest help could be days away. Macfie told me the story of George Metatawabin who, suffering from serious lacerations, was able to amputate his own leg at the knee with his knife. He was two hundred kilometres up the Albany River, far from the nearest hospital or medical assistance. He stayed alone in his cabin while the wound healed, and resumed trapping as soon as he could, using makeshift crutches he had fashioned from snowshoes. Of course, for every Metatawabin wilderness story of survival, there were many more who did not make it out alive or who were never seen again.

Traditional knowledge of the land was transmitted orally. Everything from reading the clouds and the sunsets to the type of moccasin one should wear for different activities had been tried and tested. Moccasins of dry-tanned leather, with an inner boot of rabbit skin, were best for snowshoeing; others were good for cold weather but not for the thaw, when they could become soaked and unwearable. The days of the "canoe brigades" had disappeared with the advent of air and rail, but they were still within living memory. On the journey from Fort Severn to Big Trout Lake, an eight-hundred-kilometre round trip, crews of men would travel five to a canoe carrying heavy cargo such as loads of flour, with each bag weighing forty-five kilograms.

Dogs were also essential work companions in the time before snowmobiles and all-terrain vehicles. Macfie's dog team images coincide with their swan song. In wooded terrain, the dogs were hitched in tandem to follow the trail, while in open snow-covered muskeg or tundra each dog had its own trace and the team could fan out as they pulled. Keeping the dogs healthy and properly fed was a first priority for any traveller embarking on a winter trek.

Macfie understood from the beginning of his time in the watershed region that this way of life was passing into history, and this realization inspired him to capture it in photographs—to make a record not just of the way things were done but, importantly, the people who did them. The longevity of this extended project, a full decade, is also remarkable. That and his sense of vocation created a connection to his subjects that would not have been possible were he just an outsider passing through. After a time, people knew who he was. He developed friendships. Macfie was interested in everything, and was always curious to know more about the people he met.

People of the Watershed is the first exhibition focused on Macfie's photographs. Seen together, they form an ambitious, wide-ranging visual account of the people, the lands, and the life of the watershed. Yet there is an intimacy here. This is the product of an attachment built over time: it feels less like an investigation and more like immersion, as if the photographer were trying to explore not only the community but also his own sense of belonging. "I do not propose to depict a time that is either better or worse than any other," Macfie writes with a typical lack of sentimentality. "The collection simply represents one moment in the continuing evolution of the lifestyle of the northern Algonquians of this region."[8]

One might call Macfie a journalist of the people. He had no wish to write about politicians or the powerful, but rather about working people and the land that shaped their lives. After a decade in the northwest of the province, the Macfies finally settled in Parry Sound. Macfie wrote popular columns for the Georgian Bay *Beacon* and the Parry Sound *North Star*. "Wherever John went, whether working with First Nations in Northwestern Ontario or with people here in Parry Sound, he not only listened, he specifically engaged people and sought their stories," his friend Andy Houser recalled.[9]

In the later years of his life, Macfie remained active in the community and also took up painting. In addition to his columns and activities in Parry Sound, he wrote thirteen books, including *Hudson Bay Watershed: A Photographic Memoir of the Ojibway, Cree and Oji-Cree,* in collaboration with the Anishinaabe writer Basil Johnston. Several photographs from that book are included in this exhibition. Eventually, Macfie gave his collection of prints and negatives, over twelve hundred of them, to the Archives of Ontario for posterity.

In spring 2017, the Anishinaabe artist Rebecca Belmore contacted me regarding Macfie. She hoped to get his permission to use a photograph he had taken at Pelican Falls, north of Thunder Bay, in 1955. The picture shows seven Indigenous boys, all identically dressed in coveralls and with shorn hair. They are perched on a large rock looking away from the camera at a white man, whom we can see fishing on the shoreline in the near distance. The boys are from the Pelican Falls Indian Residential School,[10] and most, if not all, are probably a long way from home. The residential school was open from 1928 through 1969, and has since been demolished, but lawsuits and testimony about abuse at the school remain part of its legacy.

It is a haunting, sobering image and it adds a poignant layer of unspoken narrative to the affirmative ones the photographer is known for. I put Belmore in touch with Macfie, who did give his permission for her to use his pictures. He also surprised her by telling her that he had known her father, whom he greatly respected for his knowledge of the land. The Pelican Falls photo inspired Belmore to travel to the residential school site with fellow artists Florene Belmore and Scott Benesiinaabandan. Her installation piece, *At Pelican Falls,* 2017, was created after that visit. It was first shown in September 2017 at the Platform Centre for Photographic and Digital Arts in Winnipeg, one of the most historically specific works in her remarkable oeuvre. About a year later, Macfie passed away peacefully in Parry Sound at the age of ninety-three.

Notes

1. The smoking of the hide has a creosote effect, making it soft and flexible, an ideal leather for clothing.

2. Birchbark biting is a traditional Cree art done by carefully separating thin pieces of birchbark, then folding the bark many times. Once the bark is folded, artists place it between their teeth and, with the desired image in mind, bite down on the bark and rotate the piece to create the artwork. At the time, birchbark biting was a dying art, with few remaining practitioners such as William Moore and Angela Merasty in Saskatchewan. It has since undergone a revival with a new generation of artists such as Kelly Church and Pat Bruderer.

3. Nabahon is a game requiring skill, patience, and practice. With Moore's nabahon, the rings are made of the knucklebones of a moose's cloven hoof. A small hole is drilled through the five pieces, which are then strung on a piece of tanned moosehide and finished with a pin. The goal is to swing the five rings upward and skewer as many rings as possible while they are airborne.

4. The Mide is a spiritual society found primarily among the Algonquians of the Upper Great Lakes region. Once widespread, the Midewiwin was suppressed by the church after the arrival of Europeans in the eighteenth and nineteenth centuries but survived by going "underground," which has led to it being erroneously called a secret society by outsiders. Today, the largest Mide Societies are found in parts of Ontario, Manitoba, Wisconsin, and Minnesota.

5. While Treaty Time was and is a time of gathering, it was predated by spring gatherings that took place every year, long before there were HBC posts or treaties.

6. The James Bay Treaty (Treaty 9) was one of the last numbered treaties signed in Canada, in 1905 and 1906, and the only treaty also signed by a province, in this case Ontario. To this day, there is little agreement among the treaty partners as to the rights entailed by Treaty 9, and dispute resolutions have gone to the courts.

7. At this time, in the 1950s, tuberculosis was still rampant in the North.

8. John Macfie, *Hudson Bay Watershed: A Photographic Memoir of the Ojibway, Cree and Oji-Cree* (Toronto: Dundurn, 1991).

9. Parry Sound *North Star*, 2018.

10. The Pelican Falls Residential School was opened near Sioux Lookout, Ontario, in 1926 and was operated by the Anglican Church of Canada. The students came from Anishinaabe, Cree, and Anisininew communities, and as in other residential schools, boys and girls were segregated. Students spent half their time in the classroom, and the boys worked on the school's farm operation for the other half of the day (the school was expected to be self-supporting), while the girls did domestic tasks such as laundry and cooking. Severe crowding, particularly in the 1930s and 1940s, led to outbreaks of tuberculosis and other infectious diseases.
At the time of Macfie's photographs, changes were being introduced, including team sports. The Pelican Falls midget hockey team, the Black Hawks, took part in the District Bantam League, and in 1951 toured to Ottawa and Toronto. In 1978, the Pelican Falls school was demolished, the Northern Nishnawbe Education Council was given control over education, and the Pelican Falls First Nations High School was built on the site. The school was initially welcomed by Cree parents in the area who wanted their children to have the opportunities afforded by a formal education. Like Pelican Falls, Bishop Horden Memorial School on Moose Factory Island, at the southern end of James Bay, suffered from overcrowding and cases of abuse, prompting some Cree families to move to Moose Factory, off the island itself, and enroll their children in the day school there. This was happening at the time of Macfie's visits to the area. More information on the history of both schools can be found at the National Centre for Truth and Reconciliation at the University of Manitoba in Winnipeg.

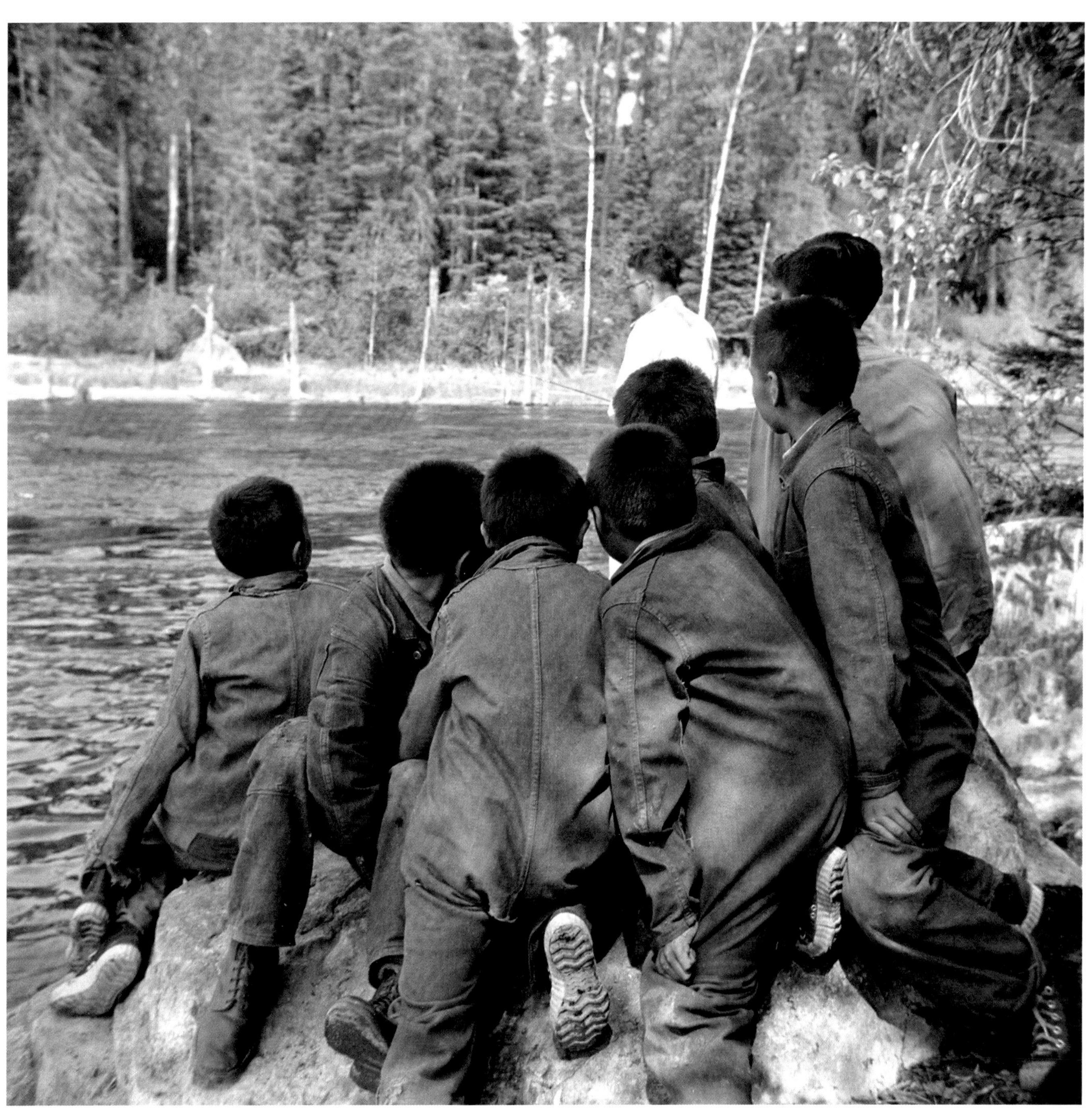

Students of Pelican Falls Indian Residential School near Sioux Lookout, watching a man trout fishing 1955

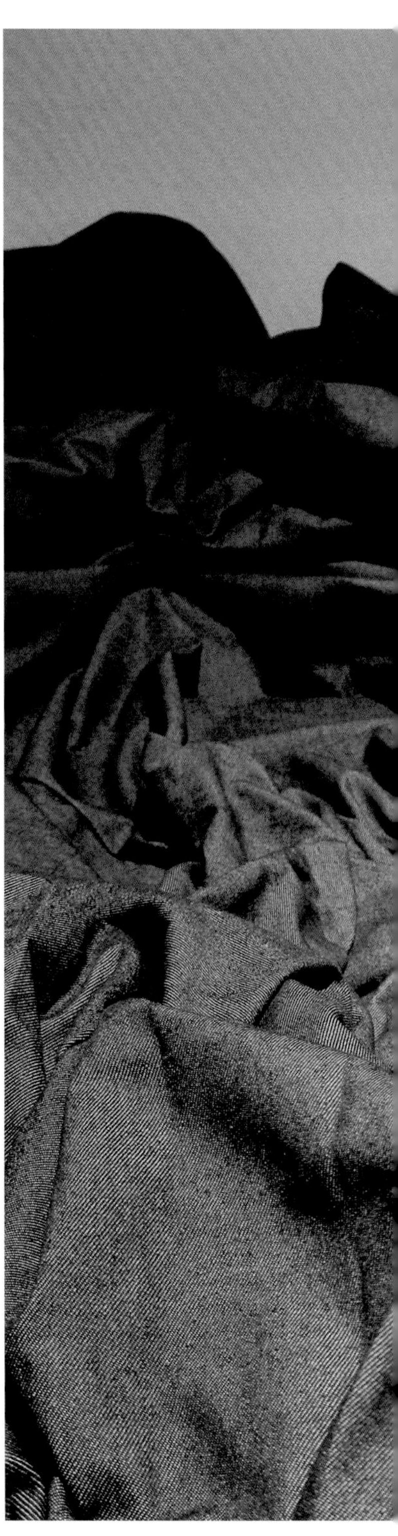

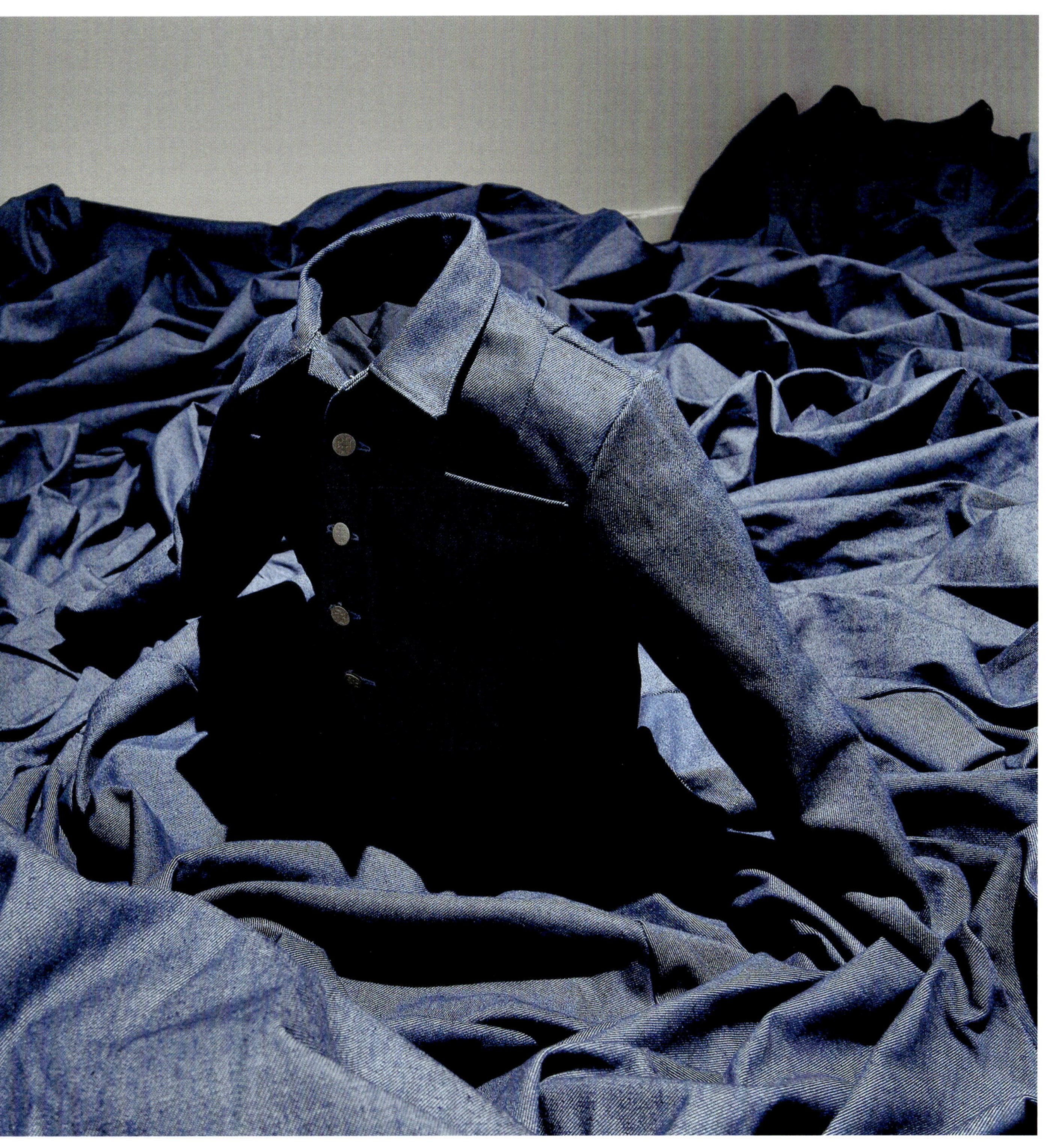

Installation view of Rebecca Belmore's *At Pelican Falls* 2017
Platform Centre for Photographic and Digital Arts, Winnipeg

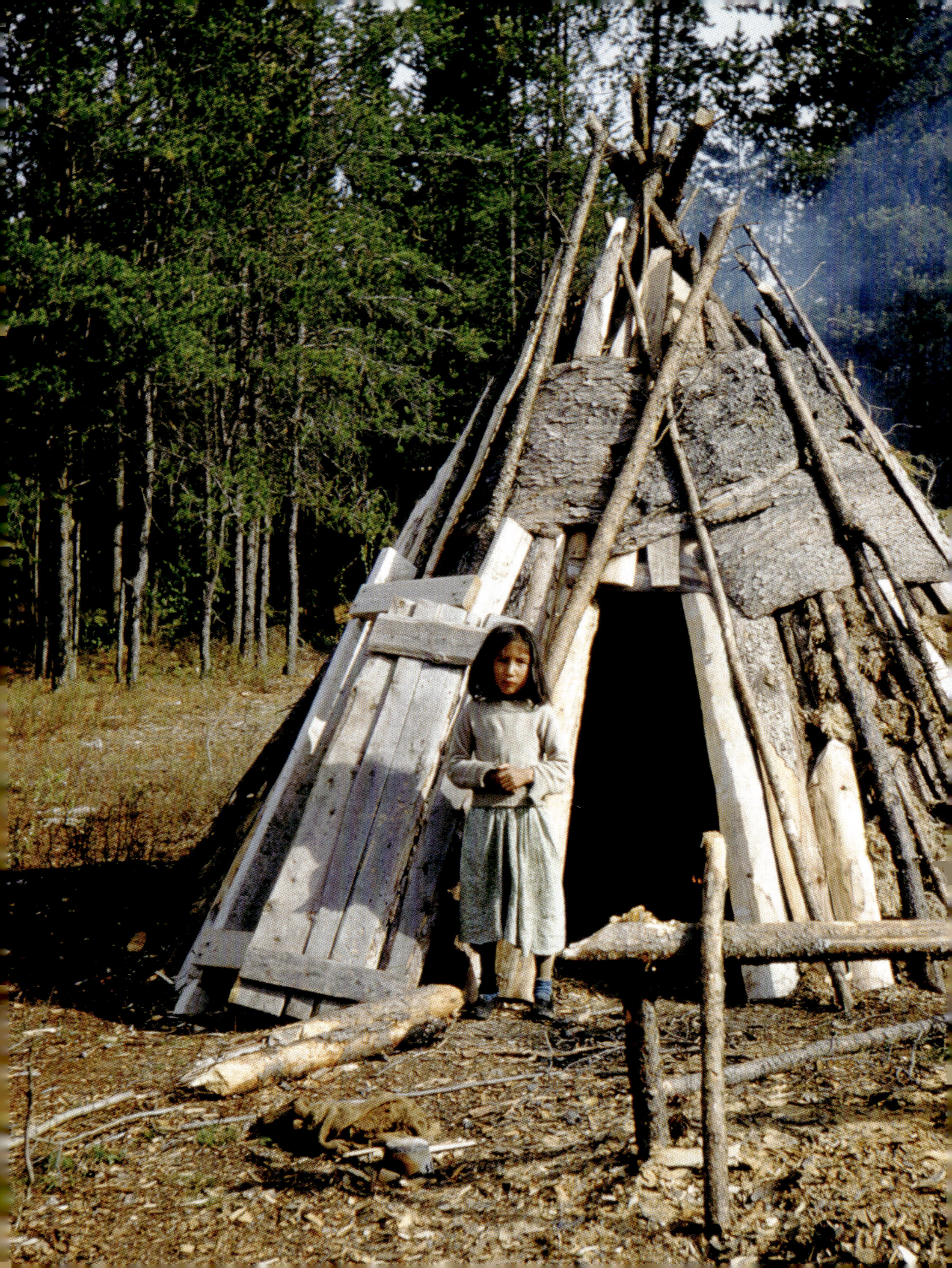

Spring/Fall

A young girl in front of a smoke lodge, Round Lake, in the Kenora District north of Sioux Lookout 1956

The daughter of Duncan Gray at Fort Severn, Kenora District c. 1955

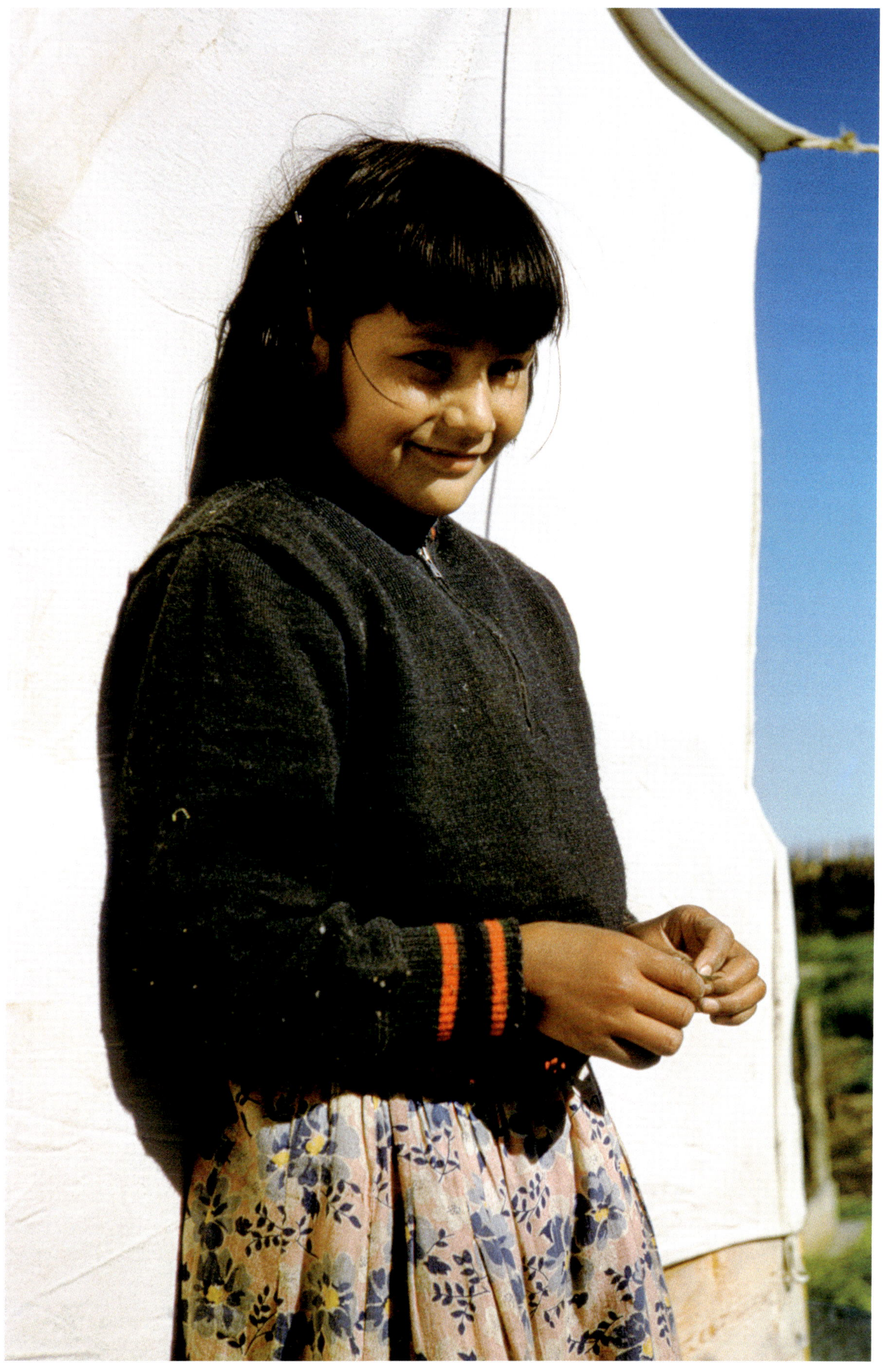

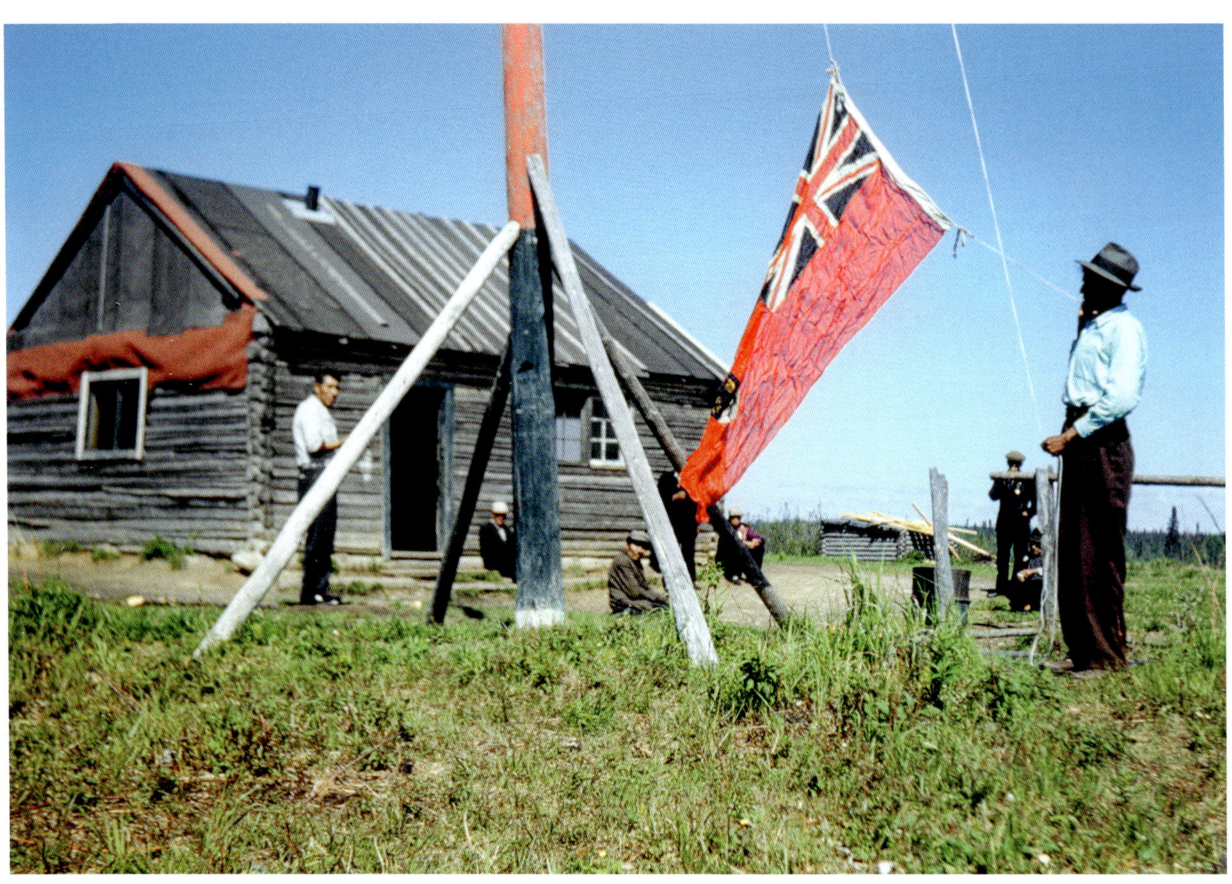

Chief Jeremiah Sainawap of Big Trout Lake (now Kitchenuhmaykoosib Inninuwug), north of Thunder Bay, raising the flag to summon trappers for a meeting 1953

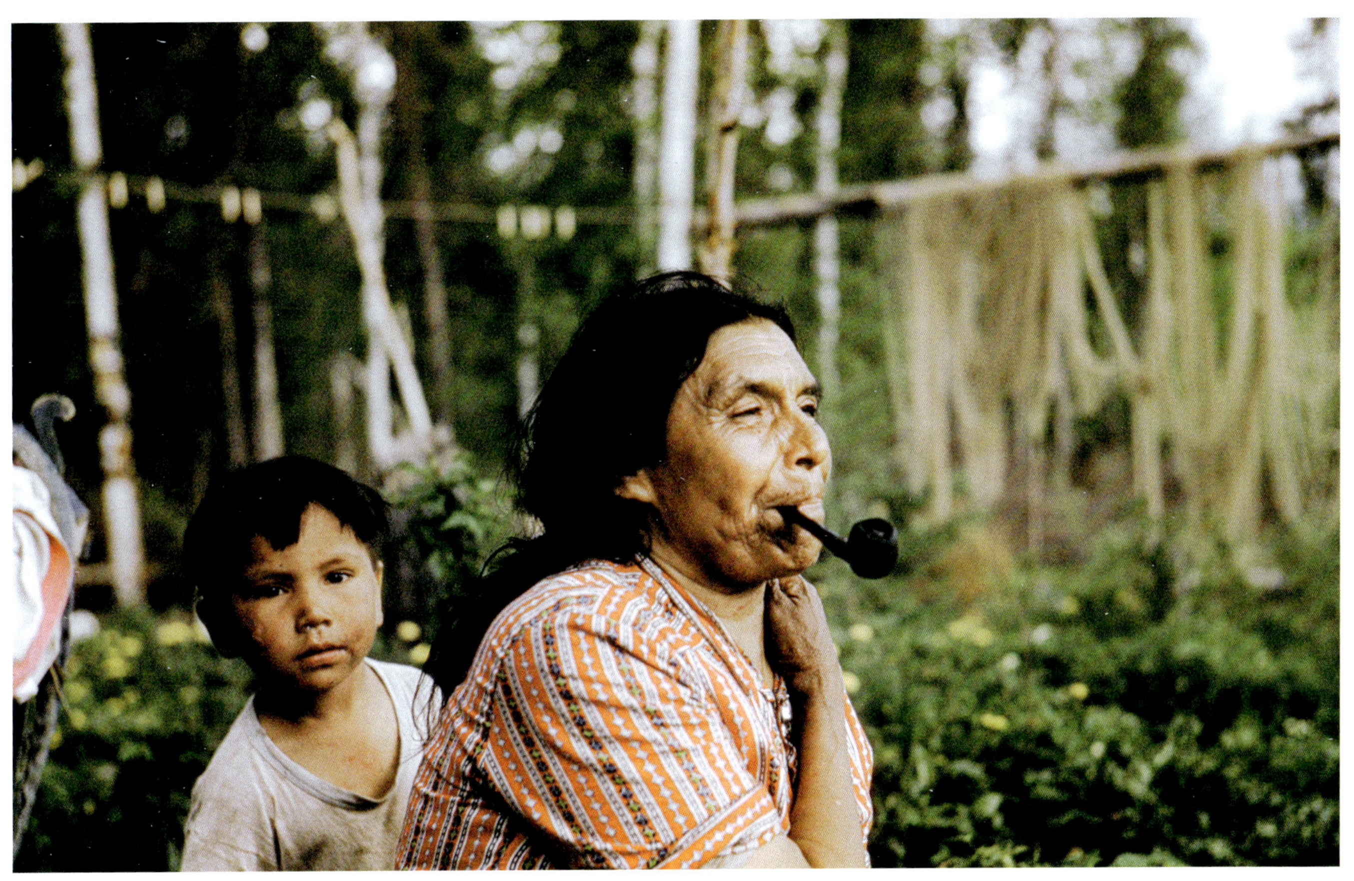

Mary Jane Rae of Sandy Lake, near the Manitoba border, and her grandson c. 1958

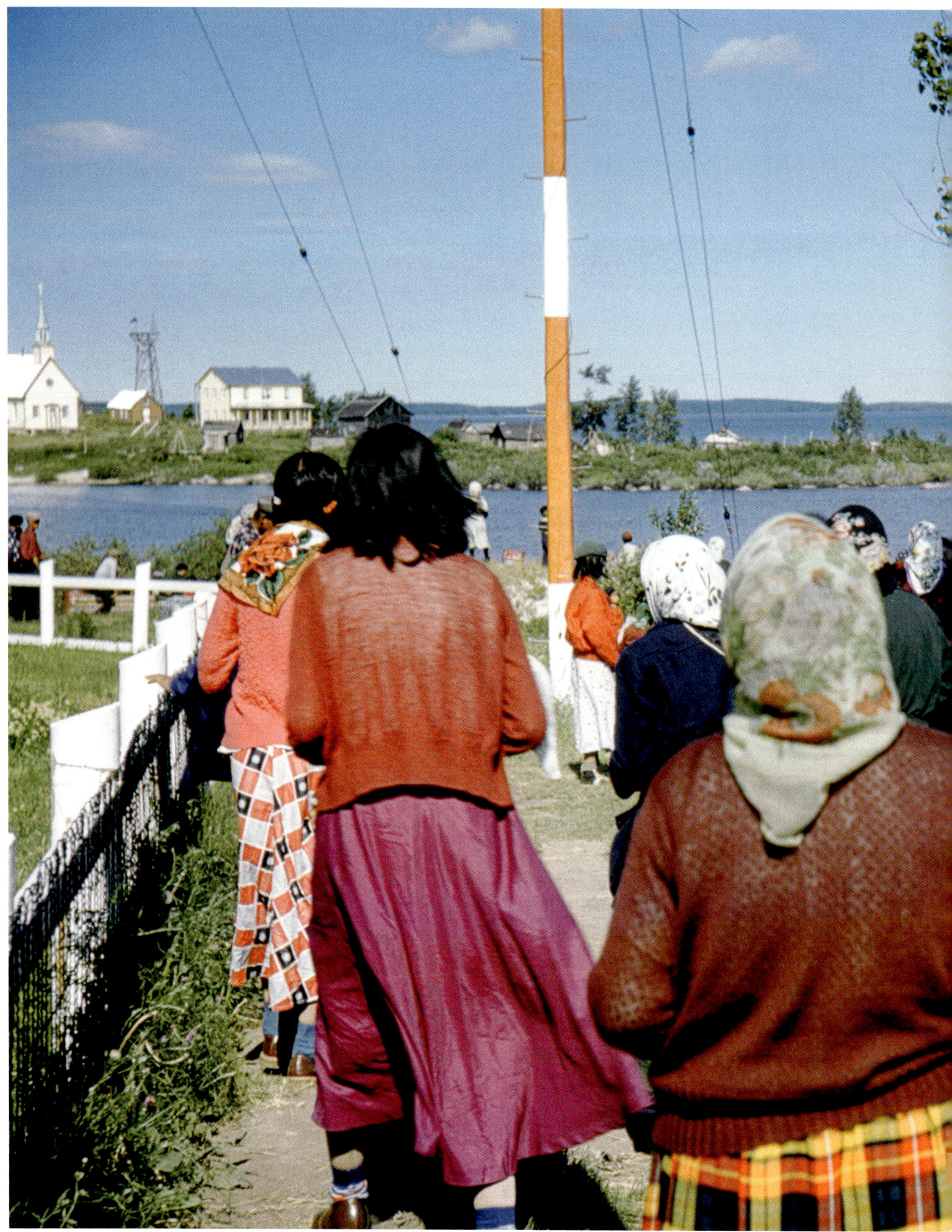

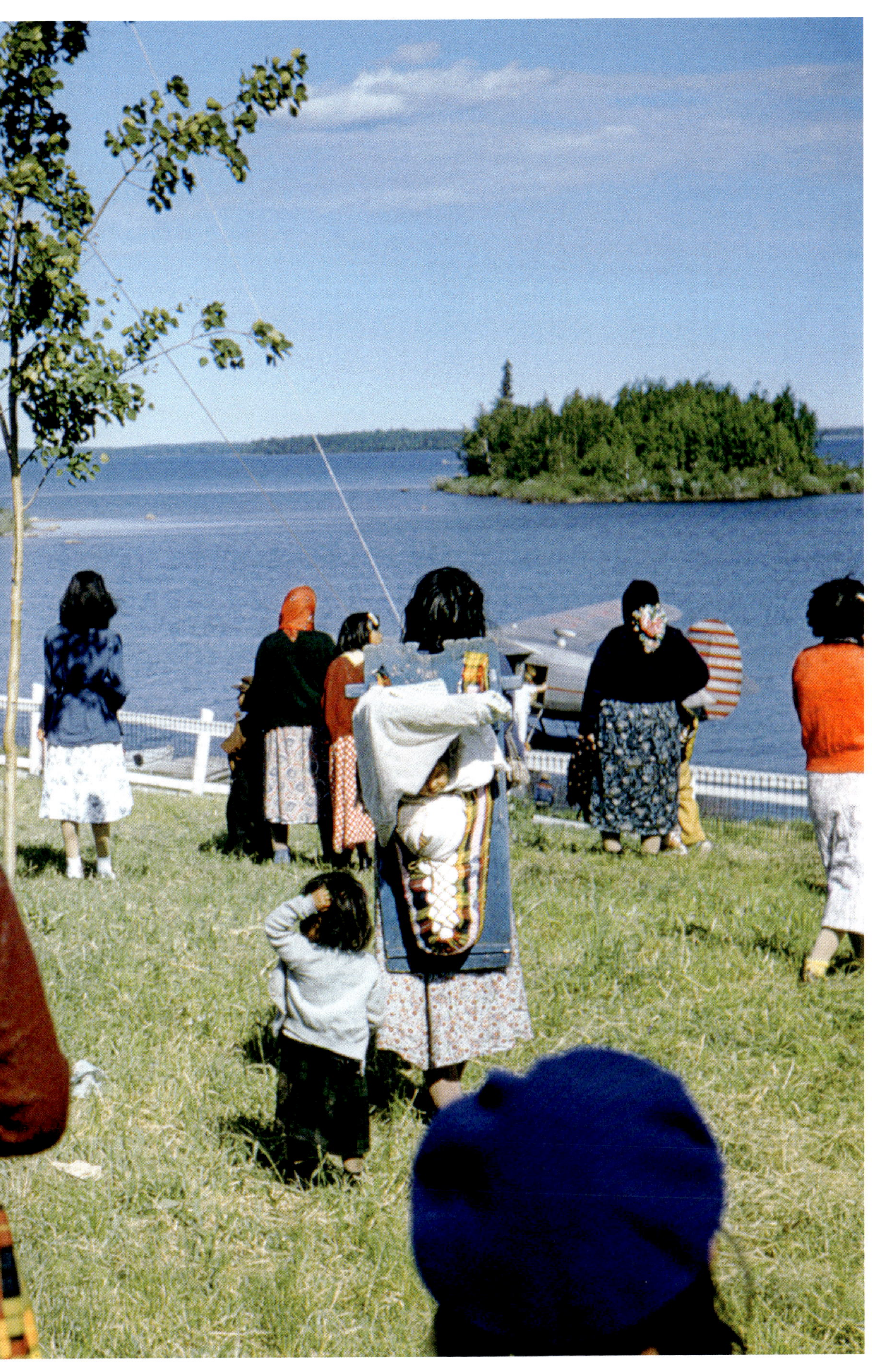

Members of the Fort Hope Band (now Eabametoong First Nation) watching a float plane arrive at the dock at Lansdowne House (now Neskantaga First Nation), Kenora District, at Treaty Time June 1956

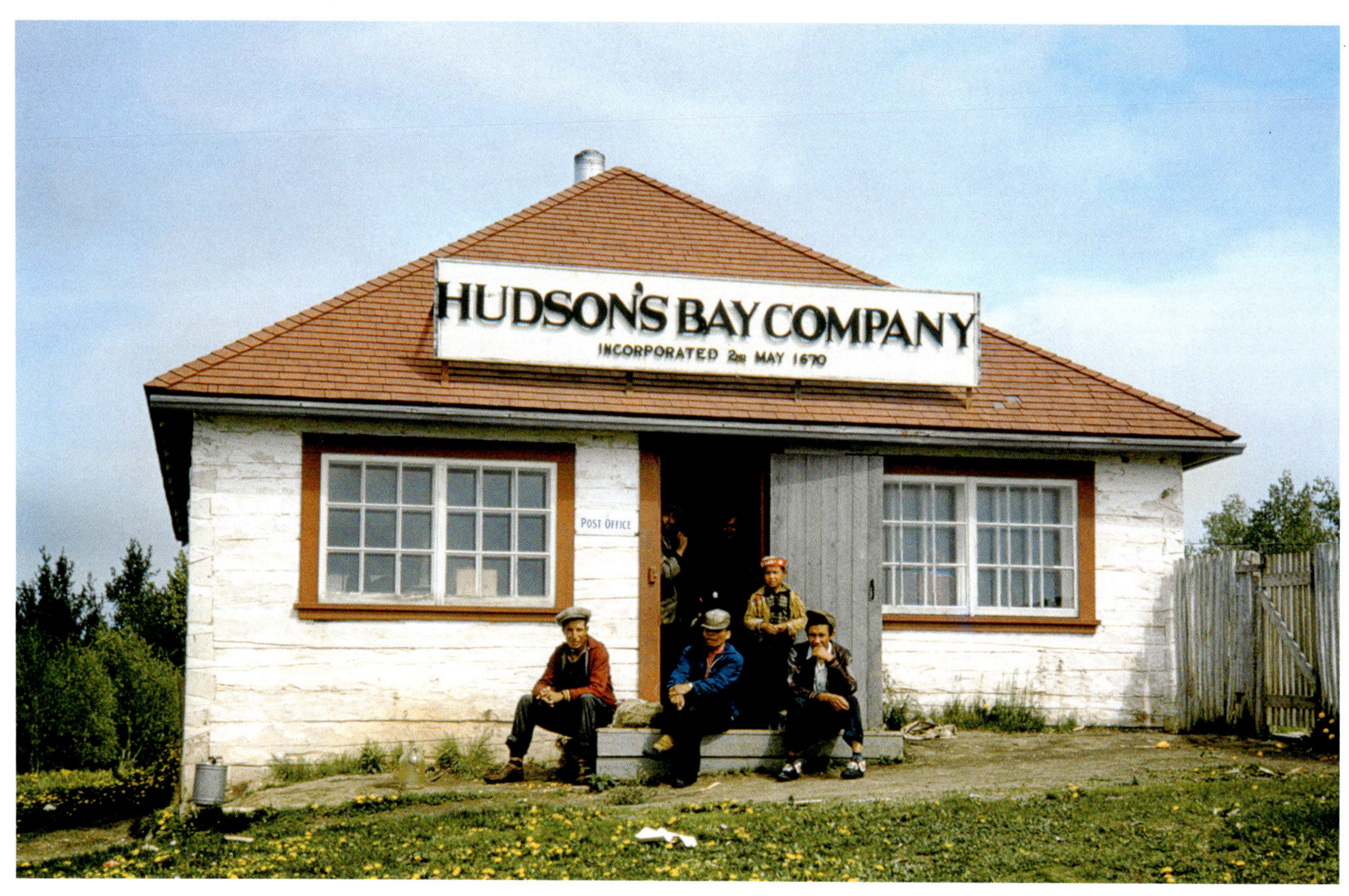

Men on the steps of the Hudson's Bay Company store in Sandy Lake 1955

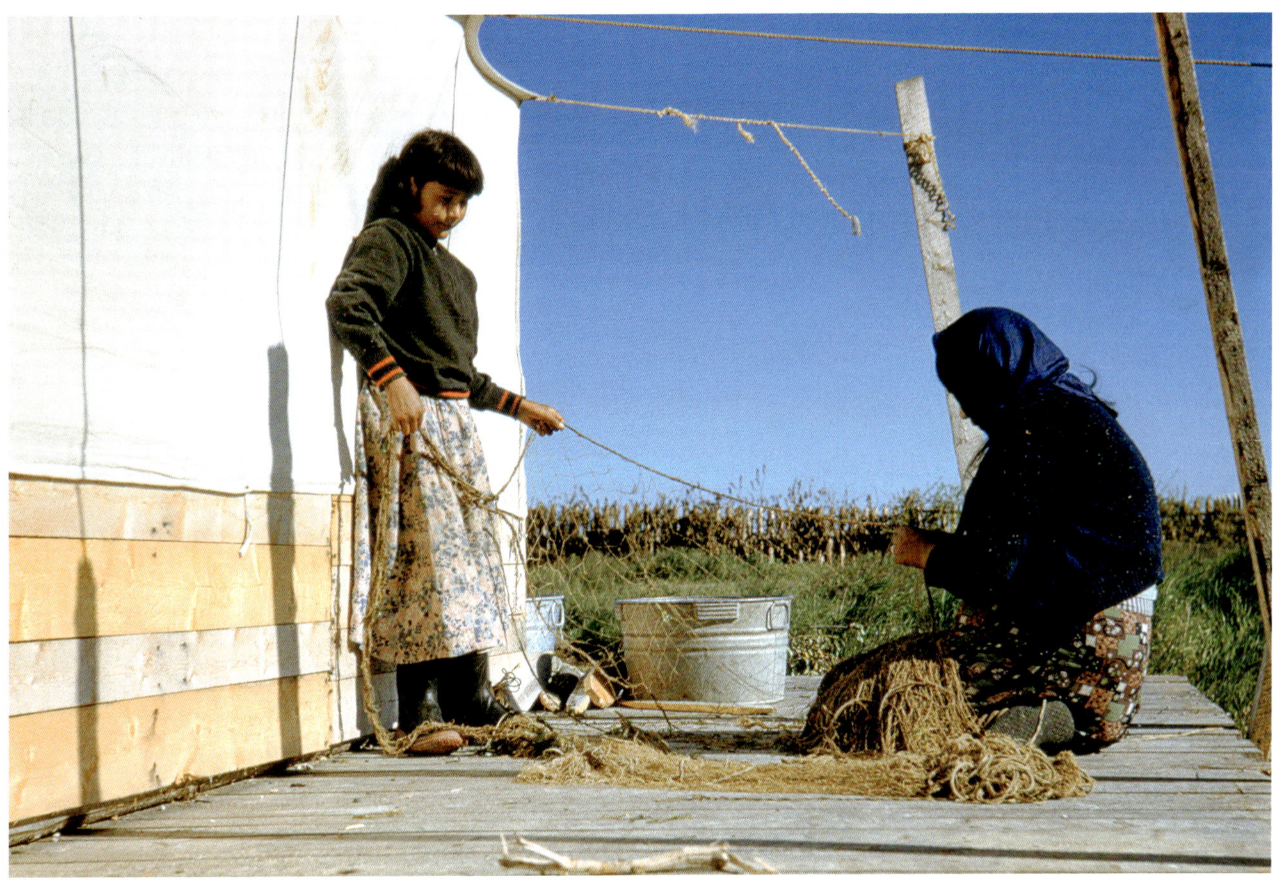

Mrs. Duncan Gray and her daughter untangle and clean a gill net at Fort Severn, on Hudson Bay 1955

Elizabeth Matthews and her daughter Charlotte in Fort Severn 1955

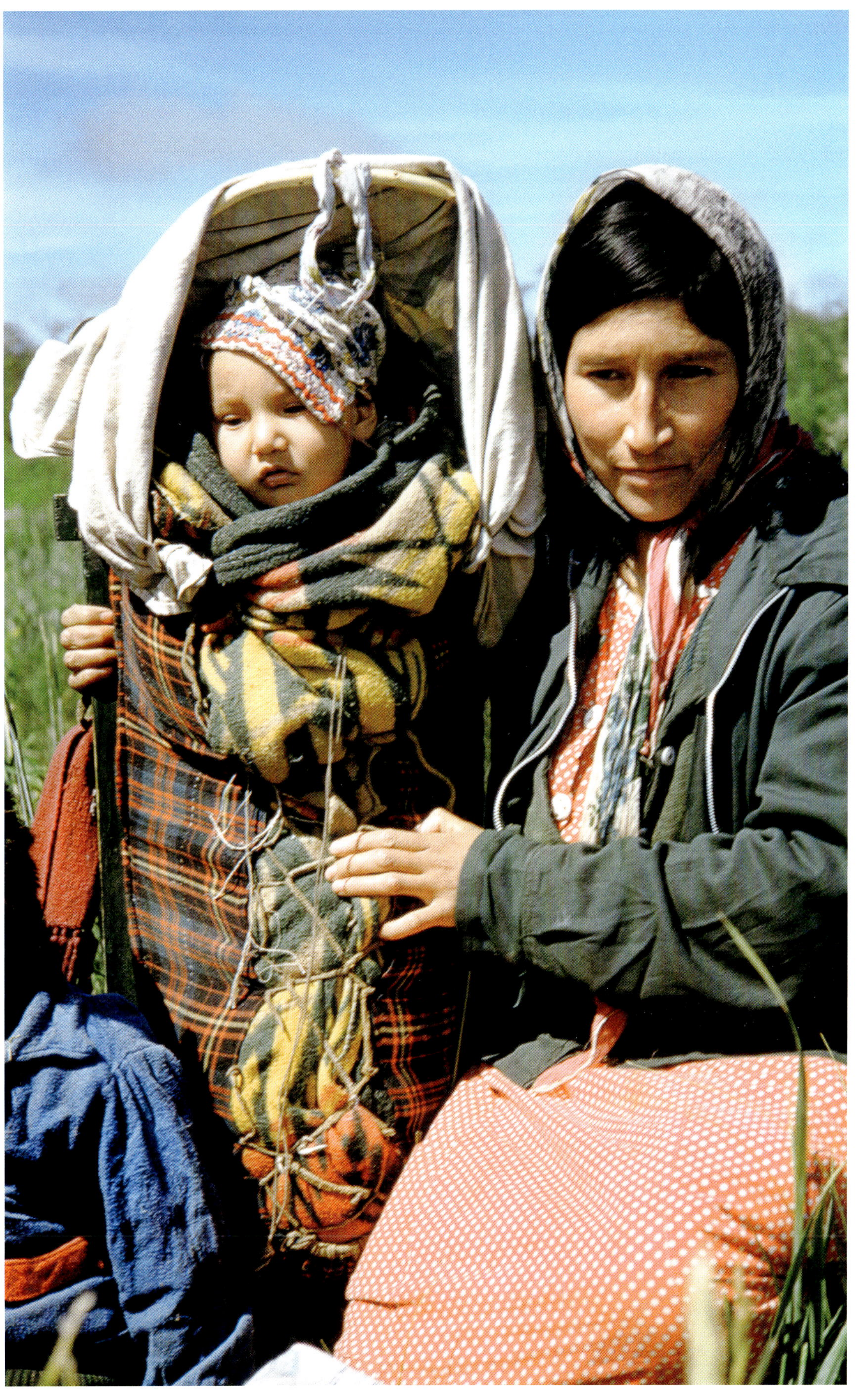

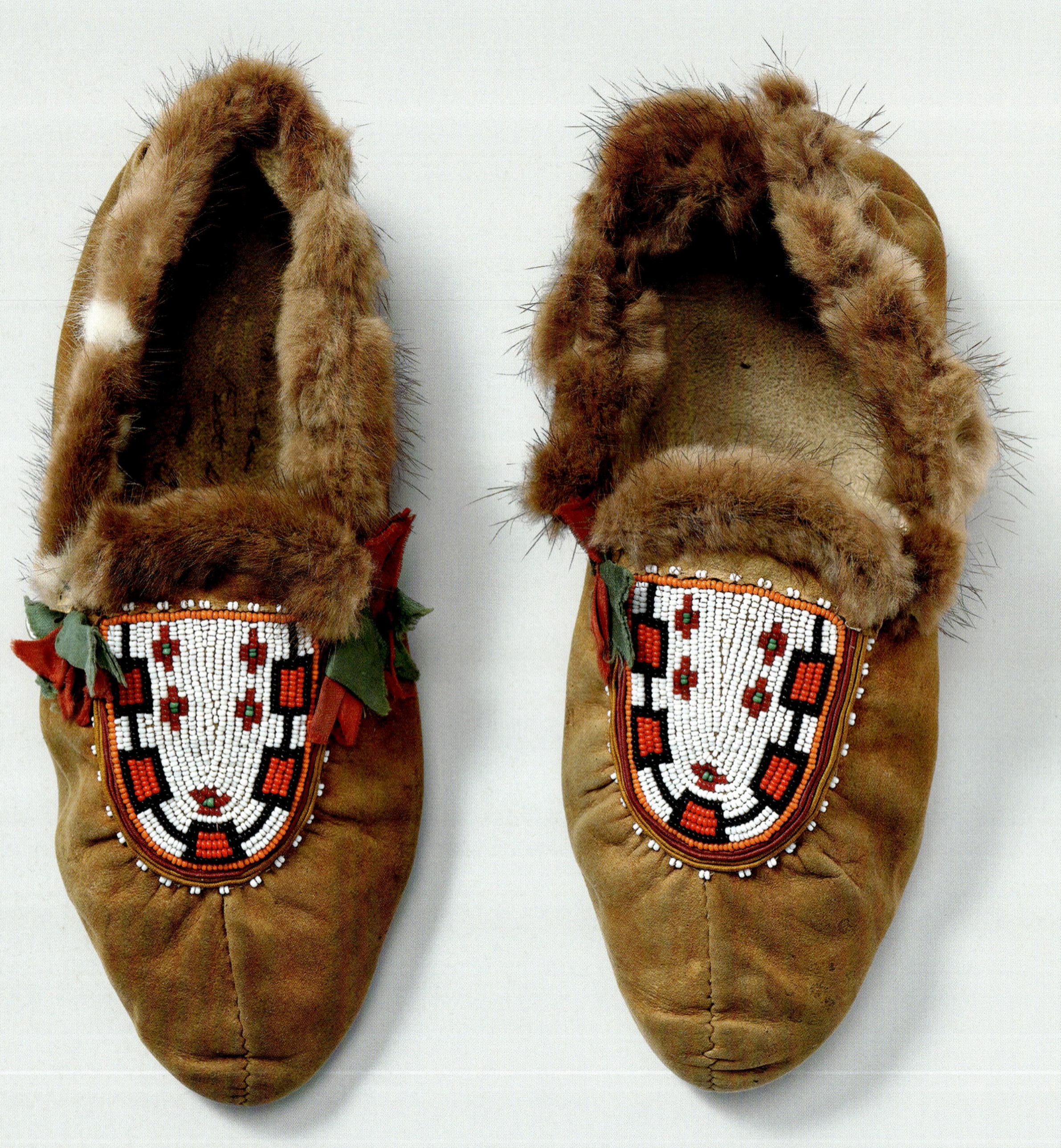

Beaded moccasins, collected by John Macfie

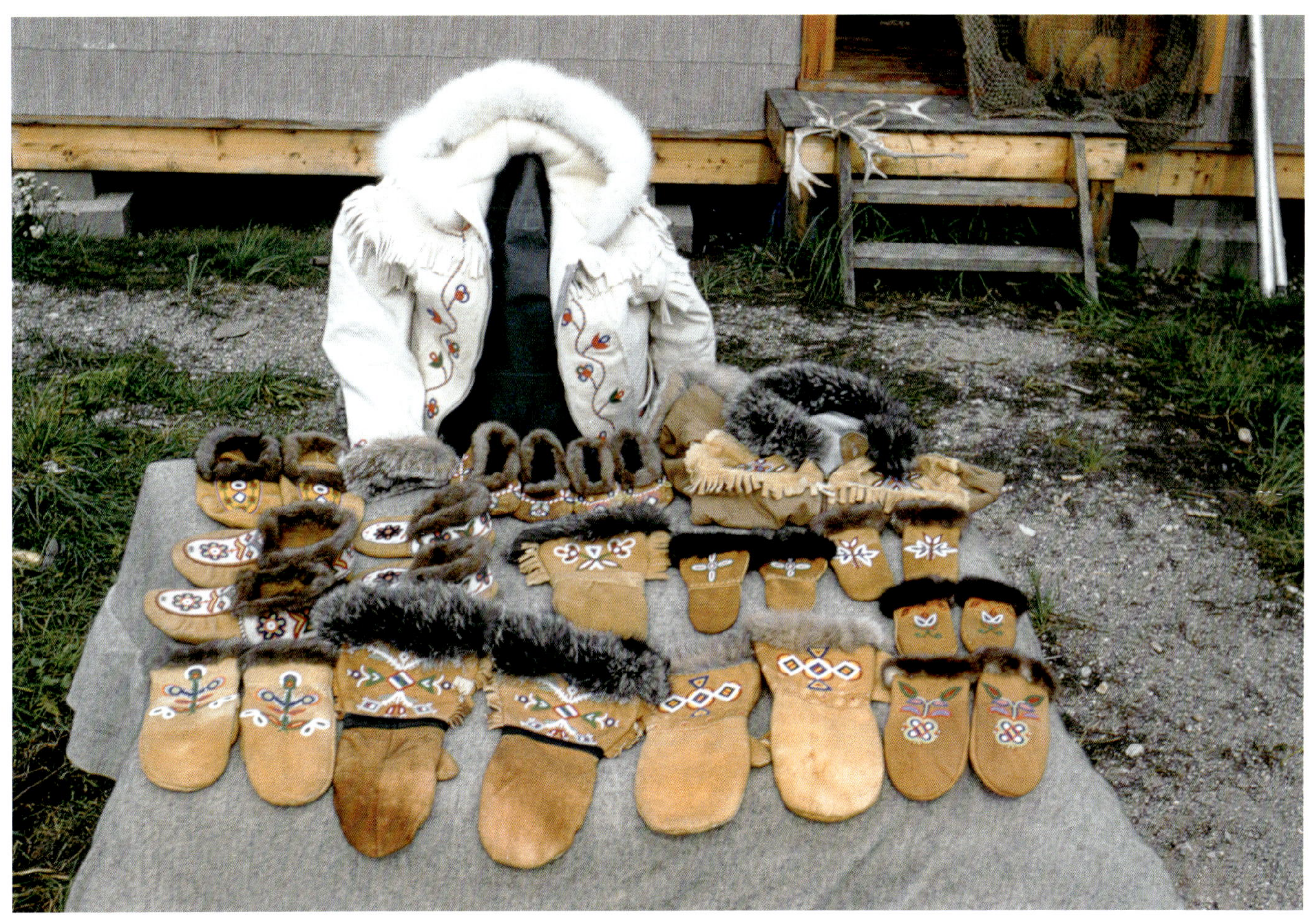

A display of leather mitts, moccasins, and a jacket decorated with beadwork c. 1955

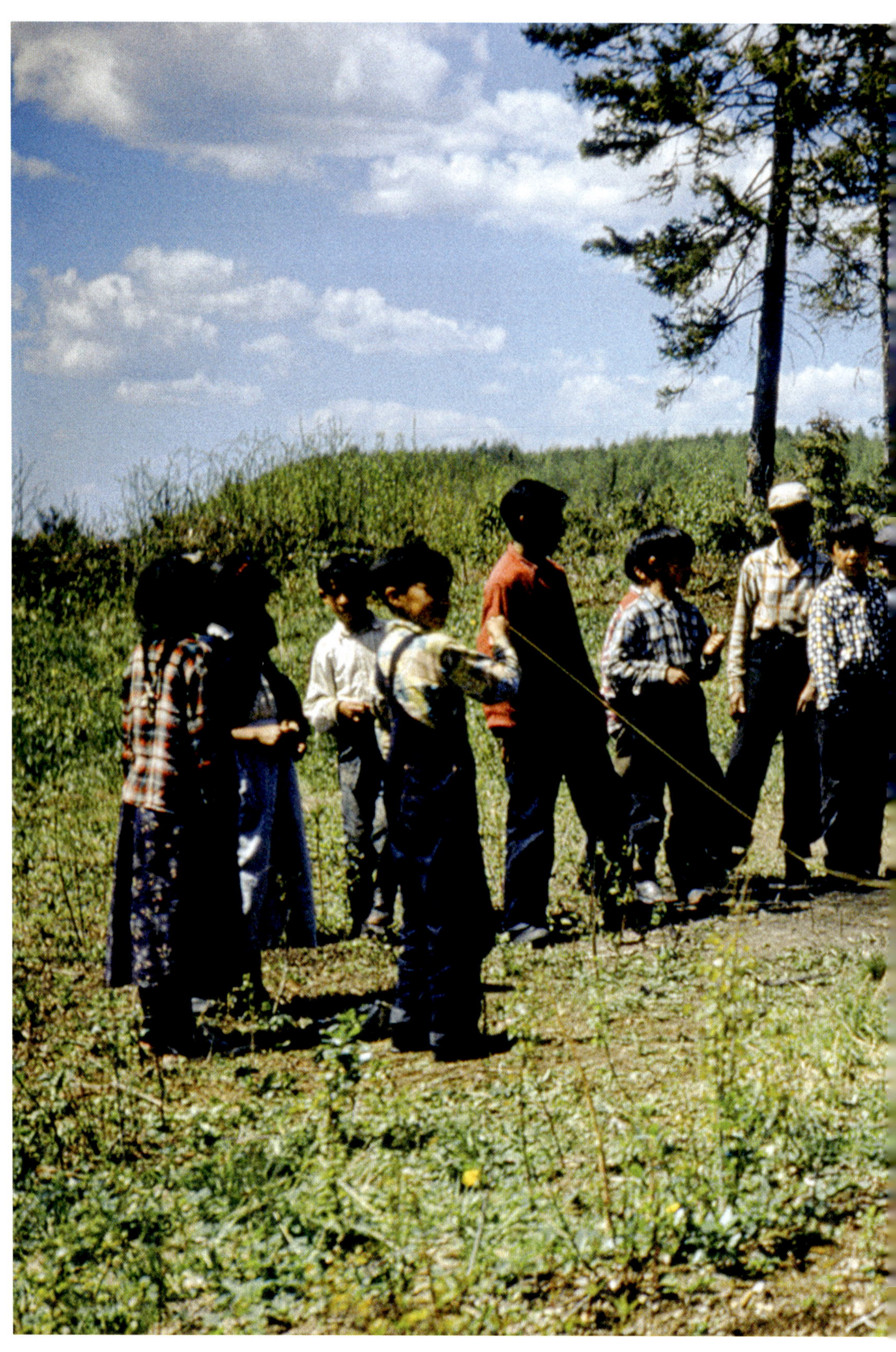

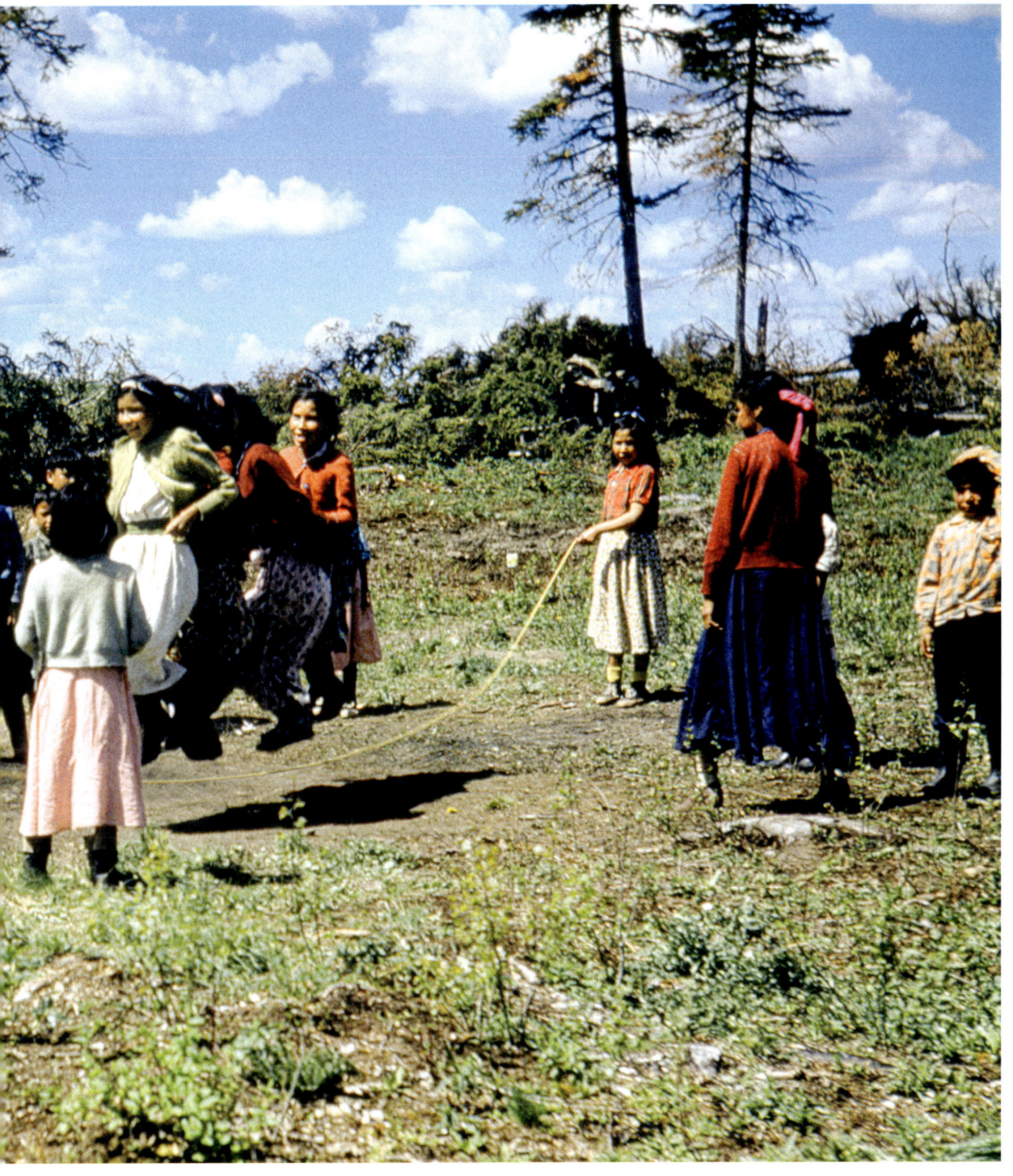

Girls skipping rope, Sandy Lake c. 1955

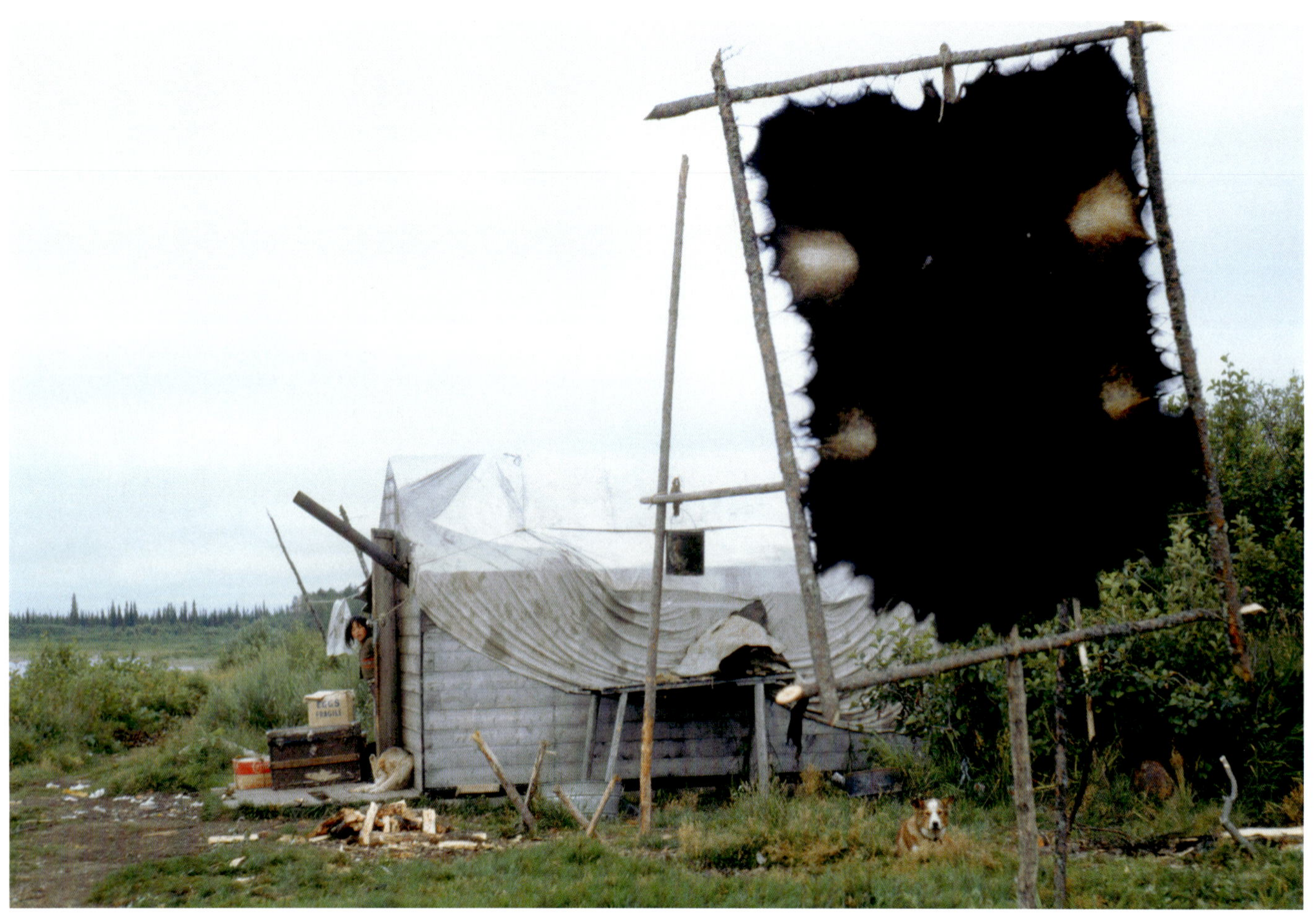

A stretched black bearskin at Attawapiskat 1964

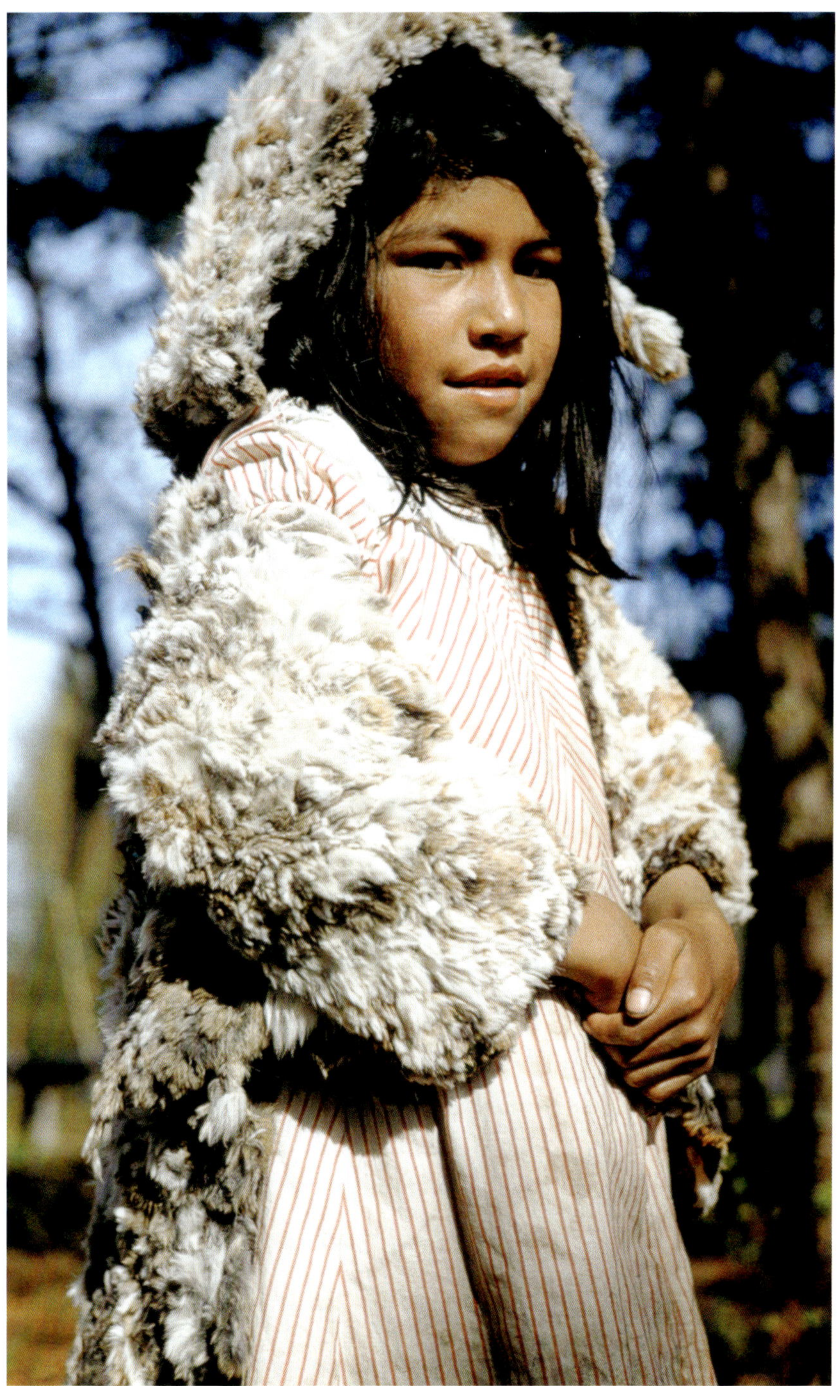

A girl wearing a hare-pelt coat, Weagamow Lake, Kenora District 1956

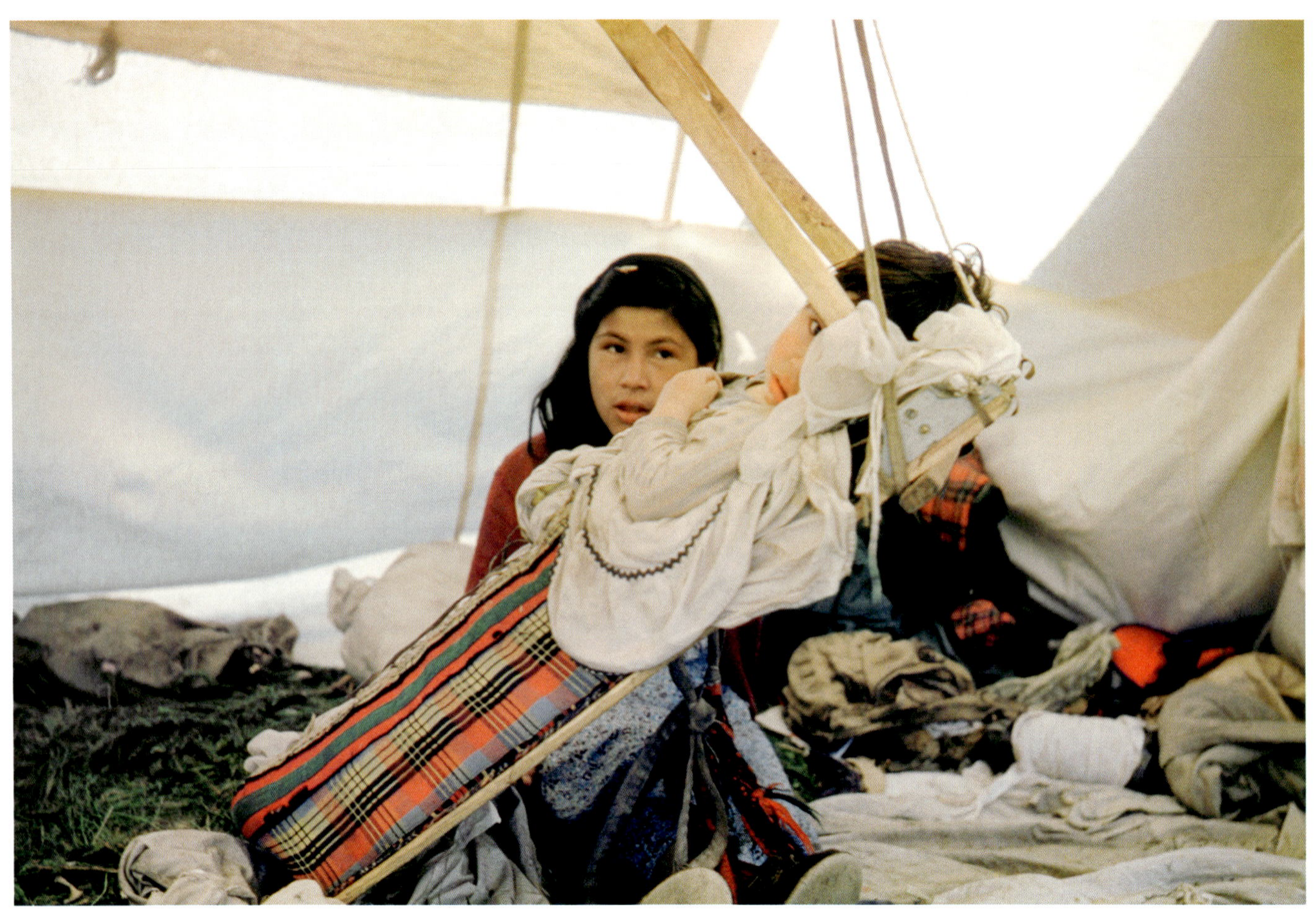

A girl watching over a sick child in a tikinagan, Eabametoong, northeast of Thunder Bay c. 1956

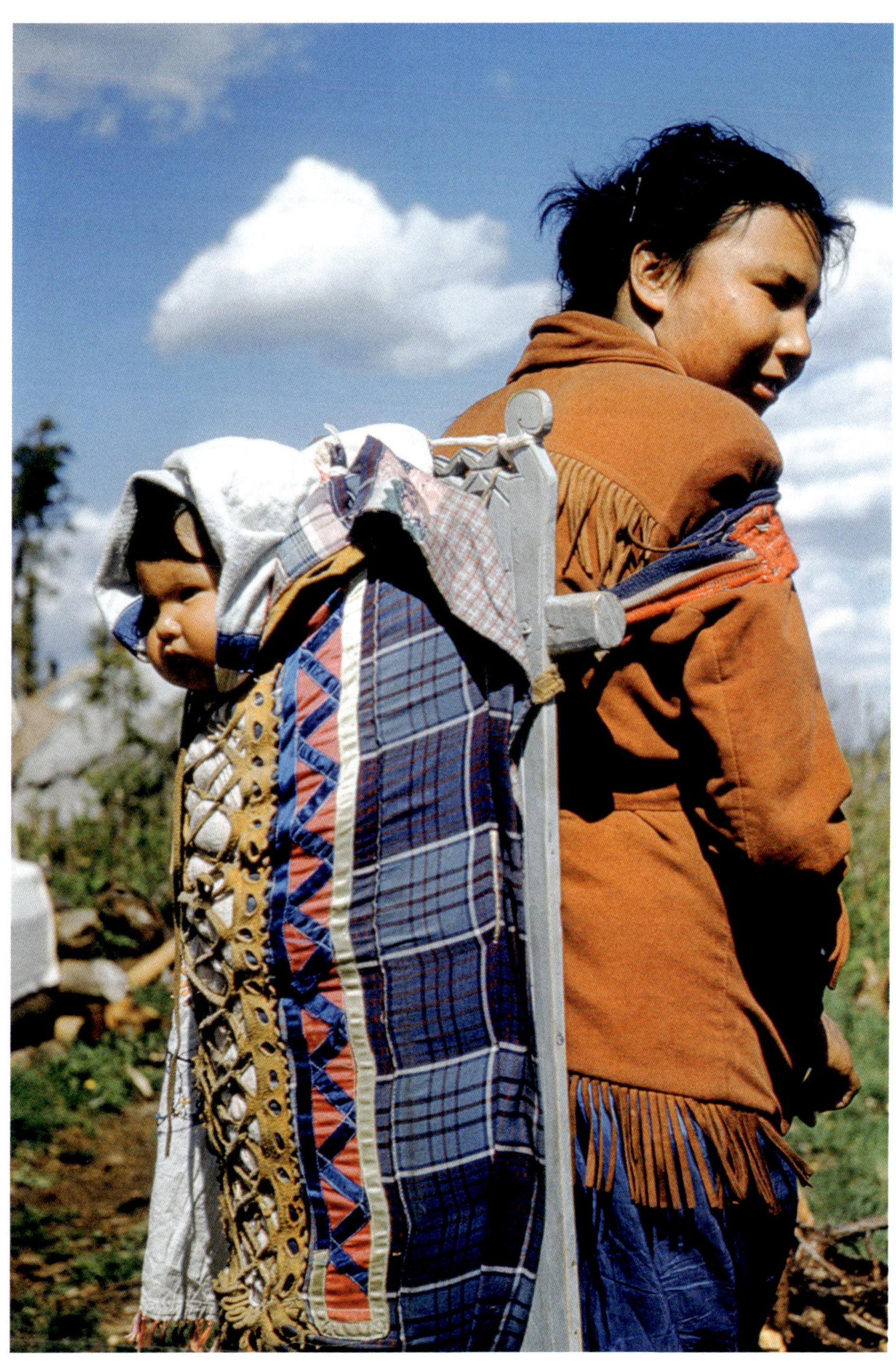

A woman with her baby in a tikinagan, Sandy Lake 1956

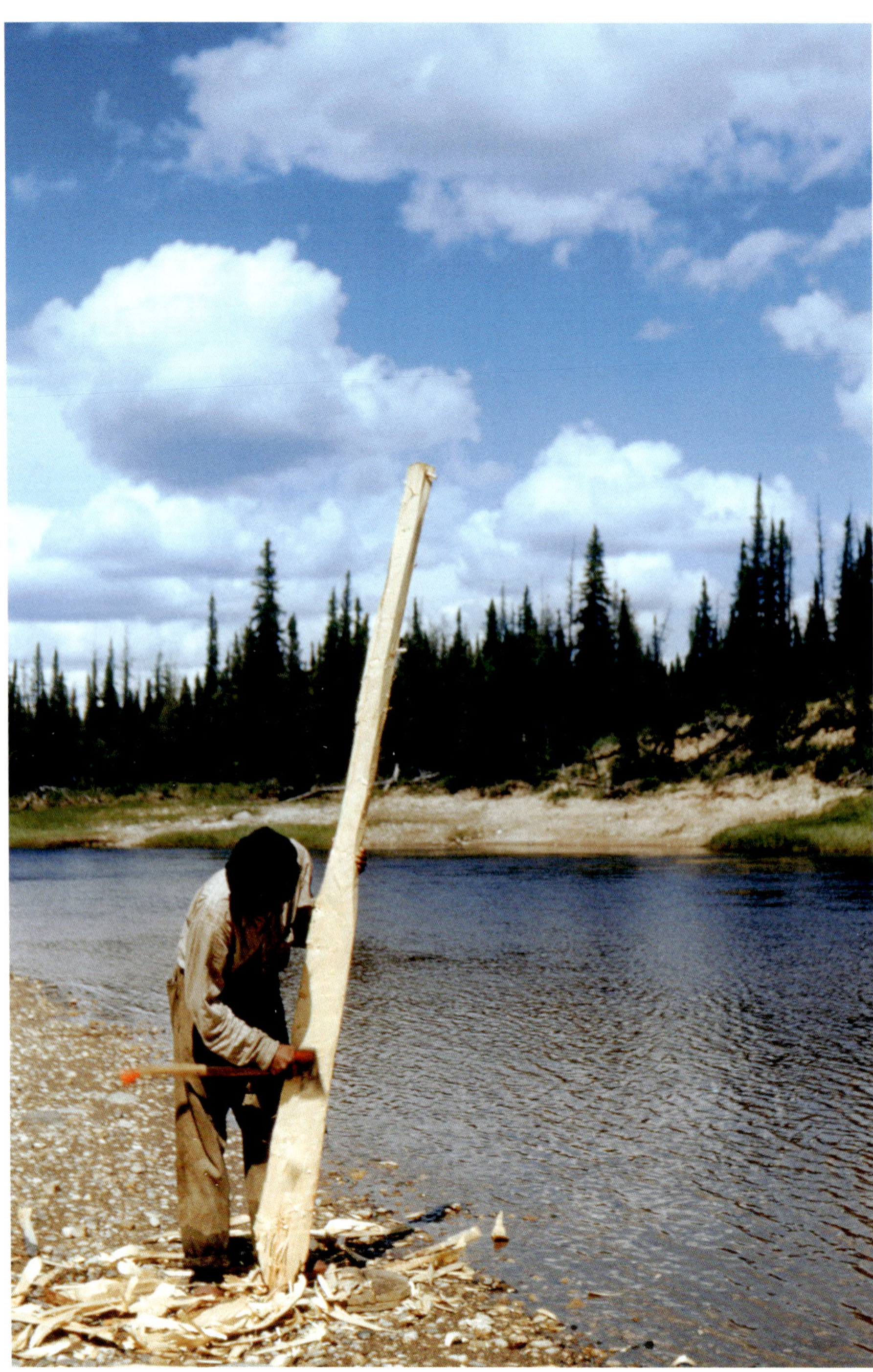

Douglas Kakekaspan of Fort Severn hewing a new paddle on the Black Duck River, Kenora District July 1953

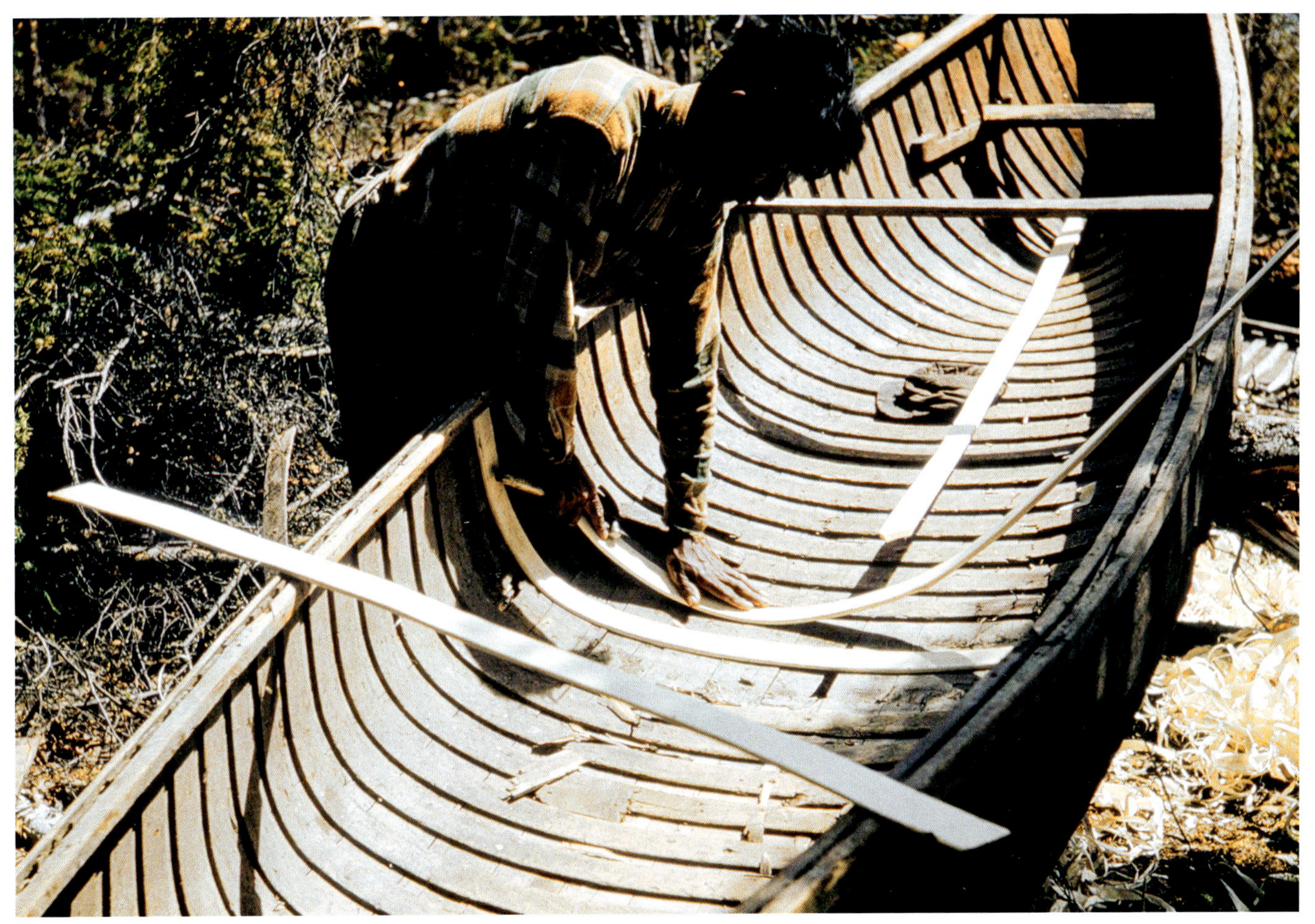

Repairing a canoe, Sandy Lake c. 1955

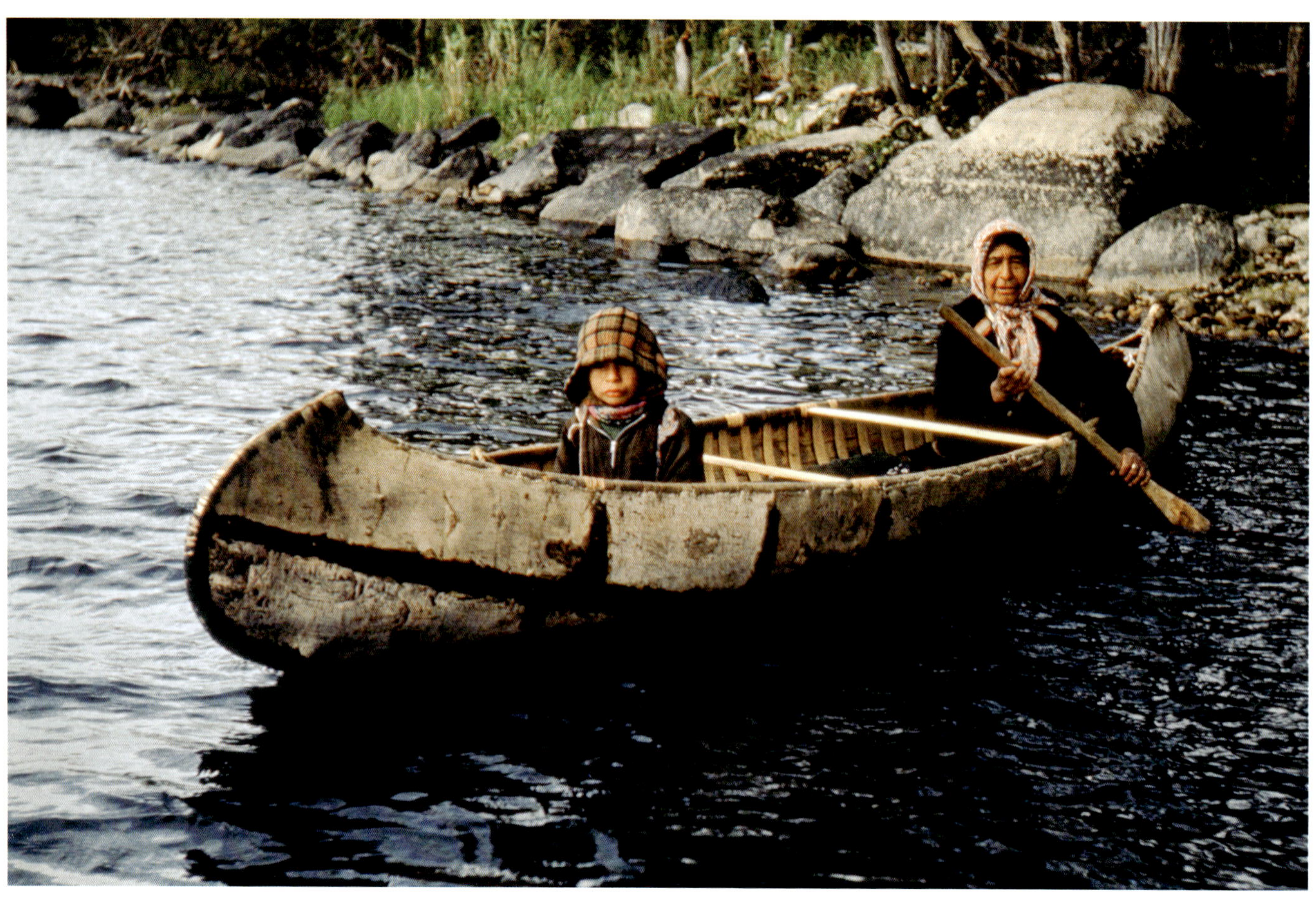

Maria Mikenak and her grandson in a birchbark canoe she made, Lake St. Joseph, Kenora and Thunder Bay Districts 1956

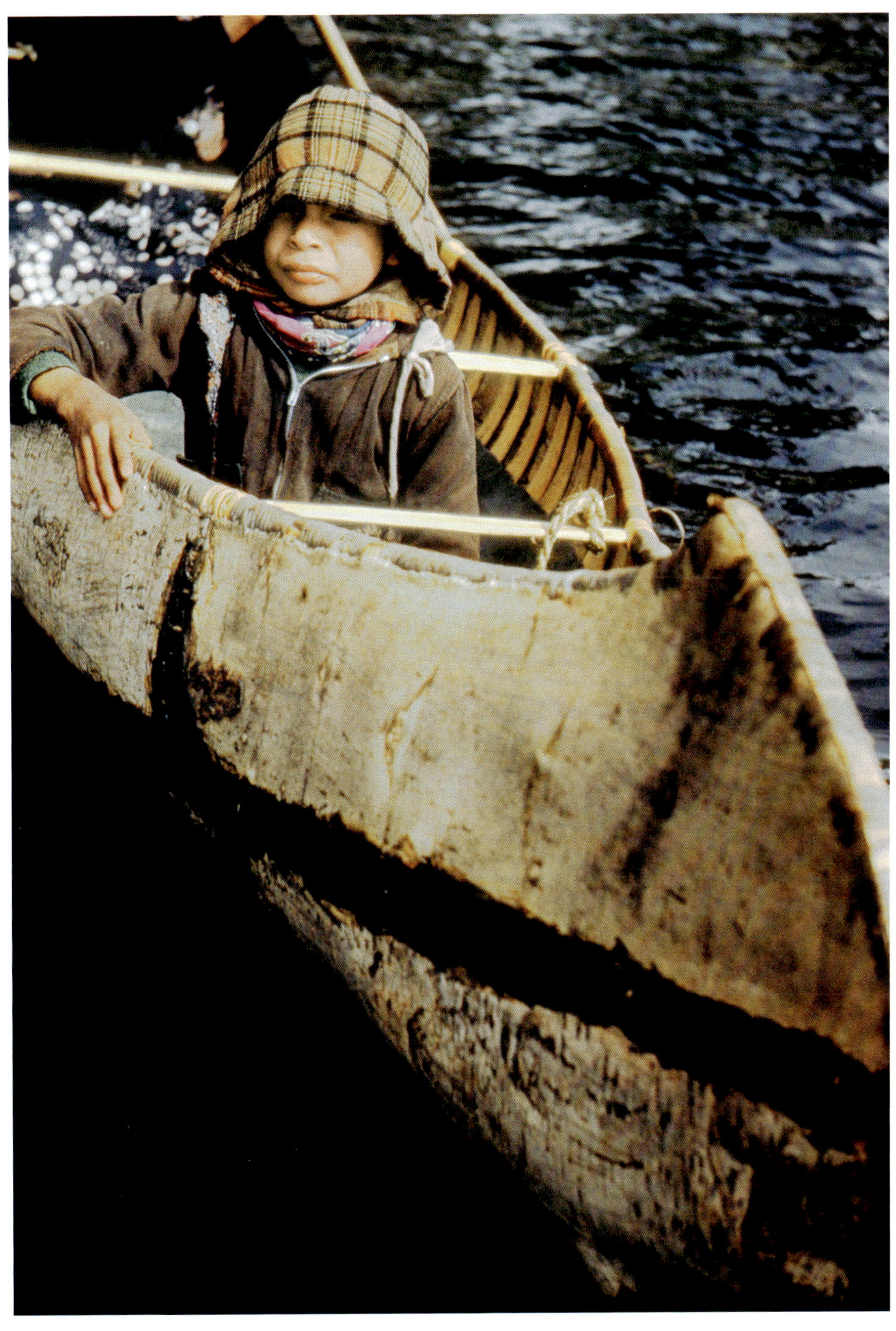

Maria Mikenak's grandson, Lake St. Joseph 1956

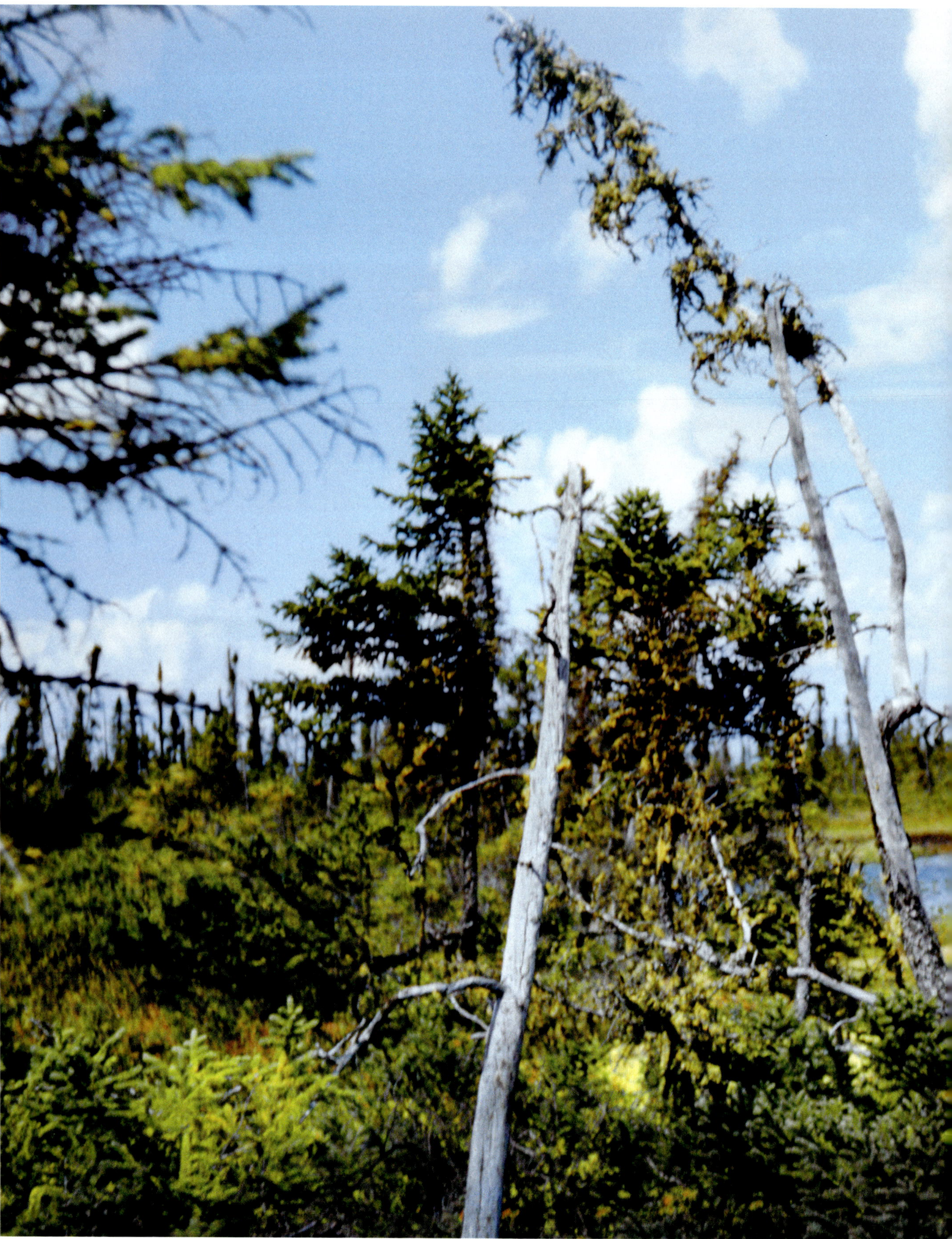

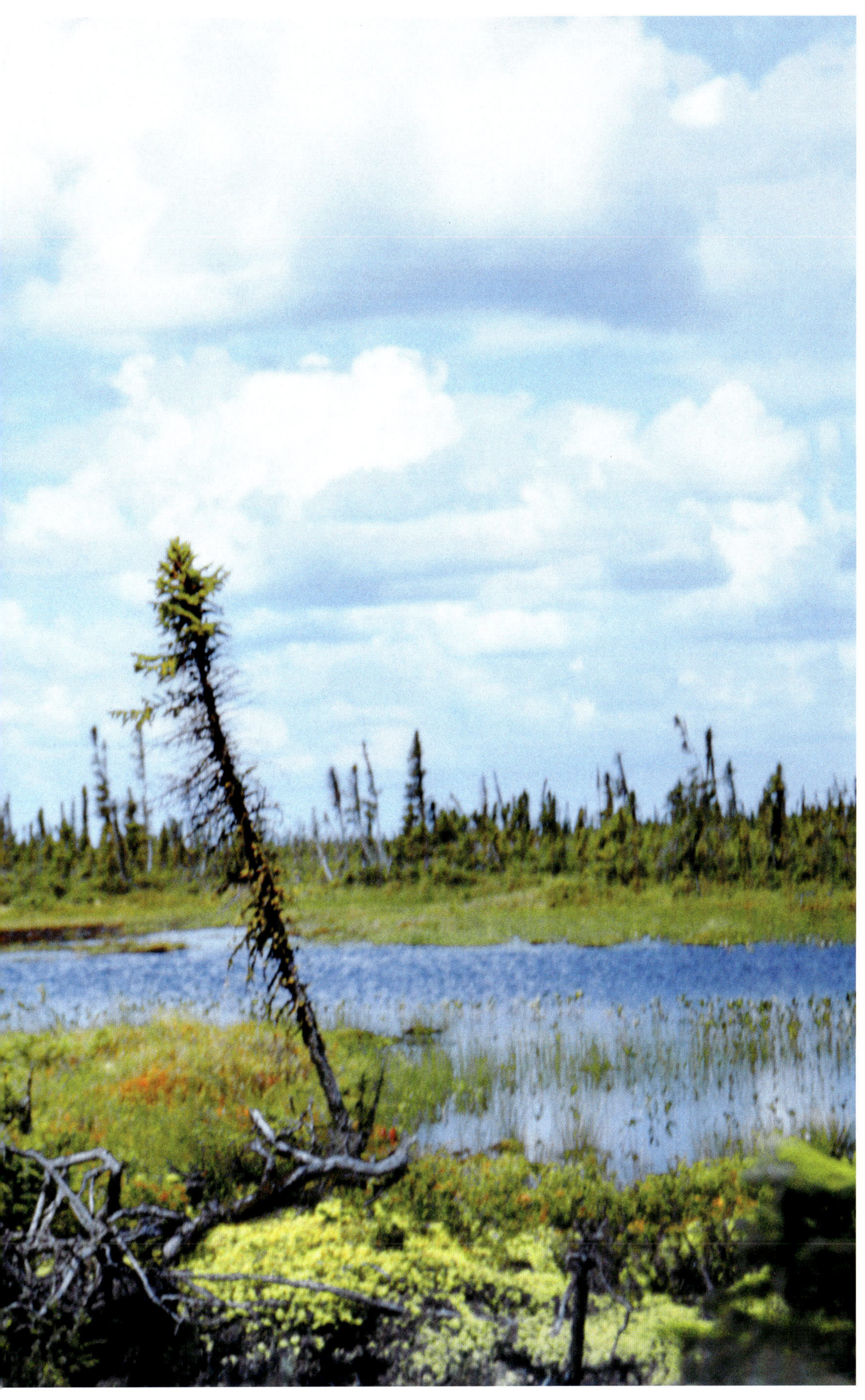

Muskeg adjacent to the Severn River, Kenora District 1952

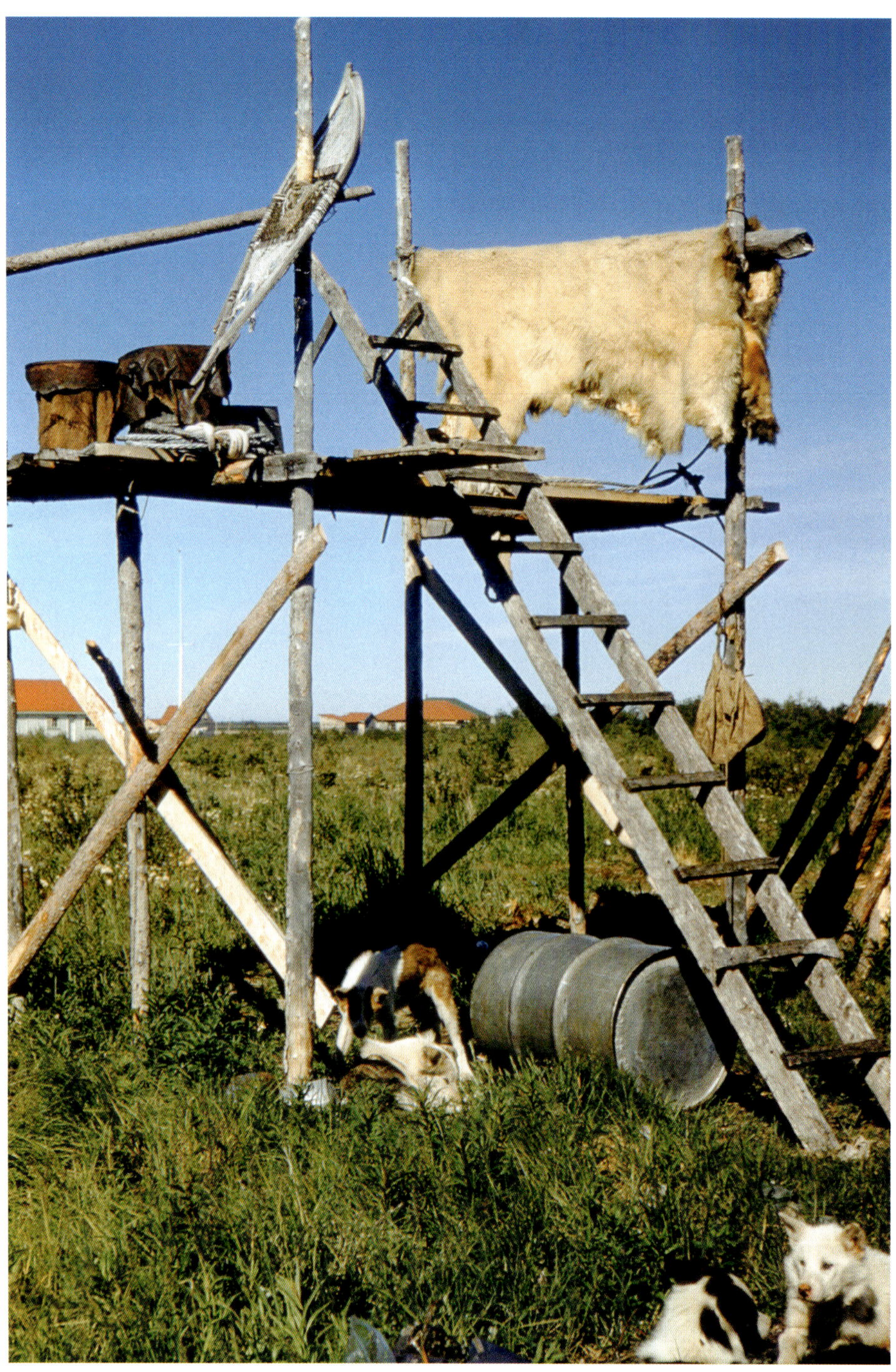

A raised cache for storing items out of the reach of dogs and wild animals at Fort Severn 1955

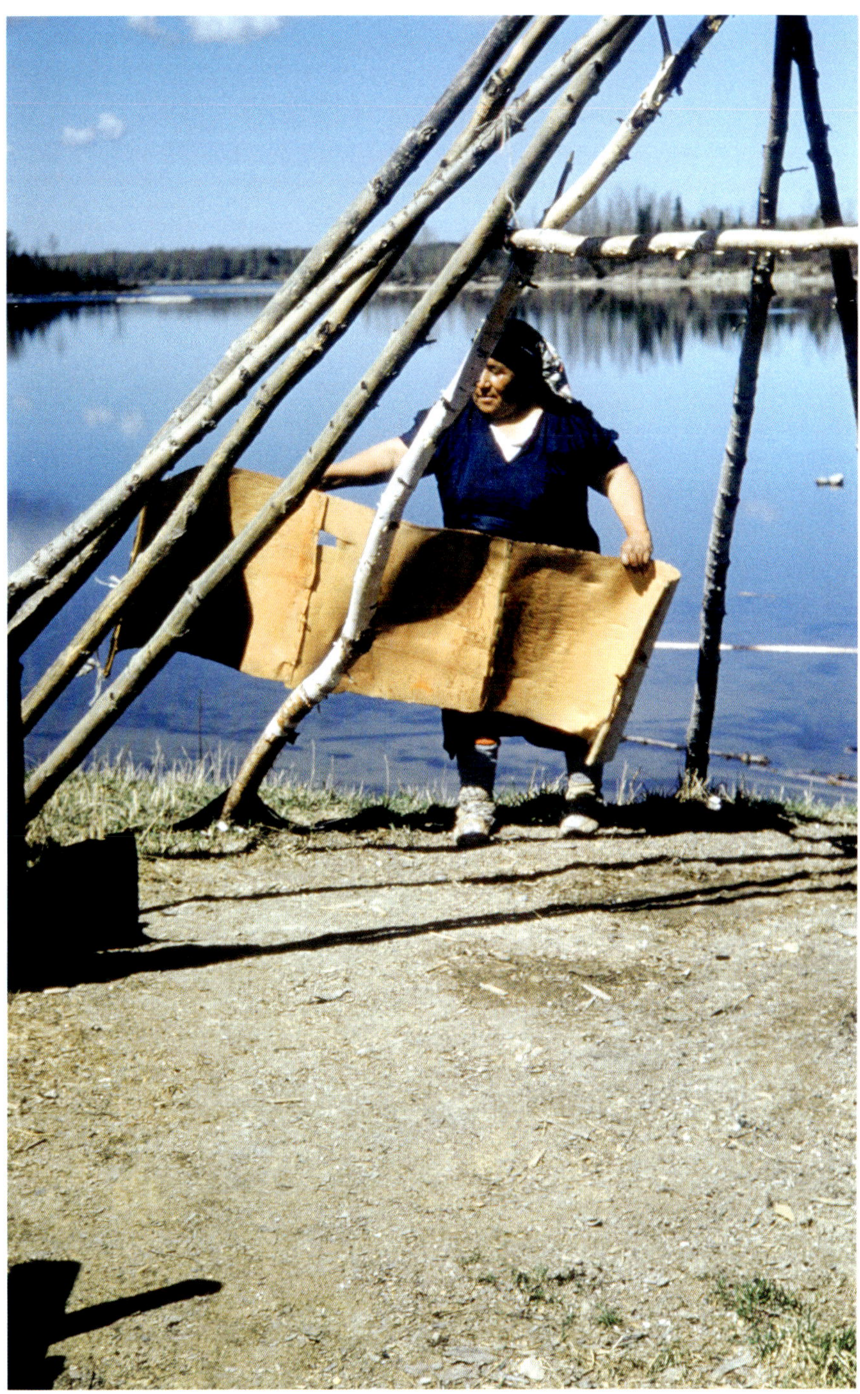

Covering a smokehouse with birchbark, Sandy Lake 1960

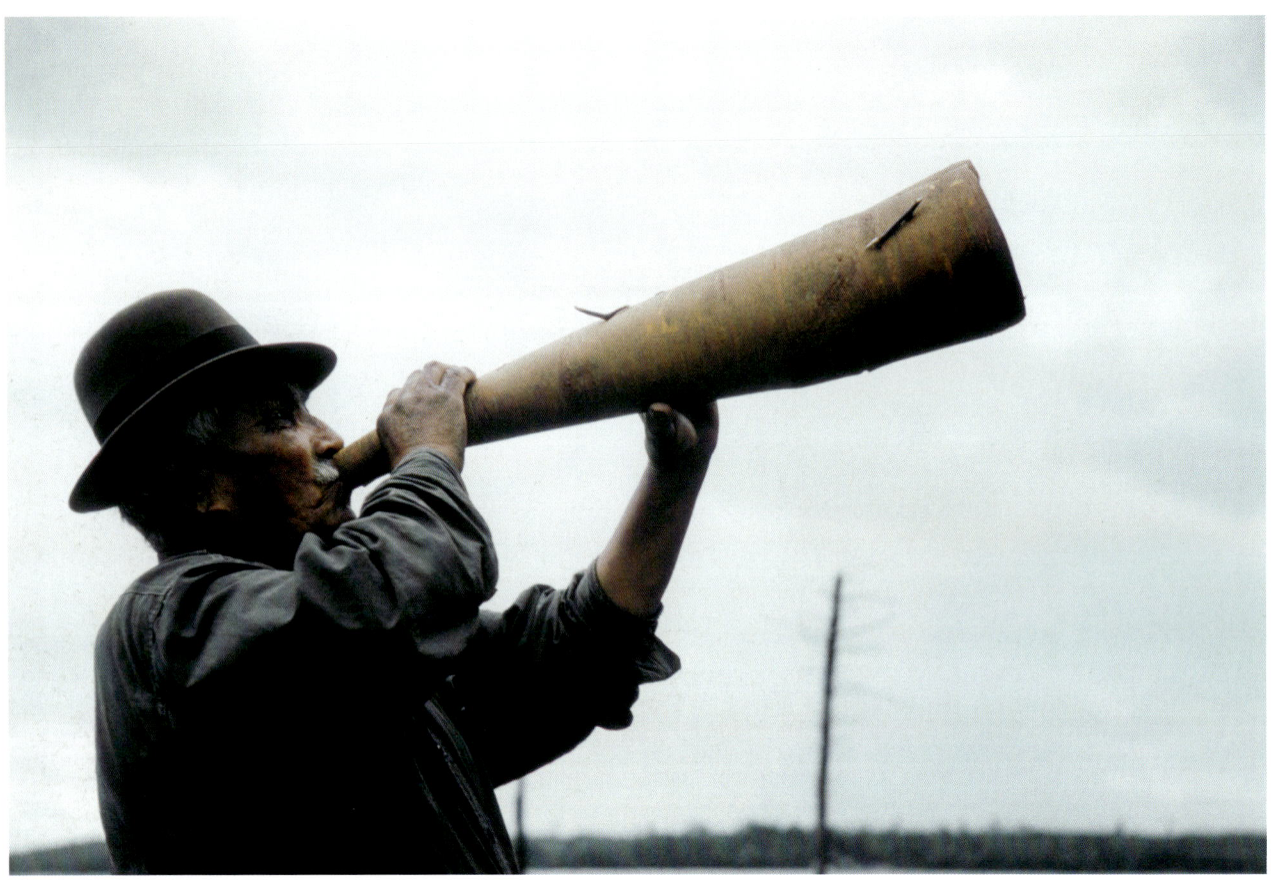

Henry Kechebra using a birchbark cone to call moose near Mattagami, Sudbury District 1959

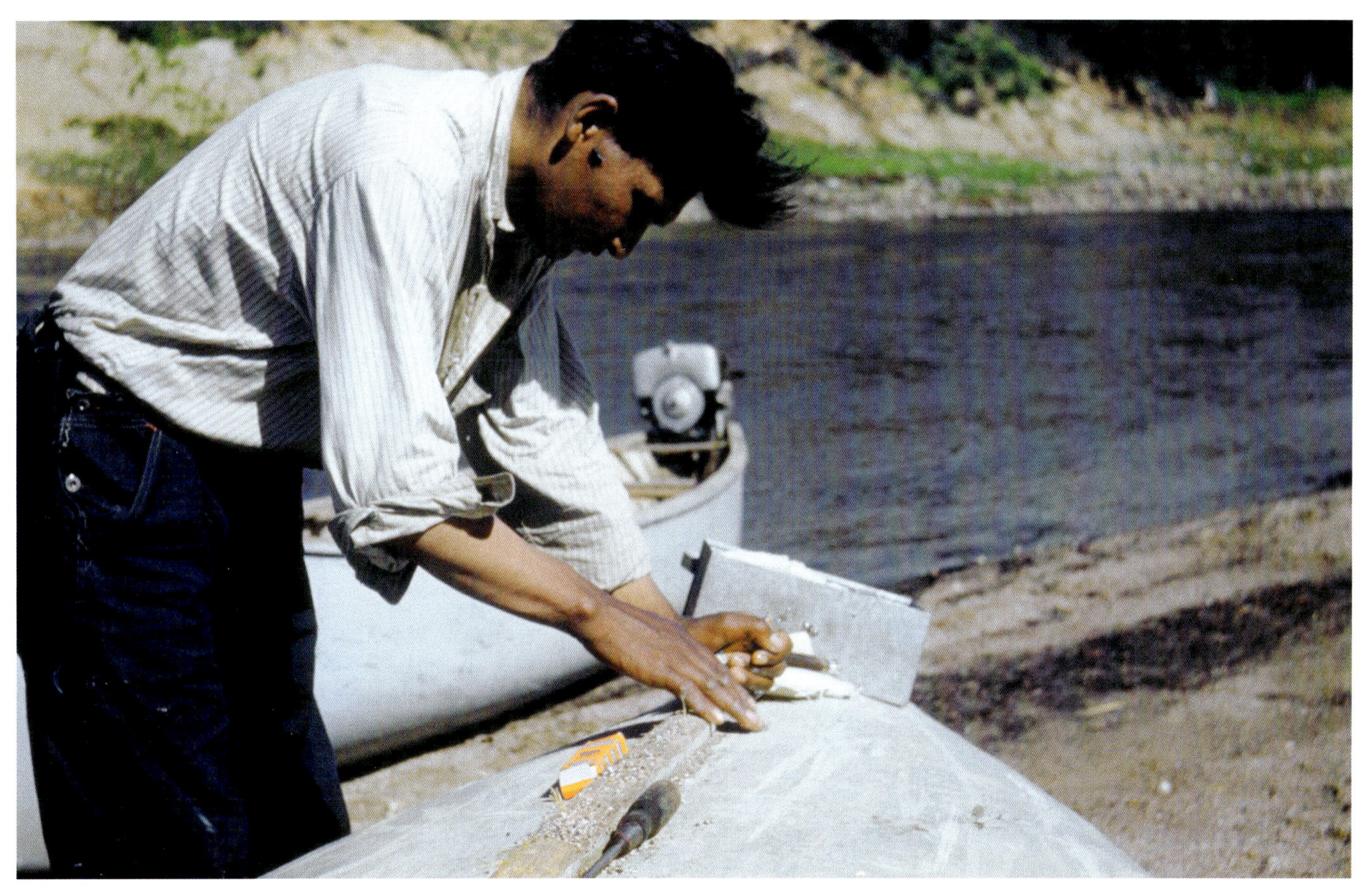

Philip "Swampy" Mathew doing seasonal repairs on a boat hull 1953

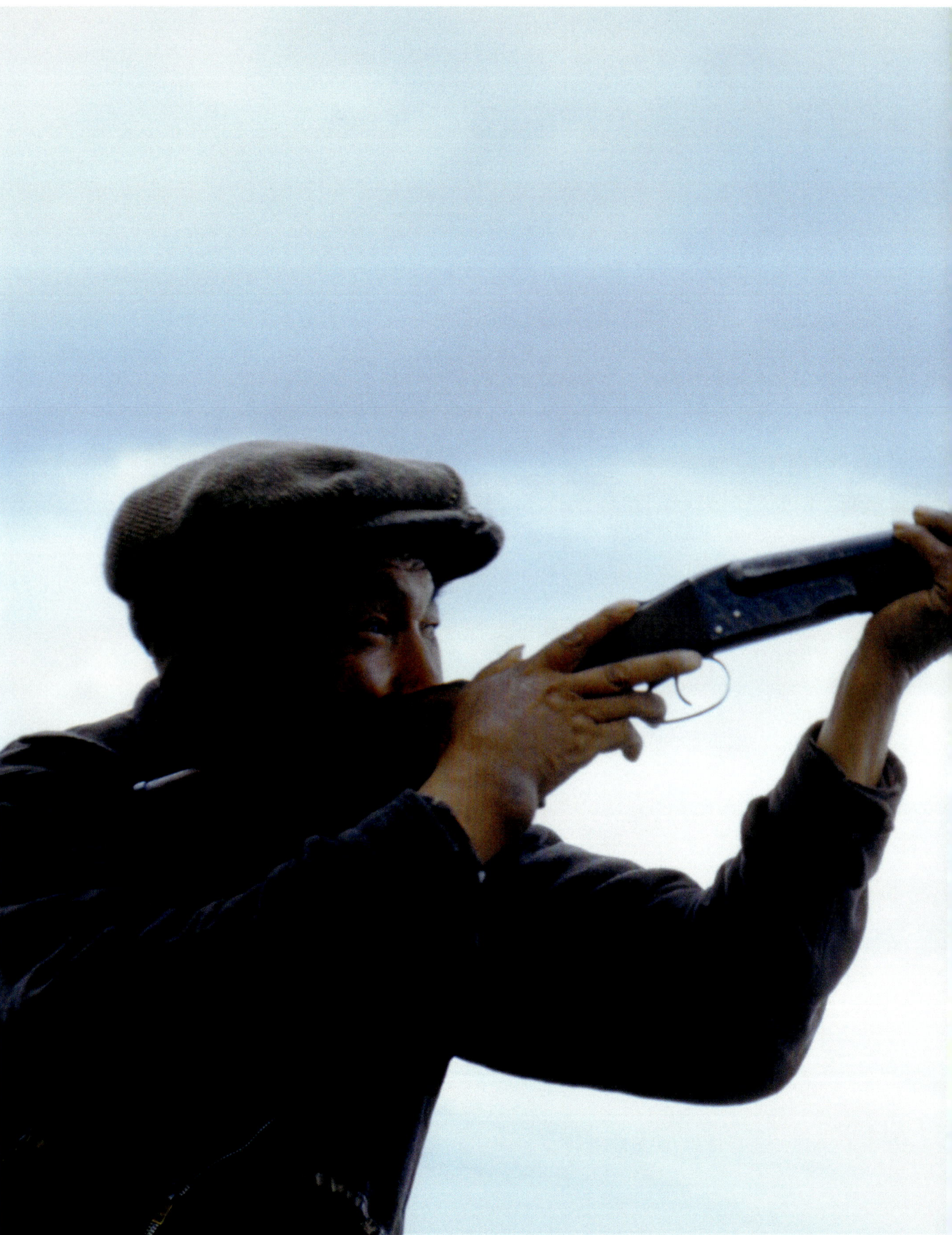

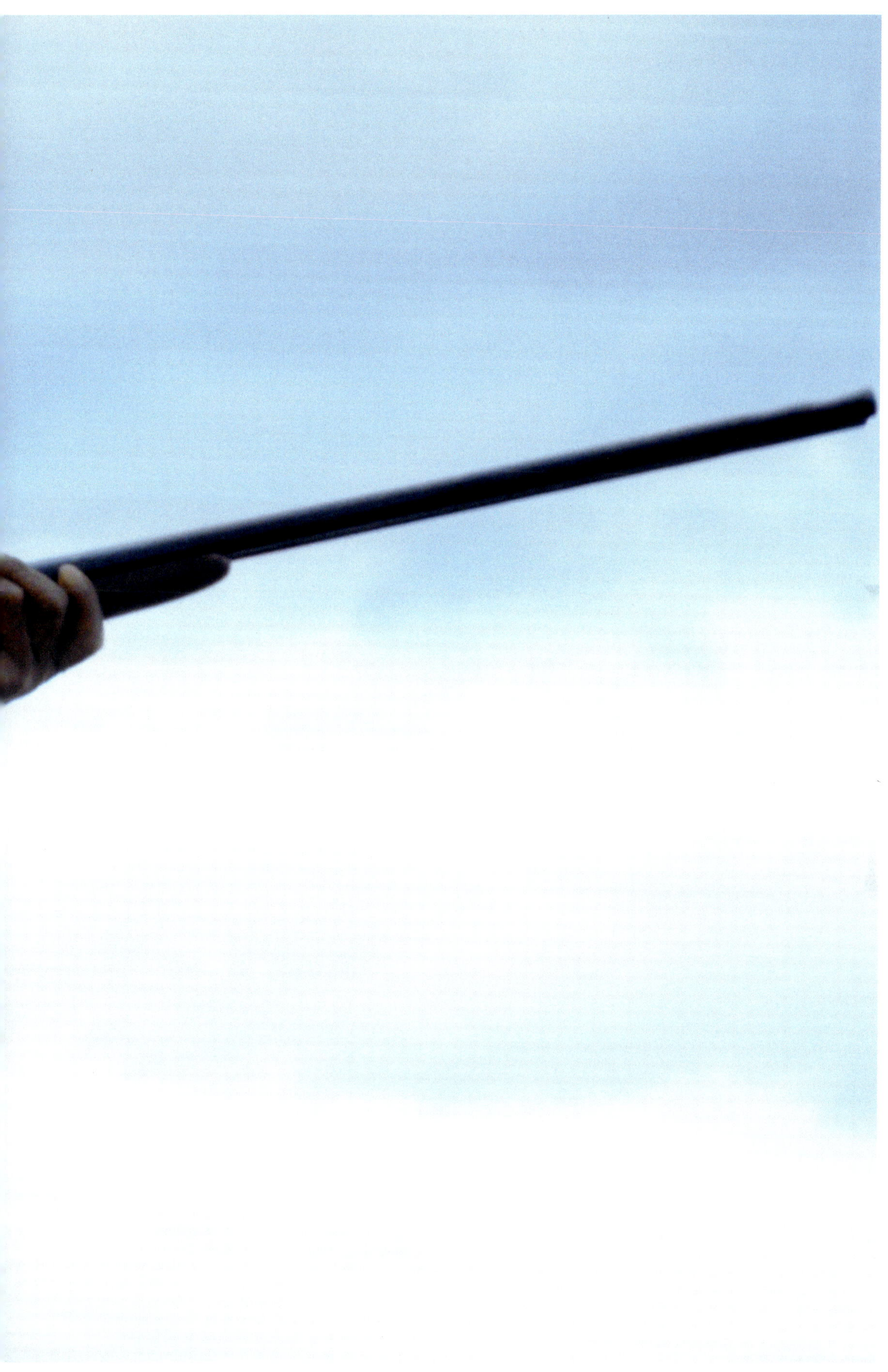

Sam Mathew showing his hunting skills, Fort Severn 1955

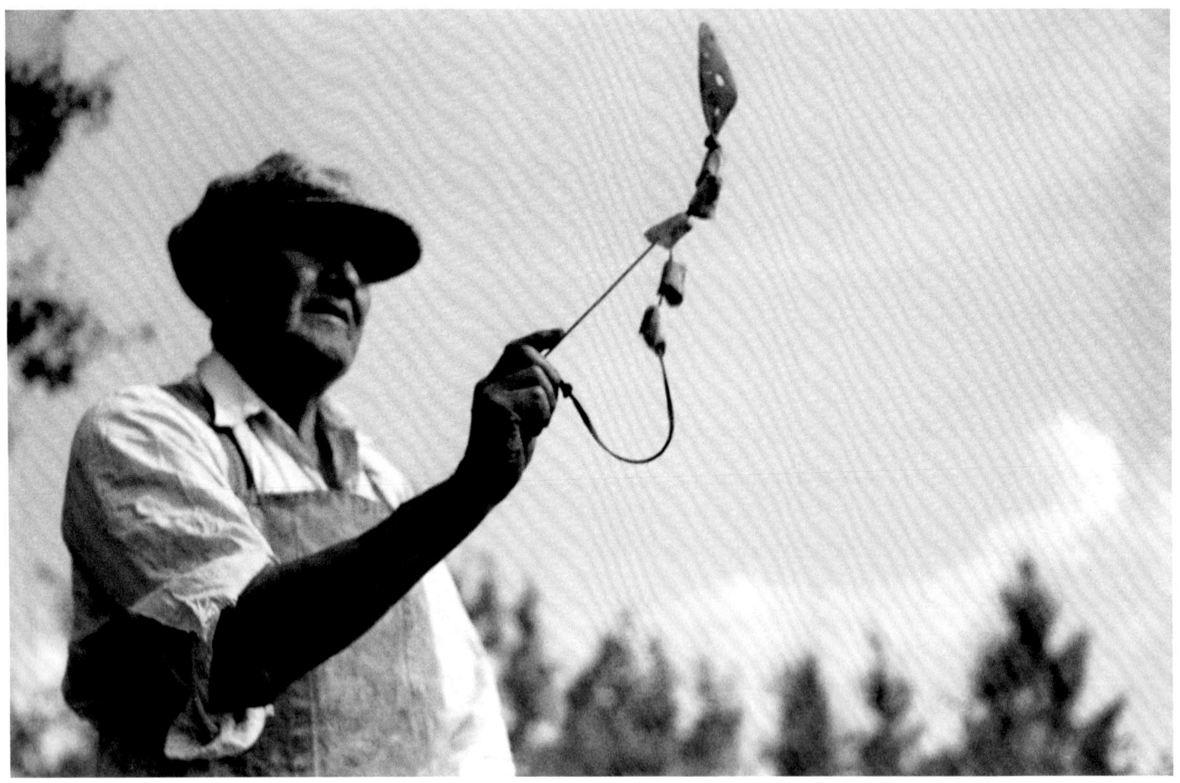

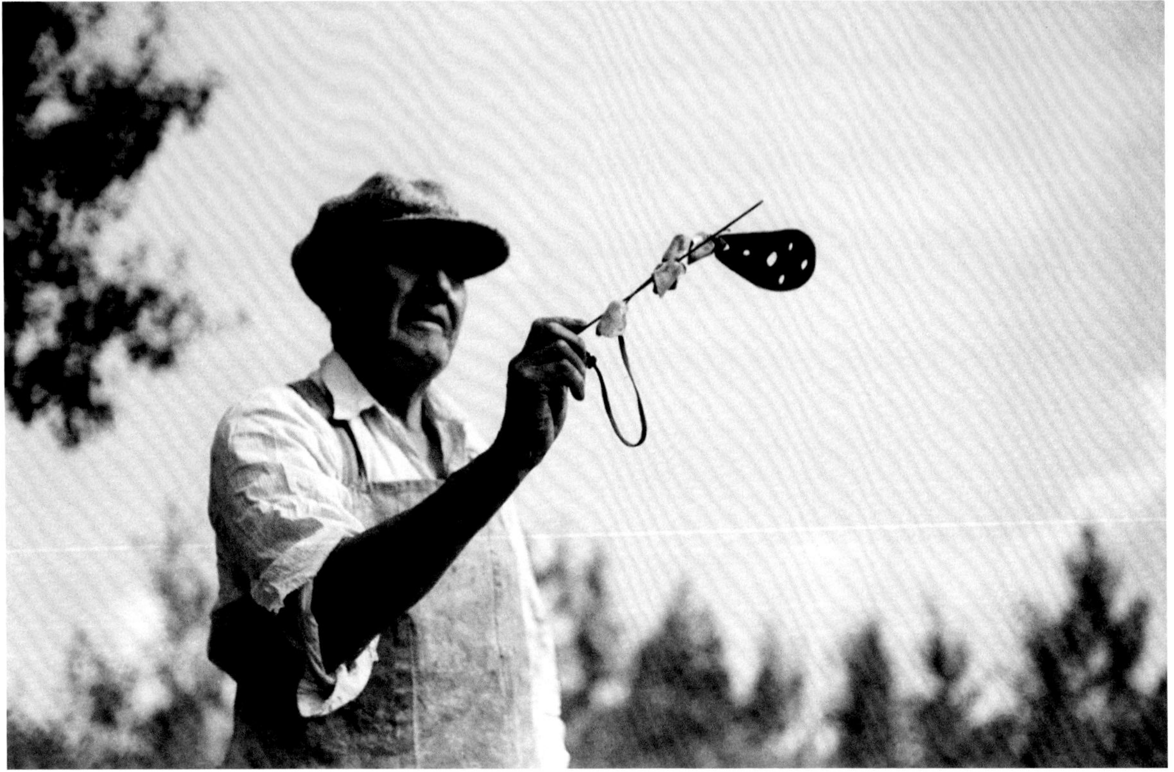

William Moore of Mattagami playing nabahon 1957

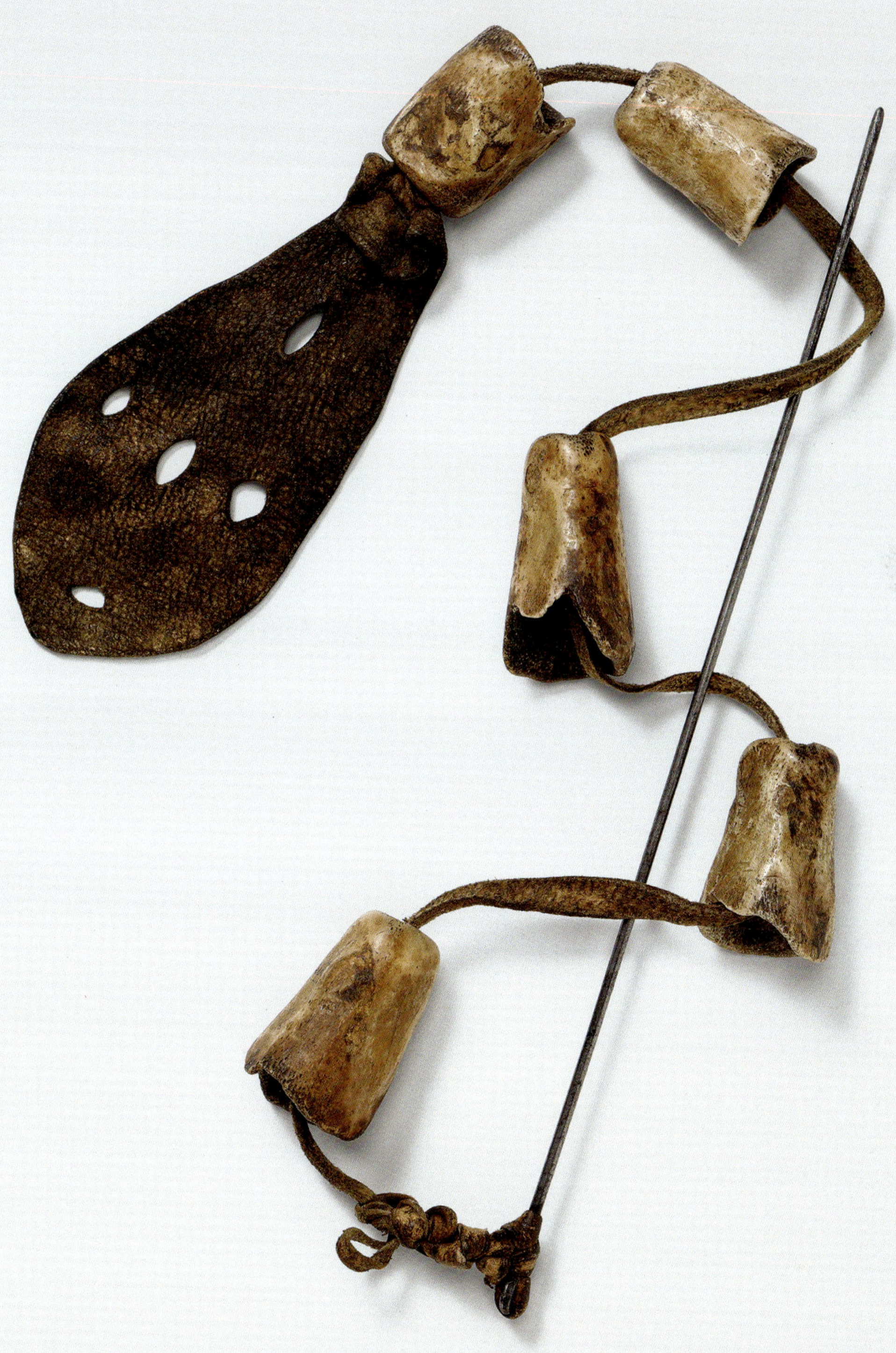

Nabahon made by William Moore, collected by John Macfie

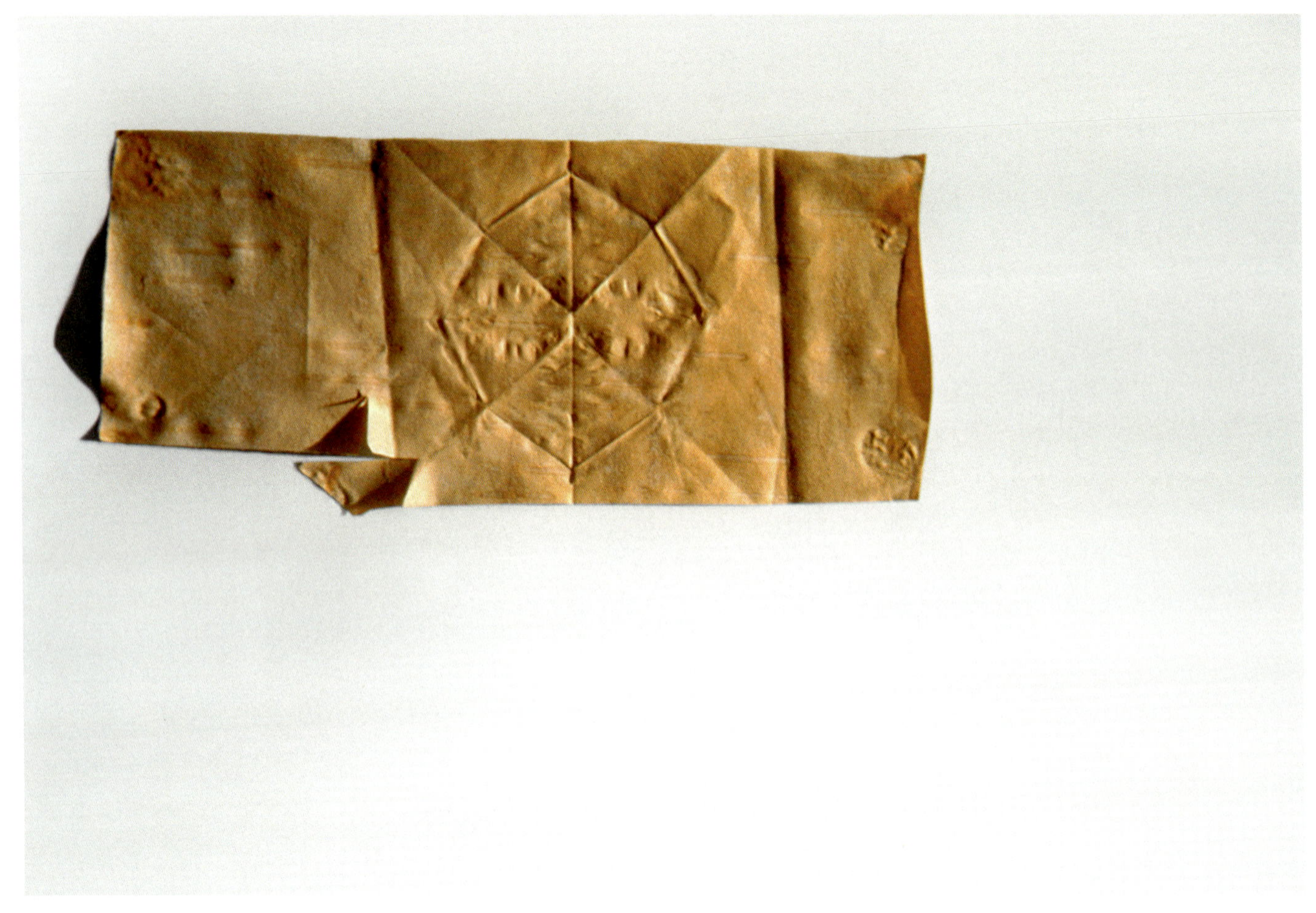

Unfolded birchbark reveals the design of a turtle 1958

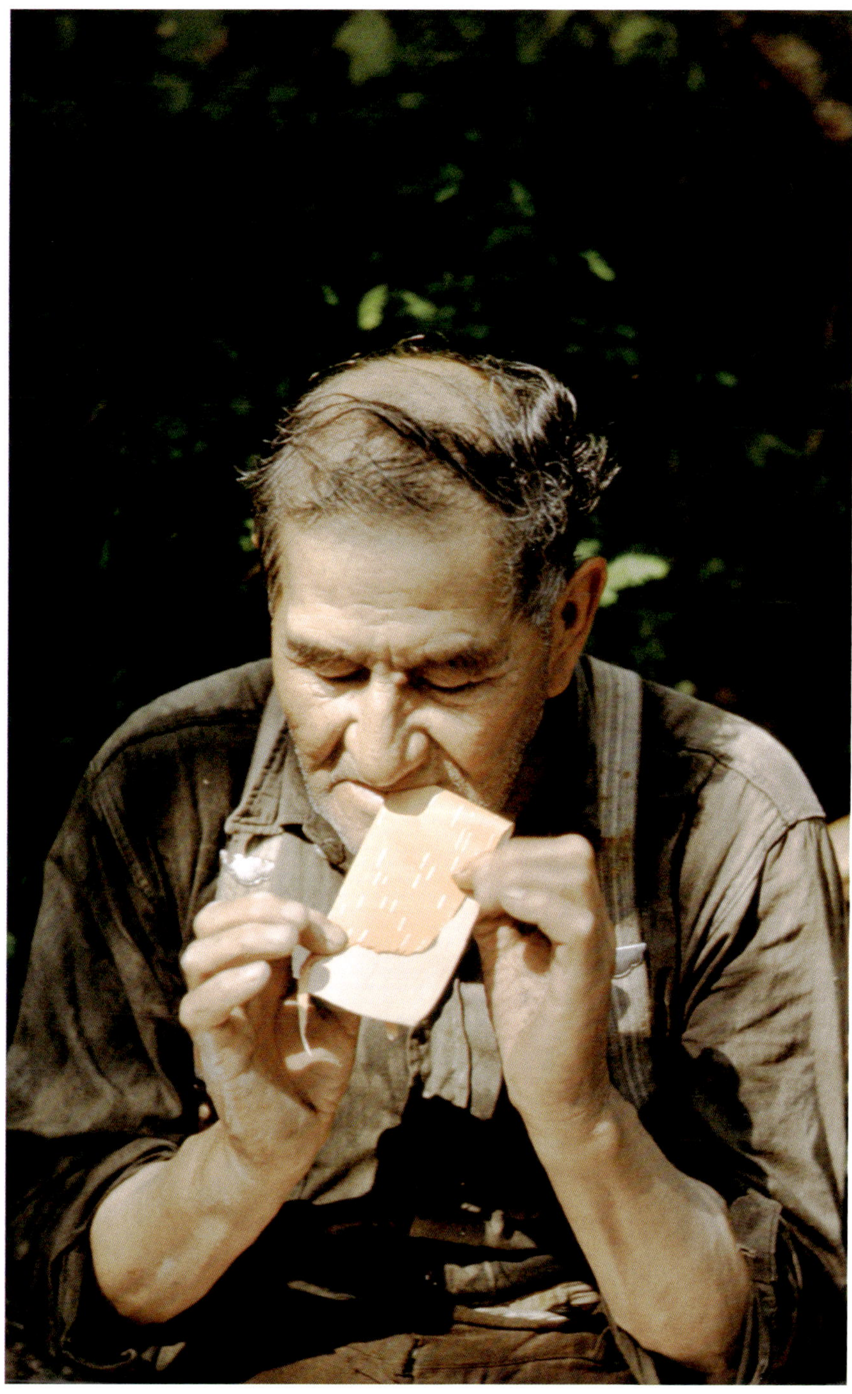

William Moore making birchbark-biting art 1958

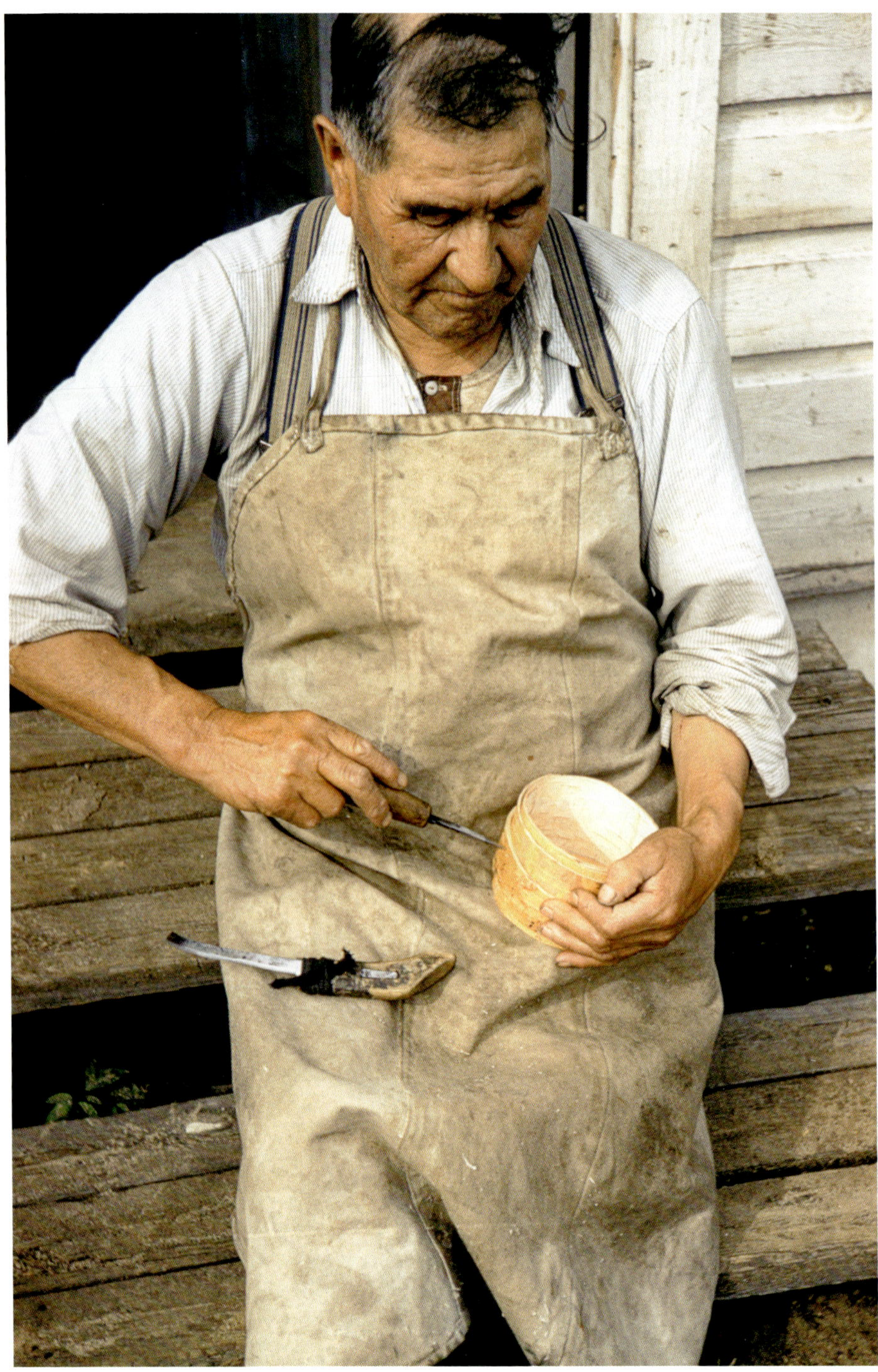

William Moore at work 1957

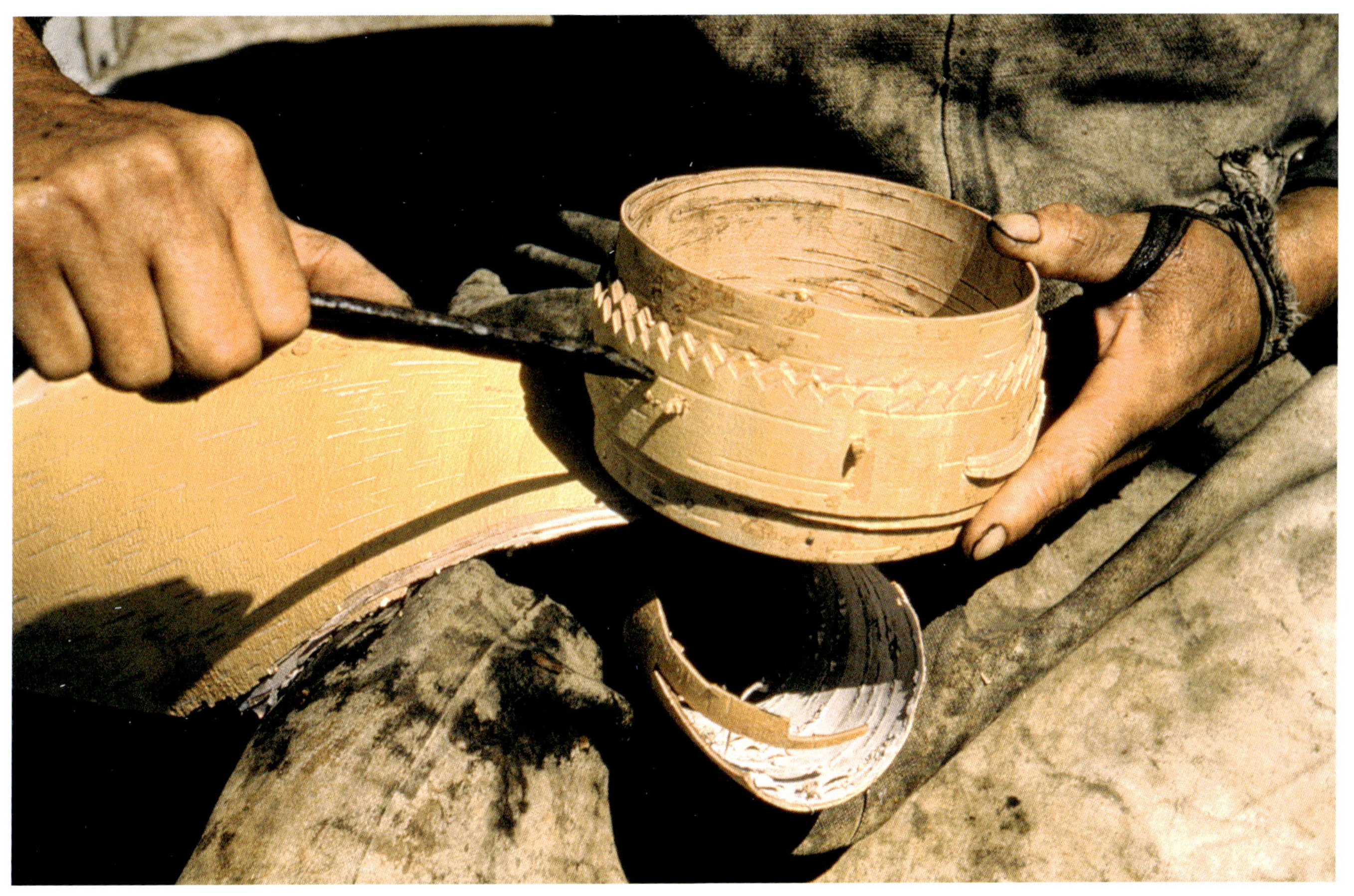

William Moore punching design holes in a circular birchbark container c. 1957

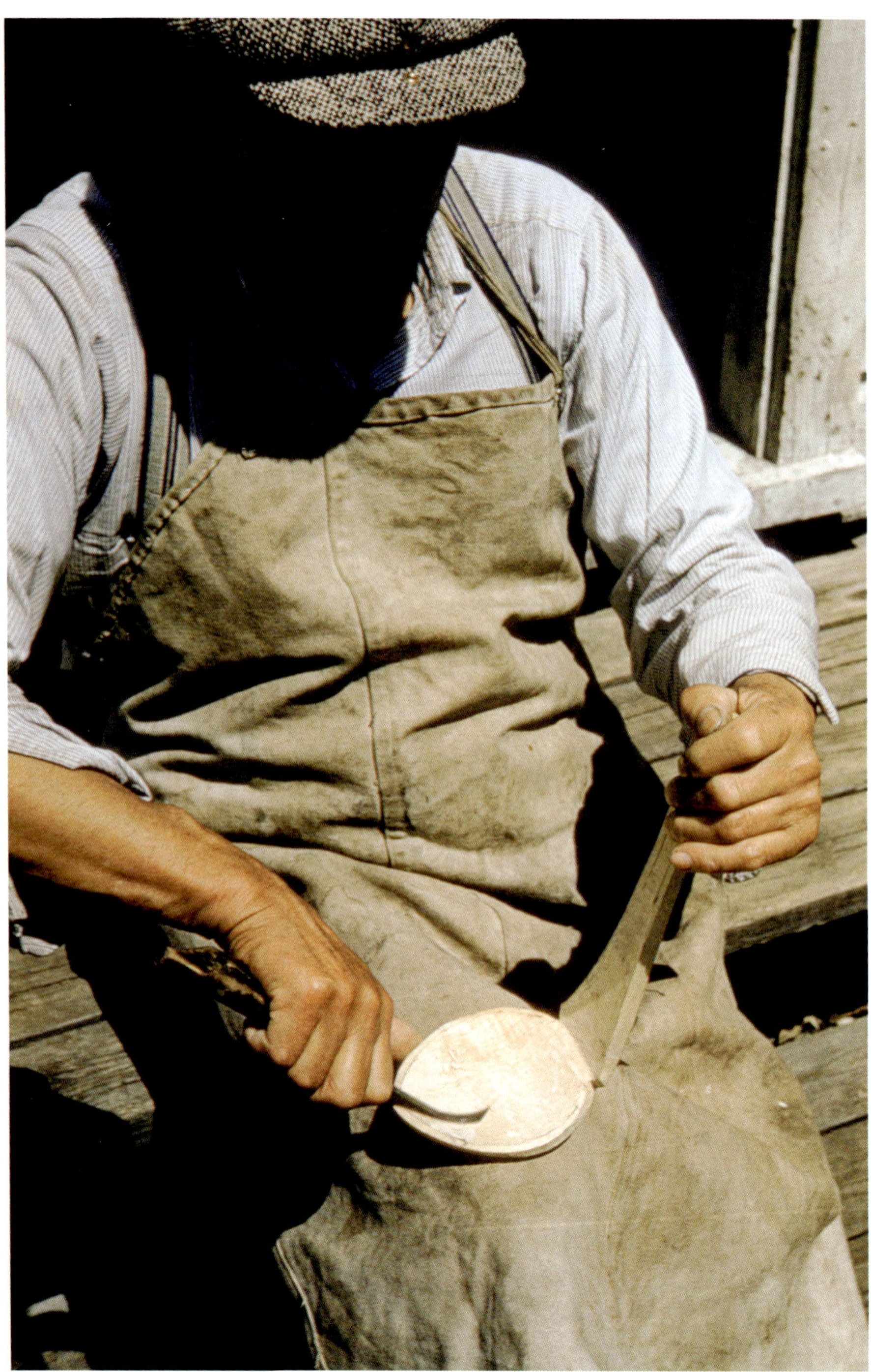

William Moore carving a ladle from birch wood, using a Hudson's Bay Company crooked knife, or canoe knife 1958

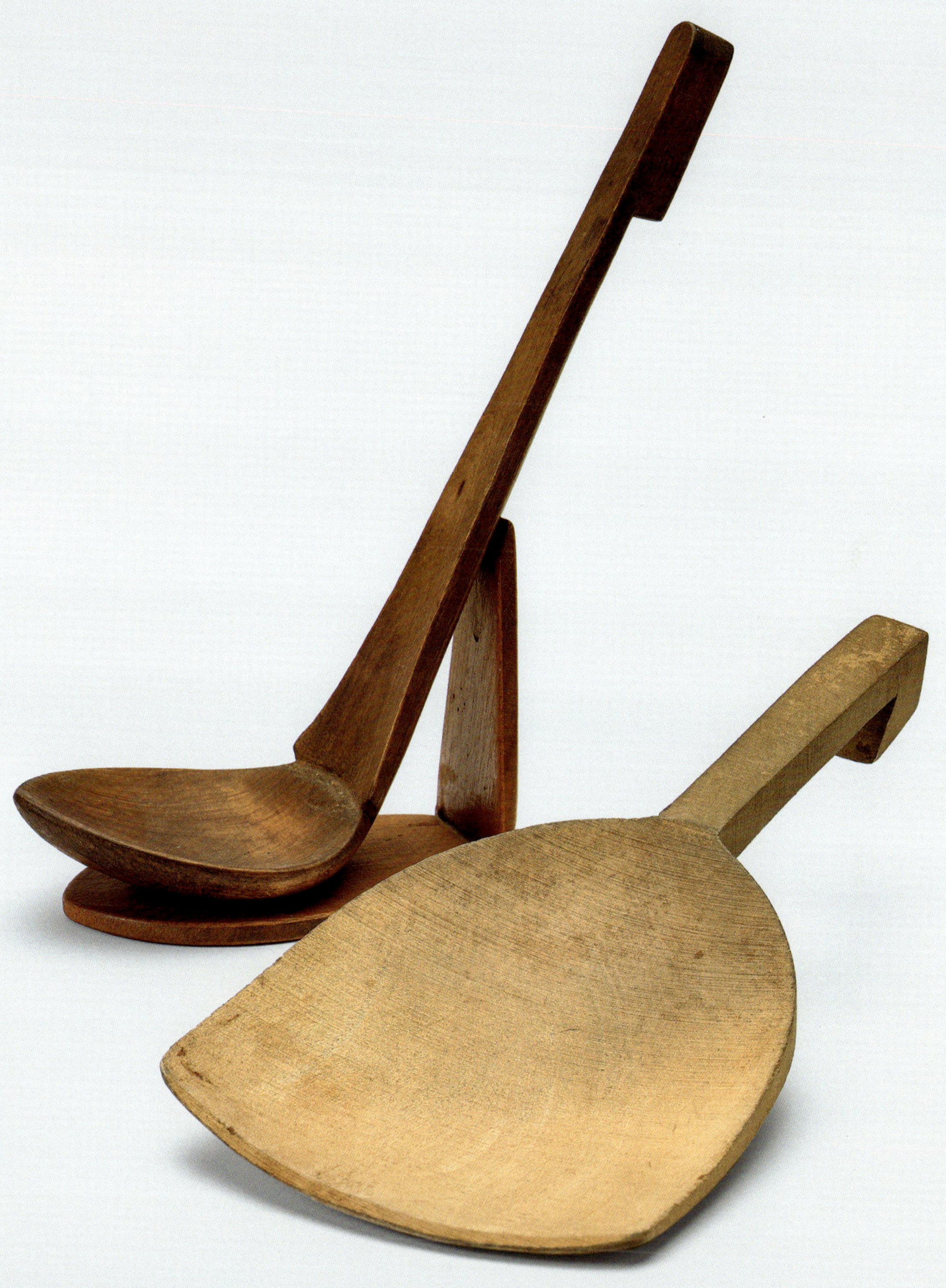

Ladle and shovel made by William Moore, collected by John Macfie

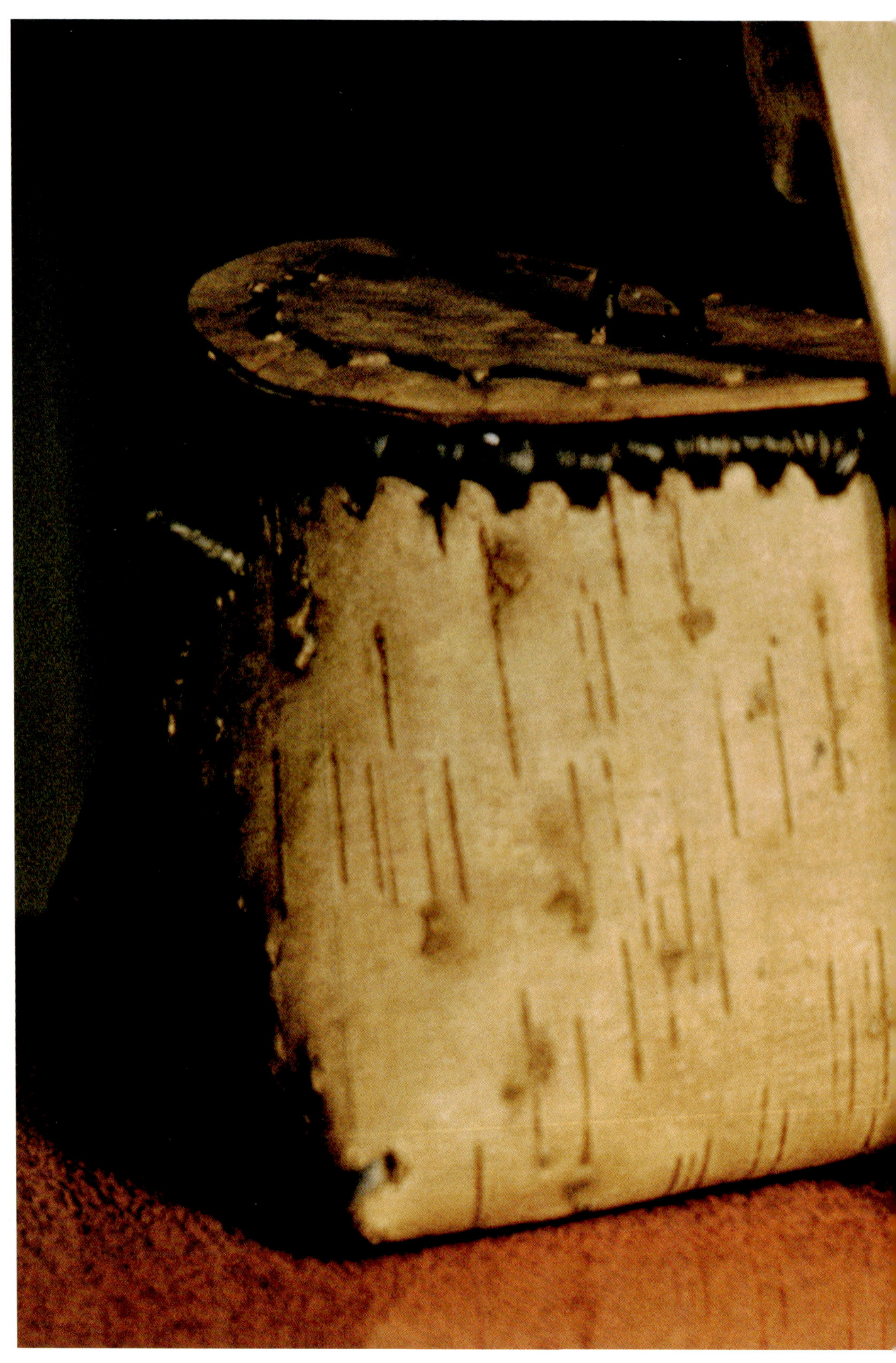

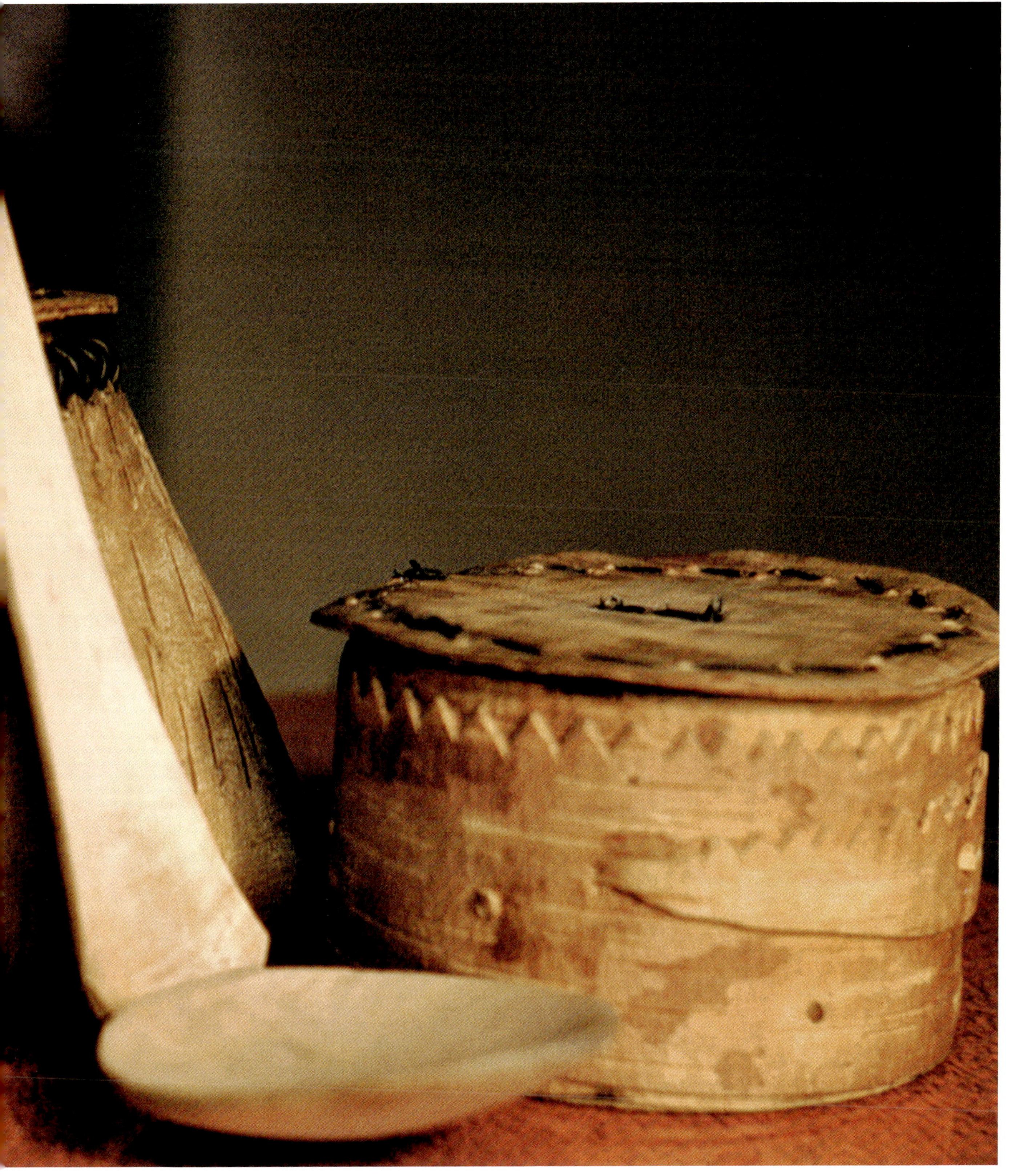

A birchbark container, basket, and wooden ladle, all made by William Moore c. 1957

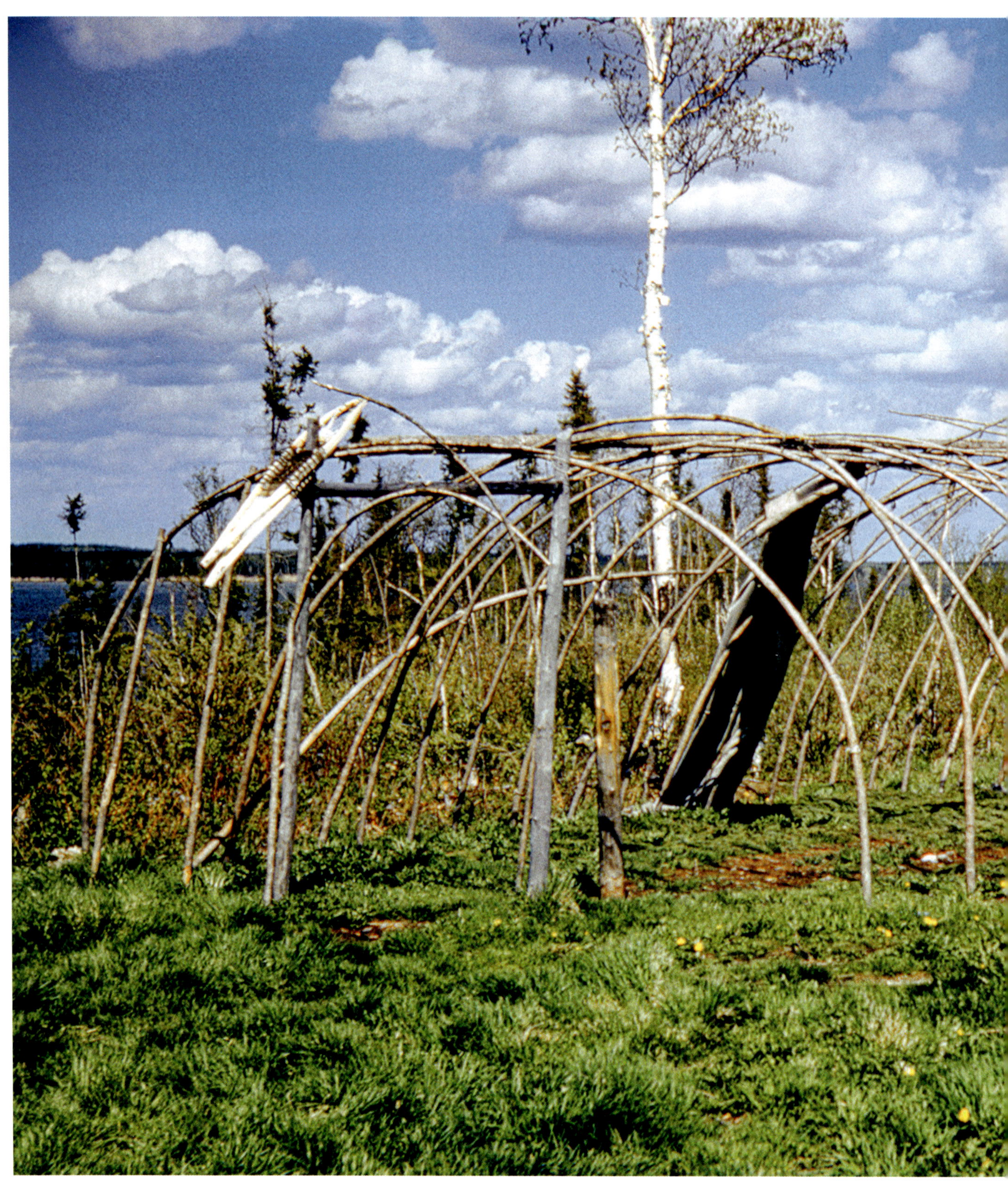

Frame of a wabinogamick, a ceremonial and feasting lodge, Sandy Lake 1956

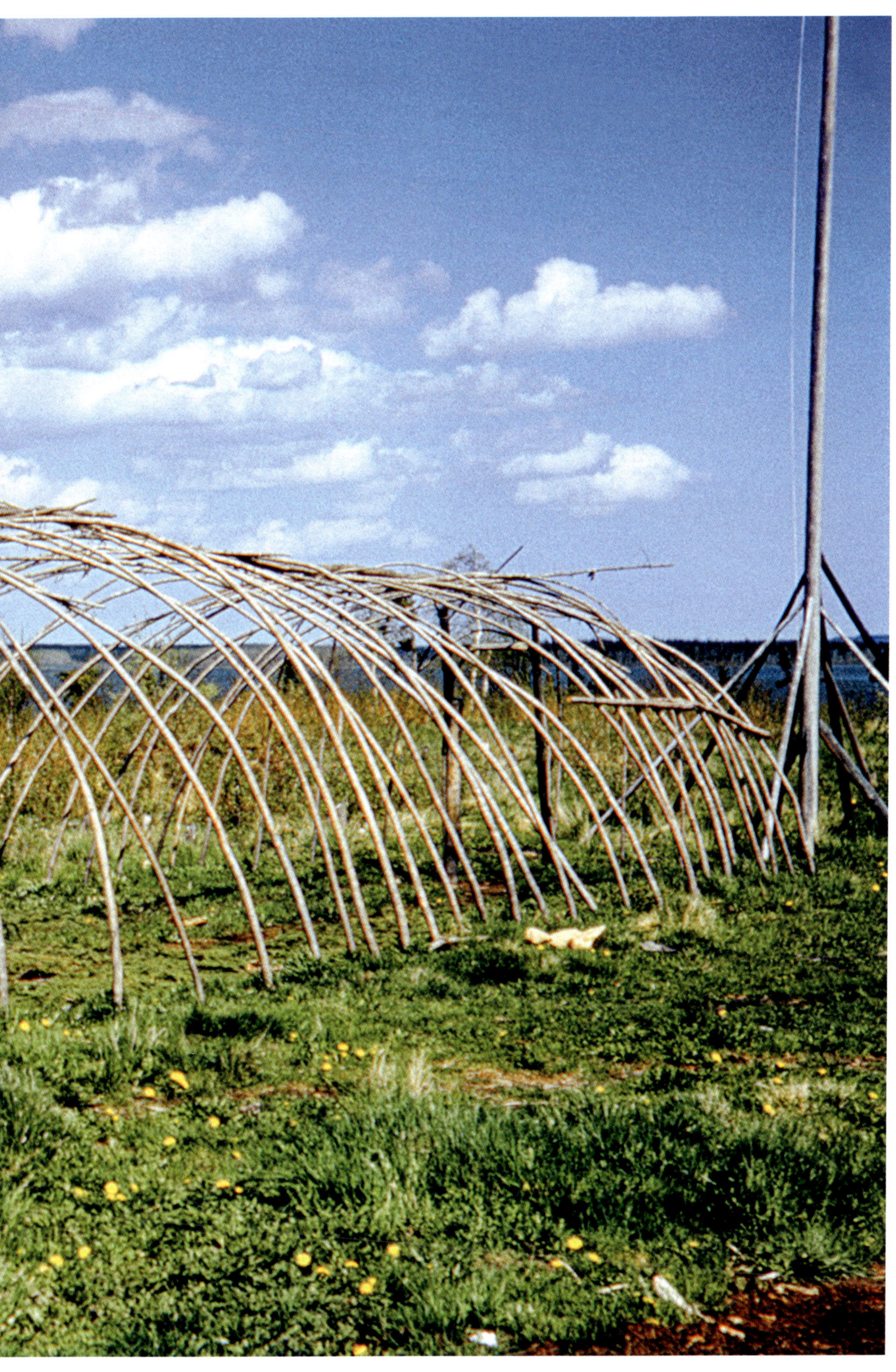

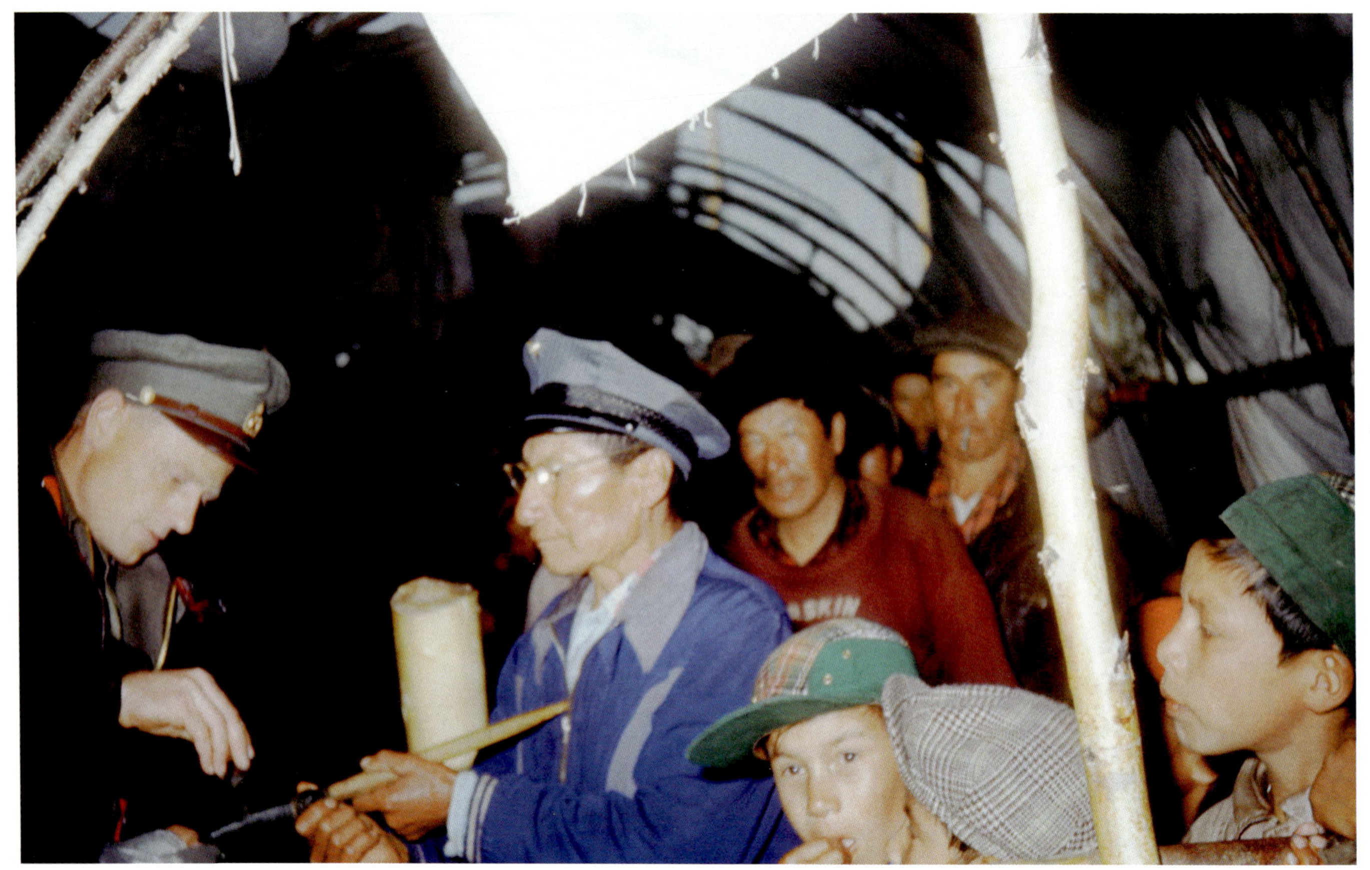

John Macfie offering tobacco for Francis Meekis's pipe 1952

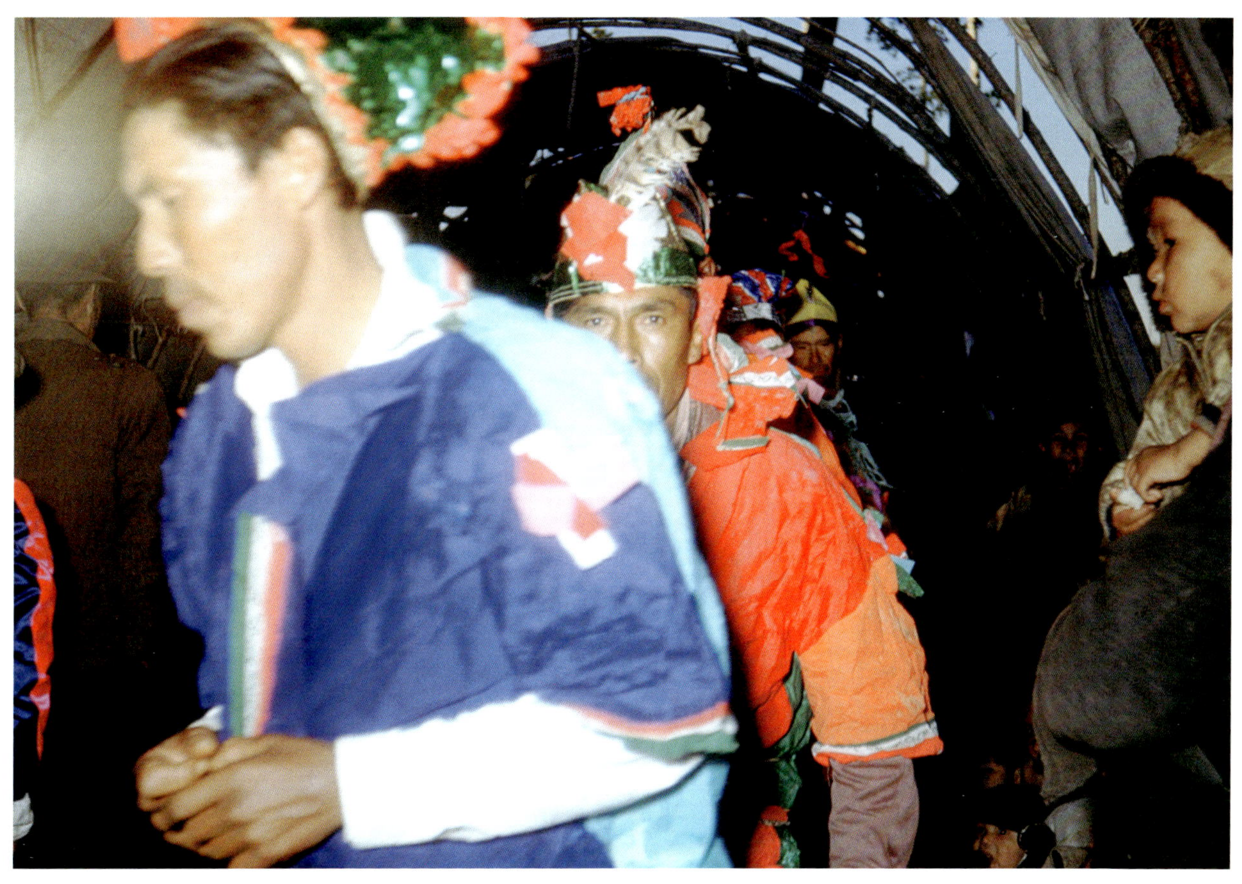

Inside the wabinogamick, Sandy Lake 1953

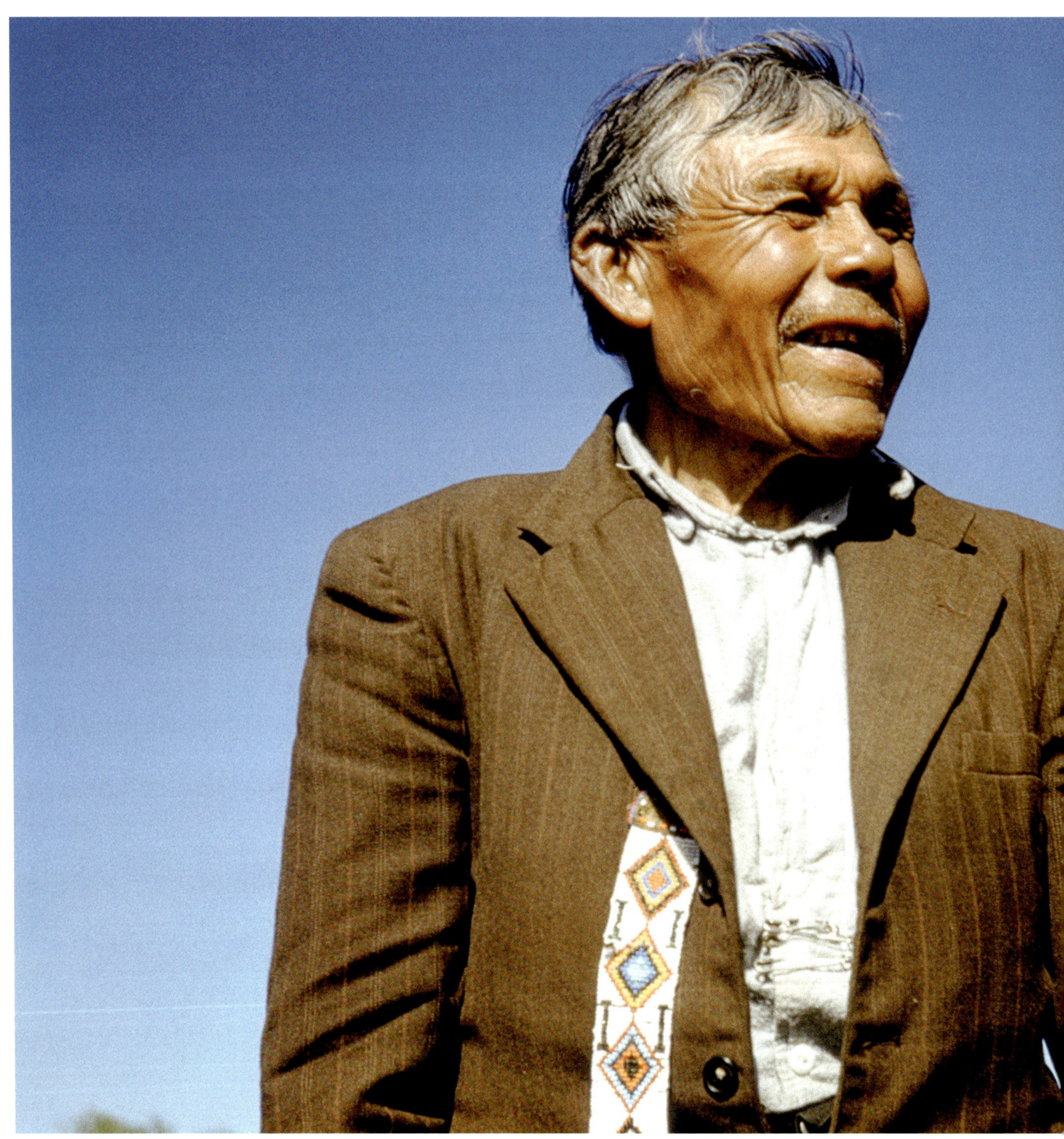

Abraham Keeper of Pikangikum, Kenora District c. 1953

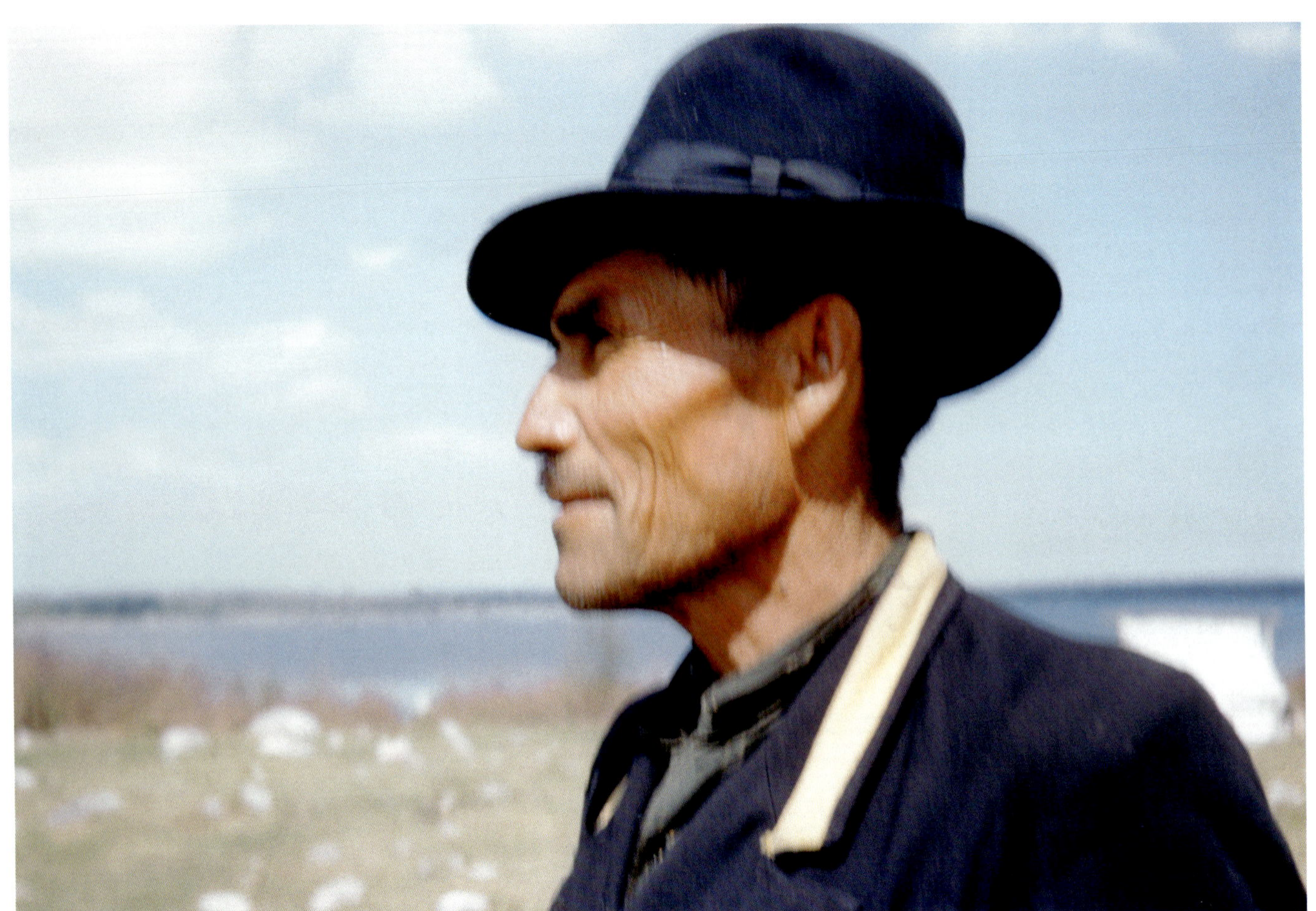

Chief Robert Wesley of Lac Seul, Kenora District c. 1953

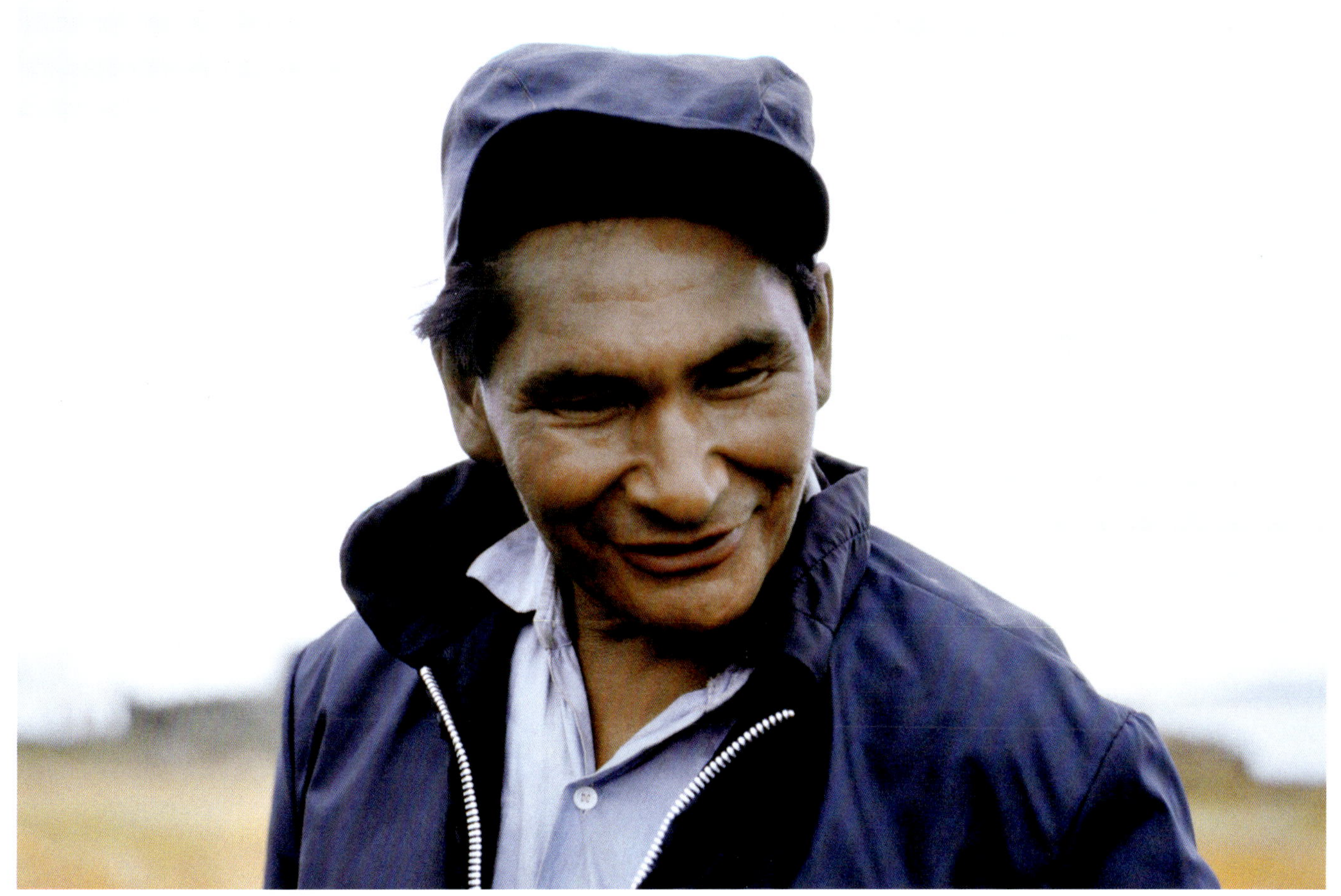

Philip "Swampy" Mathew 1963

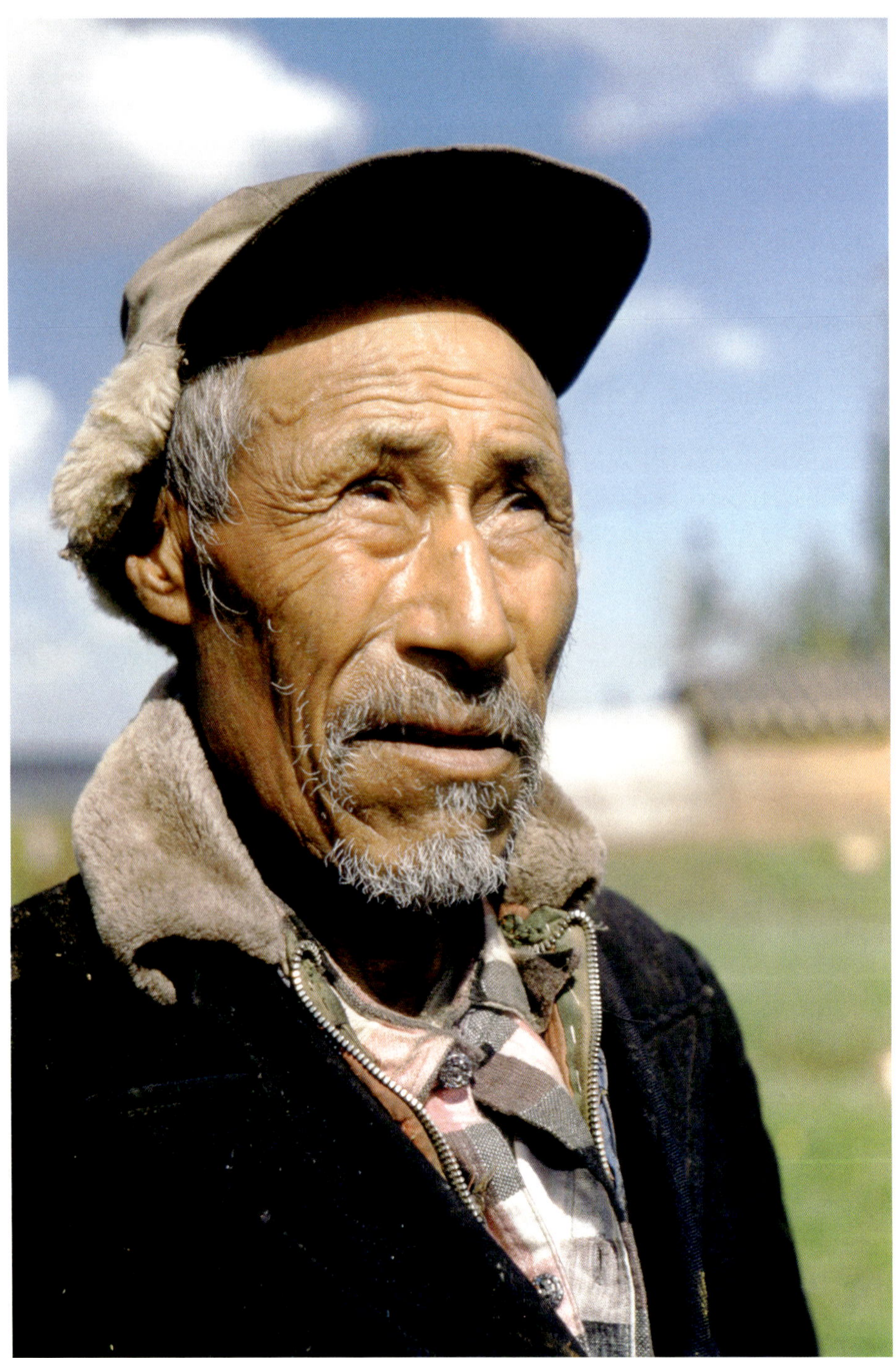

Elijah Kakegamic of Sandy Lake c. 1959

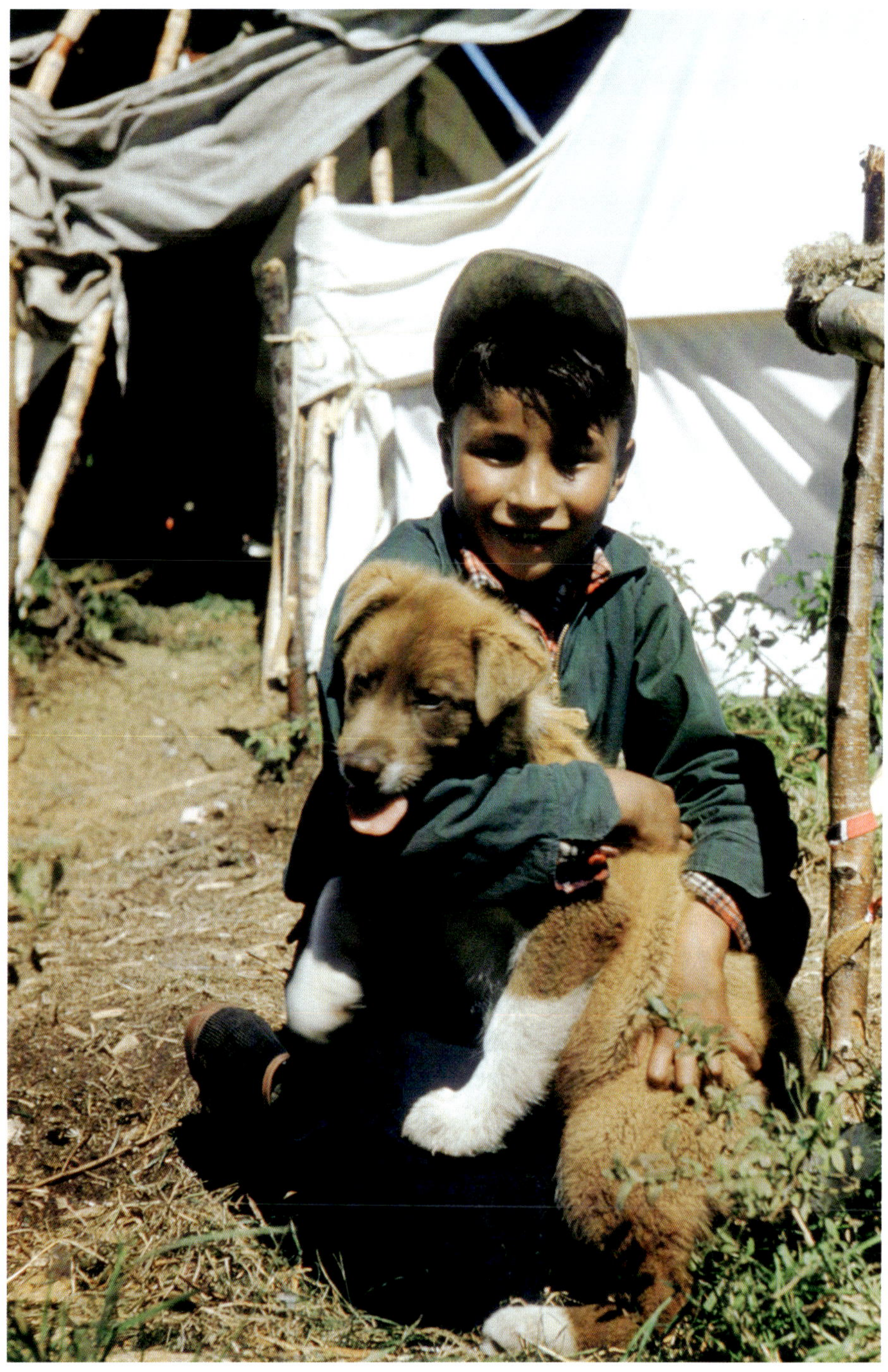

A boy with a pup at Neskantaga June 1956

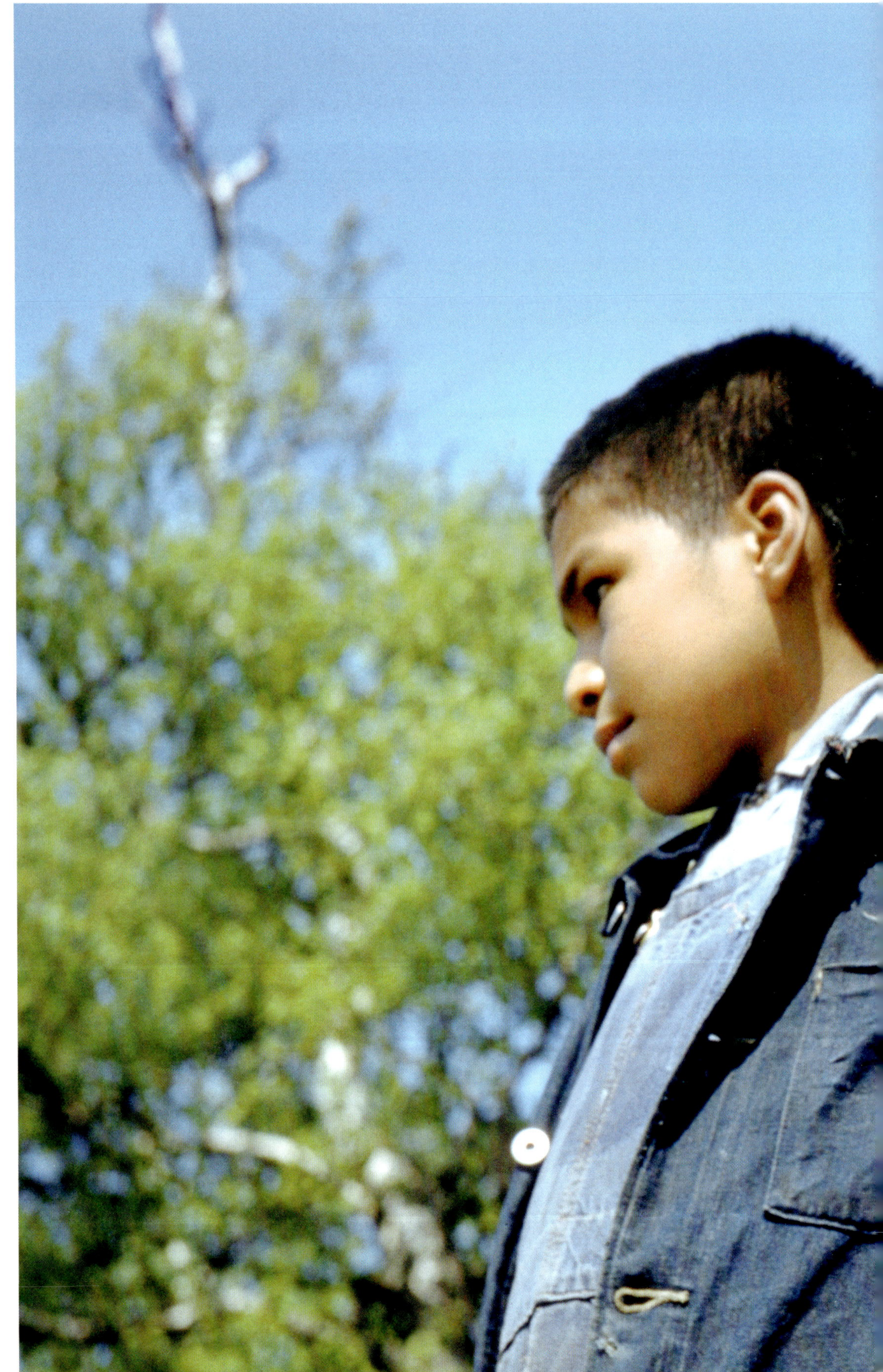

Students at Pelican Falls Indian Residential School near Sioux Lookout
c. 1953

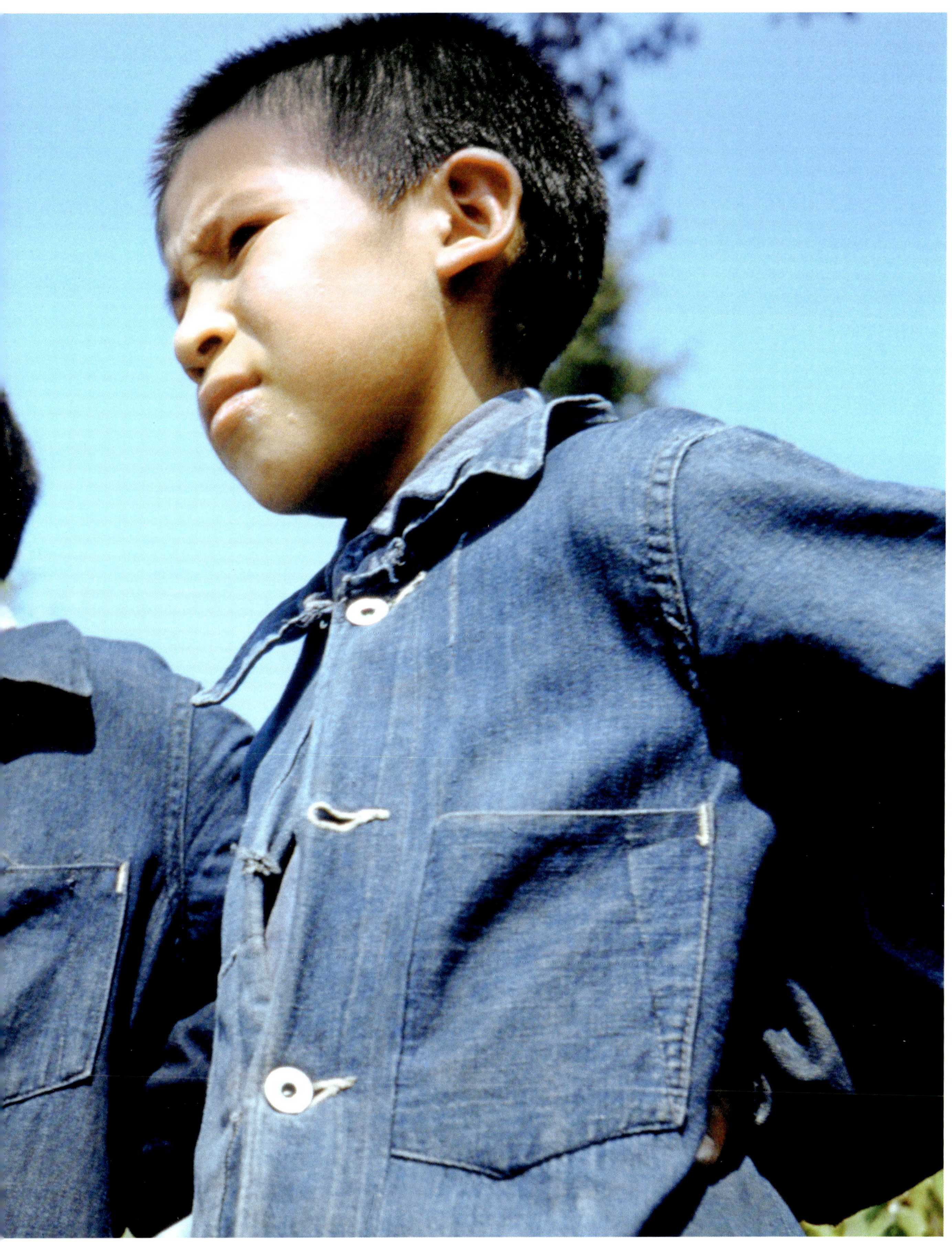

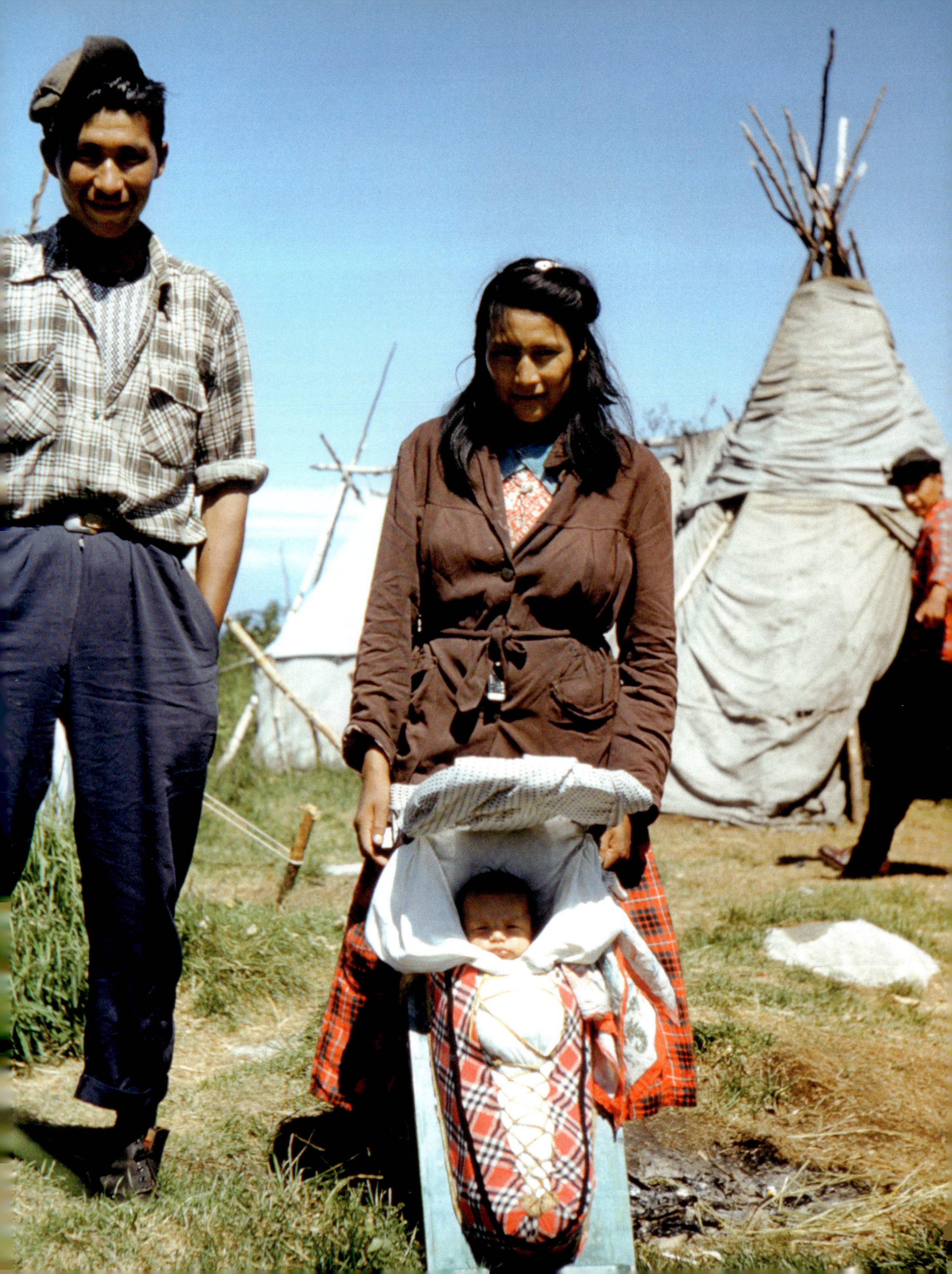

Summer

A man, a woman, and their baby at Treaty Time, near Neskantaga on the shore of Attawapiskat Lake in the Kenora District 1956

Family walking down the boardwalk at Neskantaga 1956

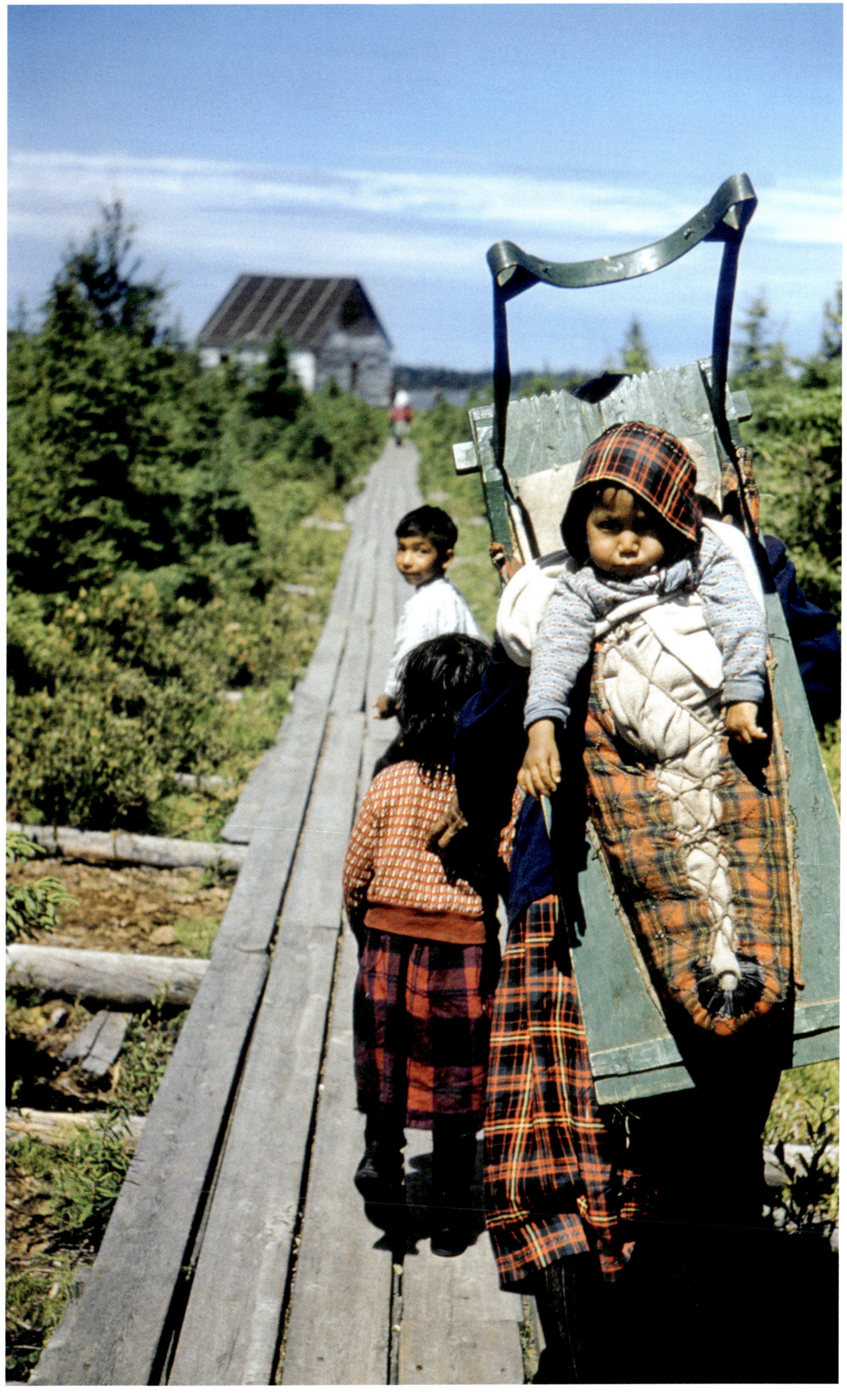

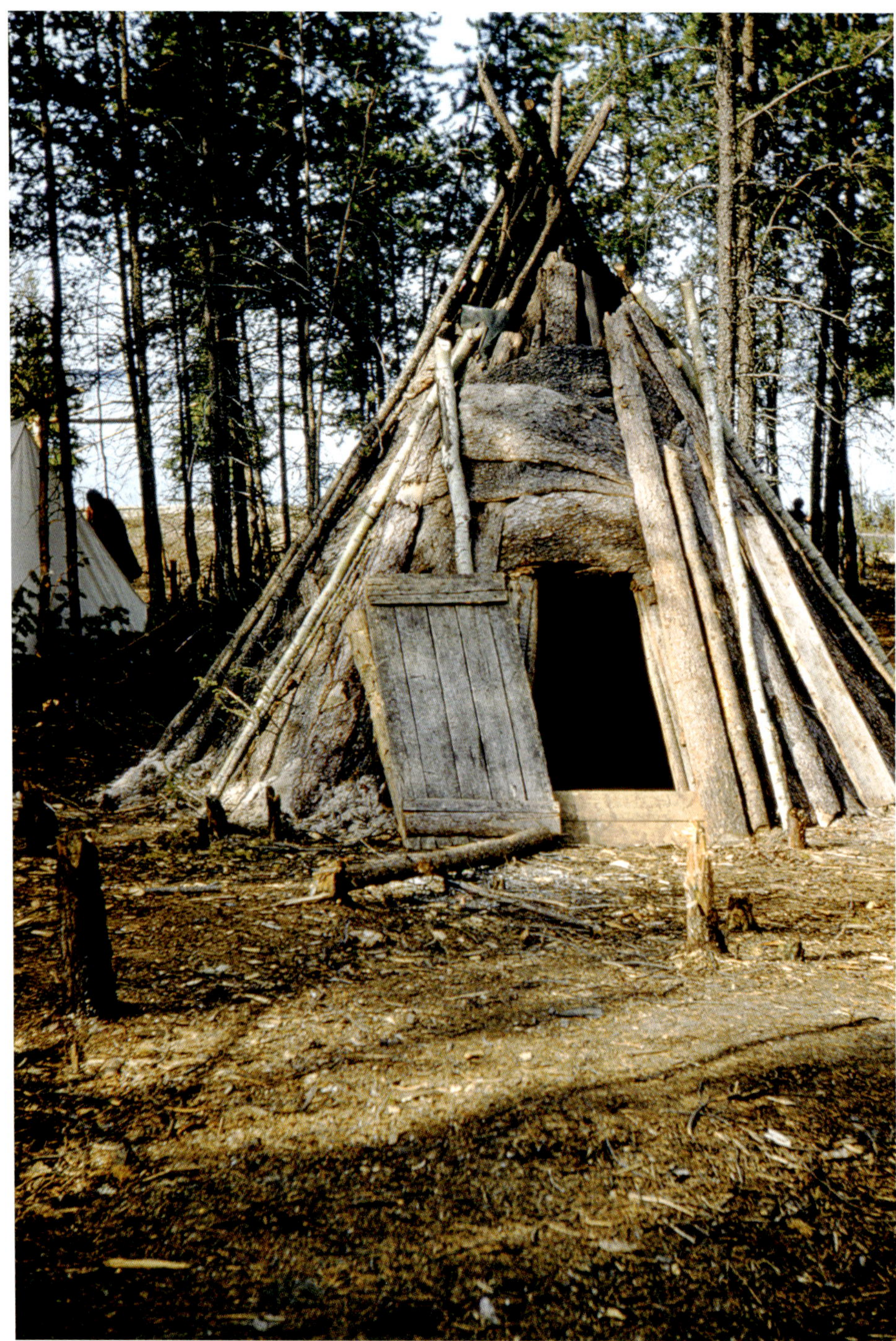

A smokehouse, Weagamow Lake (Round Lake), Kenora District c. 1955

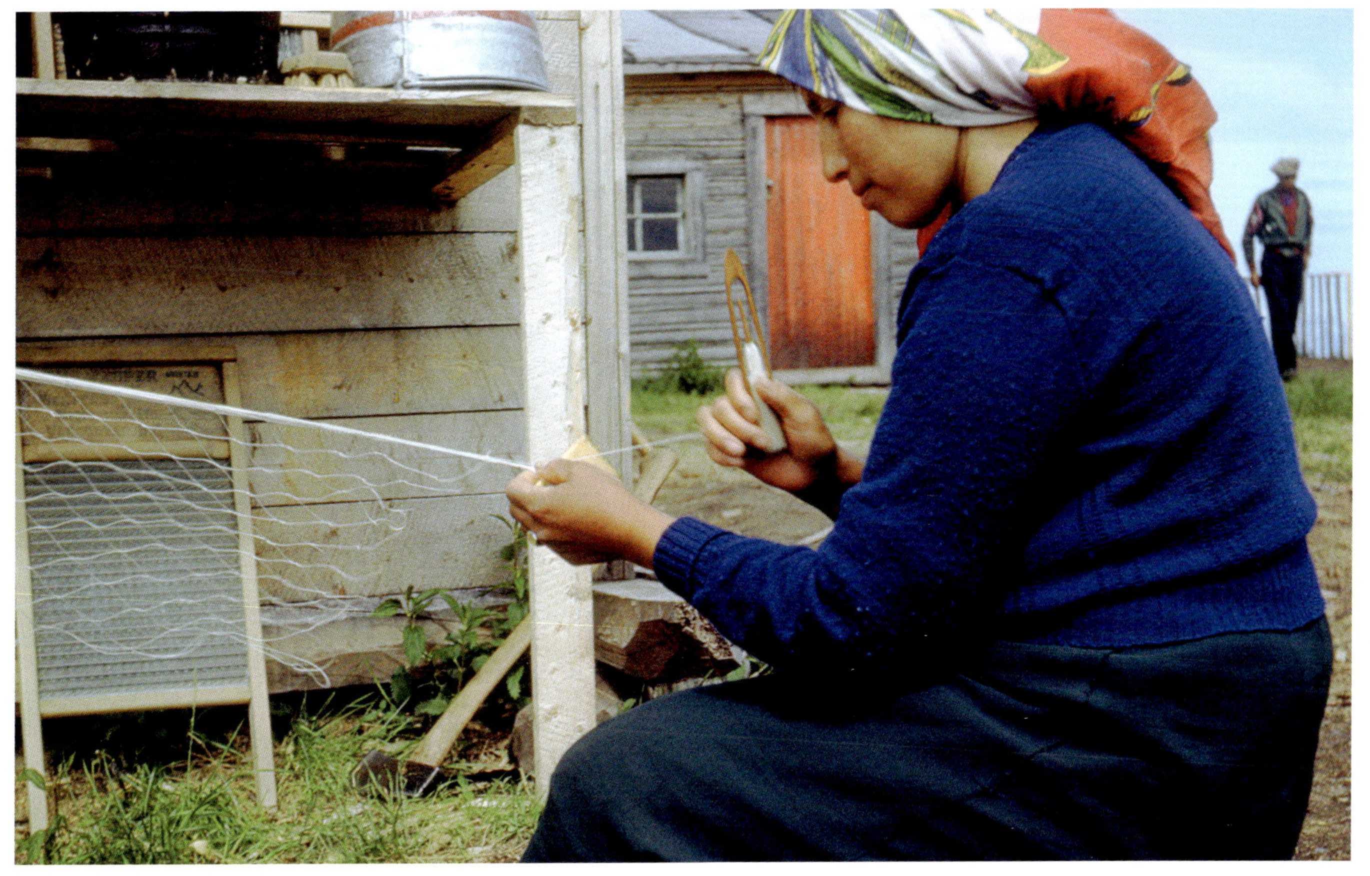

Repairing a gill net, Kasabonika, Kenora District c. 1952

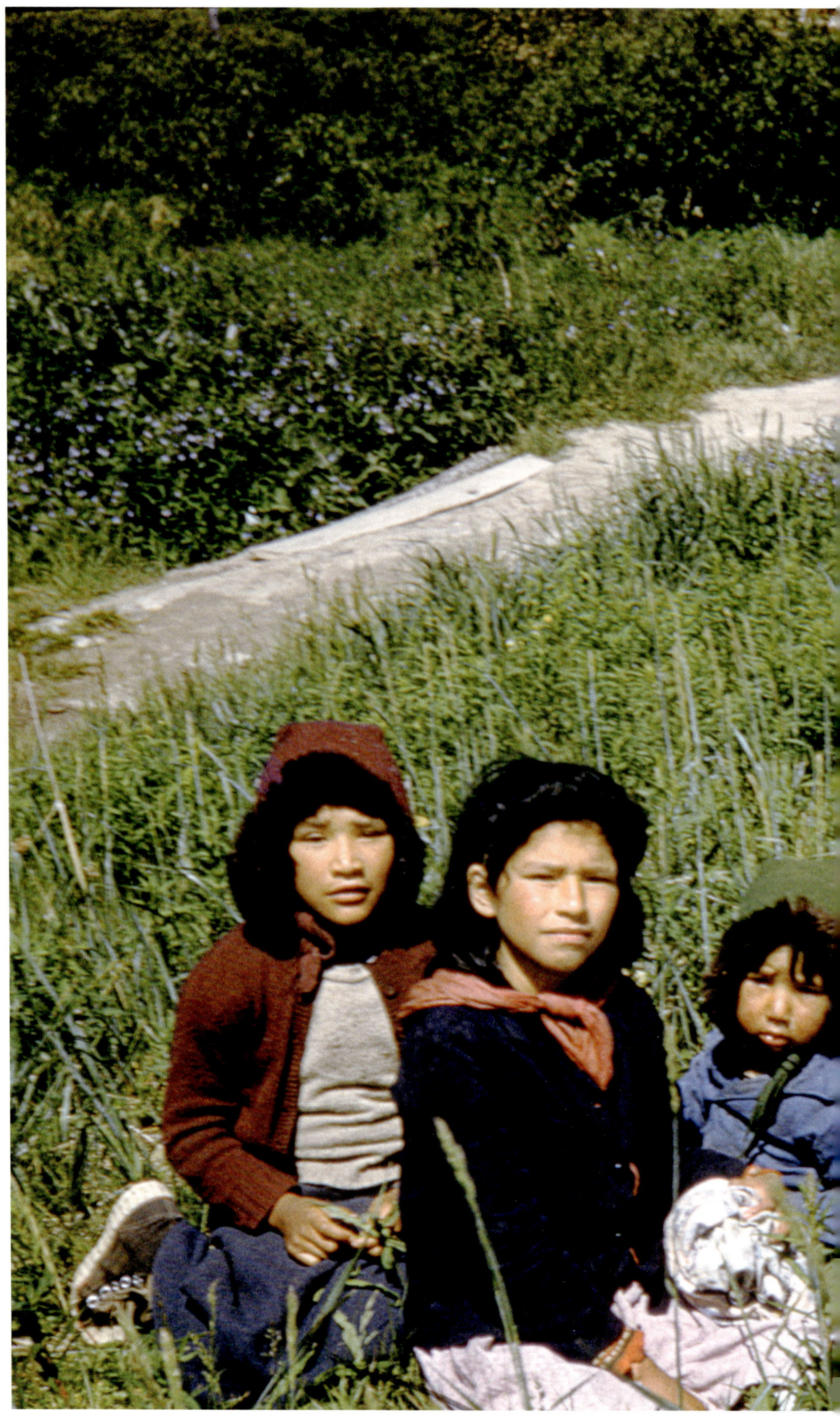

Sitting in the grass at Fort Severn 1955

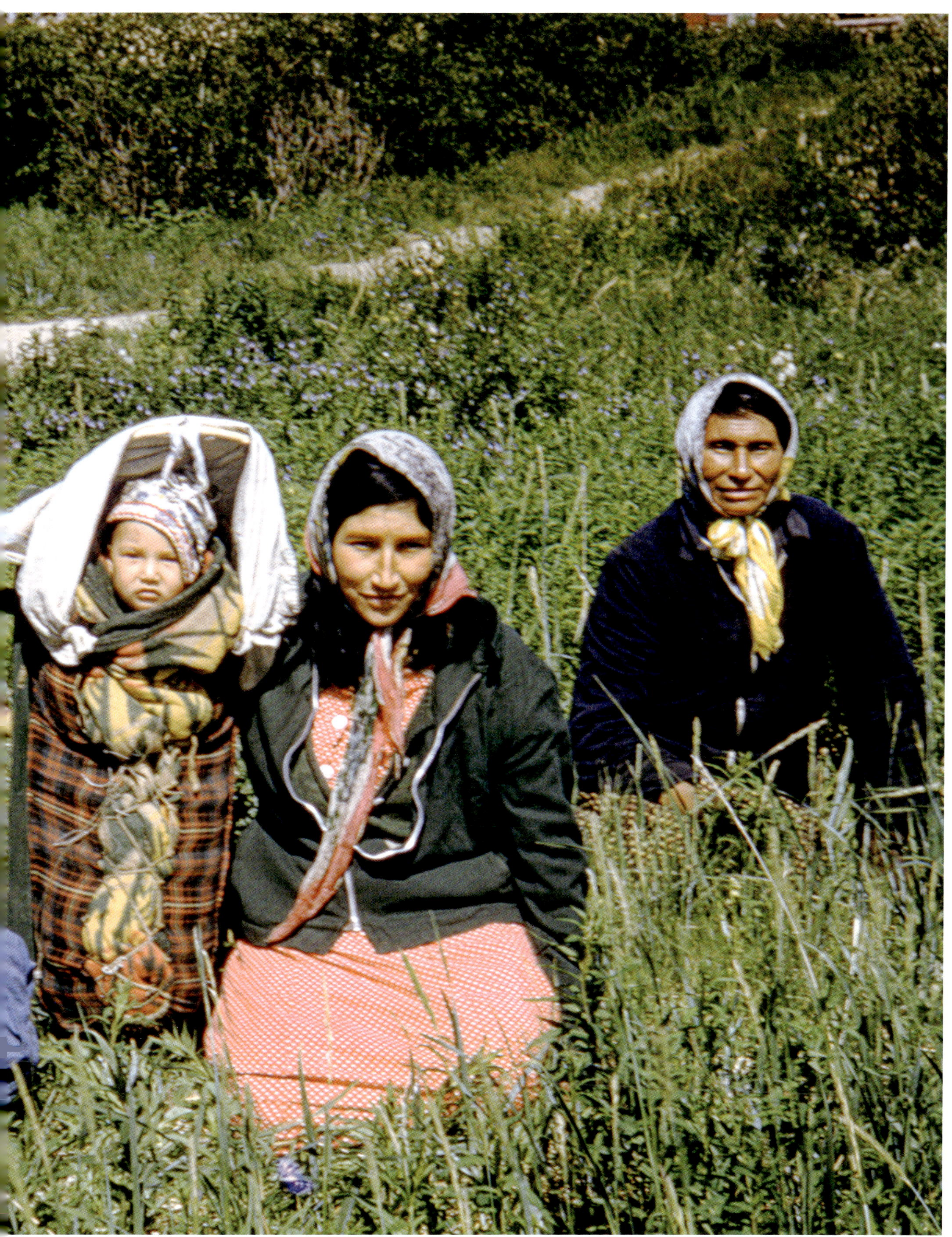

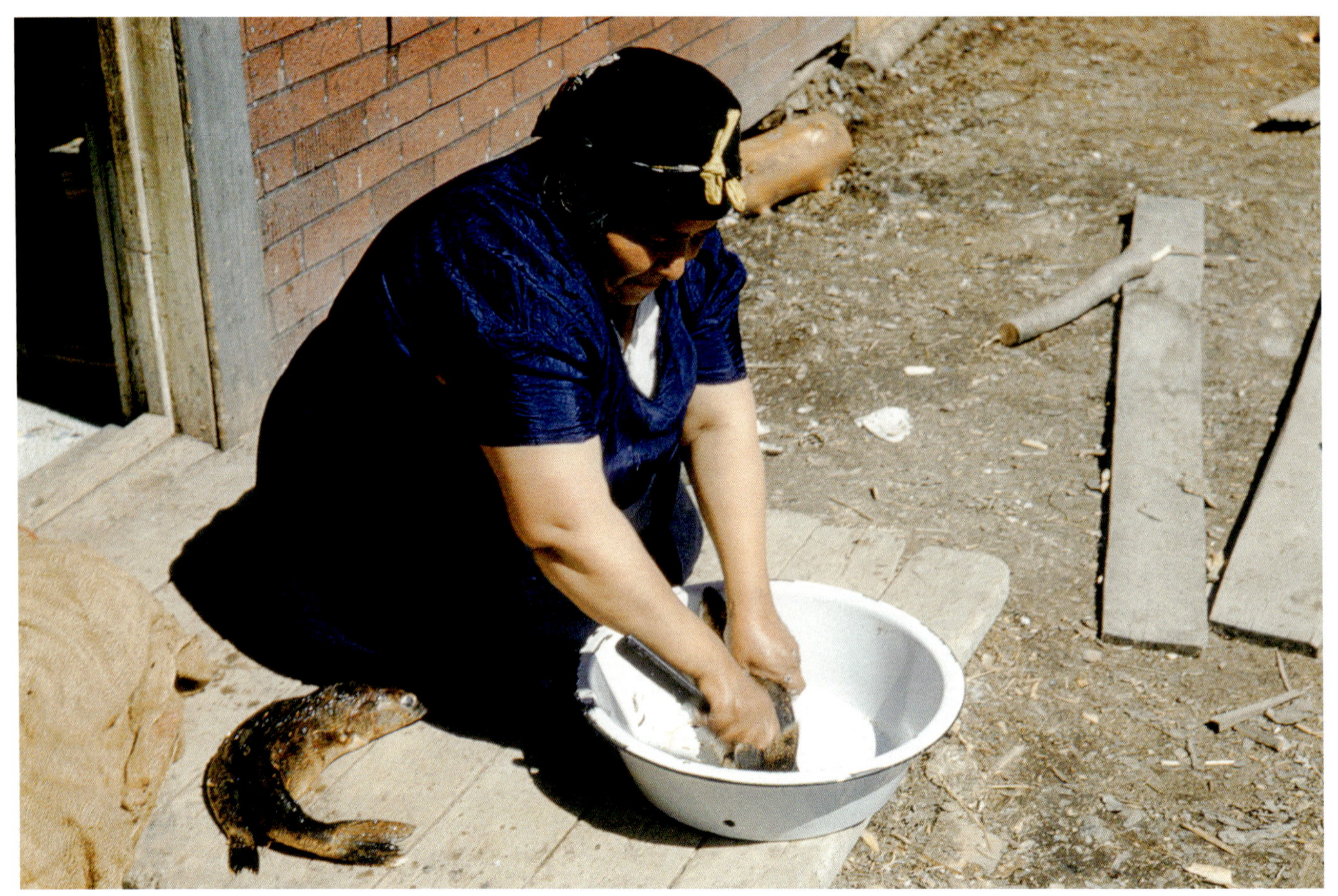

A woman cleaning a pickerel, Longlac, Thunder Bay District c. 1955

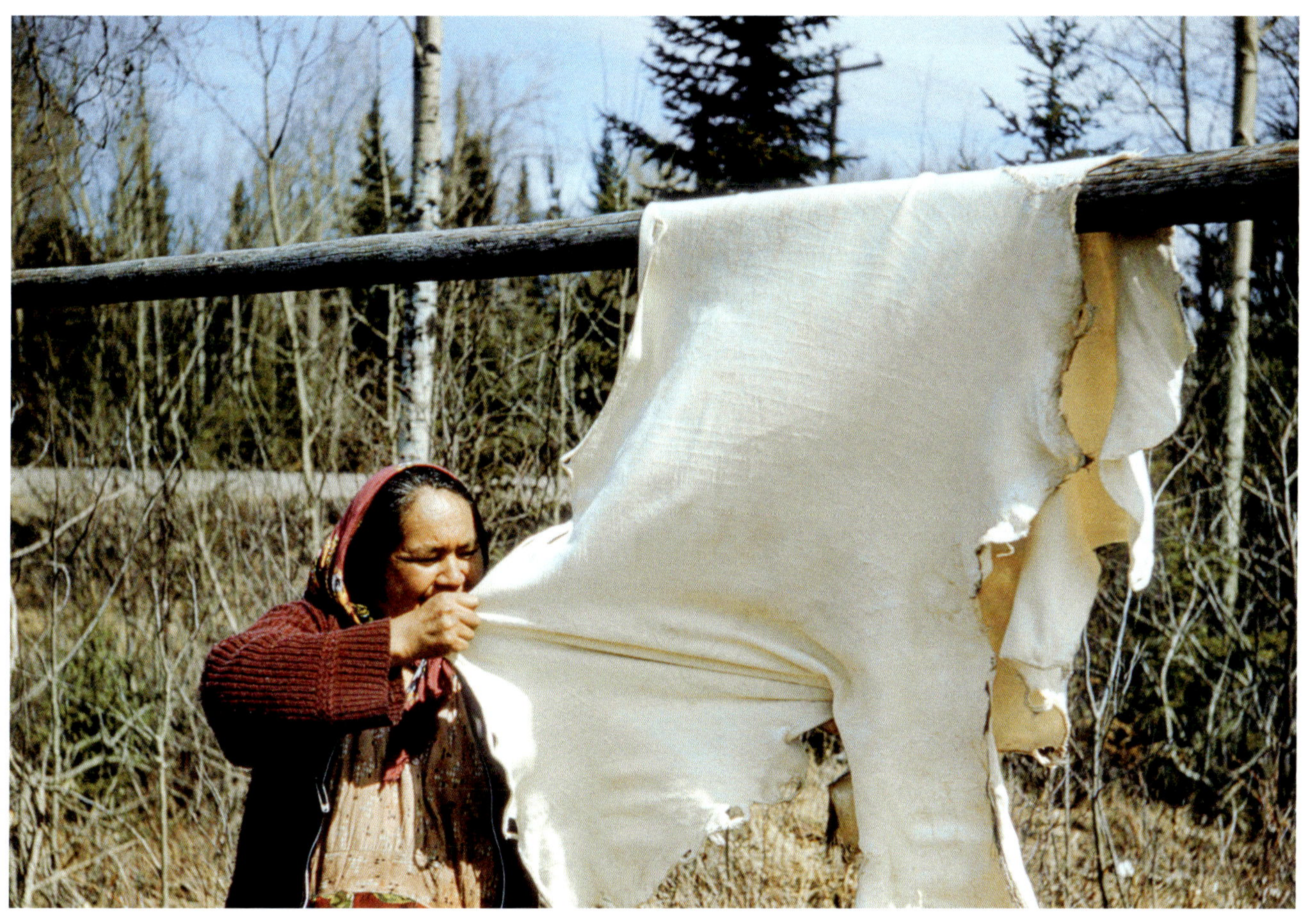

Mrs. Dan Suganaqueb working a newly tanned moose hide, Longlac May 1960

Woman with a child in a tikinagan, Sandy Lake c. 1952

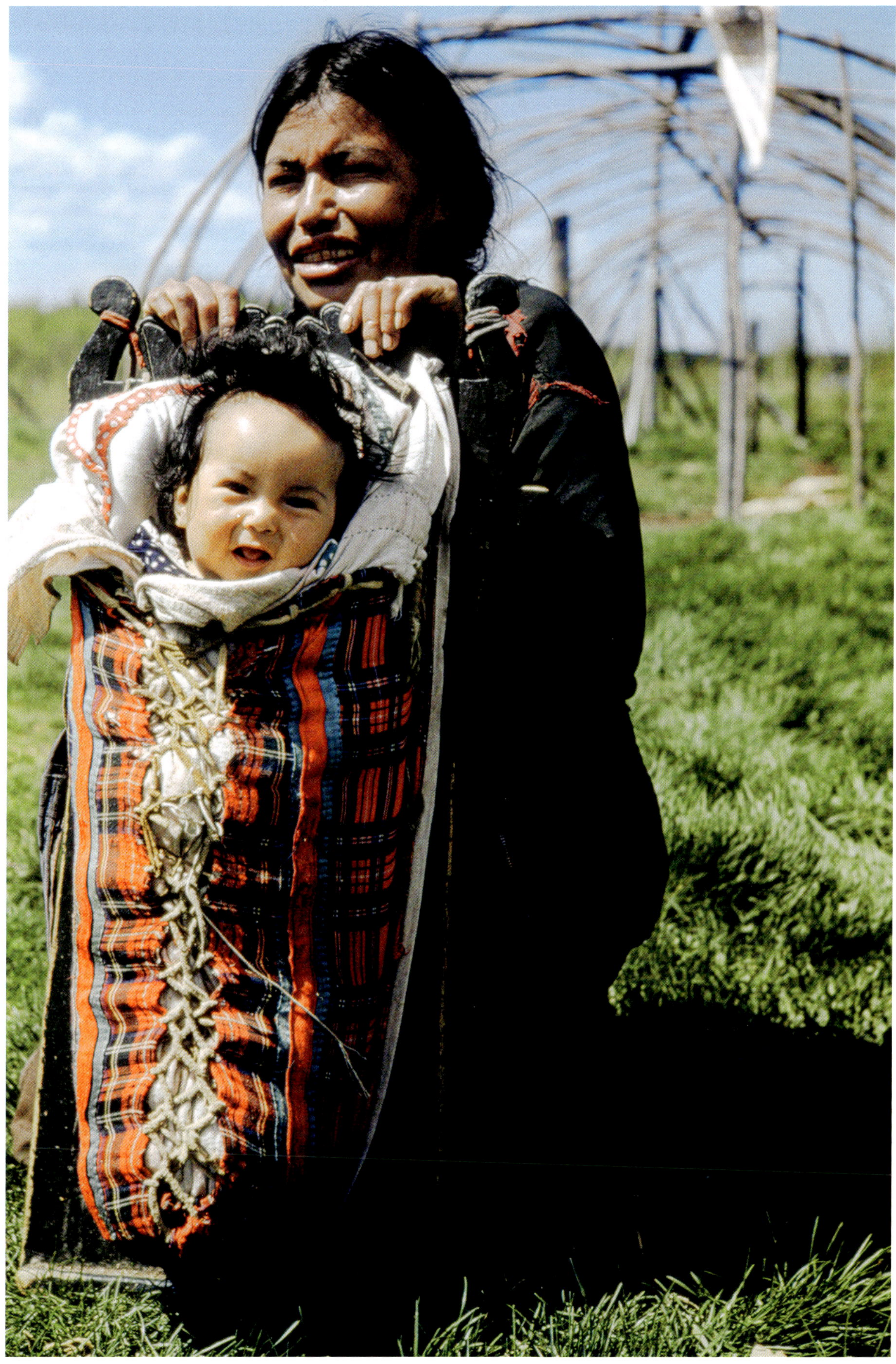

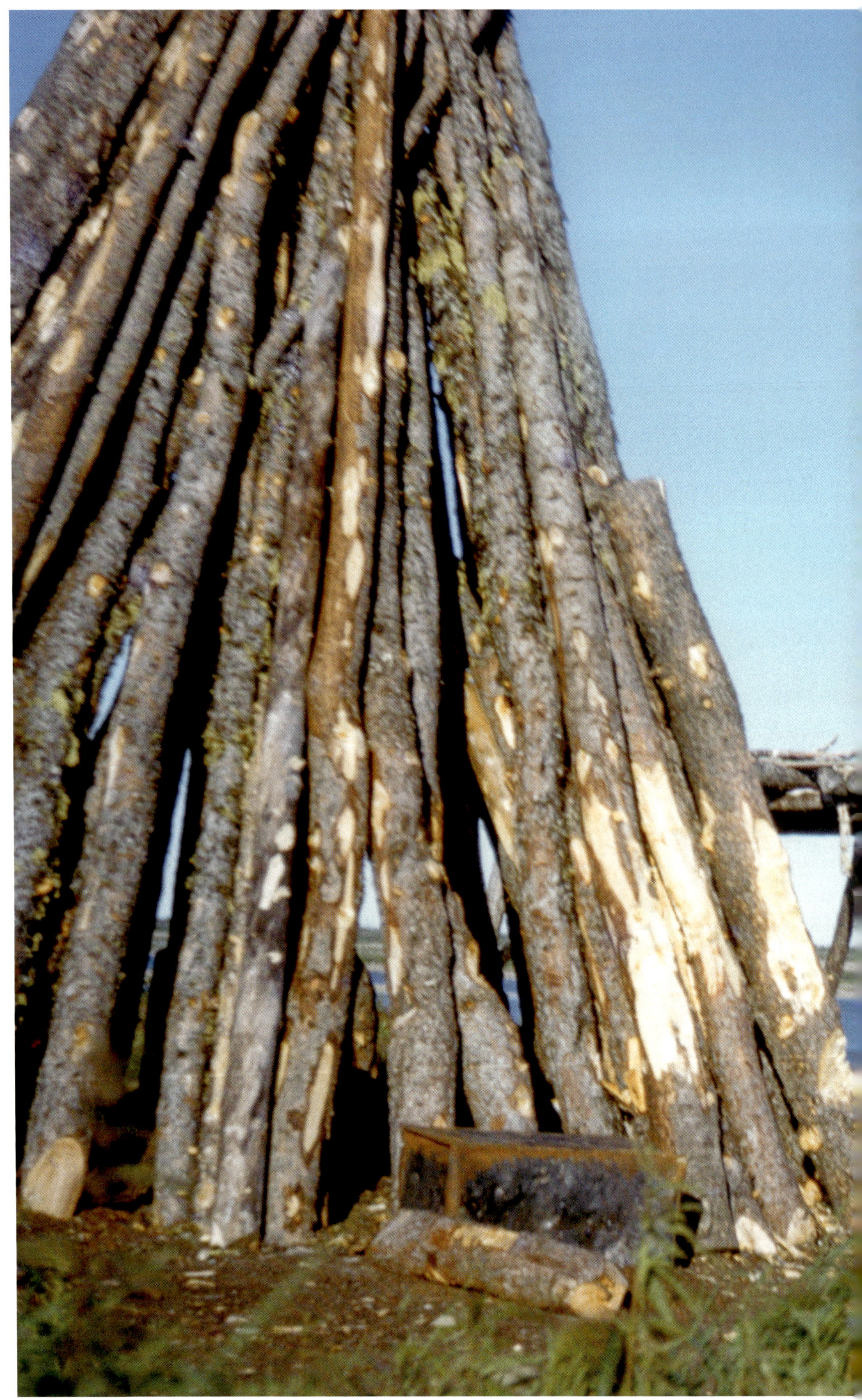

Jane Miles chopping wood, Fort Severn c. 1955

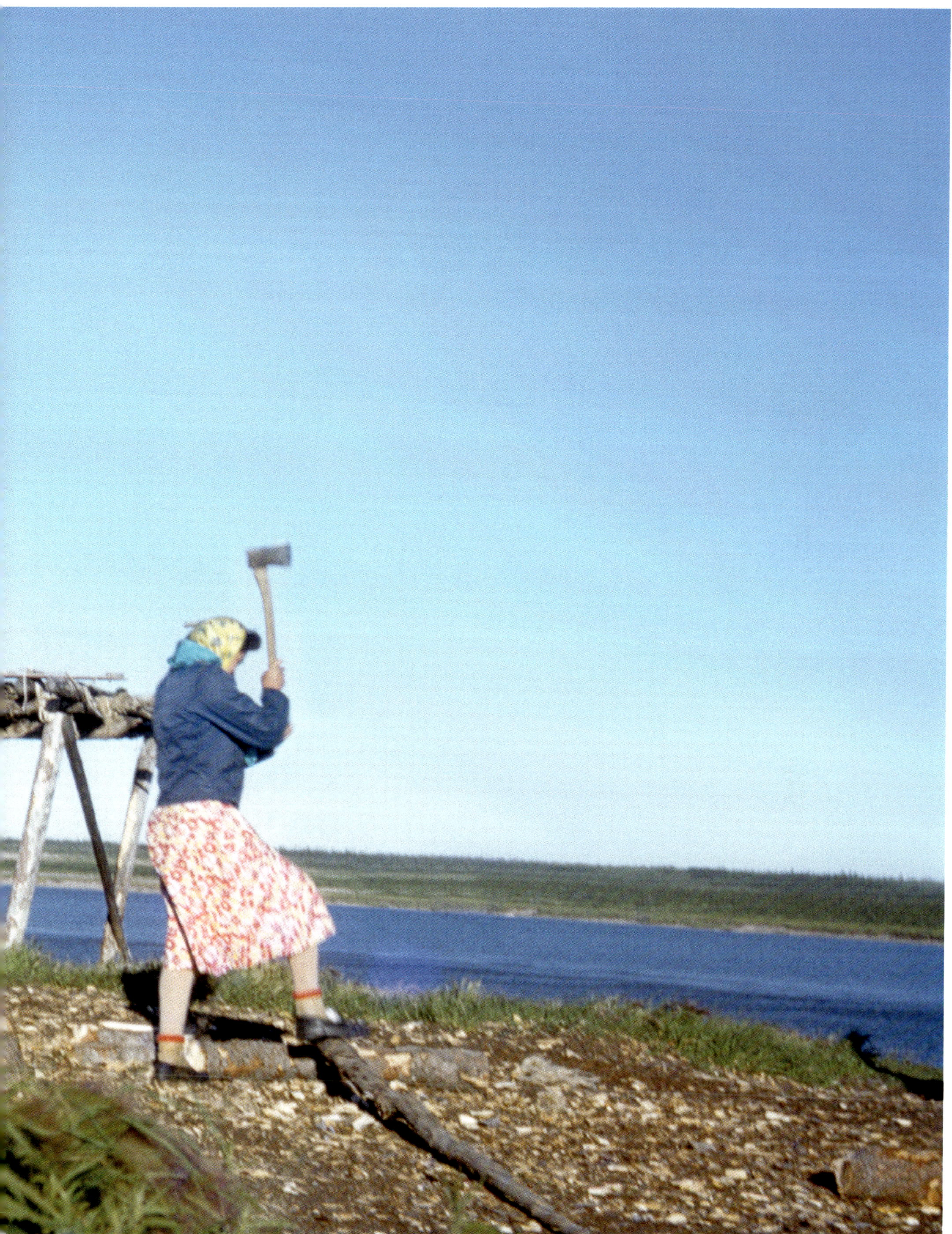

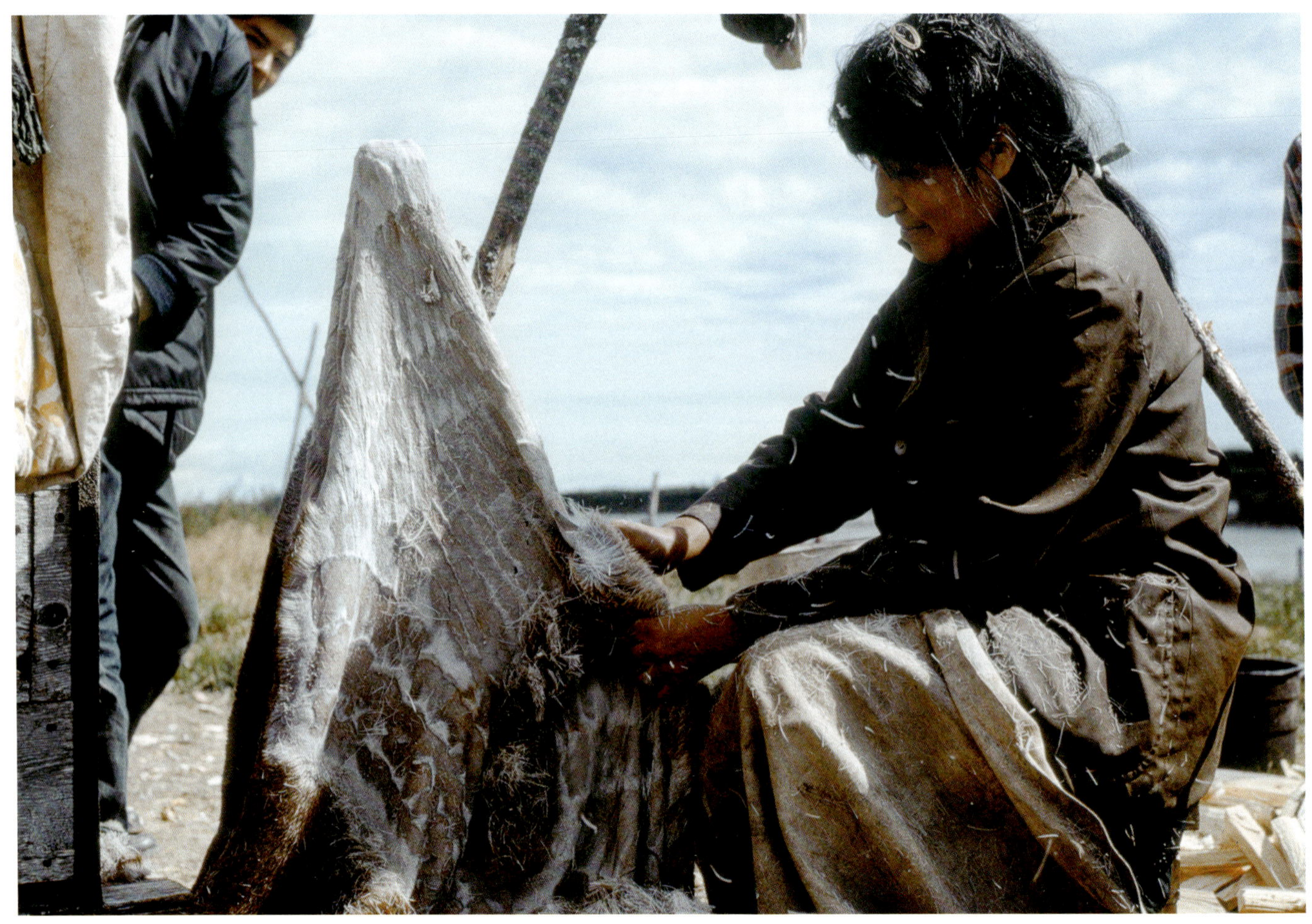

Dehairing a caribou hide, Attawapiskat, Kenora District September 1963

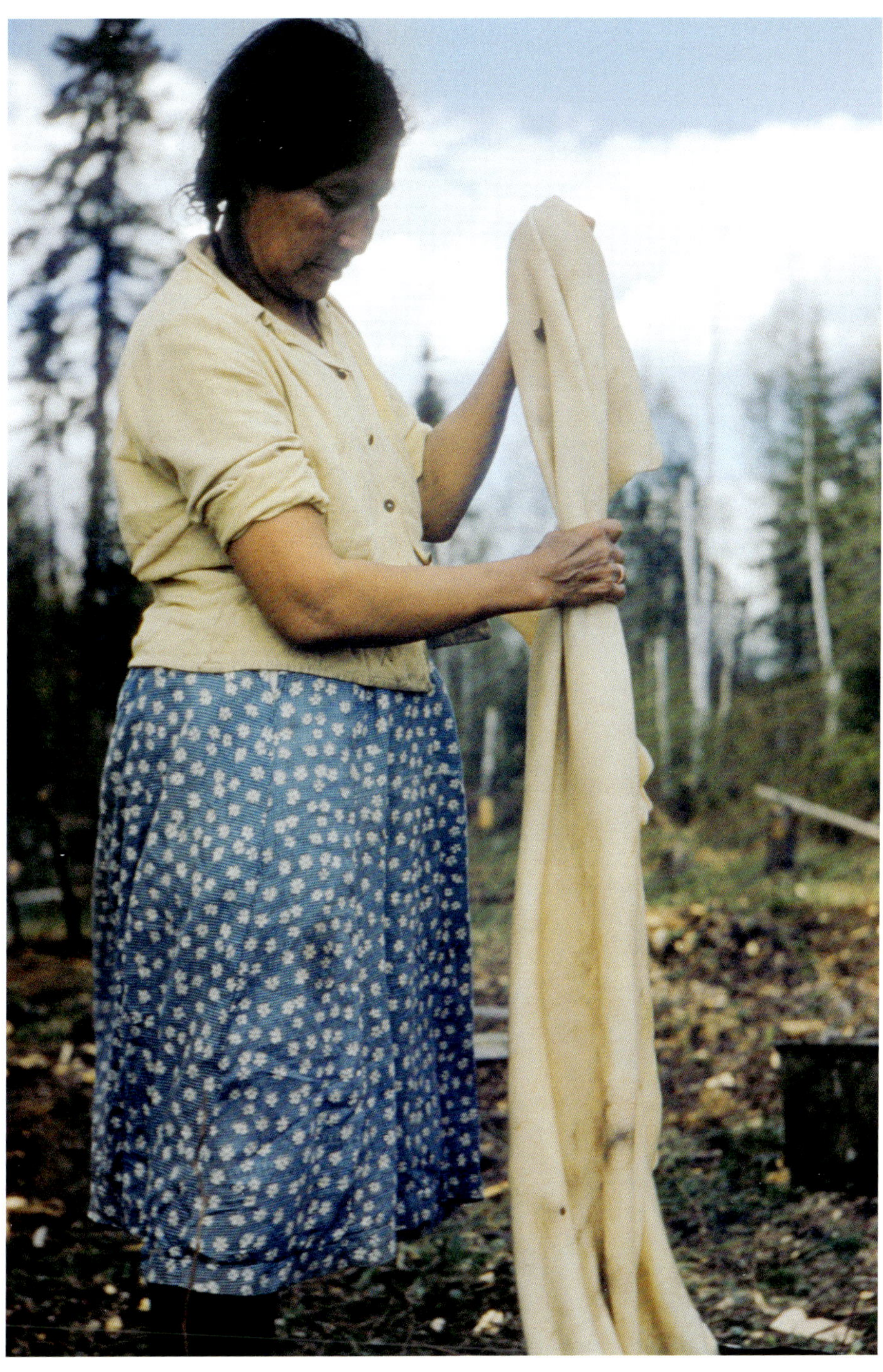

Wringing out a moosehide in preparation for tanning c. 1955

A Webequie girl standing in front of a tipi at Neskantaga 1956

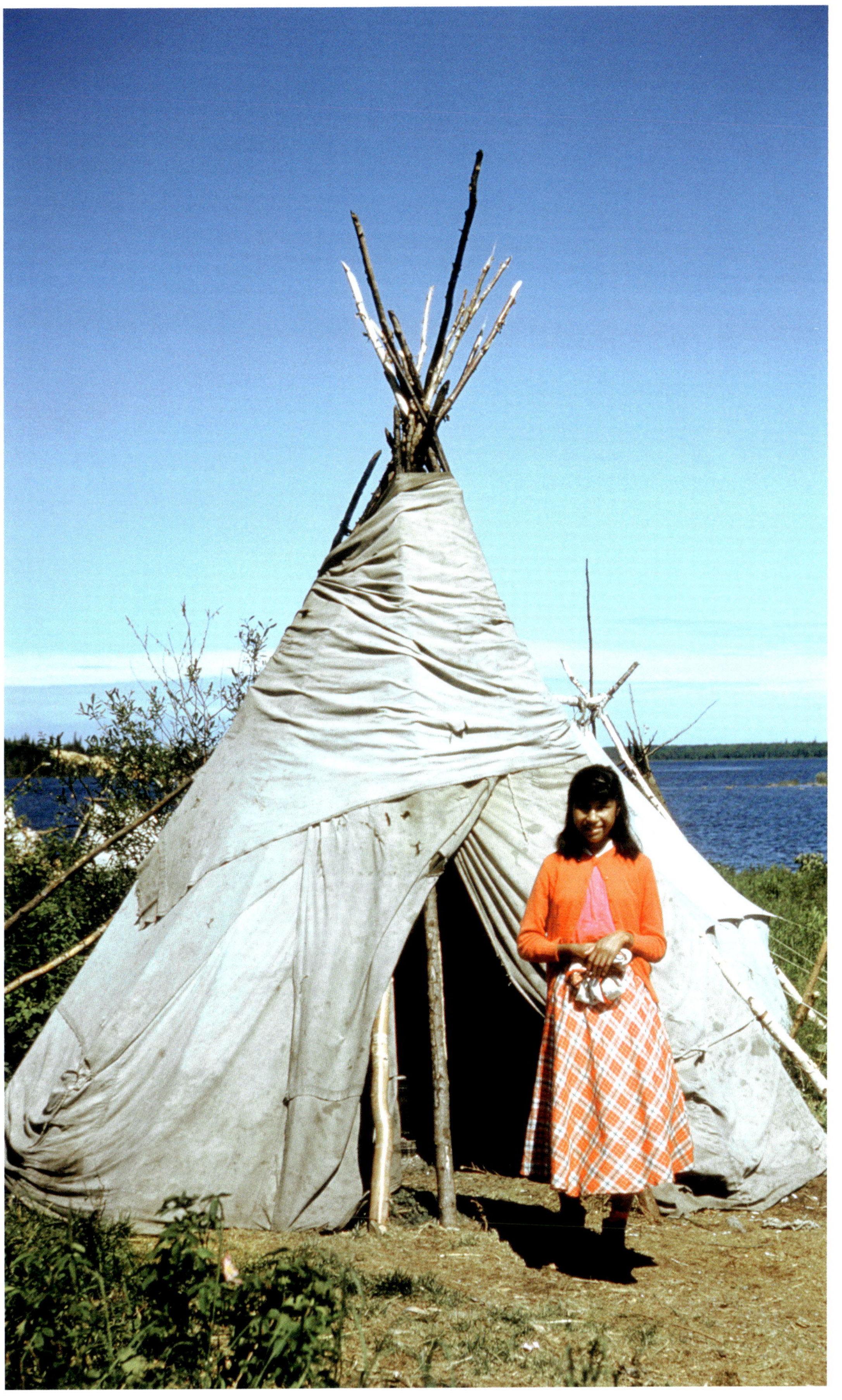

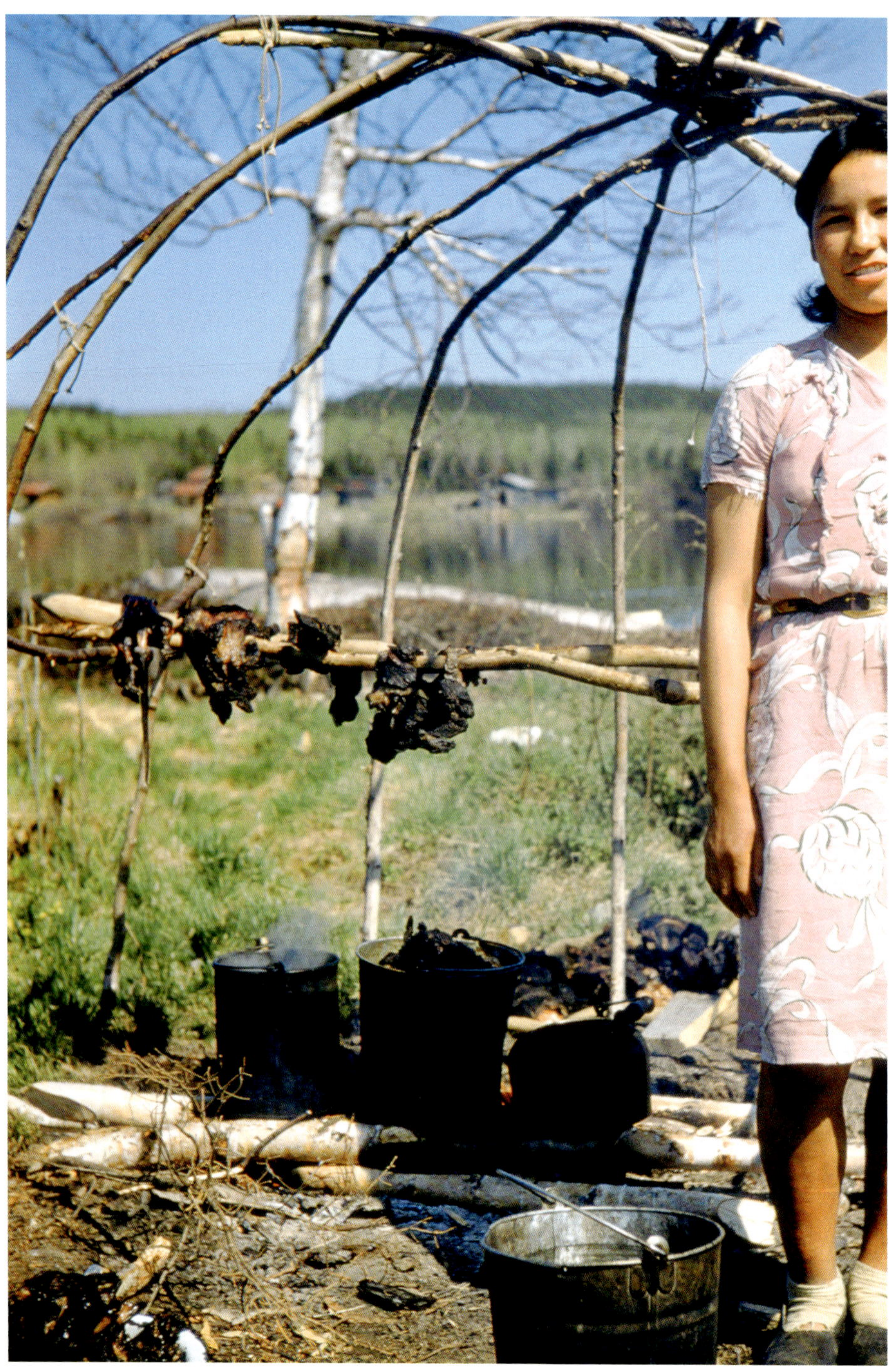

Bear meat being smoked, Deer Lake, Kenora District June 1956

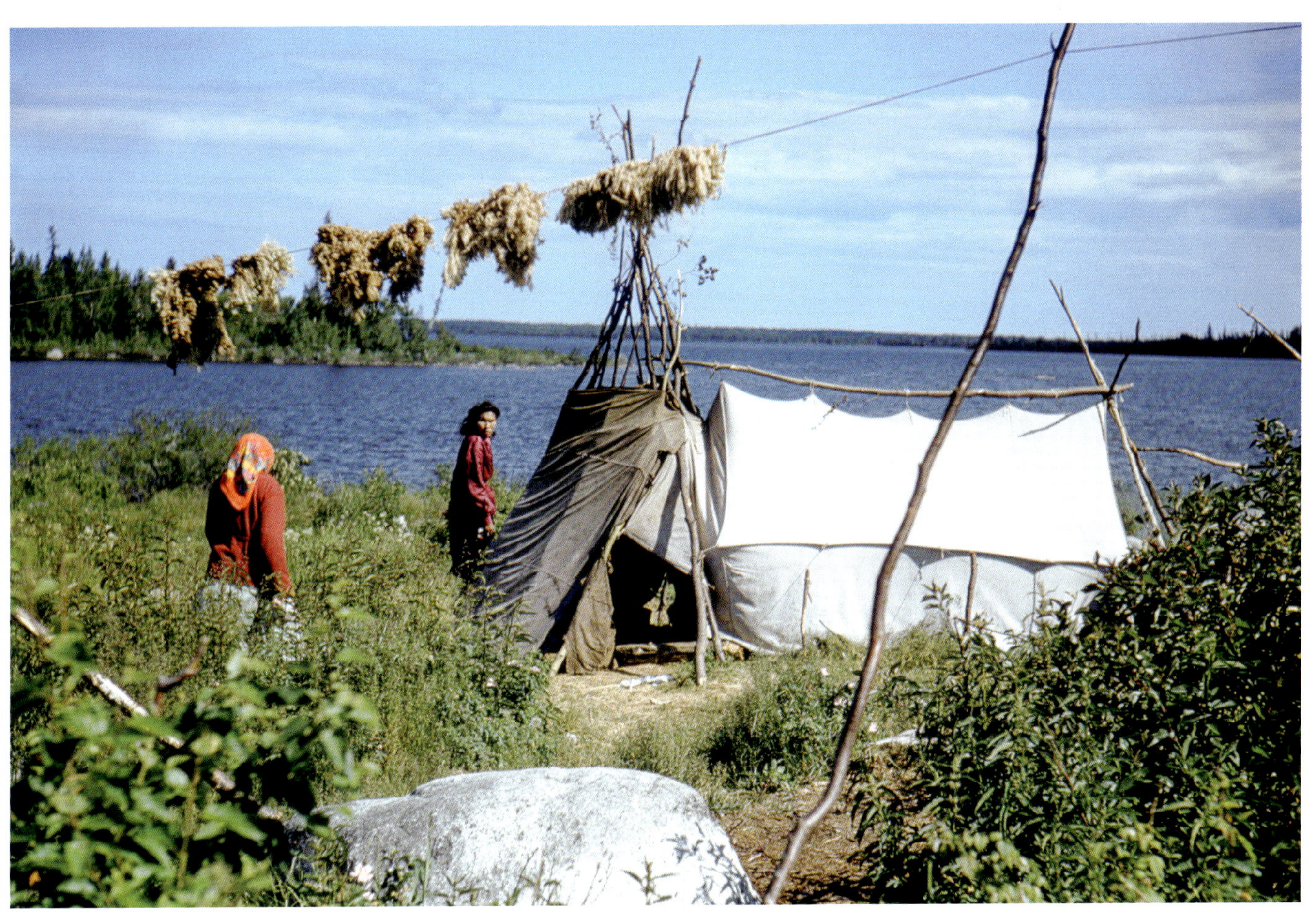

Drying sphagnum moss for use as an antiseptic absorbant, near Neskantaga 1956

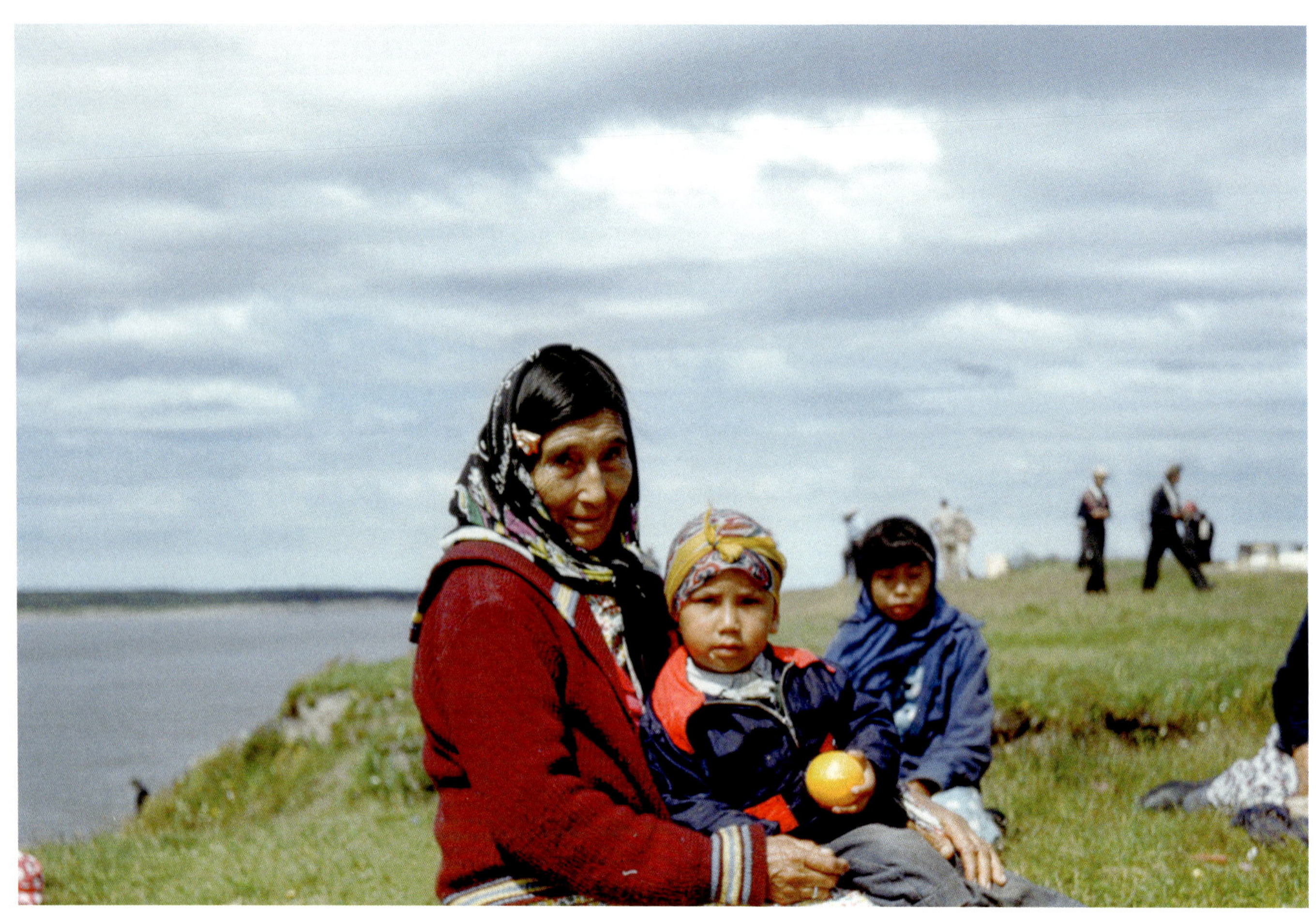

A woman and children resting on the riverbank at Fort Severn 1955

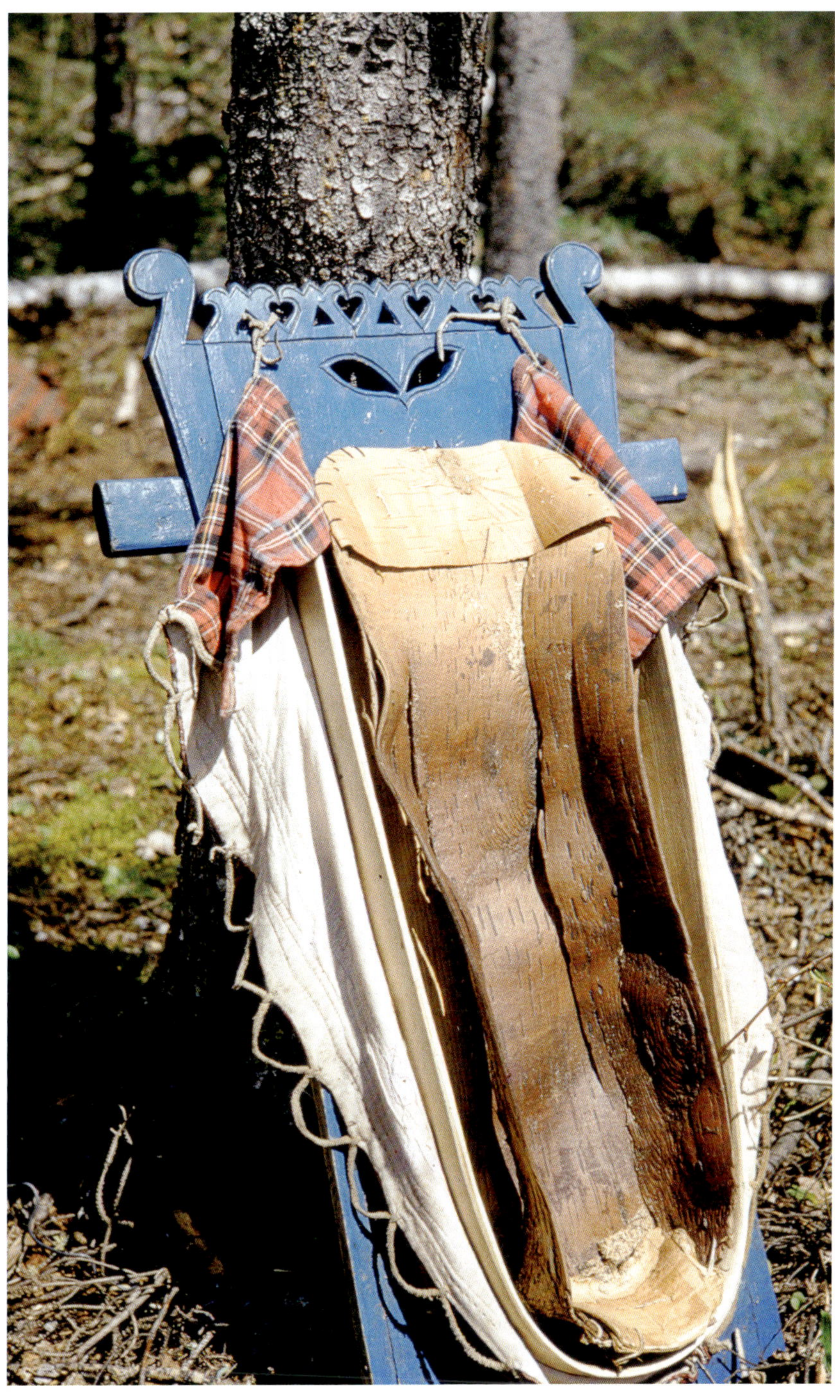

A tikinagan, Sandy Lake, northwest of Thunder Bay c. 1955

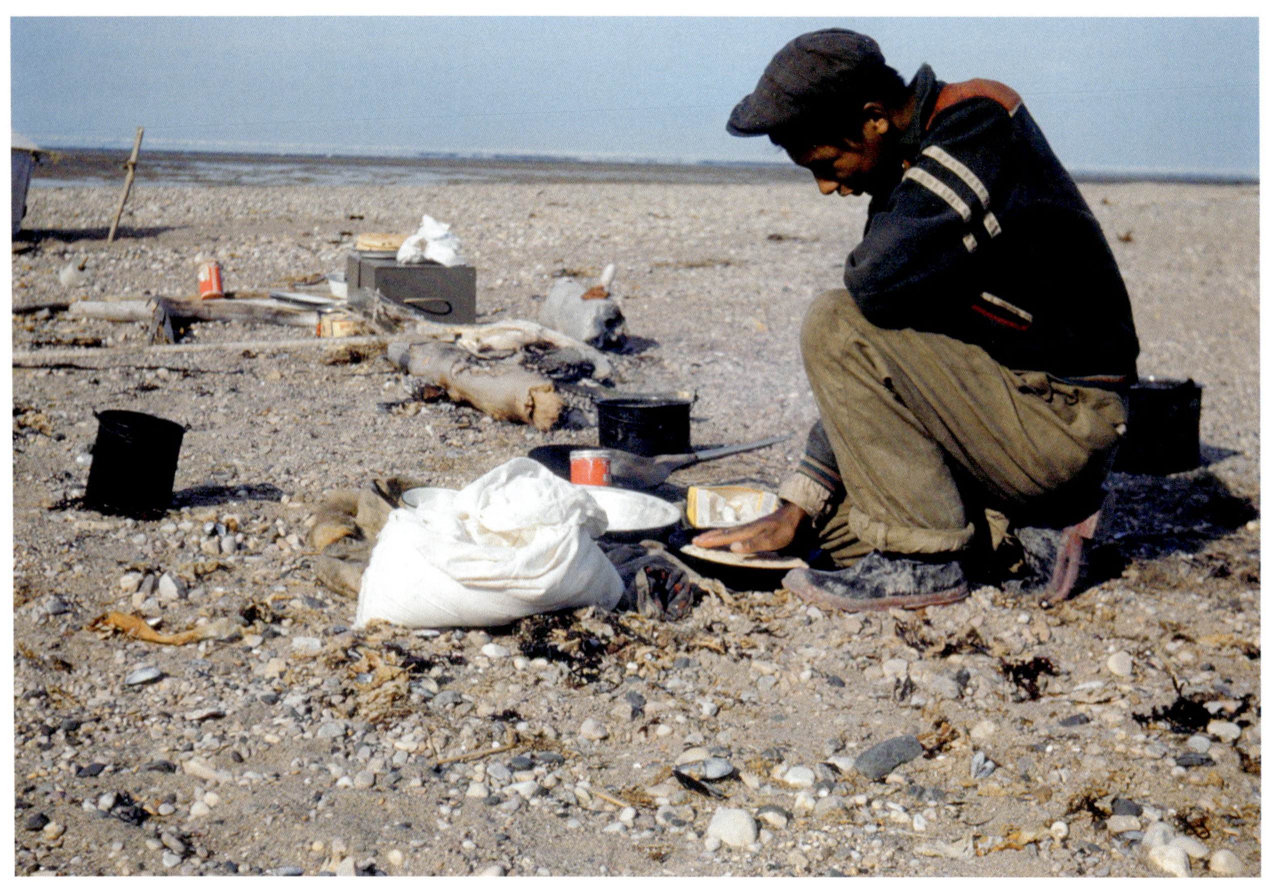

Douglas Kakekaspan of Fort Severn making bannock, Hudson Bay 1953

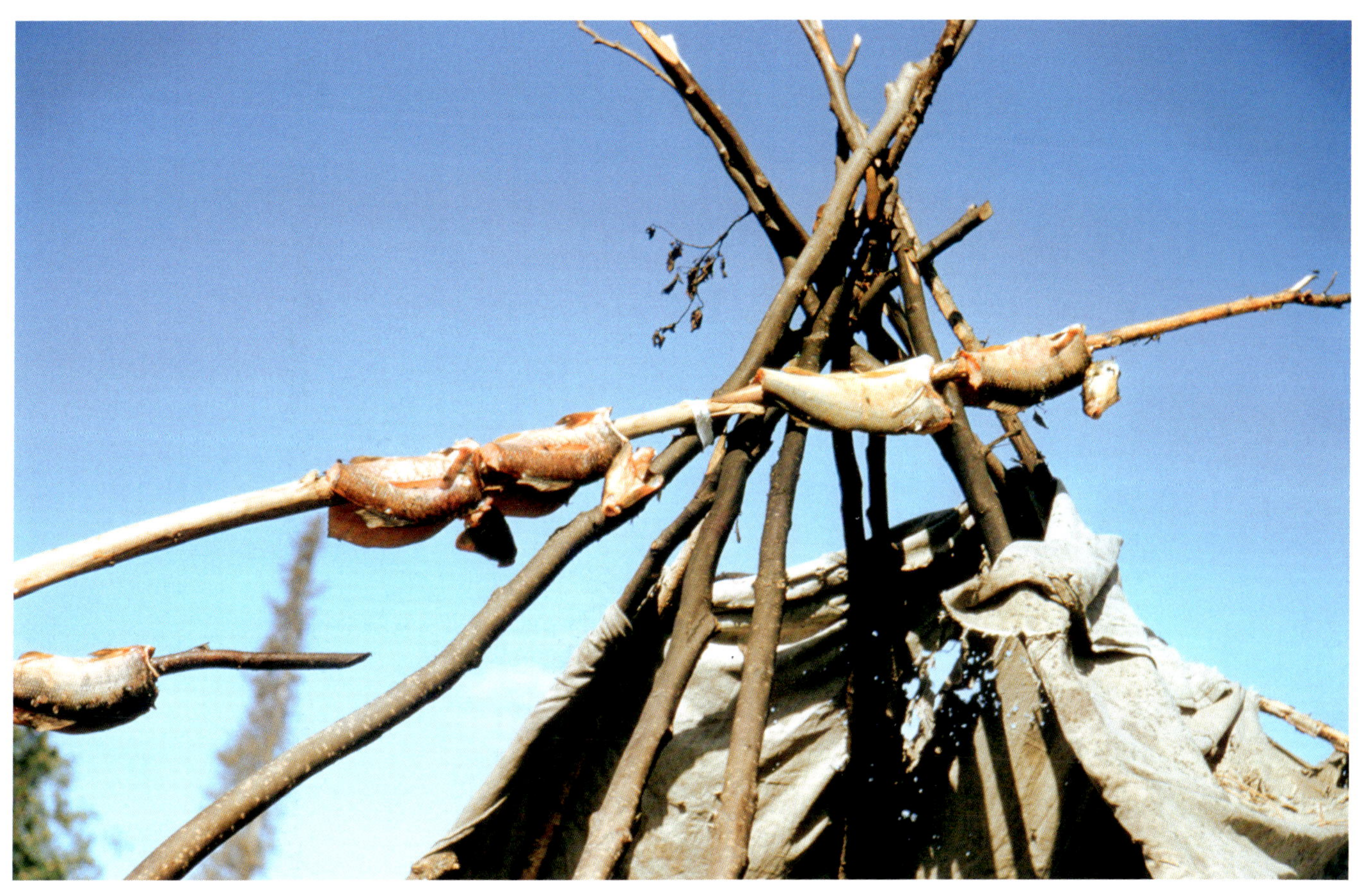

Fish being dried at Neskantaga June 1956

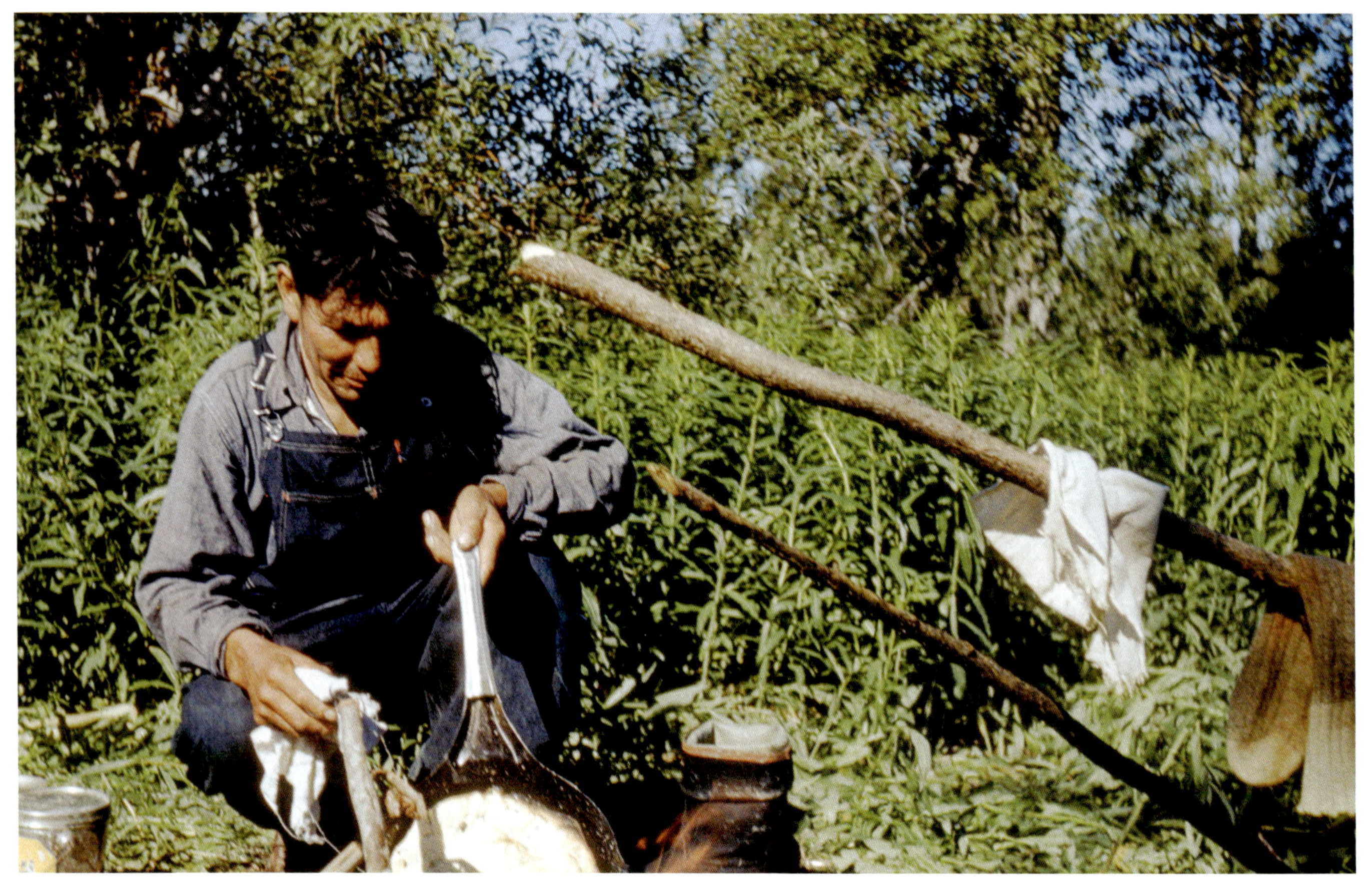

Henry Cutfeet cooking bannock in a cast iron pan by an open fire c. 1955

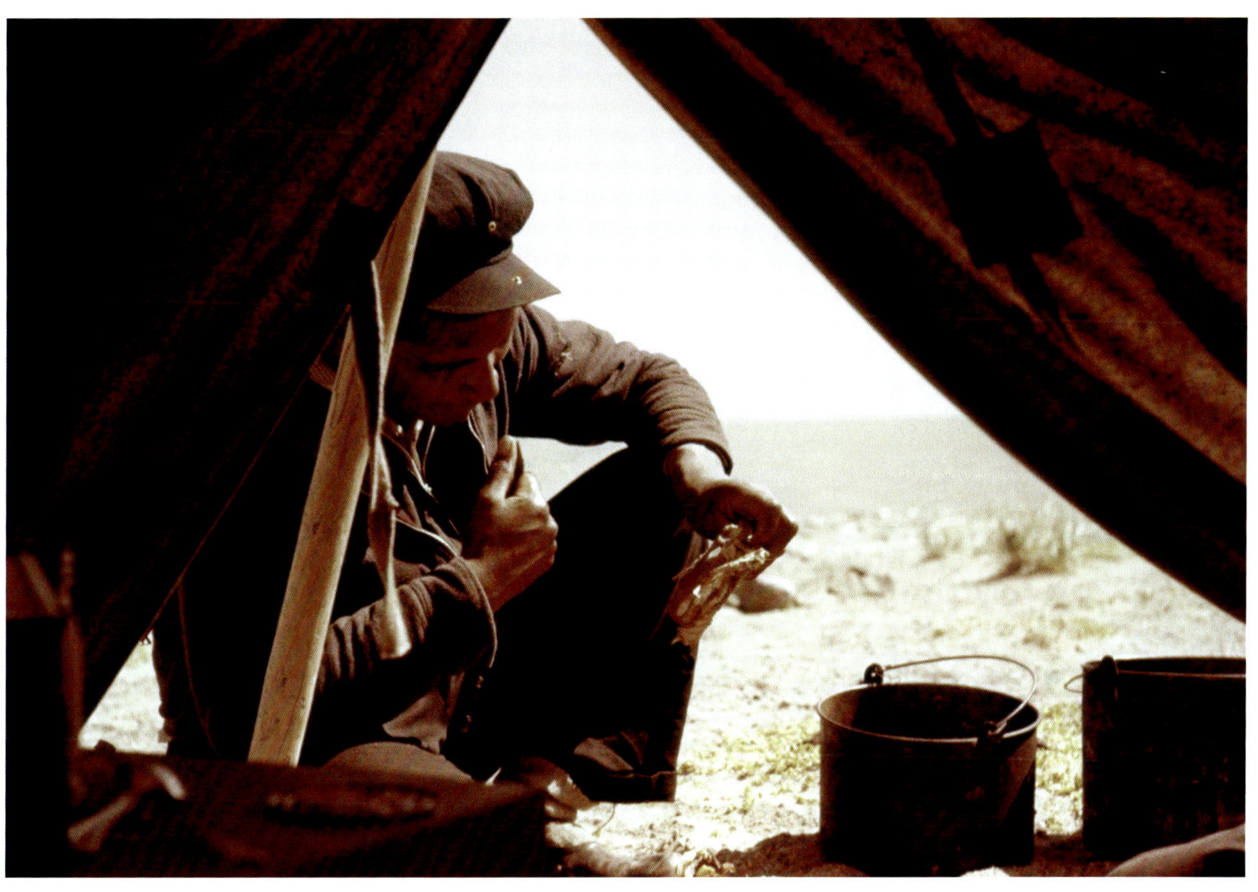

Philip "Swampy" Mathew eating from the broiled carcass of a duck, Hudson Bay coast 1955

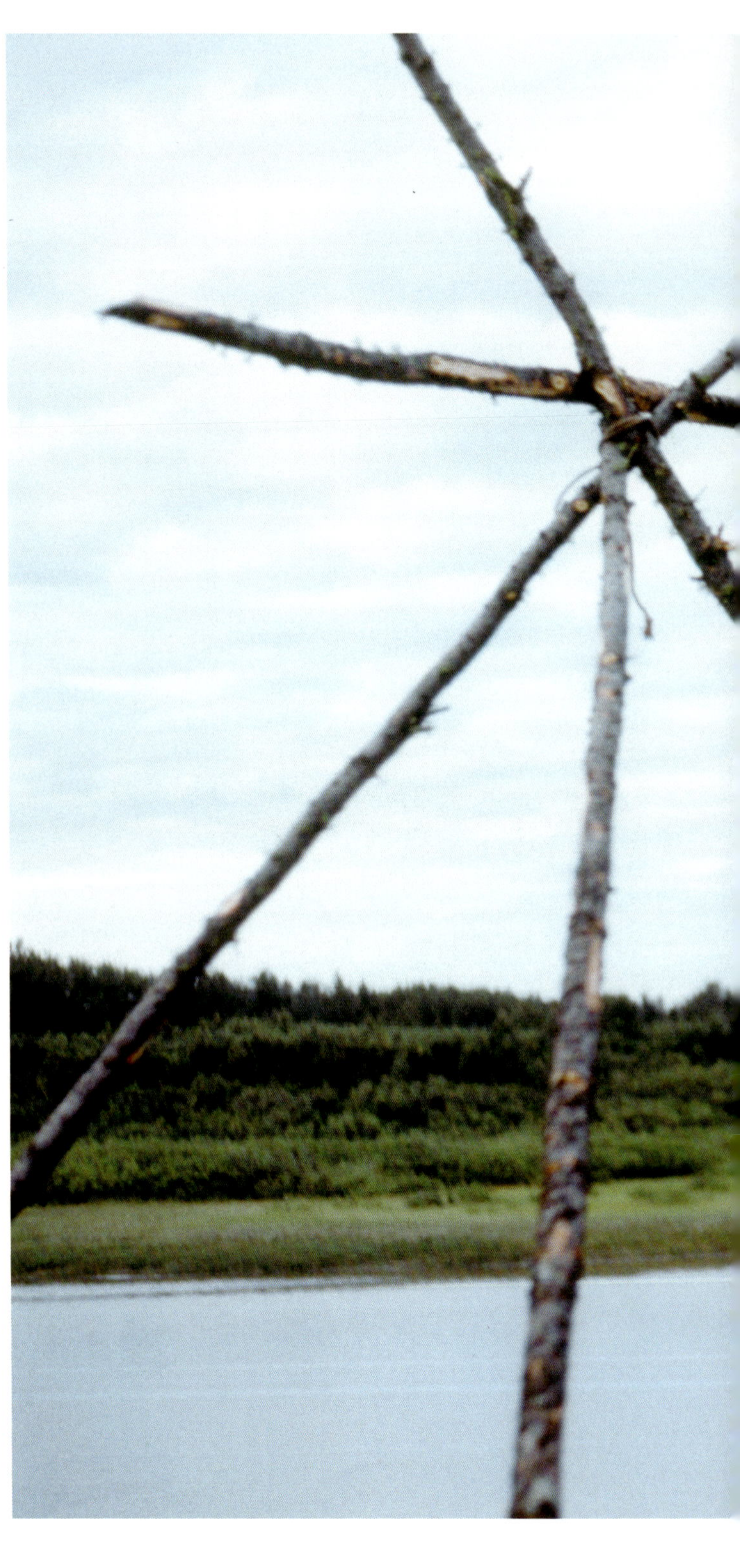

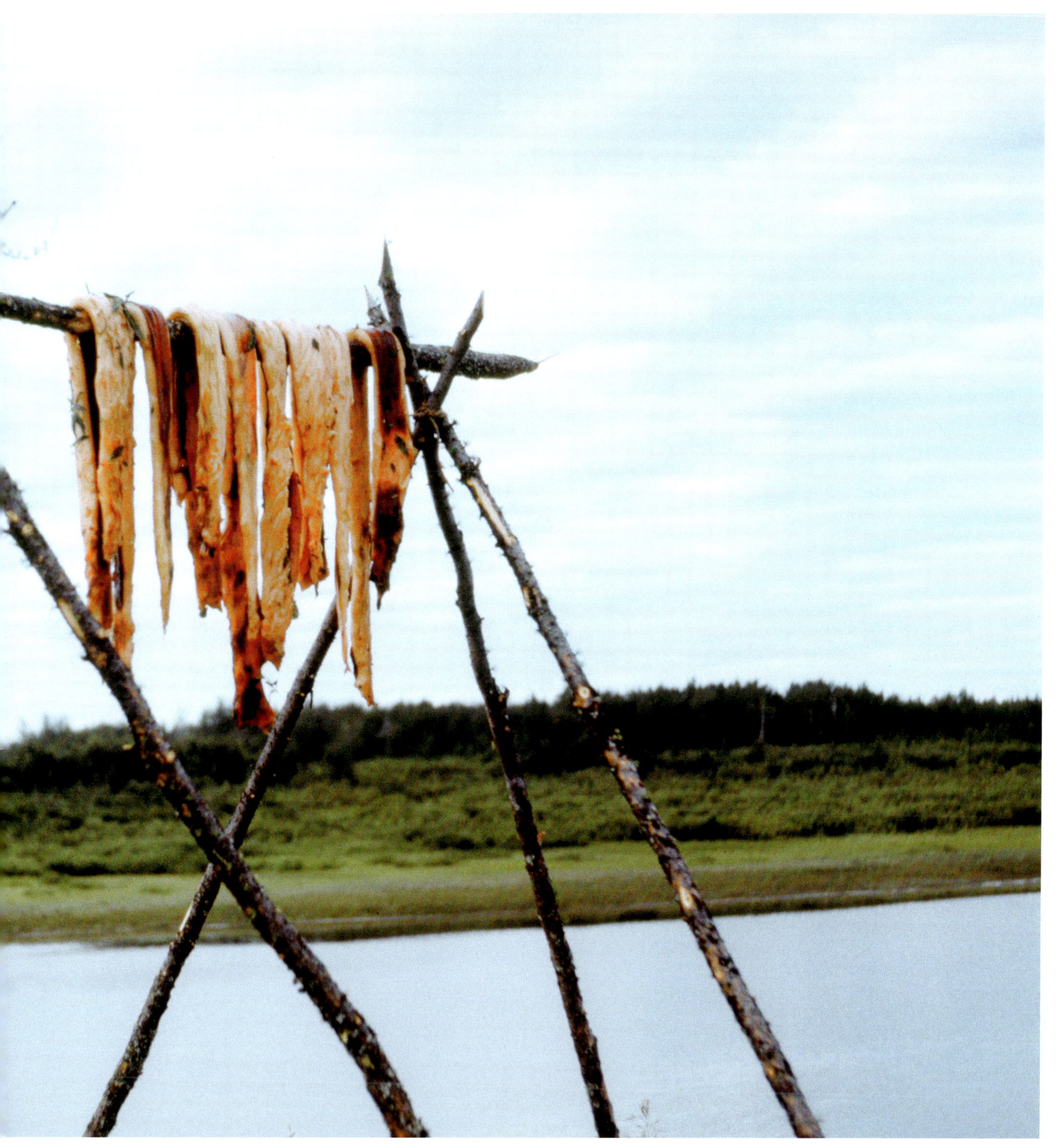

Seal blubber hanging to dry in Attawapiskat August 29, 1963

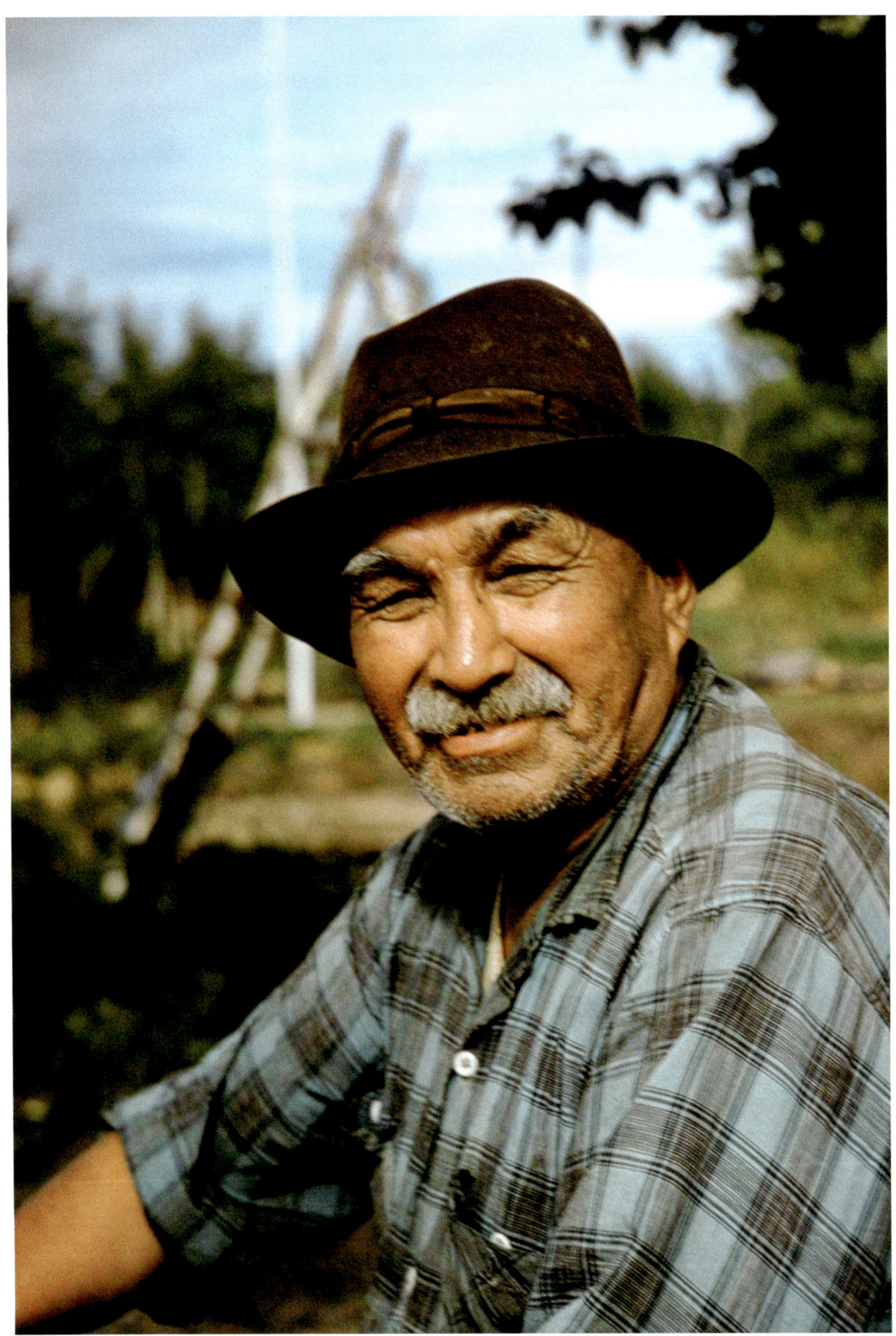

Henry Kechebra of Mattagami 1957

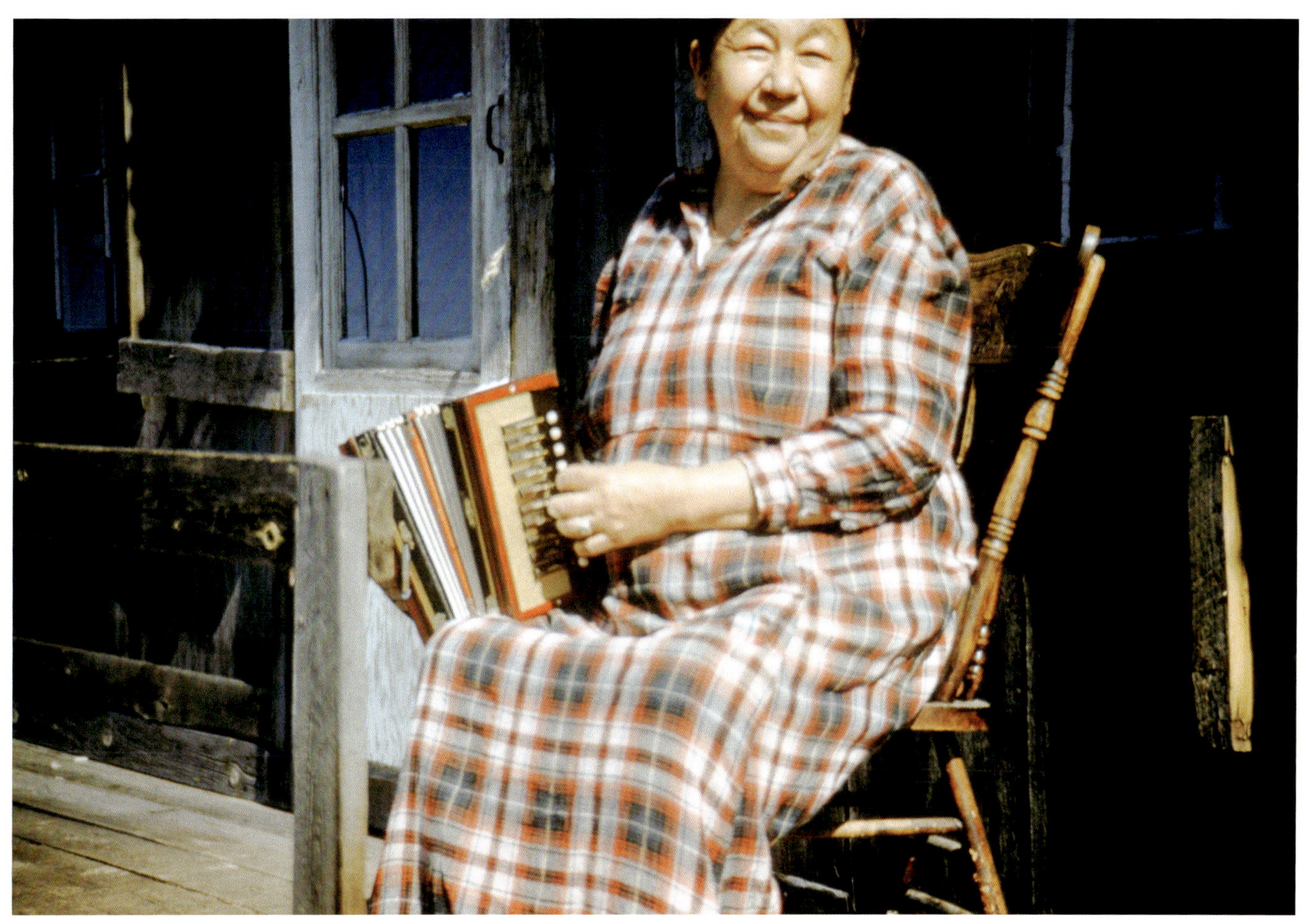

Jessie Mann playing her Concordia, Gogama, Lake Minisinakwa, Sudbury District 1957

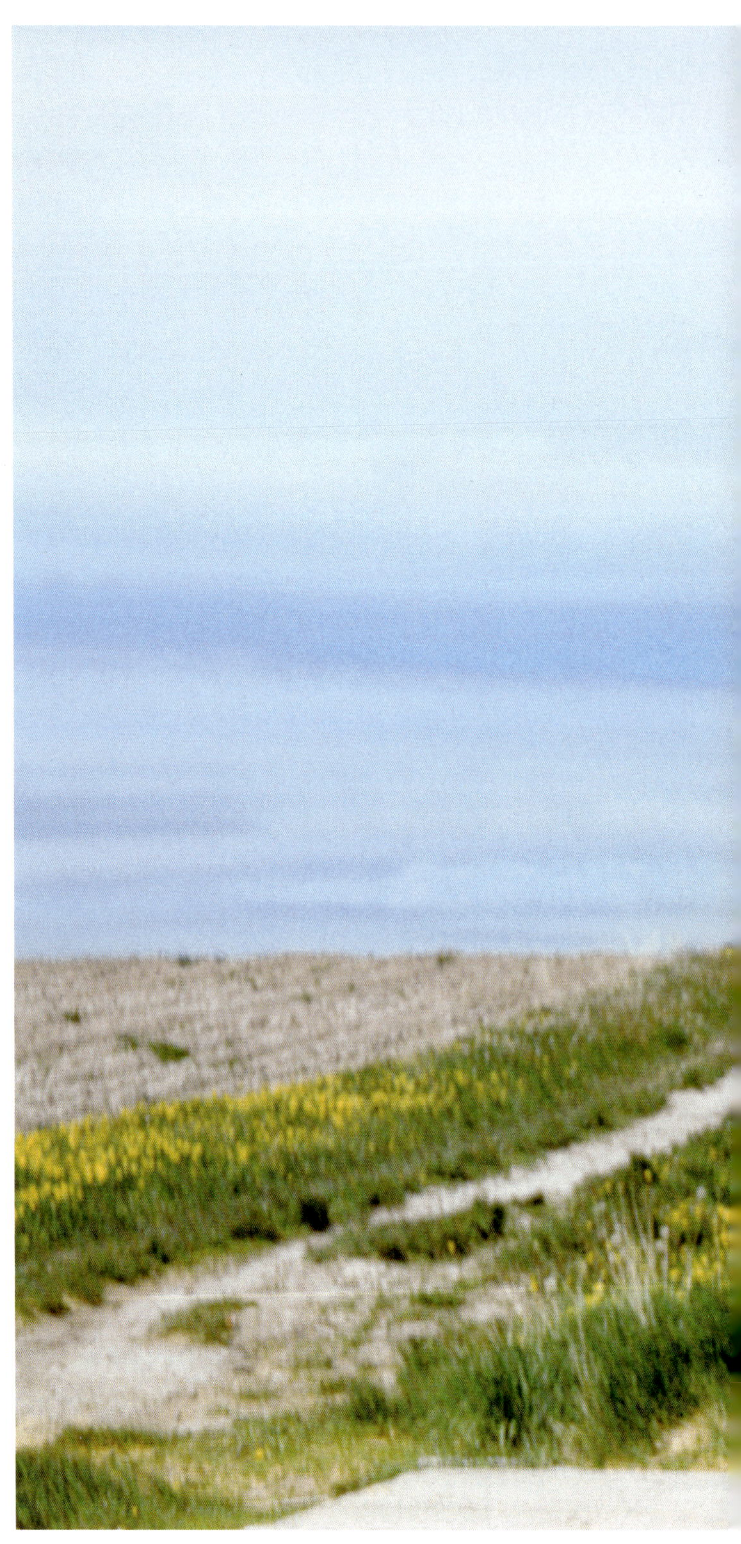

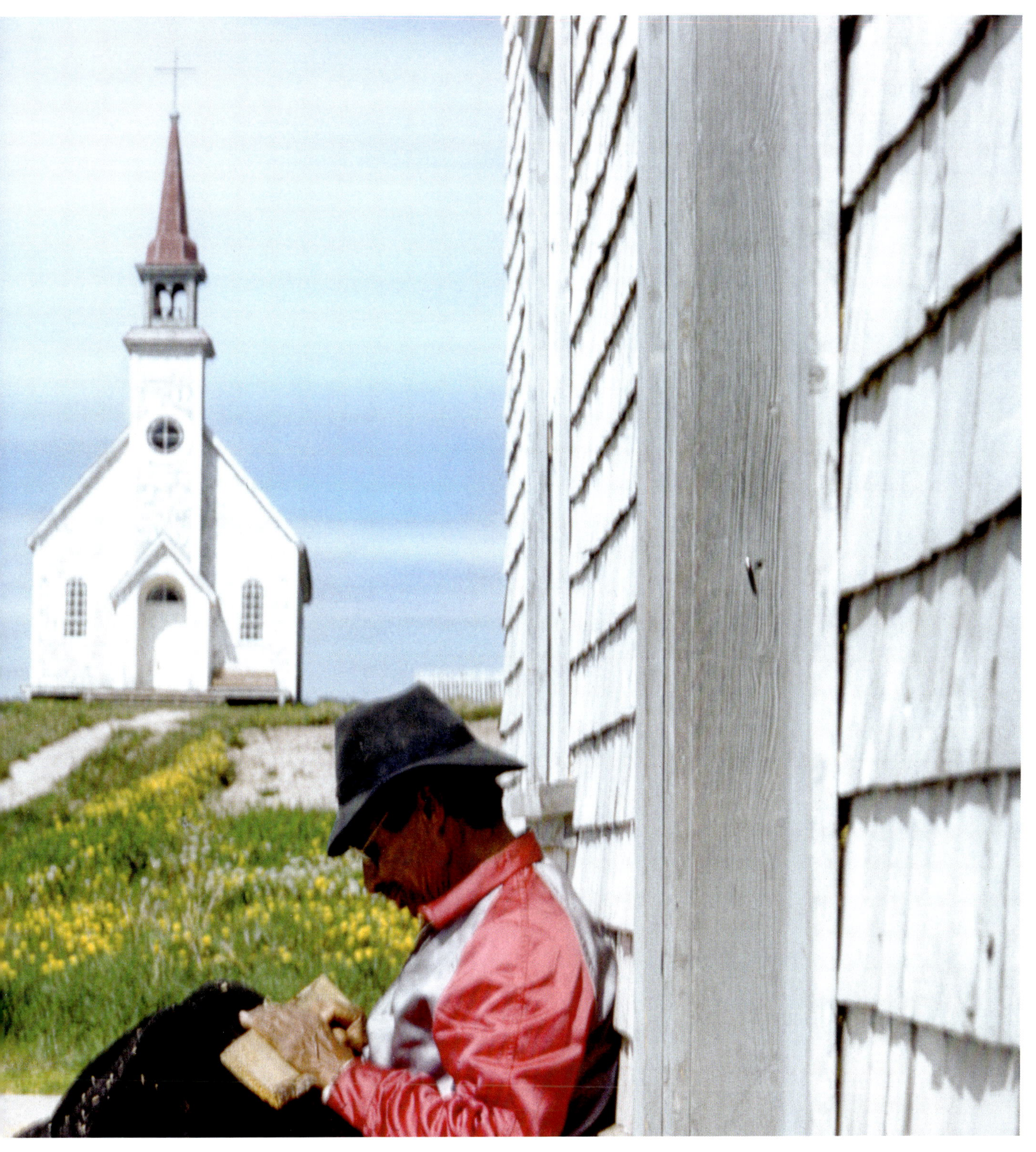

A man resting at Sandy Lake c. 1952

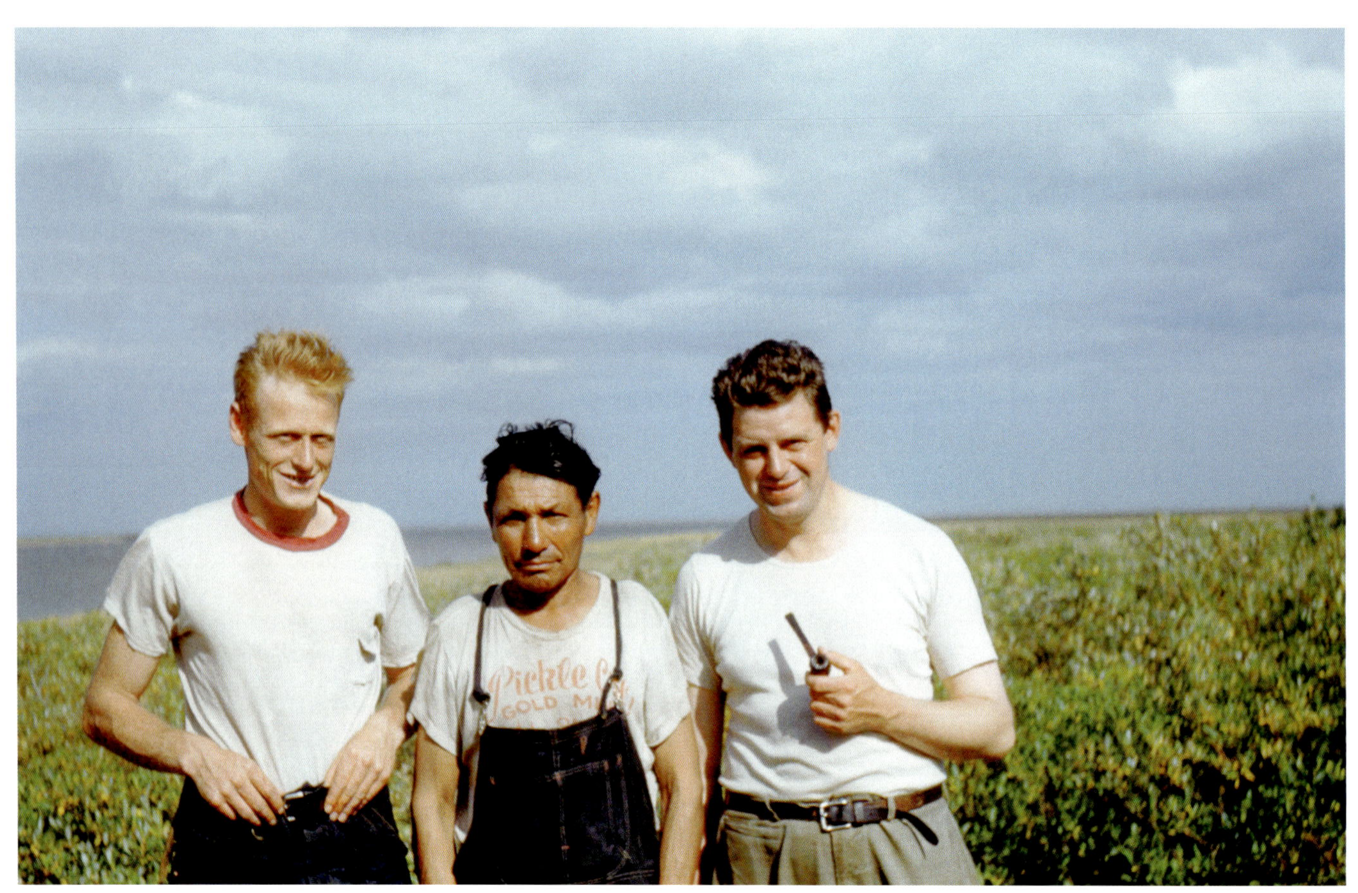

John Macfie, Henry Cutfeet, and Ross Moir, near Hudson Bay 1952

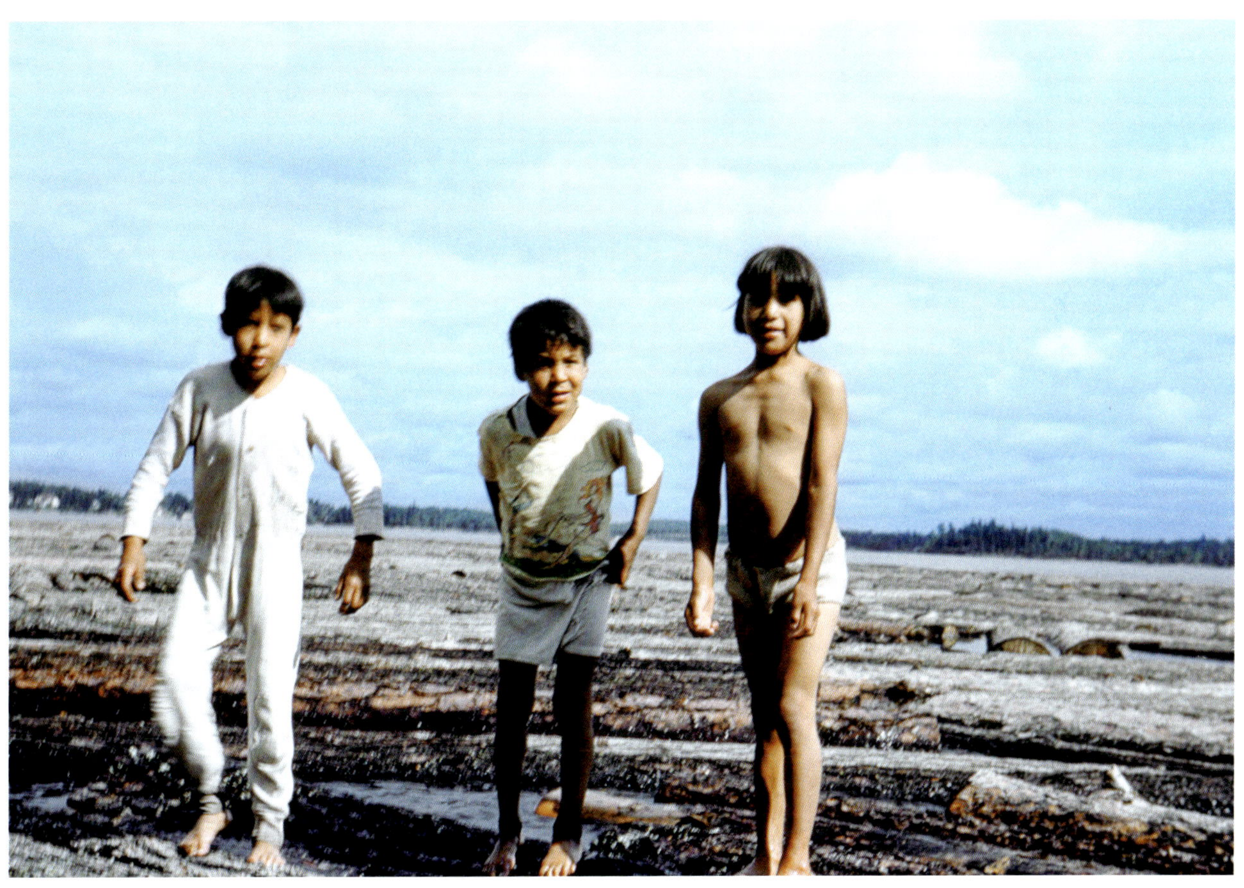

Children playing on logs at Farlinger's sawmill, Sioux Lookout c. 1955

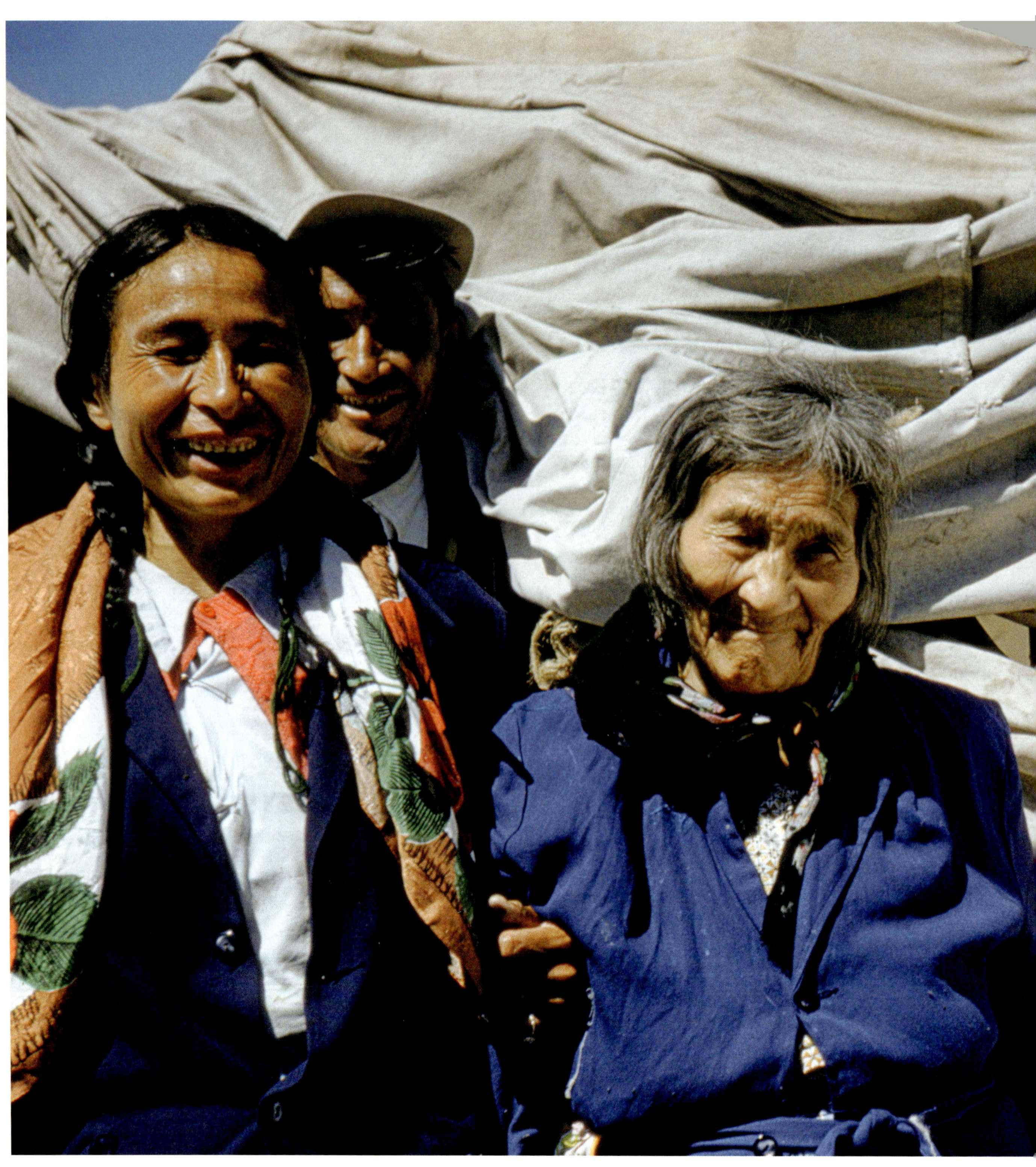

The Suganaqueb family at Neskantaga for Treaty Time; the women are
Matilda Suganaqueb, a midwife, and Nancy Suganaqueb, a medicine woman c. 1955

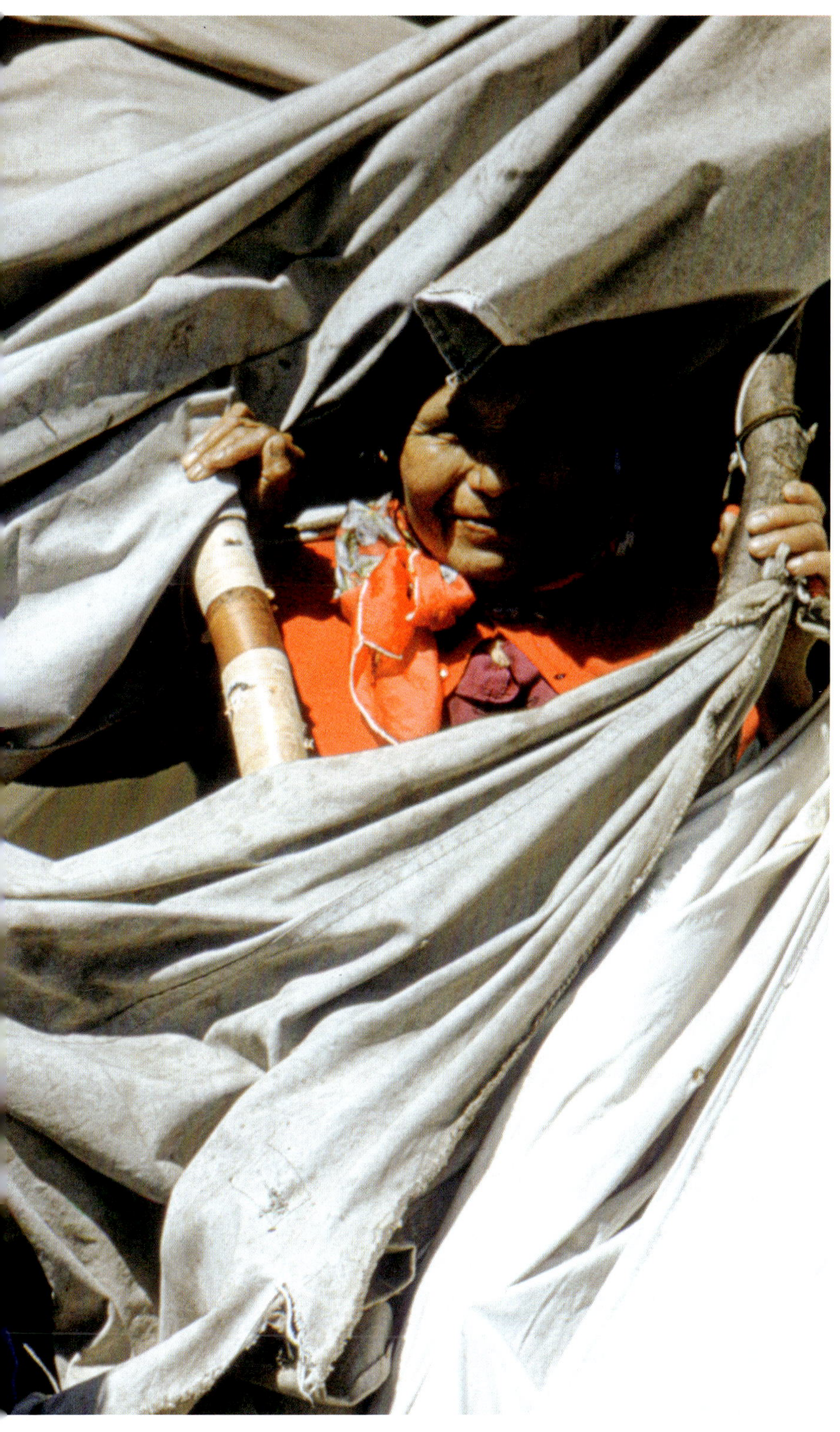

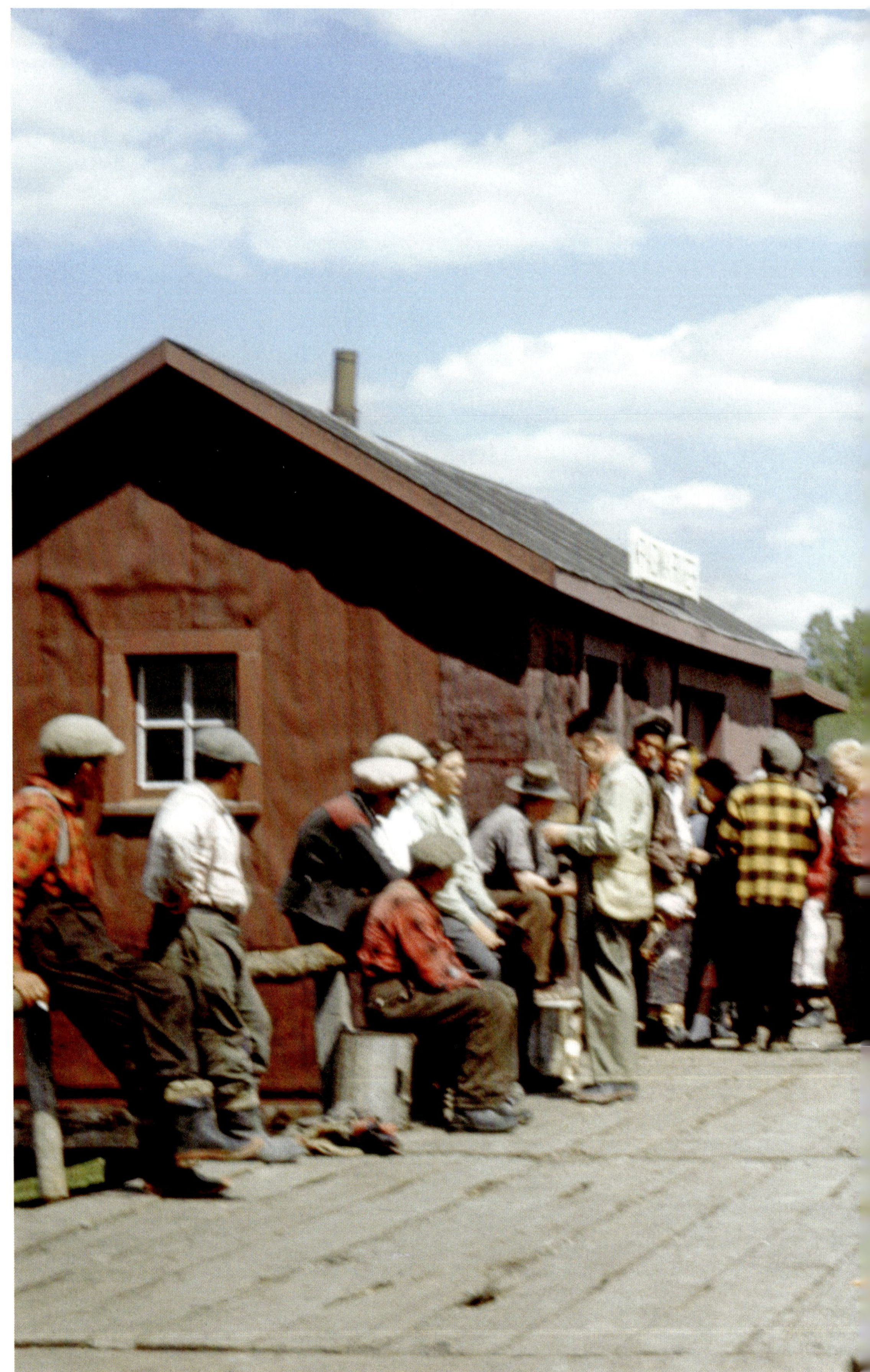

Treaty Party arriving at the train station in Pagwa River, Cochrane District 1951

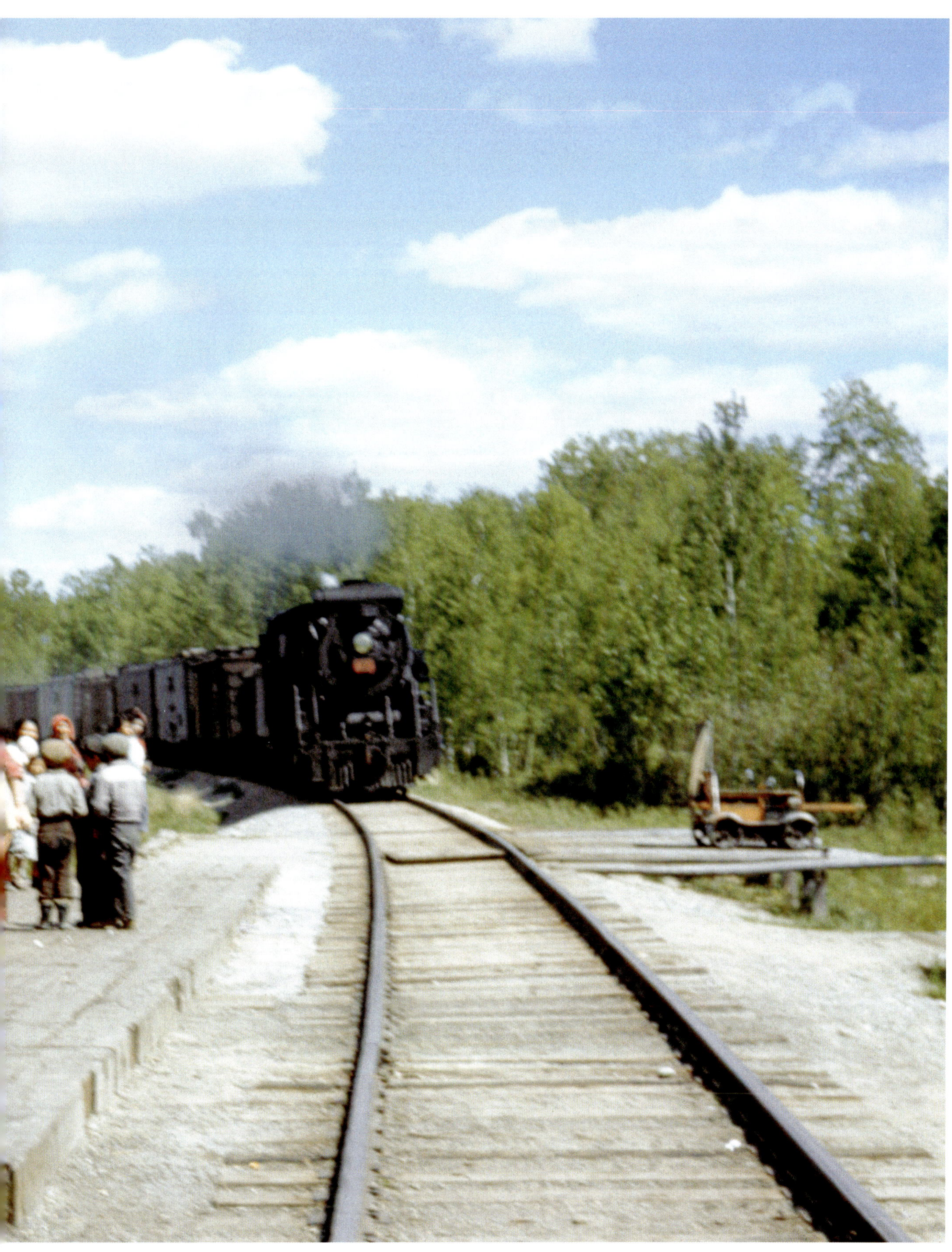

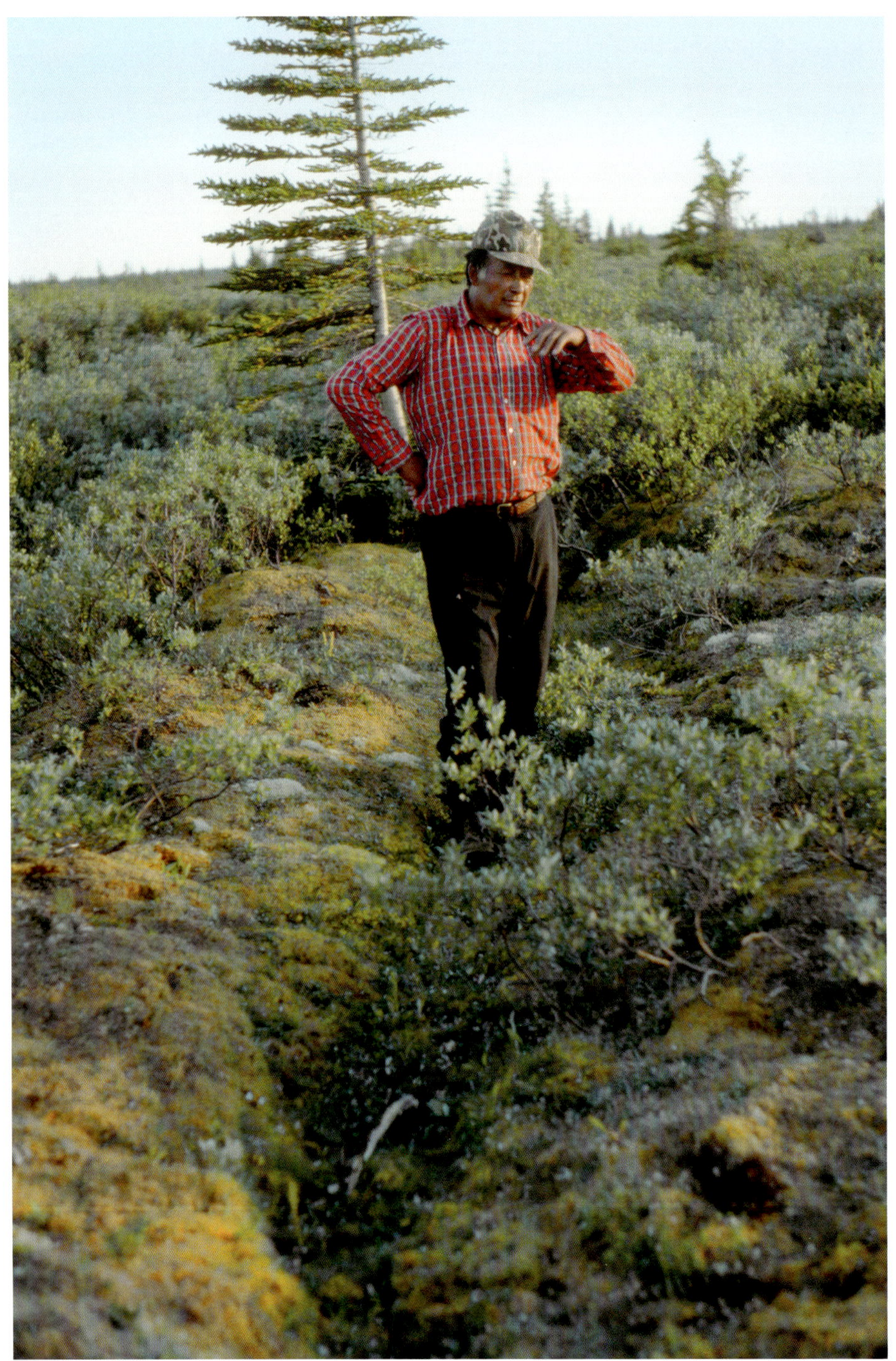

John George Koostachin standing in the trench of an old walking trail July 1958

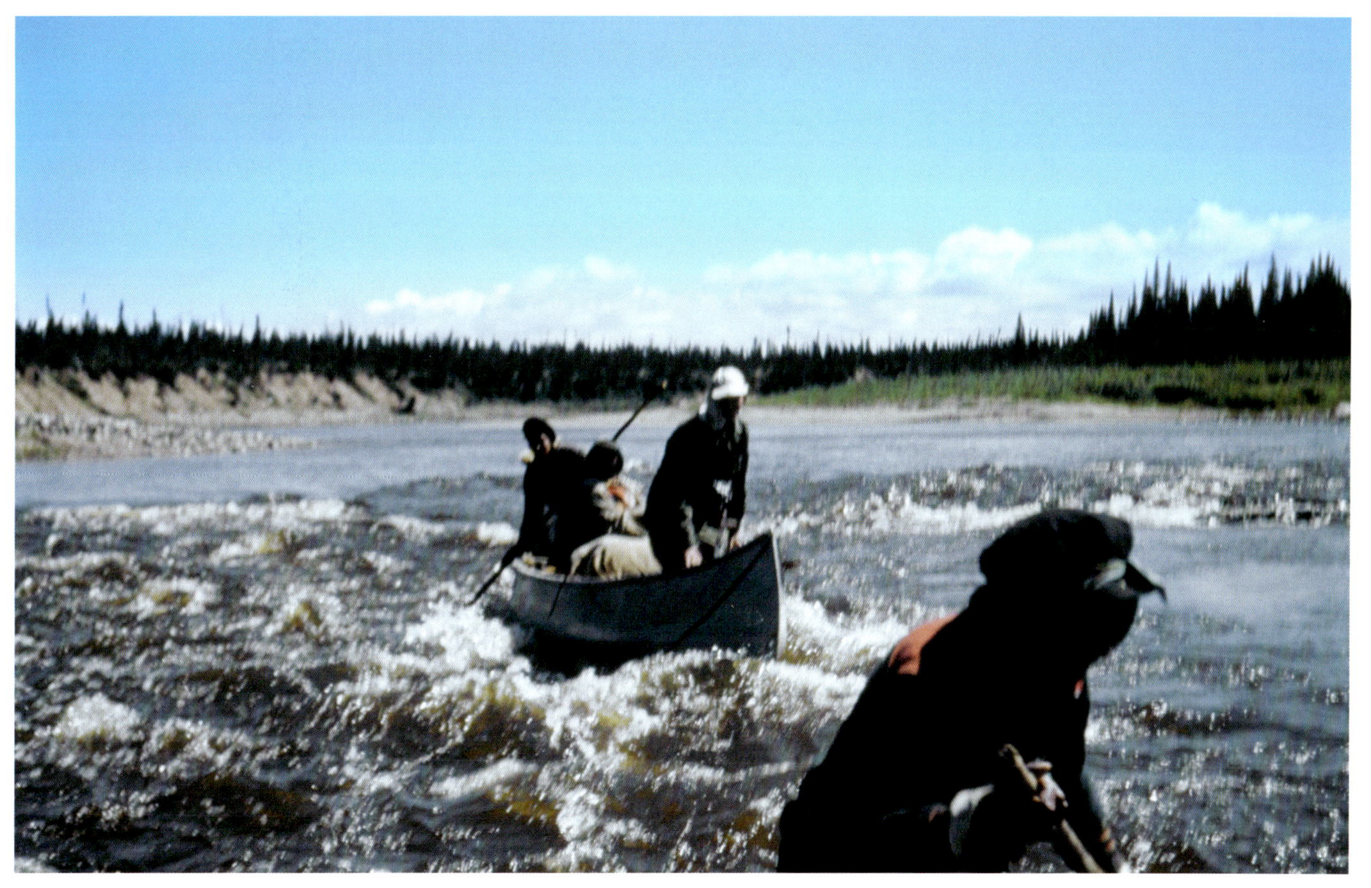

Rafting rapids in canoes on the Black Duck River, Kenora District July 25, 1953

Roderick Fiddler of Sandy Lake c. 1955

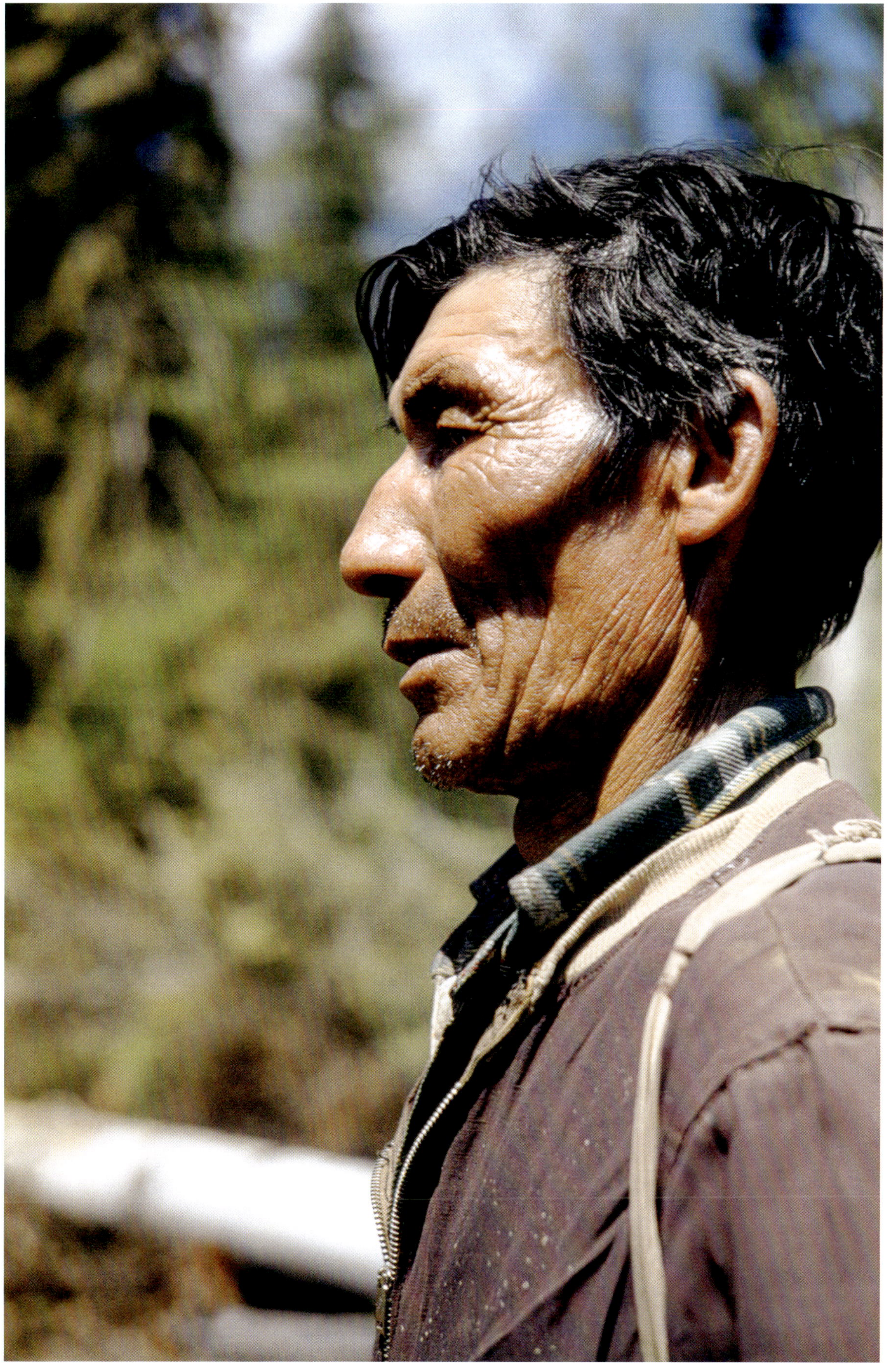

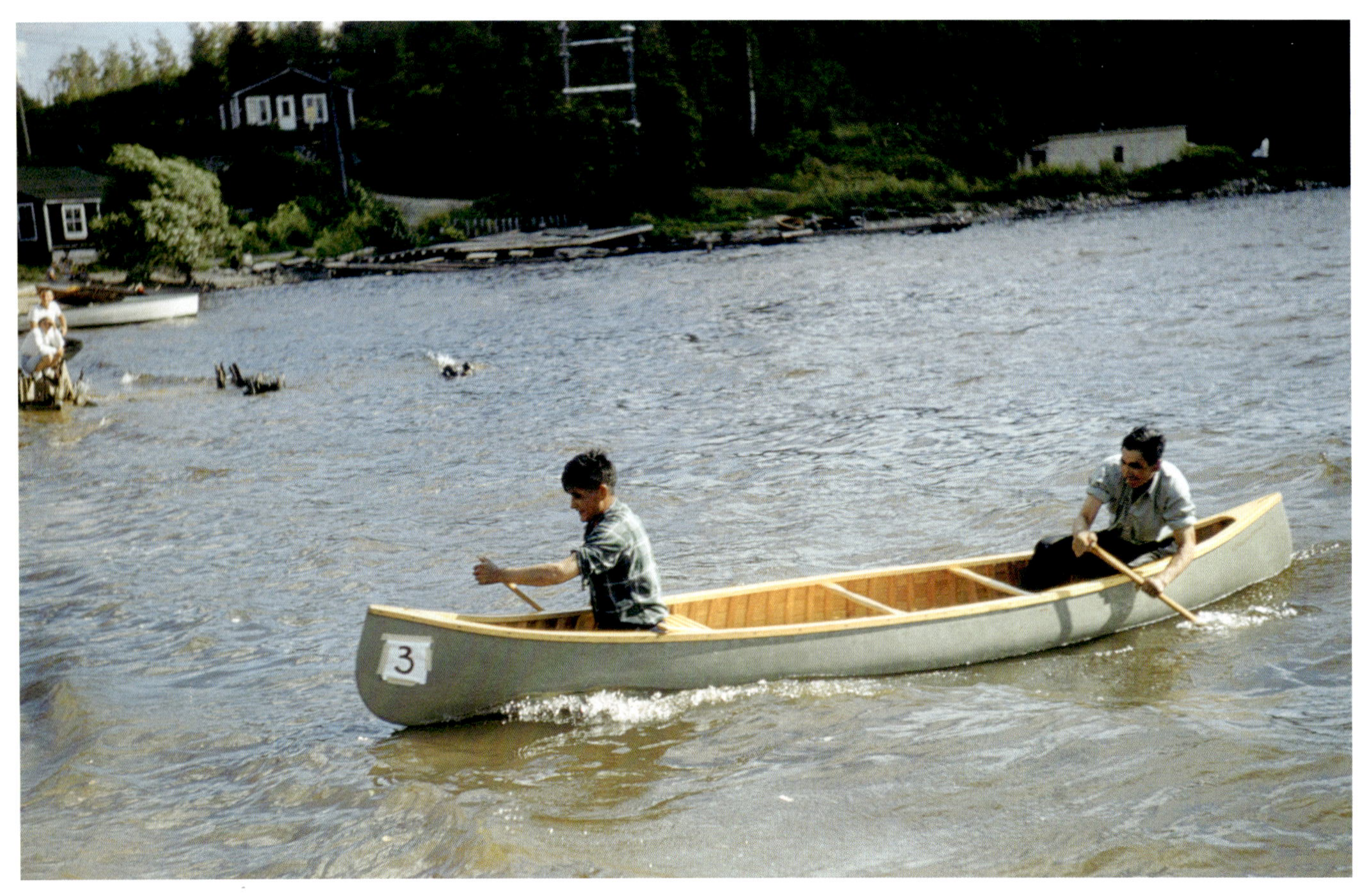

Elijah Batter in the bow of a canoe at the regatta, Sioux Lookout c. 1953

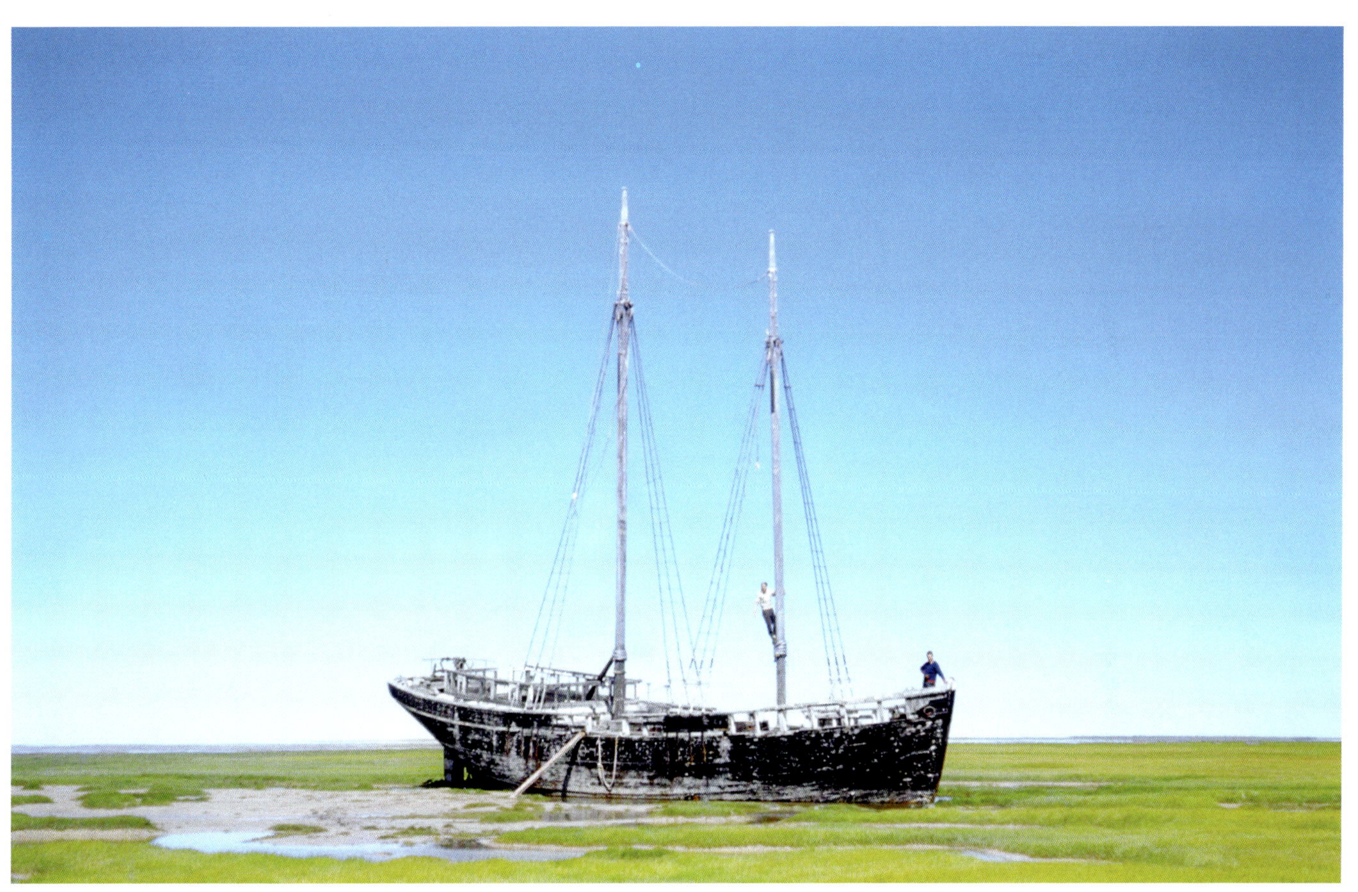

The Hudson's Bay Company schooner *York Fort,* stranded where it was blown onto mud flats just west of the mouth of the Severn River in 1931 1955

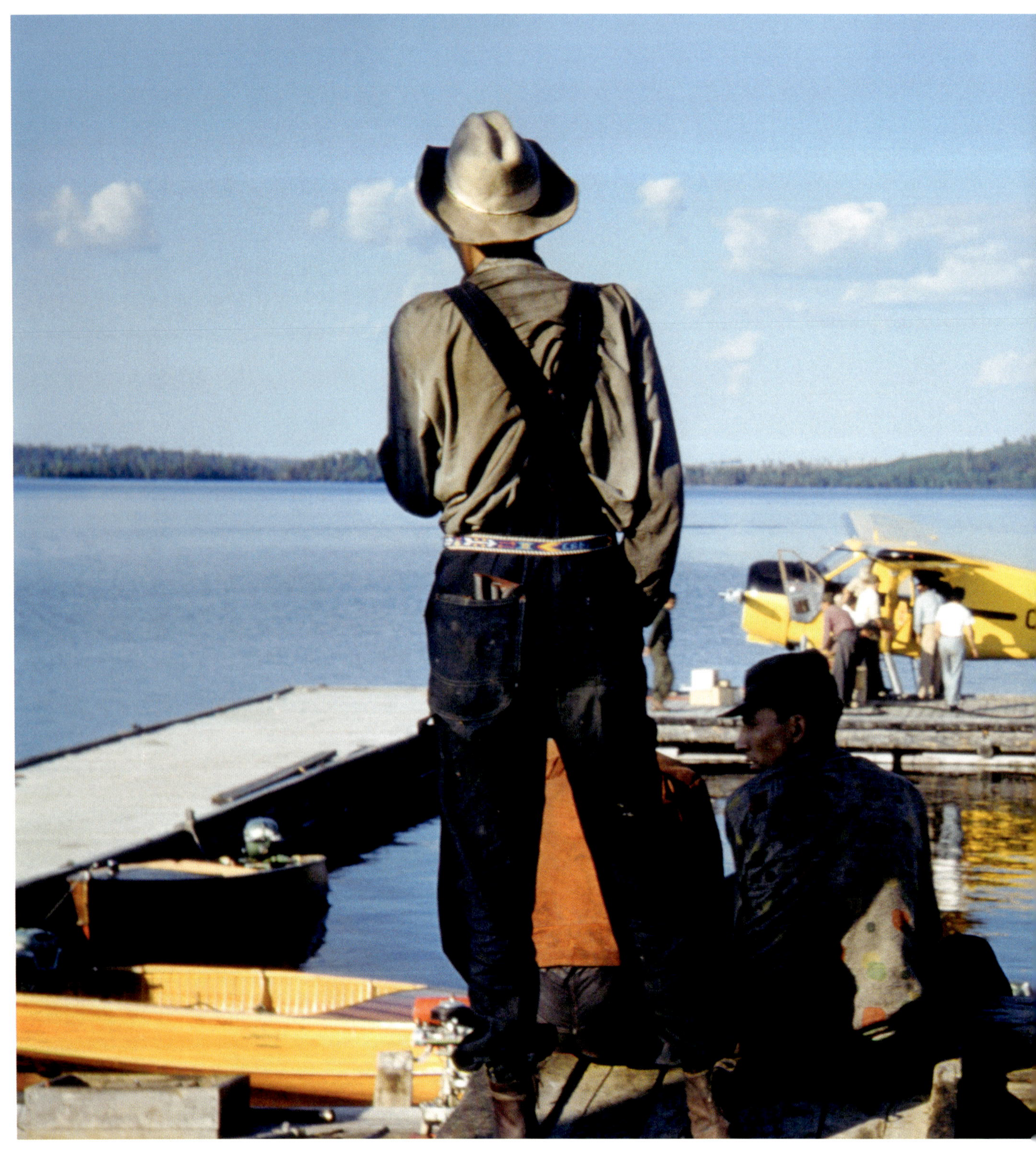

Watching distant forest fires at Red Lake, Kenora District 1956

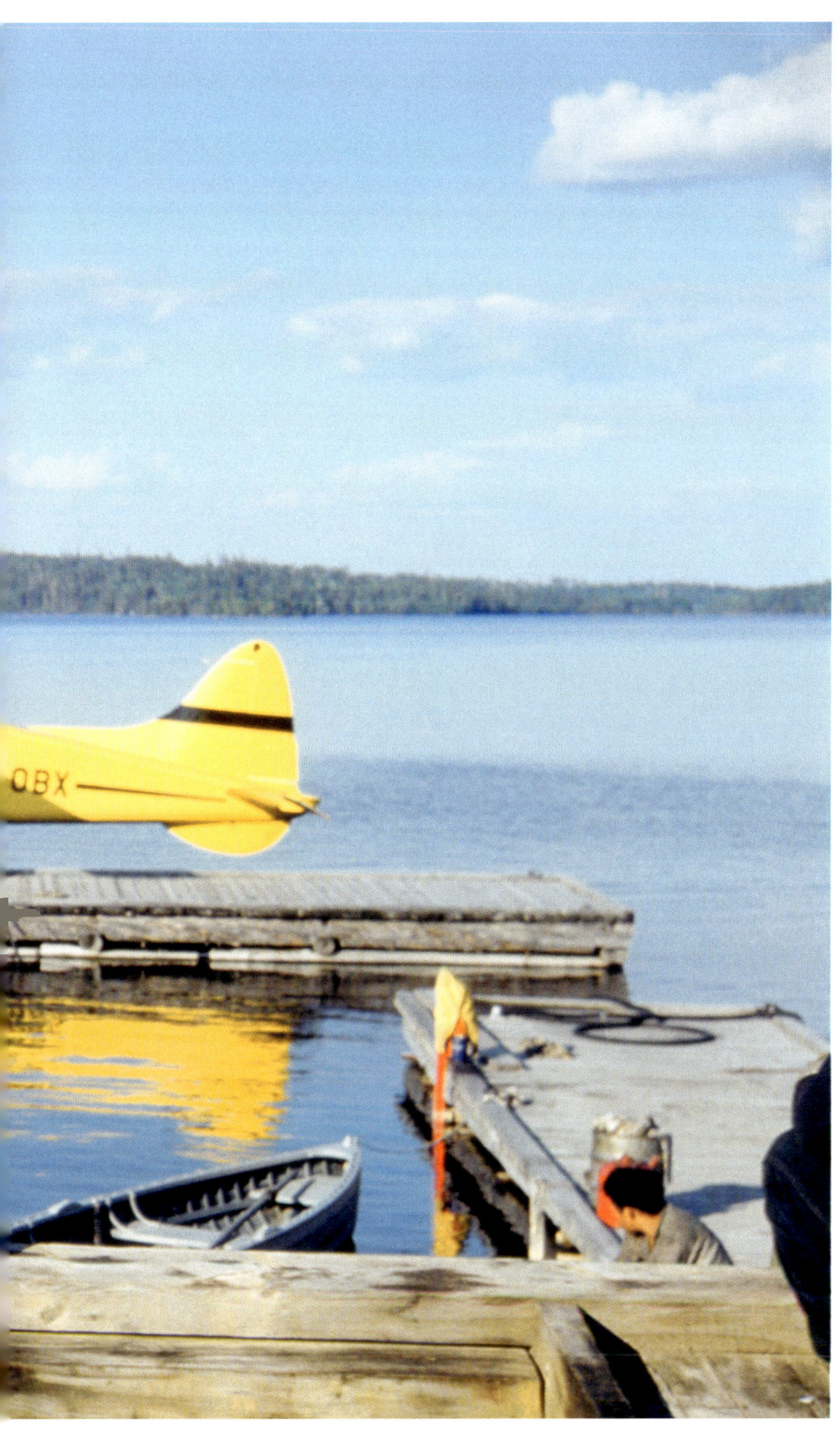
OBX

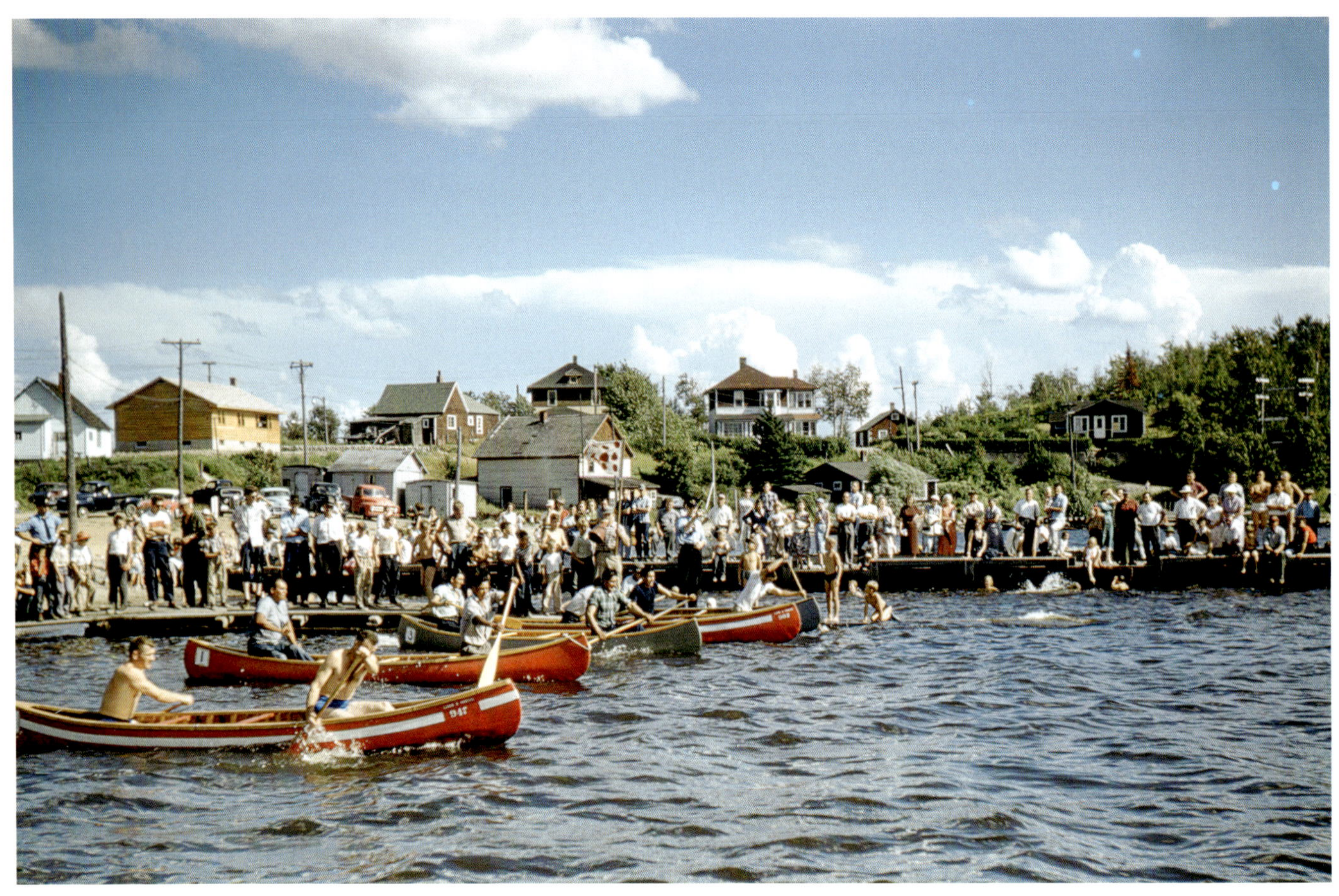

A crowd watching the canoe regatta at Sioux Lookout c. 1953

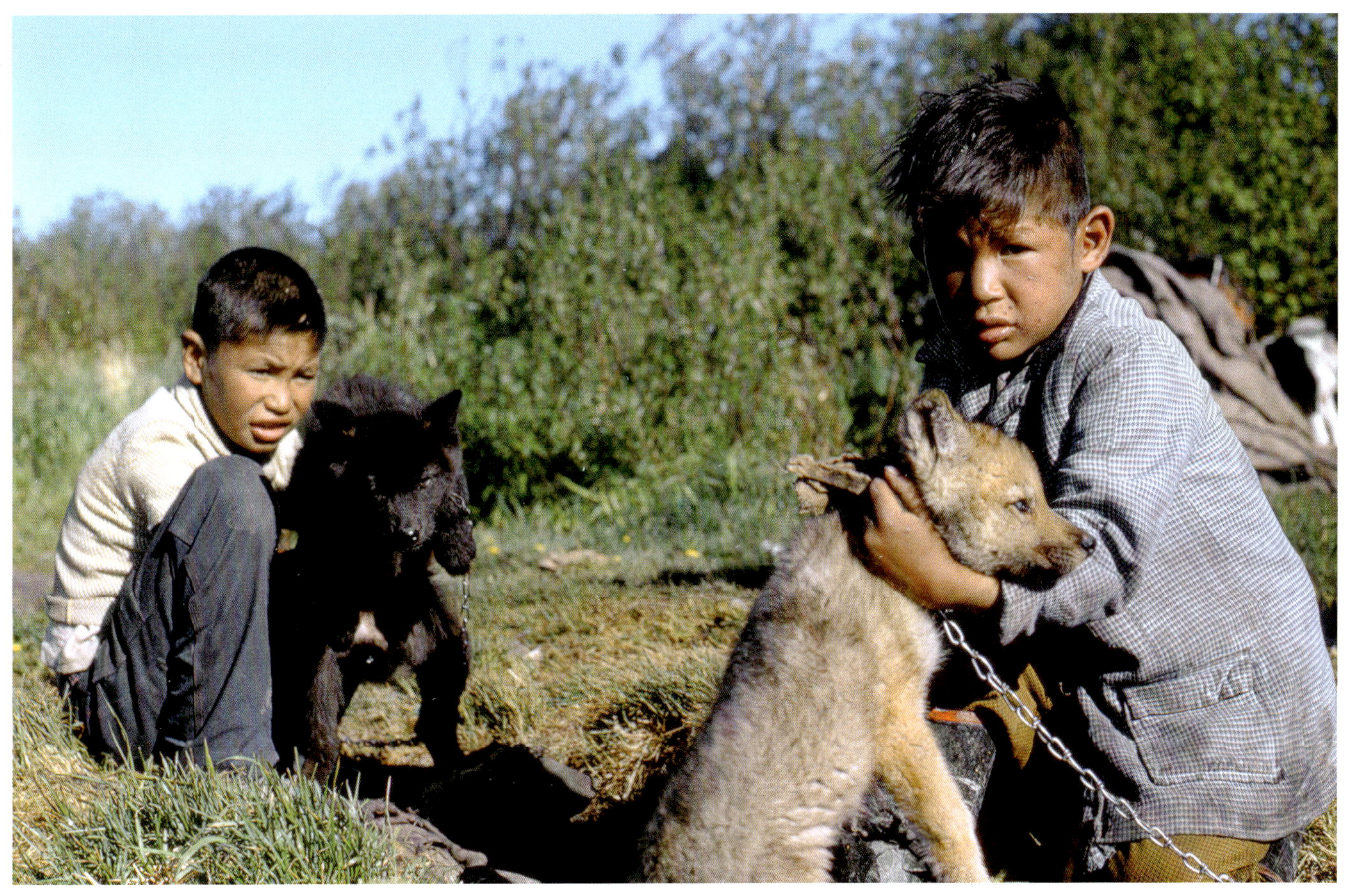

Boys with wolf pups in Attawapiskat 1963

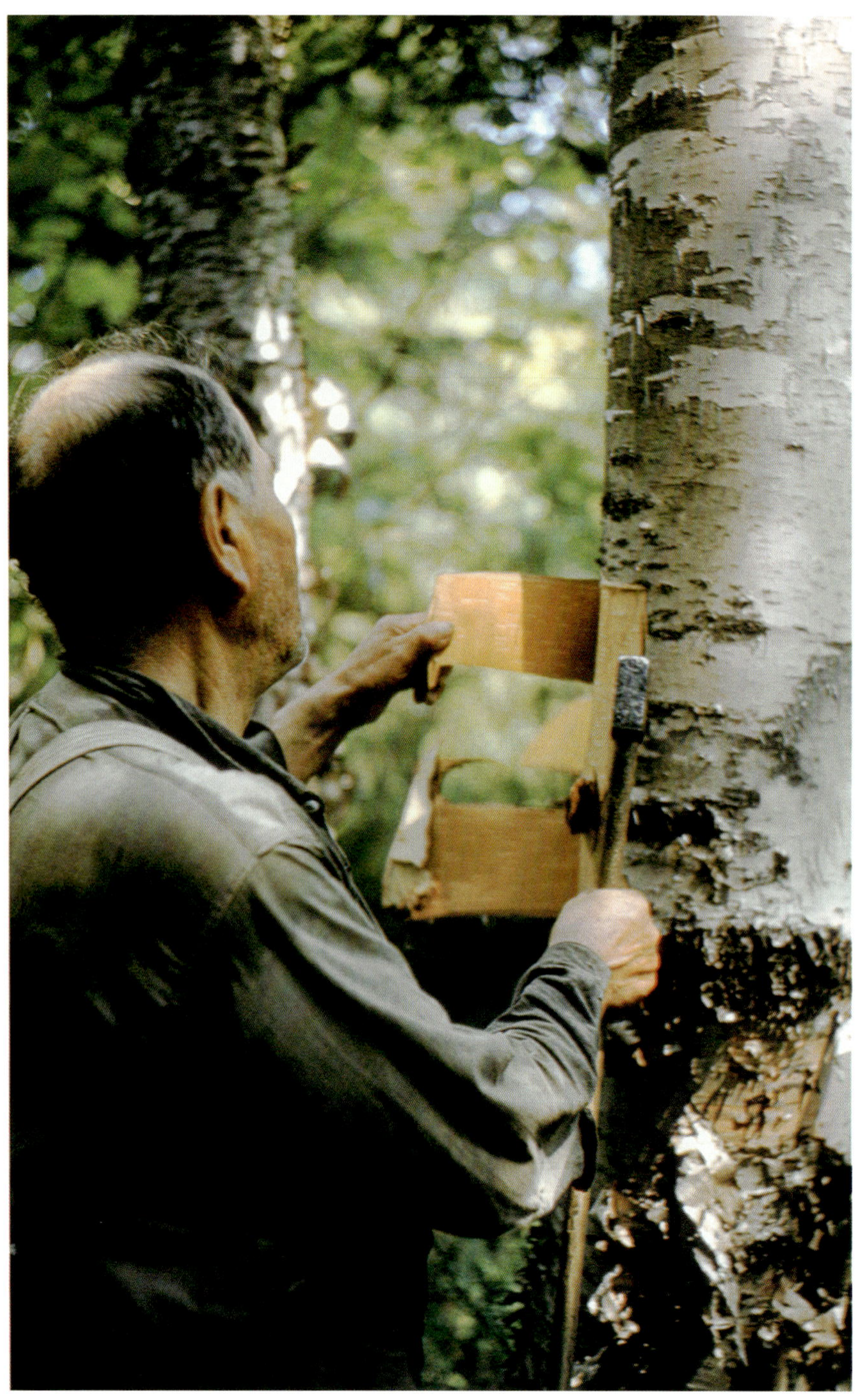

William Moore checking the condition of birchbark before deciding whether to harvest it 1958

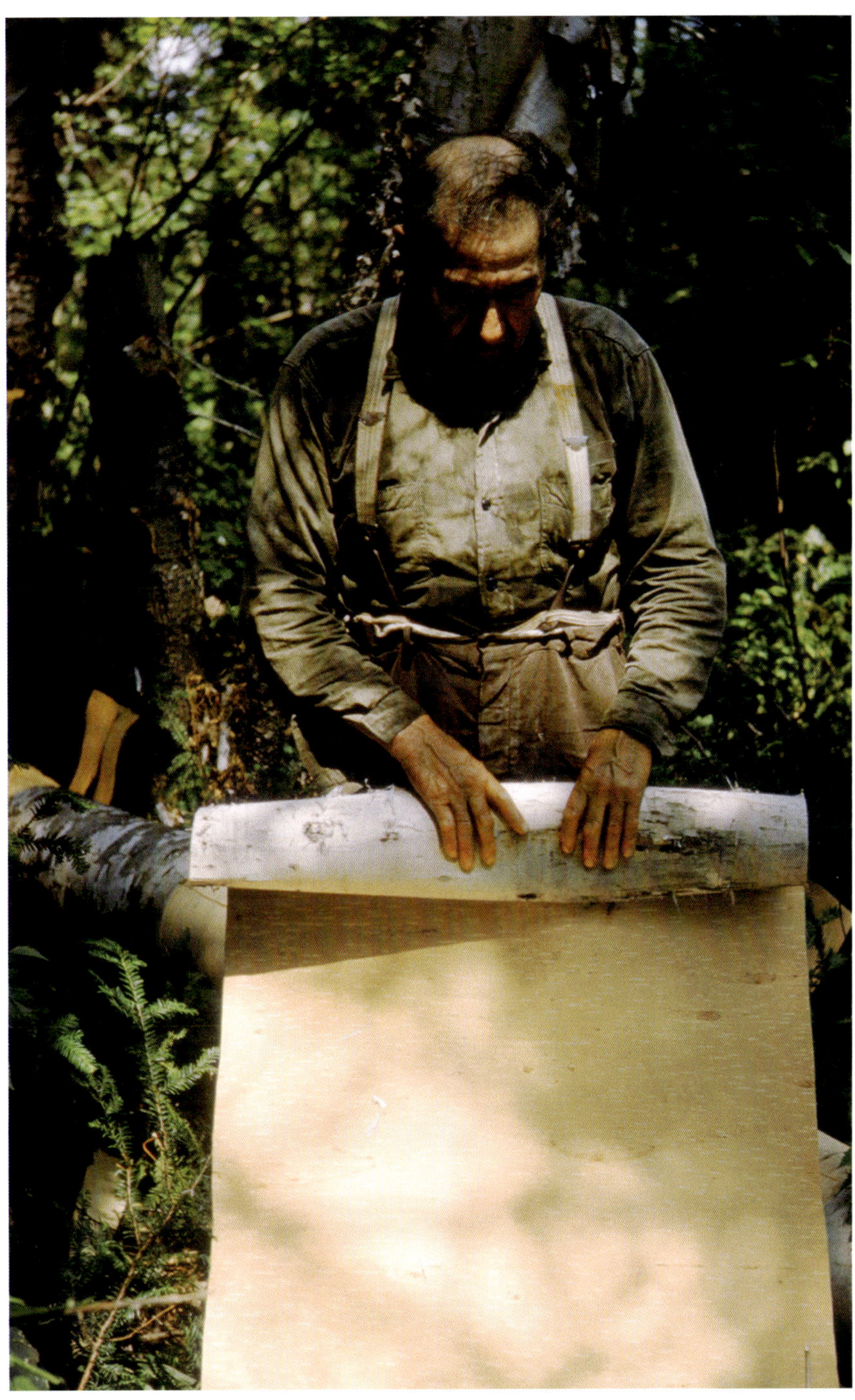

William Moore rolling birchbark to carry home 1958

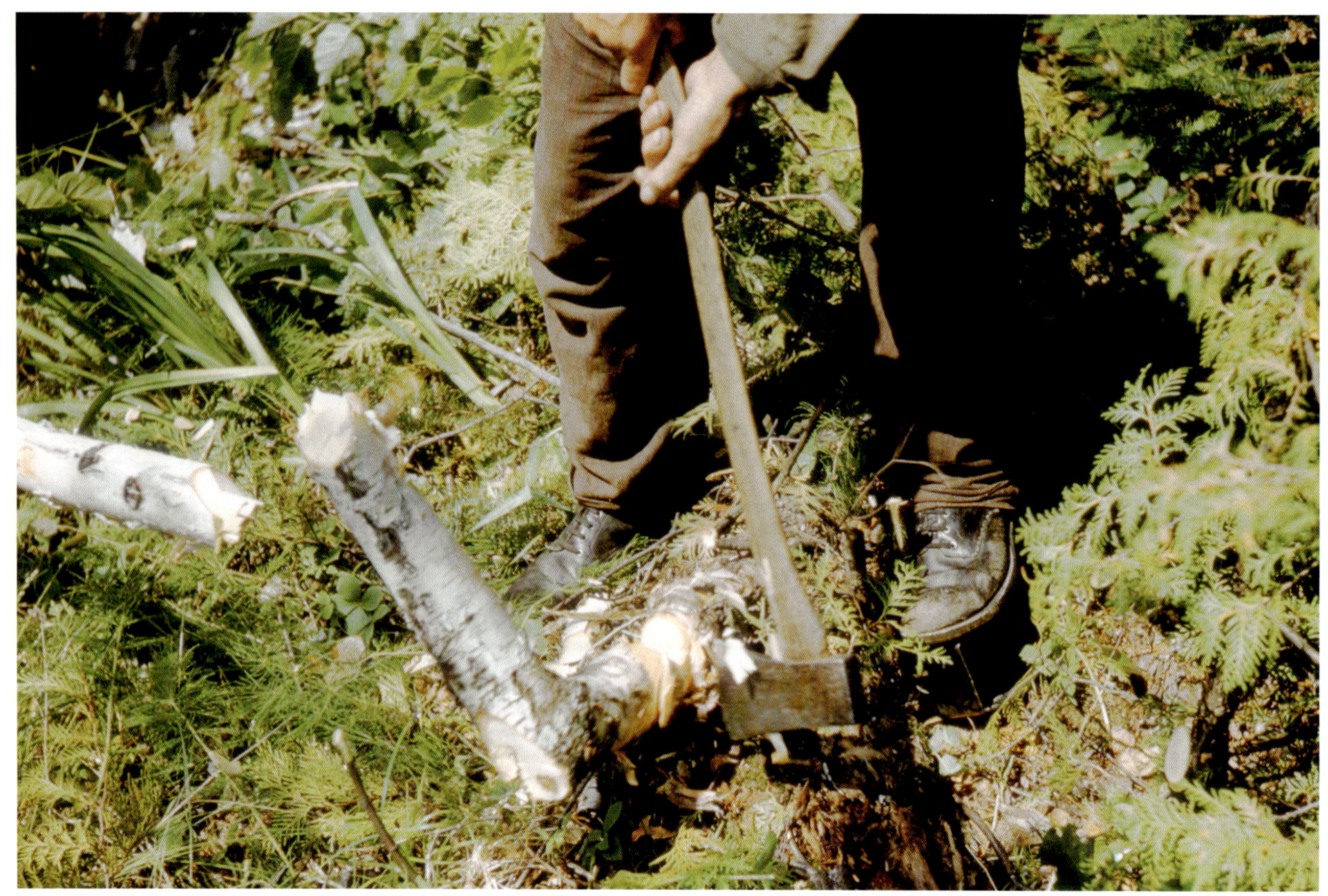

William Moore digging up bent birch for his crafts 1958

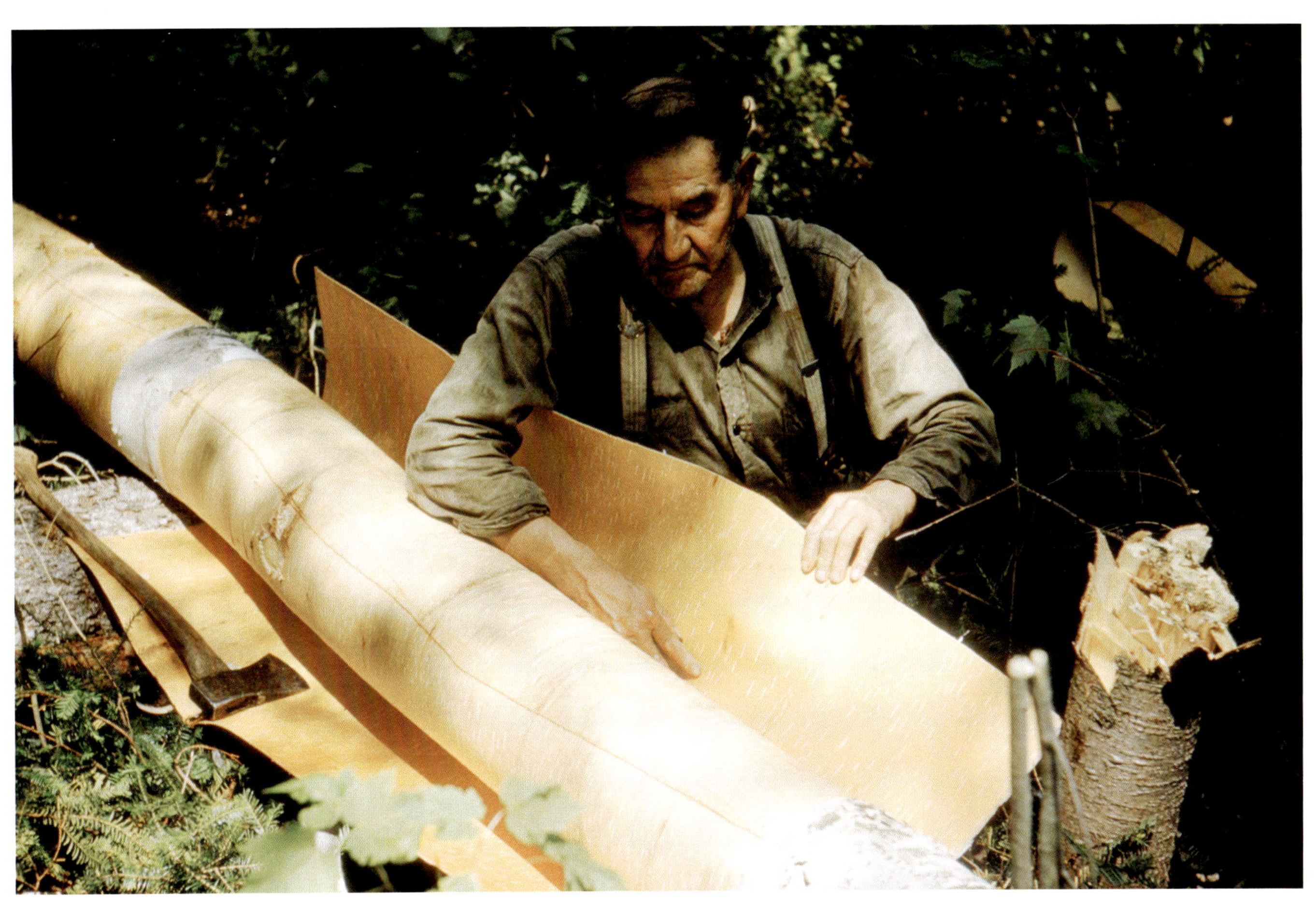

William Moore peeling birchbark from a felled tree for making baskets 1958

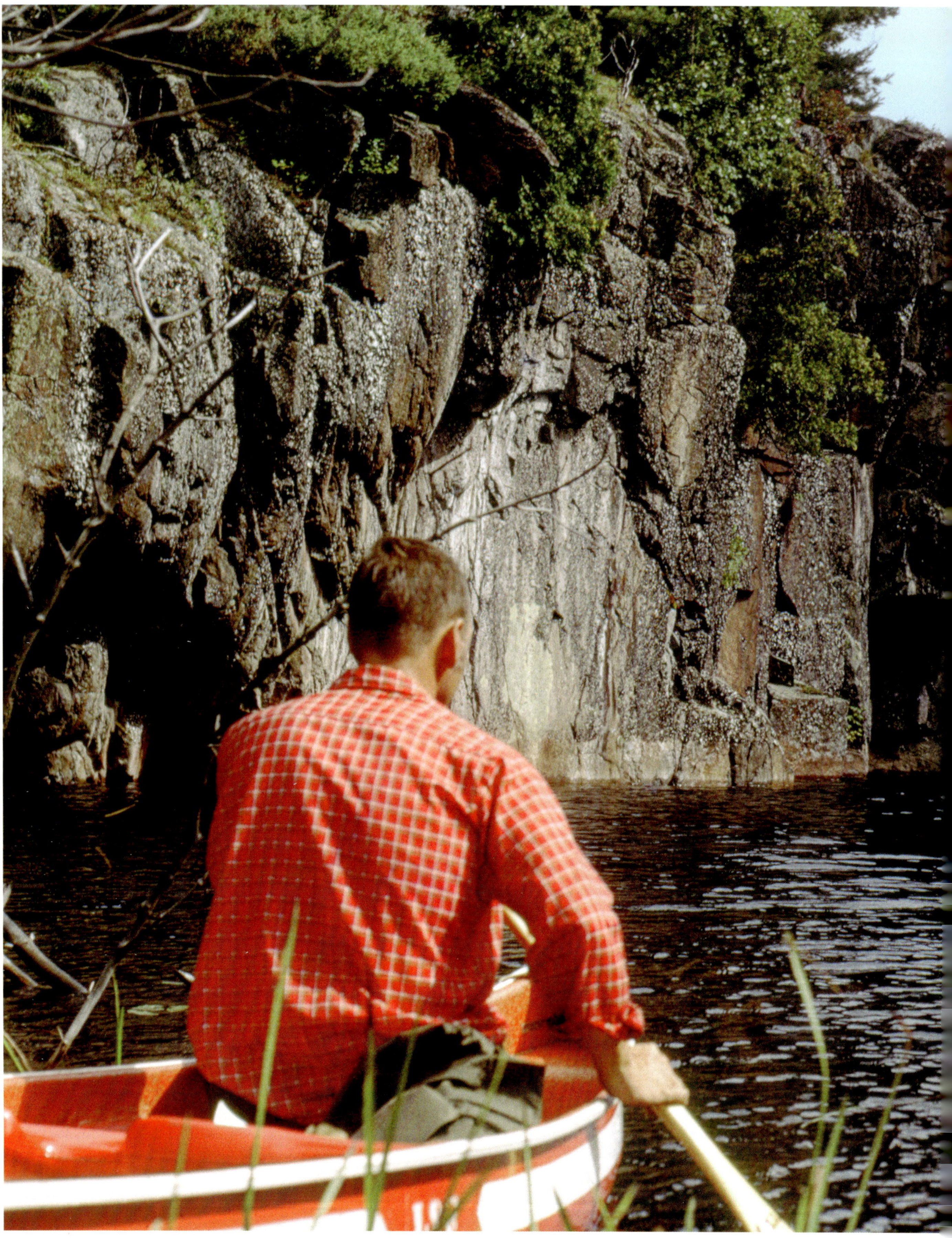

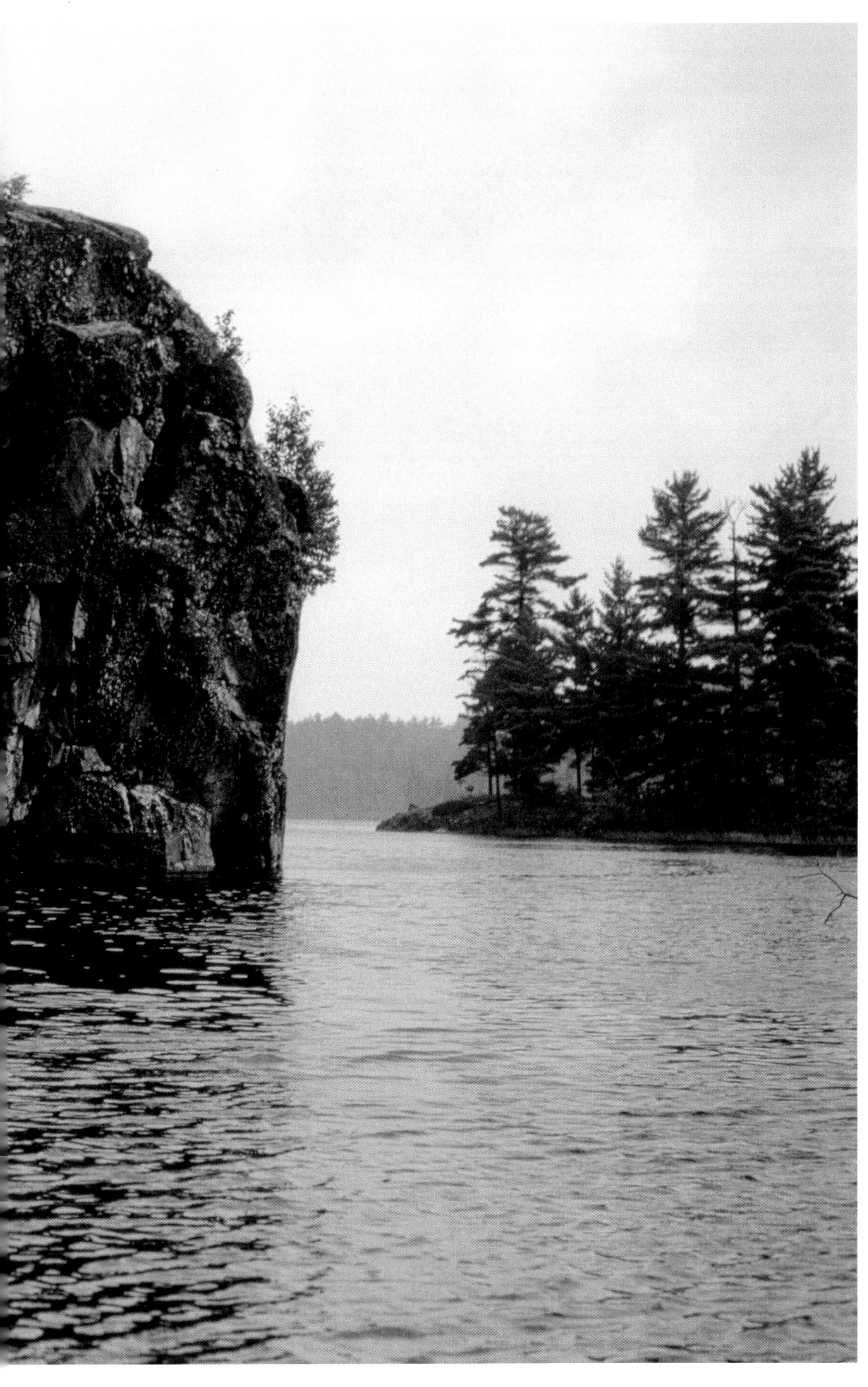

Pictograph rock, Lone Tree Lake, Harrison Township, Parry Sound District 1971

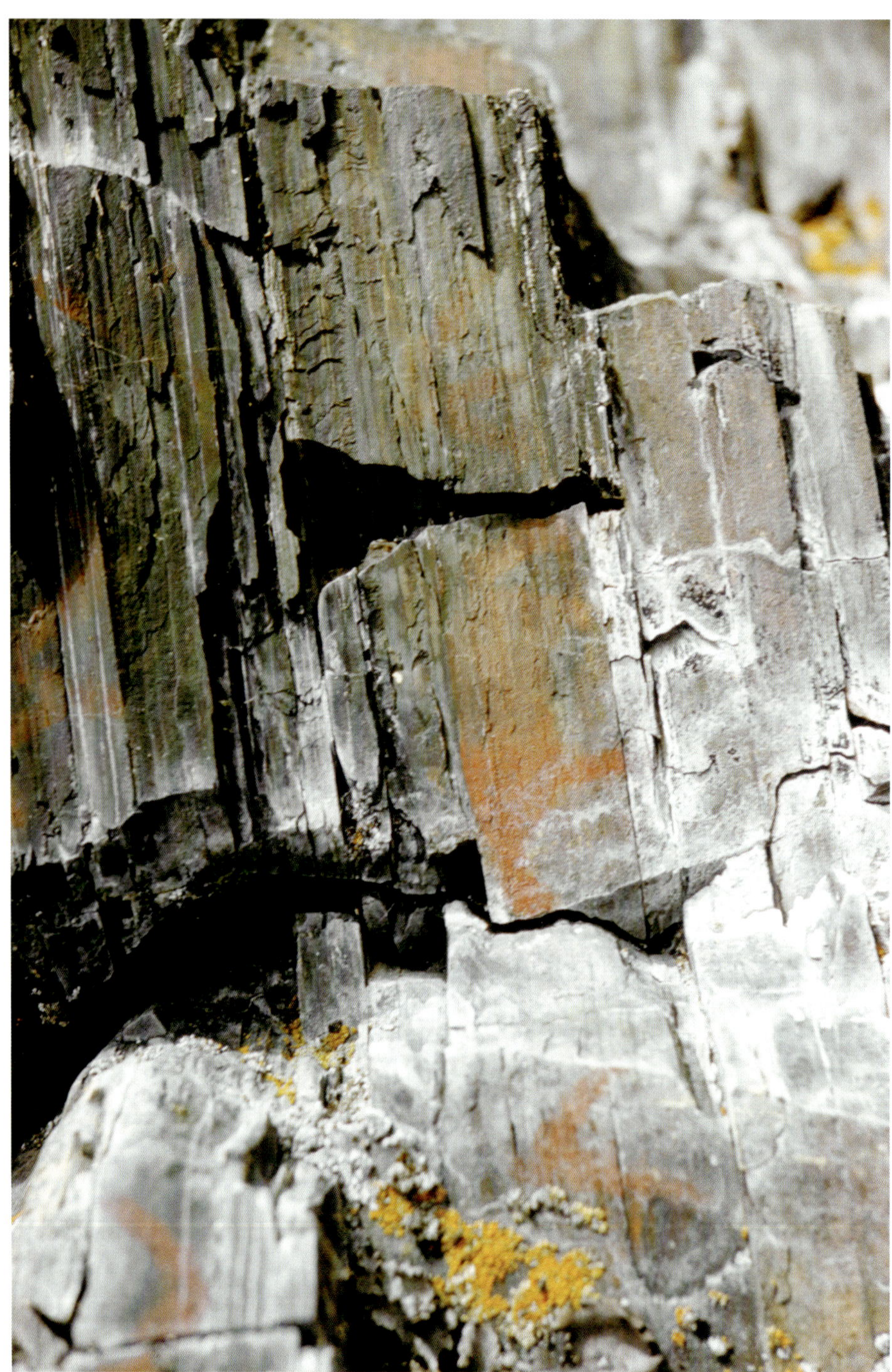

Rock pictographs at Ferris Lake, Mond Township, between Mattagami Lake and Matachewan, Timiskaming District March 1958

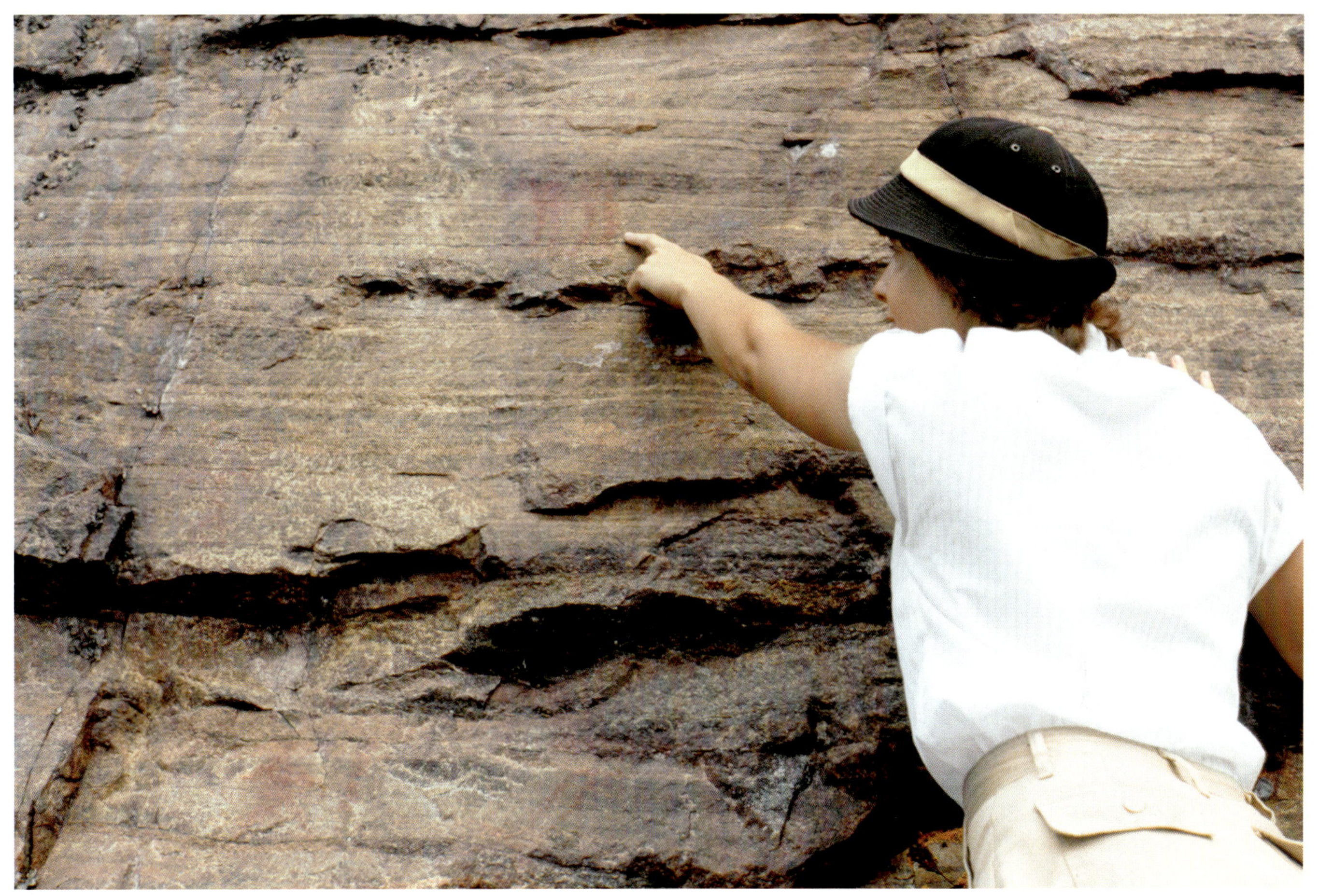

Beth Macfie, John Macfie's daughter, pointing to a pictograph on the Pickerel River, in the French River system between Parry Sound and Georgian Bay 1980

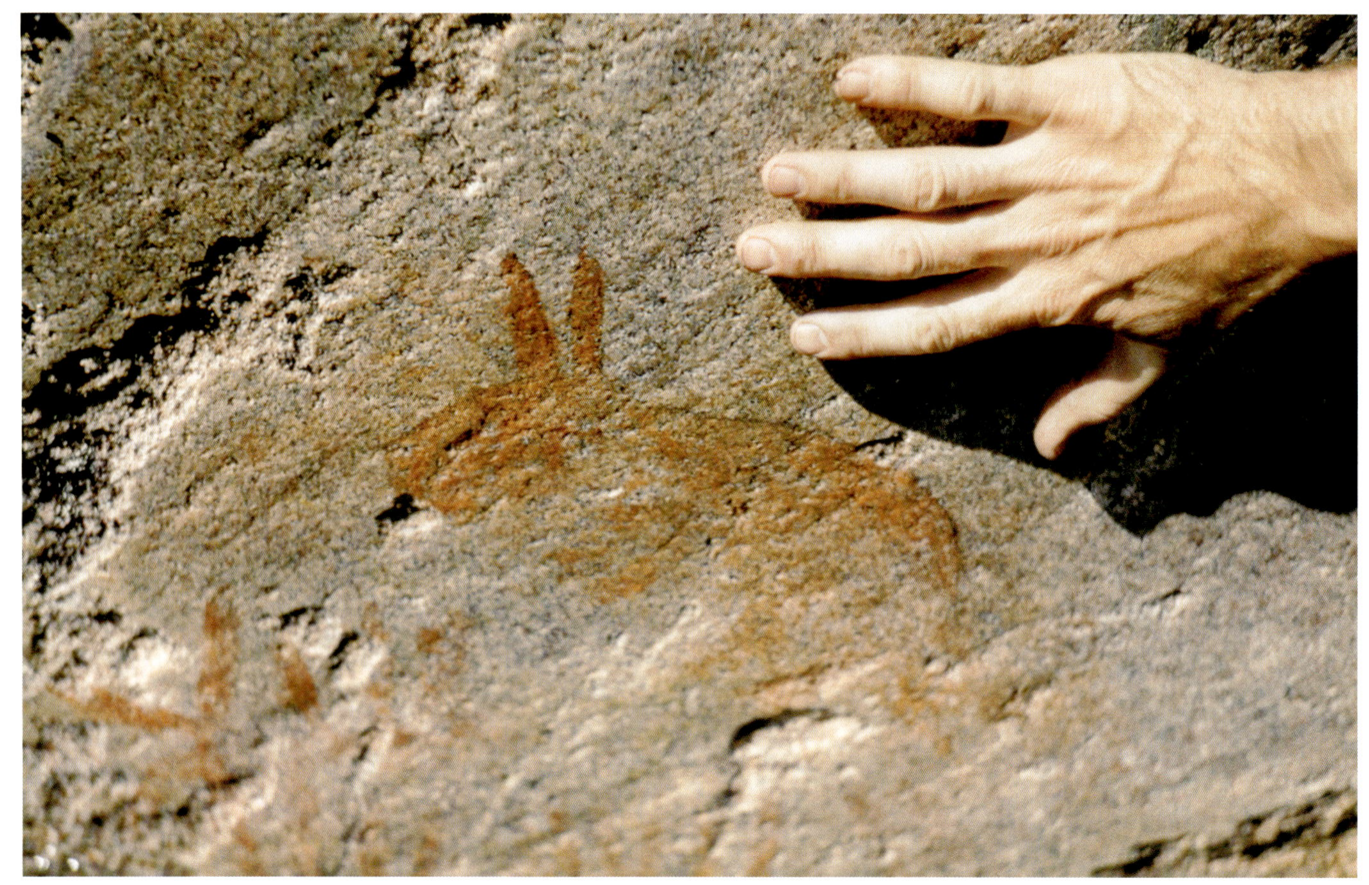

Rabbit pictograph at Deer Lake, Kenora District June 1956

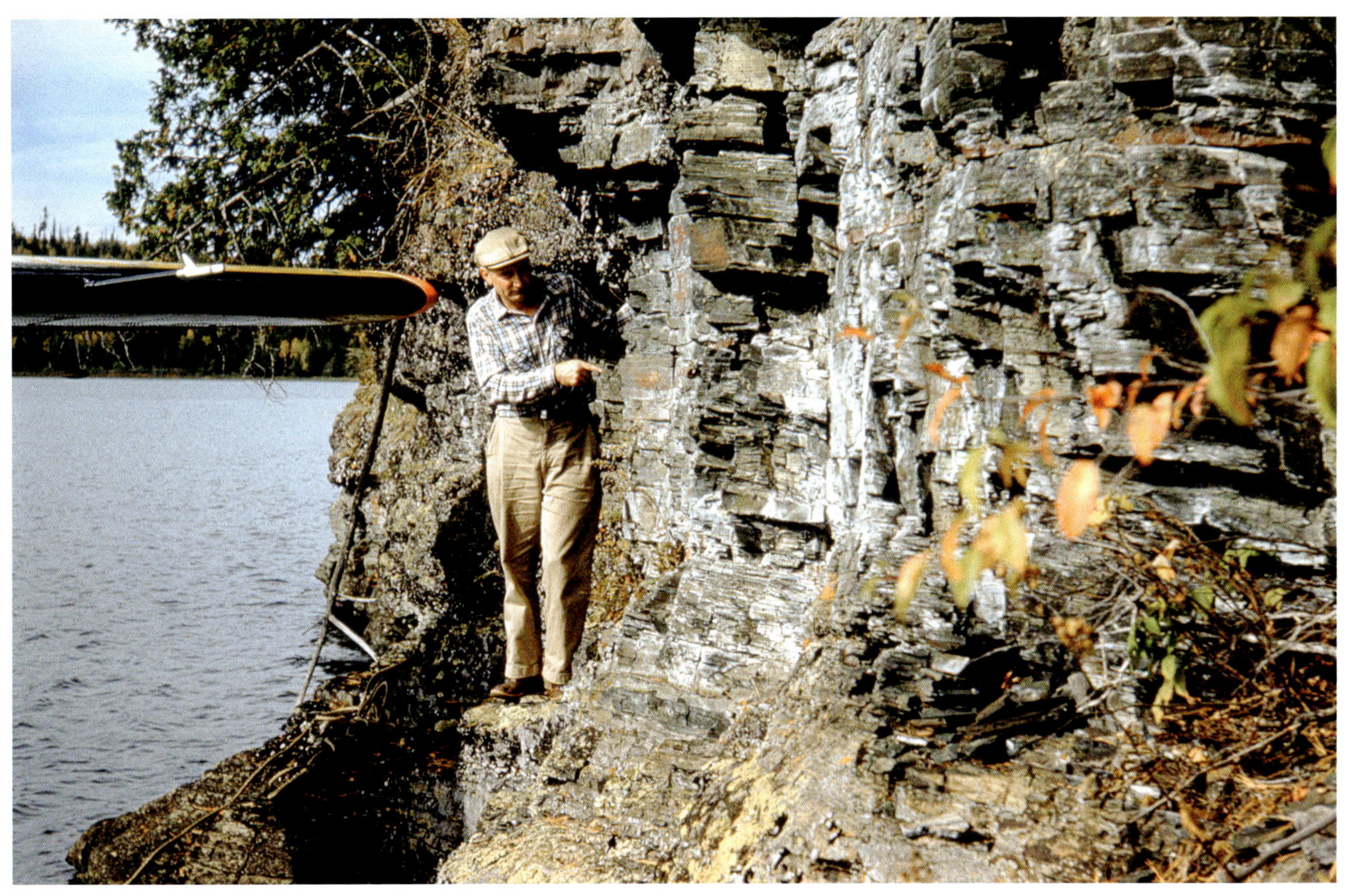

Provincial Air Service pilot George Campbell beside a pictograph site at Ferris Lake, Mond Township between Mattagami Lake and Matachewan, Timiskaming District September 26, 1958

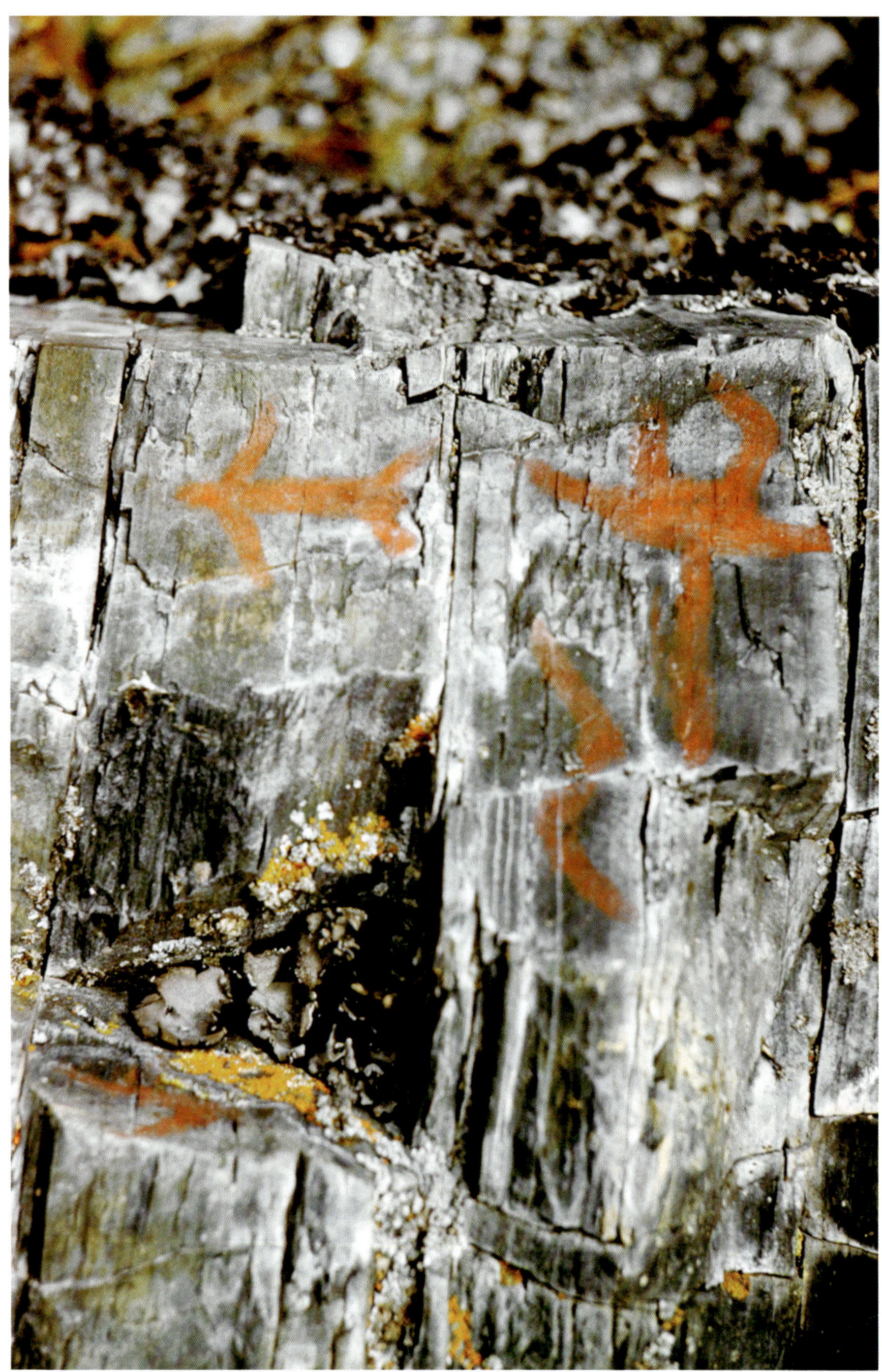

Rock pictographs at Ferris Lake east of Gogama September 26, 1958

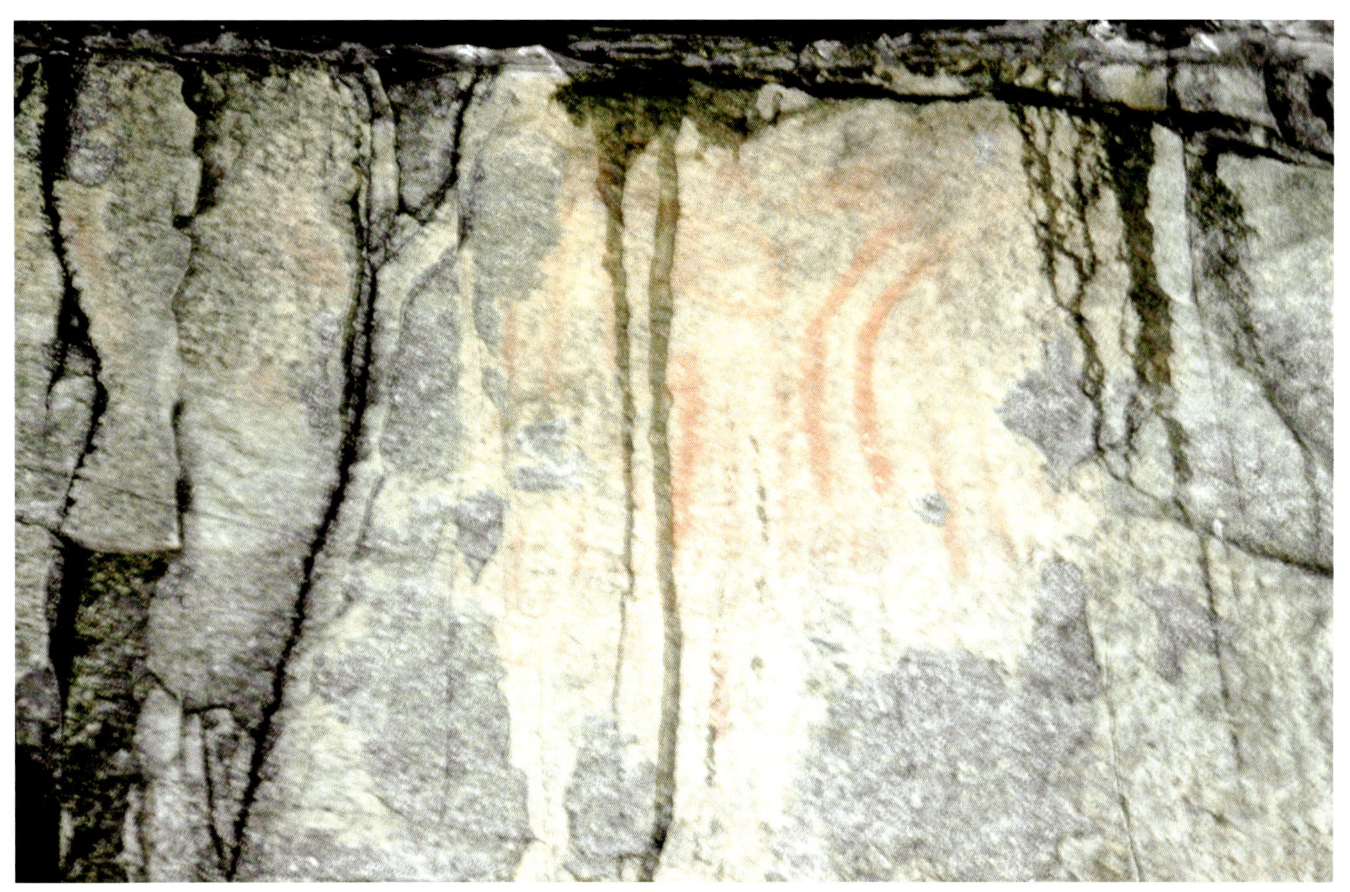

Pictographs at Hardimon Bay site, Sudbury District March 1958

Albert Carpenter offering tobacco at a pictograph site, Carling Lake, Kenora District 1954

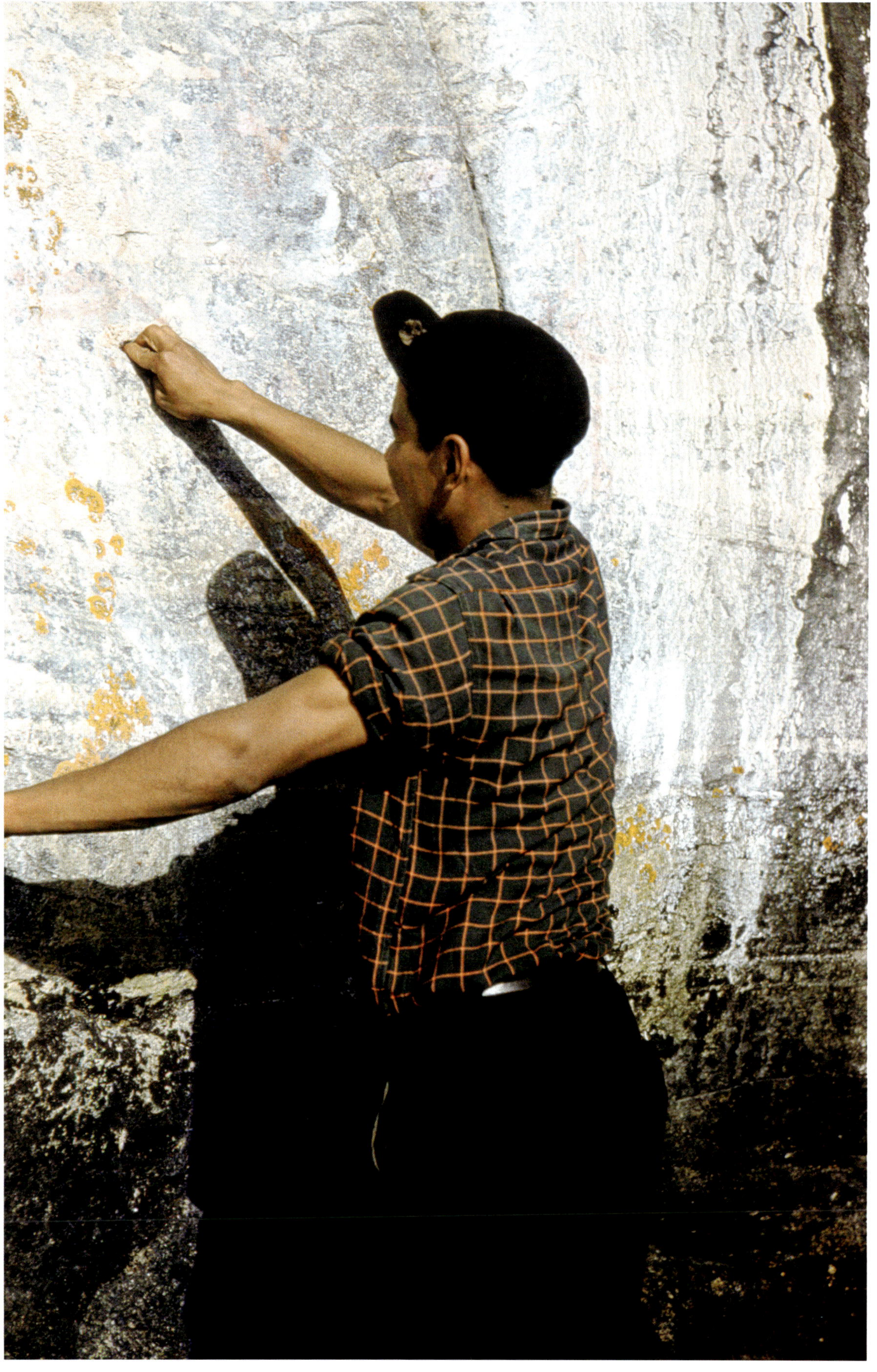

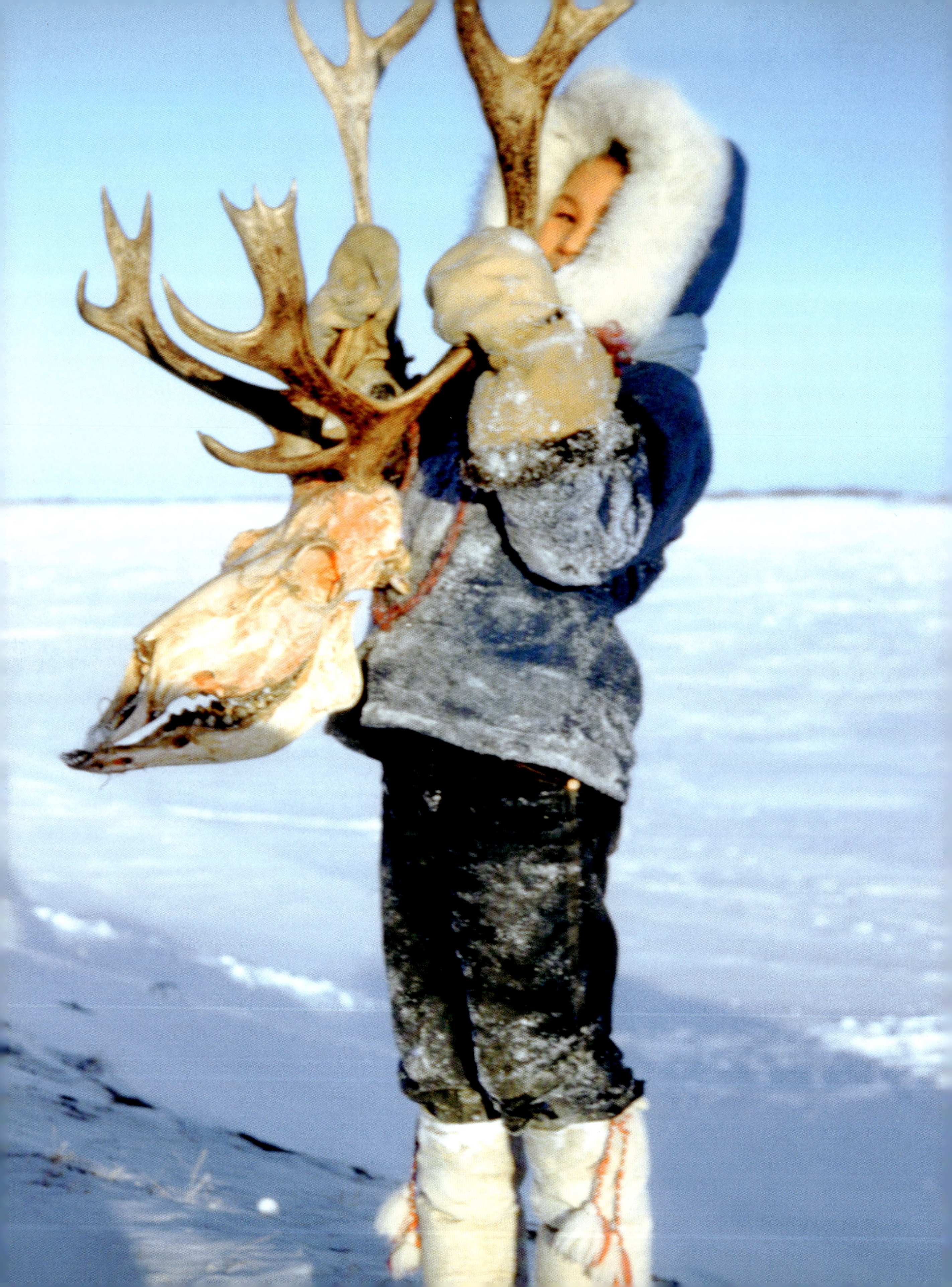

Winter

A boy holding a caribou skull at Weenusk, on the western shore of Hudson Bay February 20, 1955

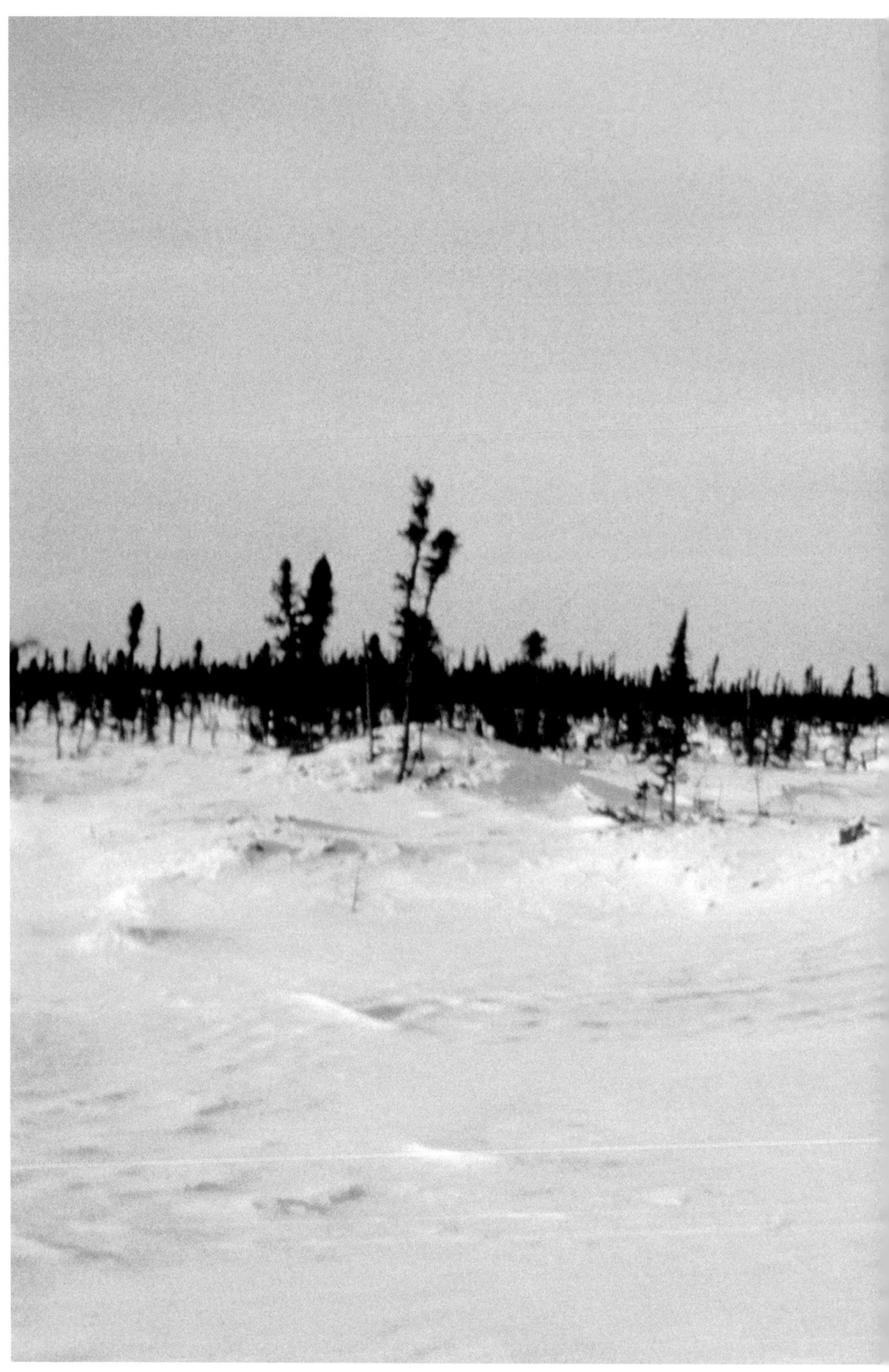

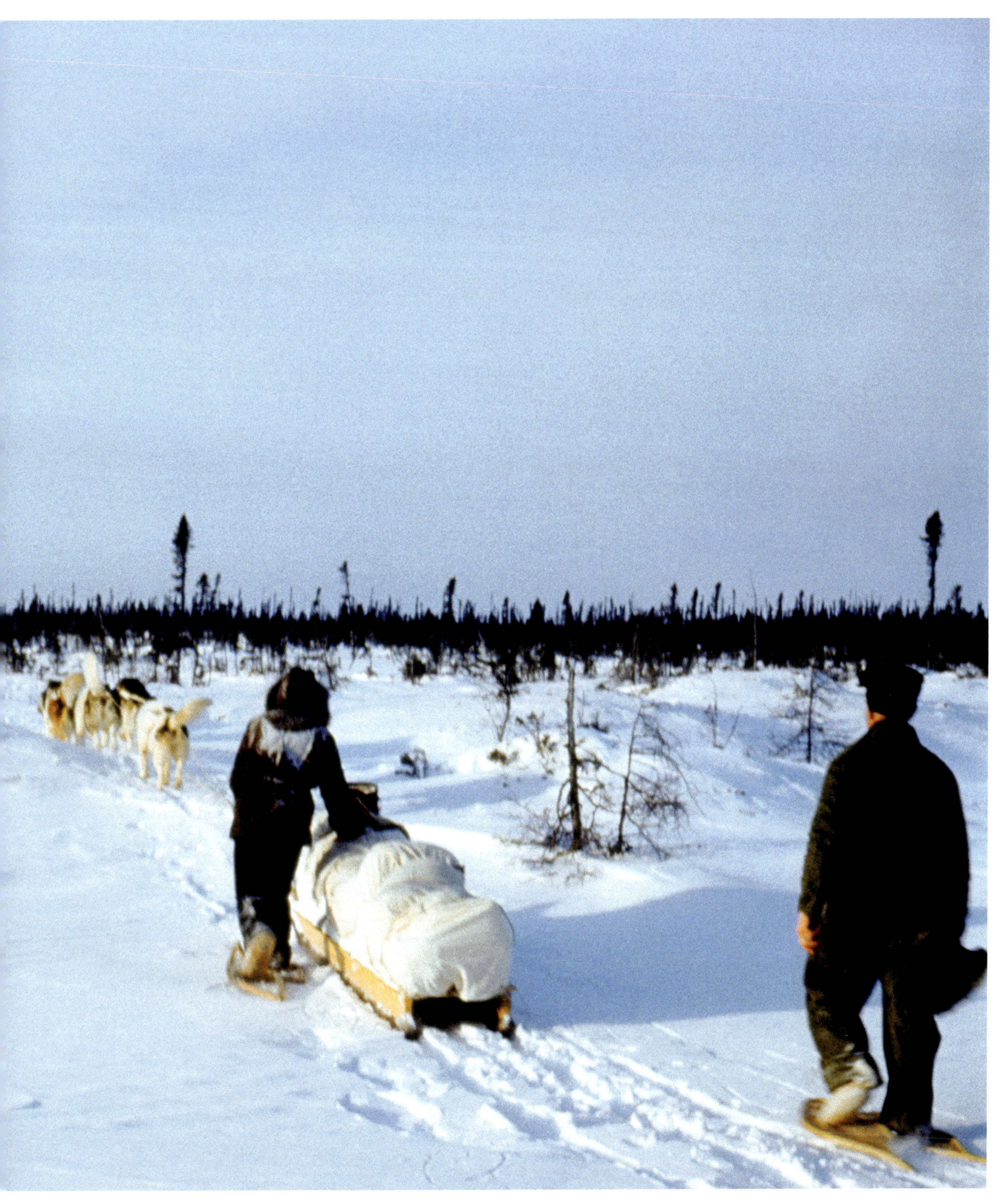

Moses Koostachin driving a dog team from Weenusk to Hawley Lake, Kenora District February 1955

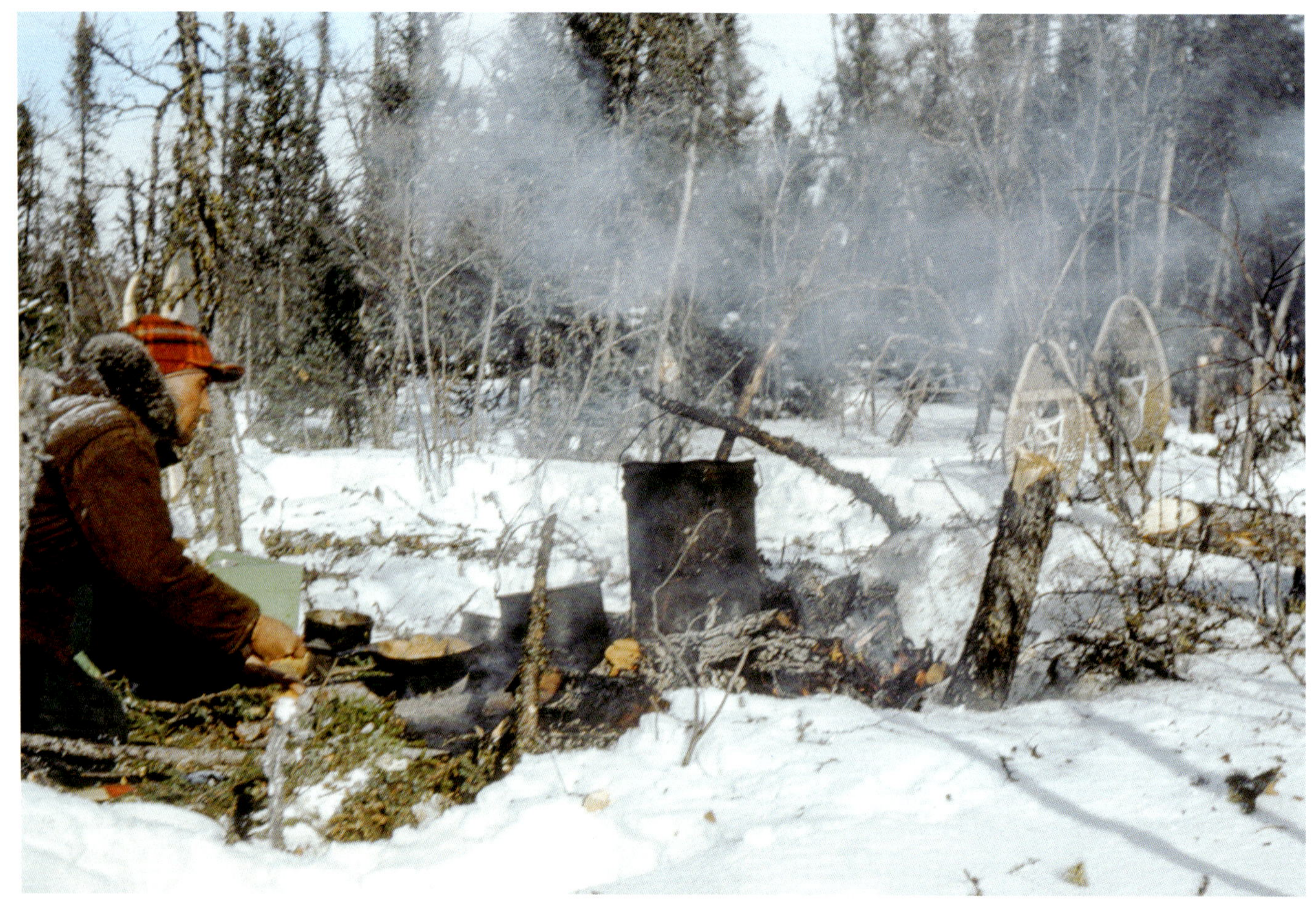

Moses Koostachin at a noon stop en route from Weenusk to Hawley Lake February 1955

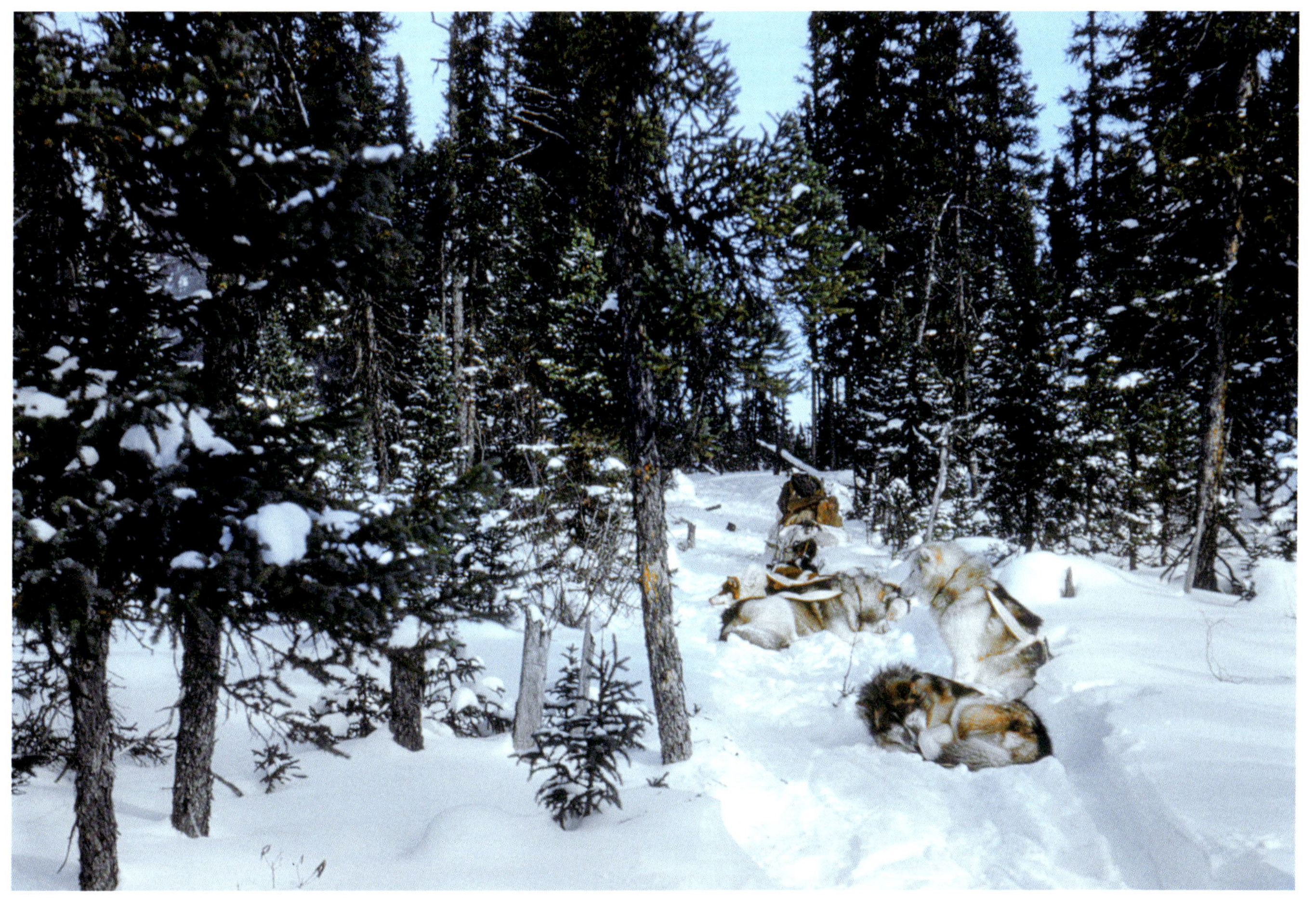

Father Gagnon's dog team resting during a trip from Weenusk to Hawley Lake February 1955

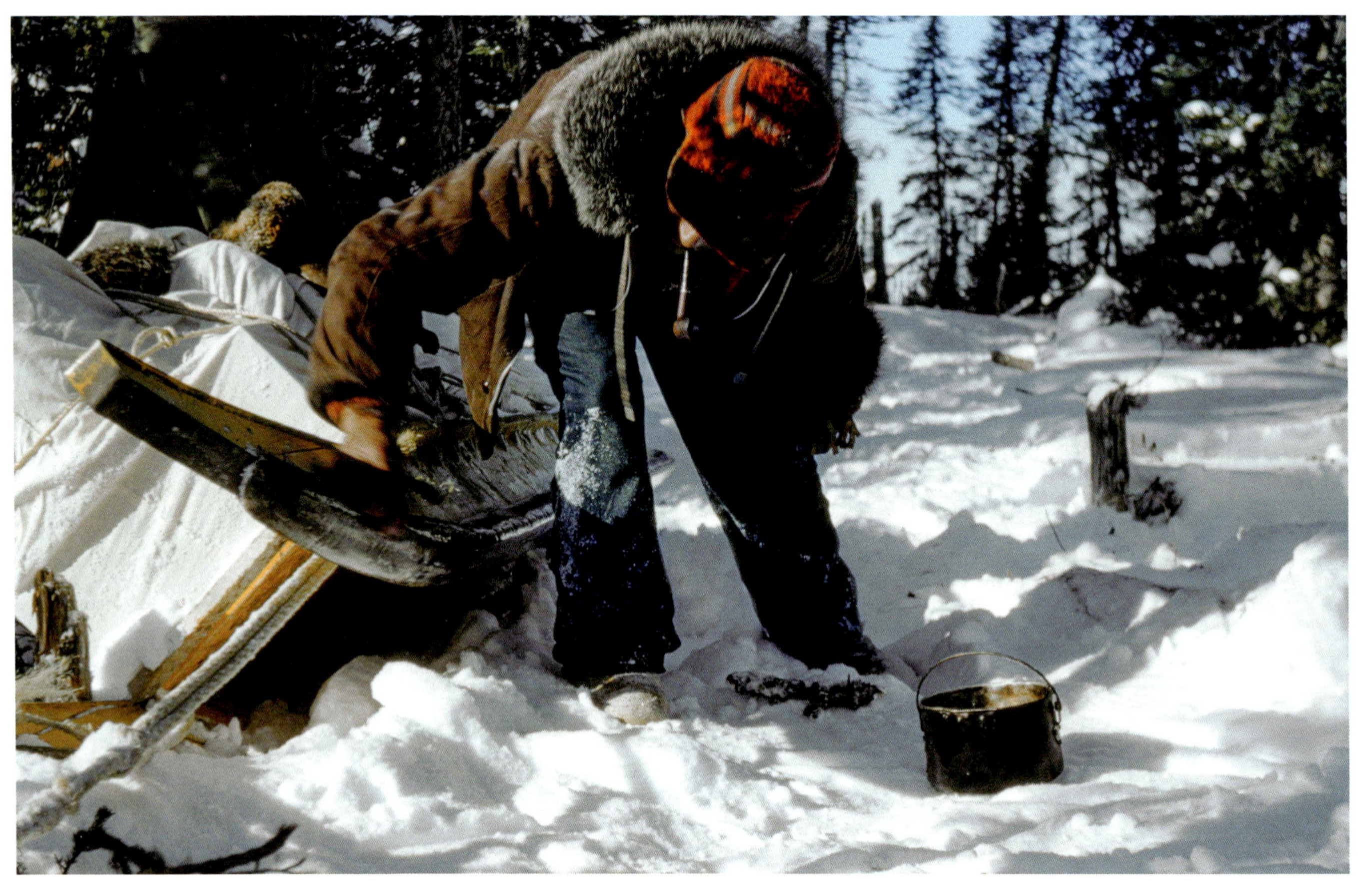

Moses Koostachin of Weenusk icing the muddied runners of the sled with tea during a stop in the muskeg between Weenusk and Hawley Lake February 1955

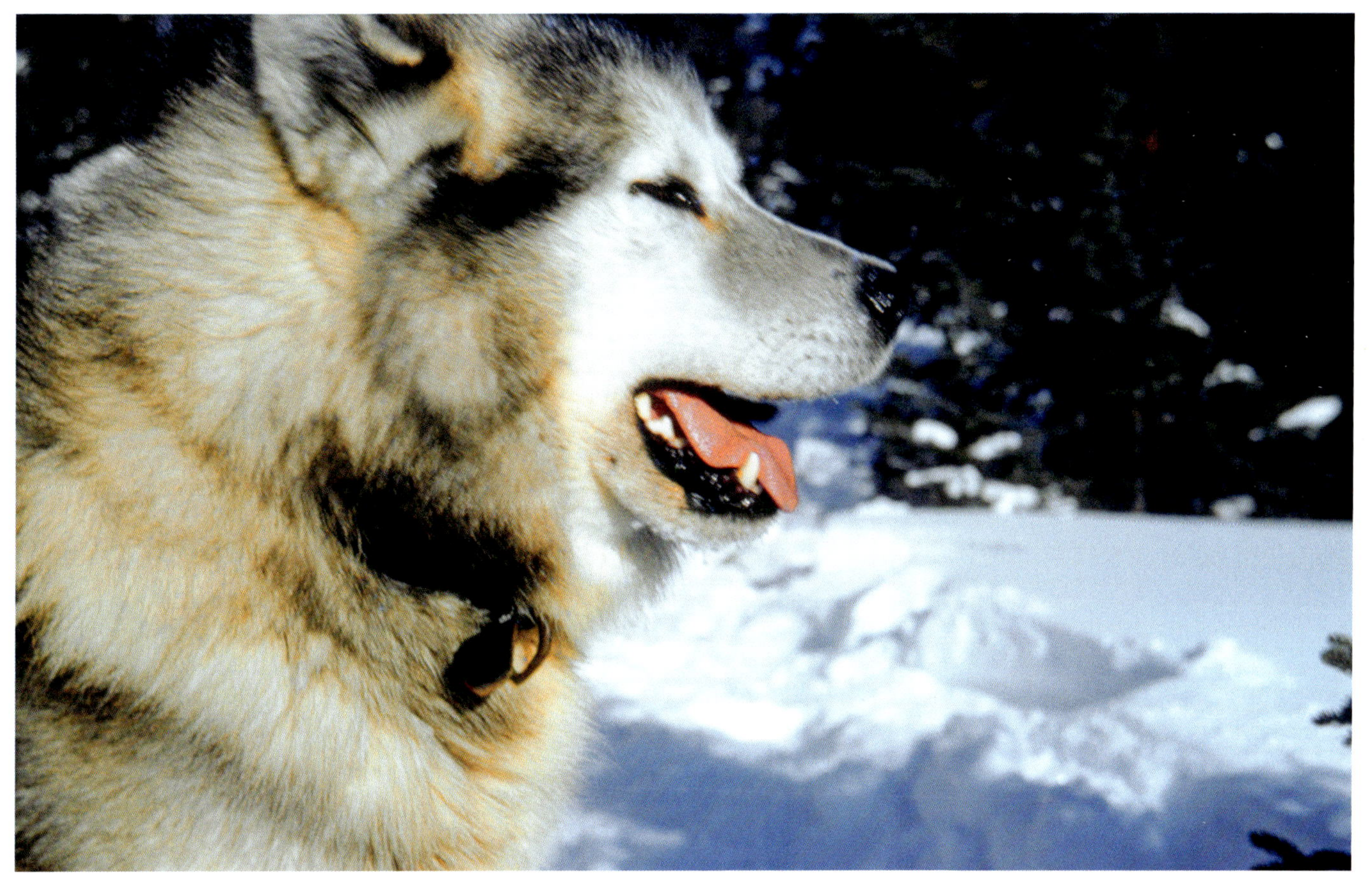

Jumbo, the lead dog of a seven-dog team belonging to the Roman Catholic mission at Weenusk 1955

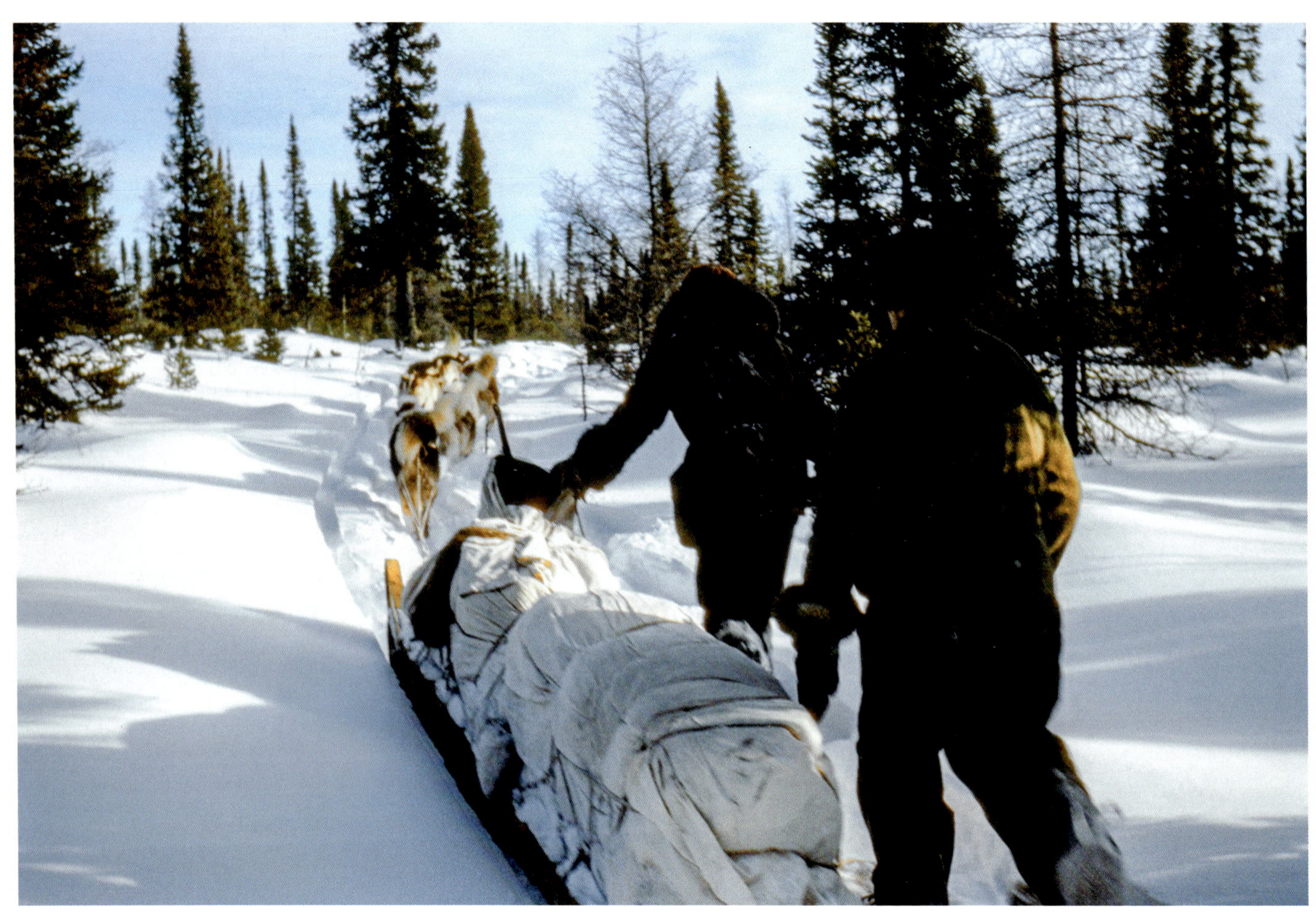

Moses Koostachin and Father Gagnon travelling between Weenusk and Hawley Lake February 1955

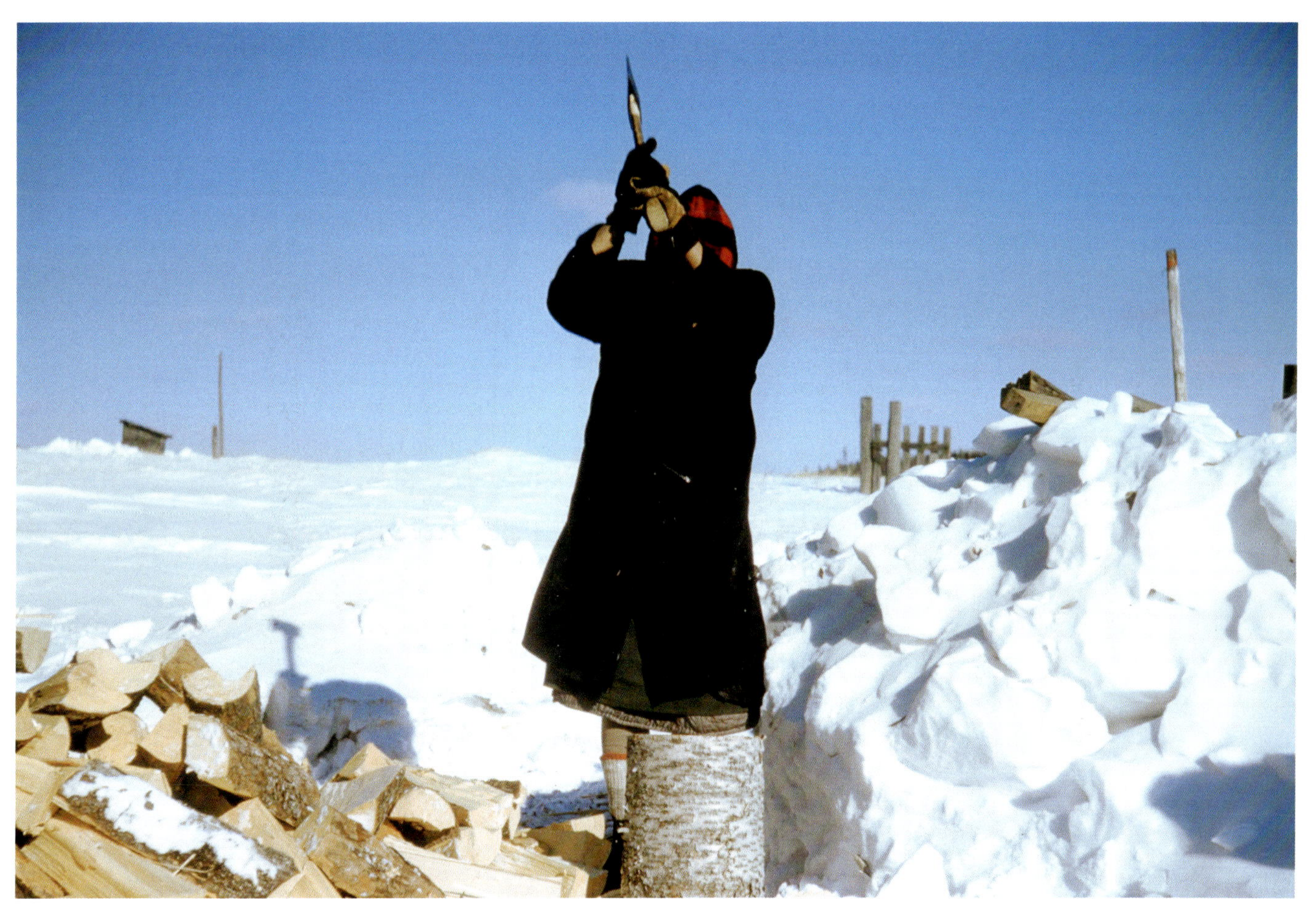

Mrs. Restoule chopping firewood at Gogama c. 1955

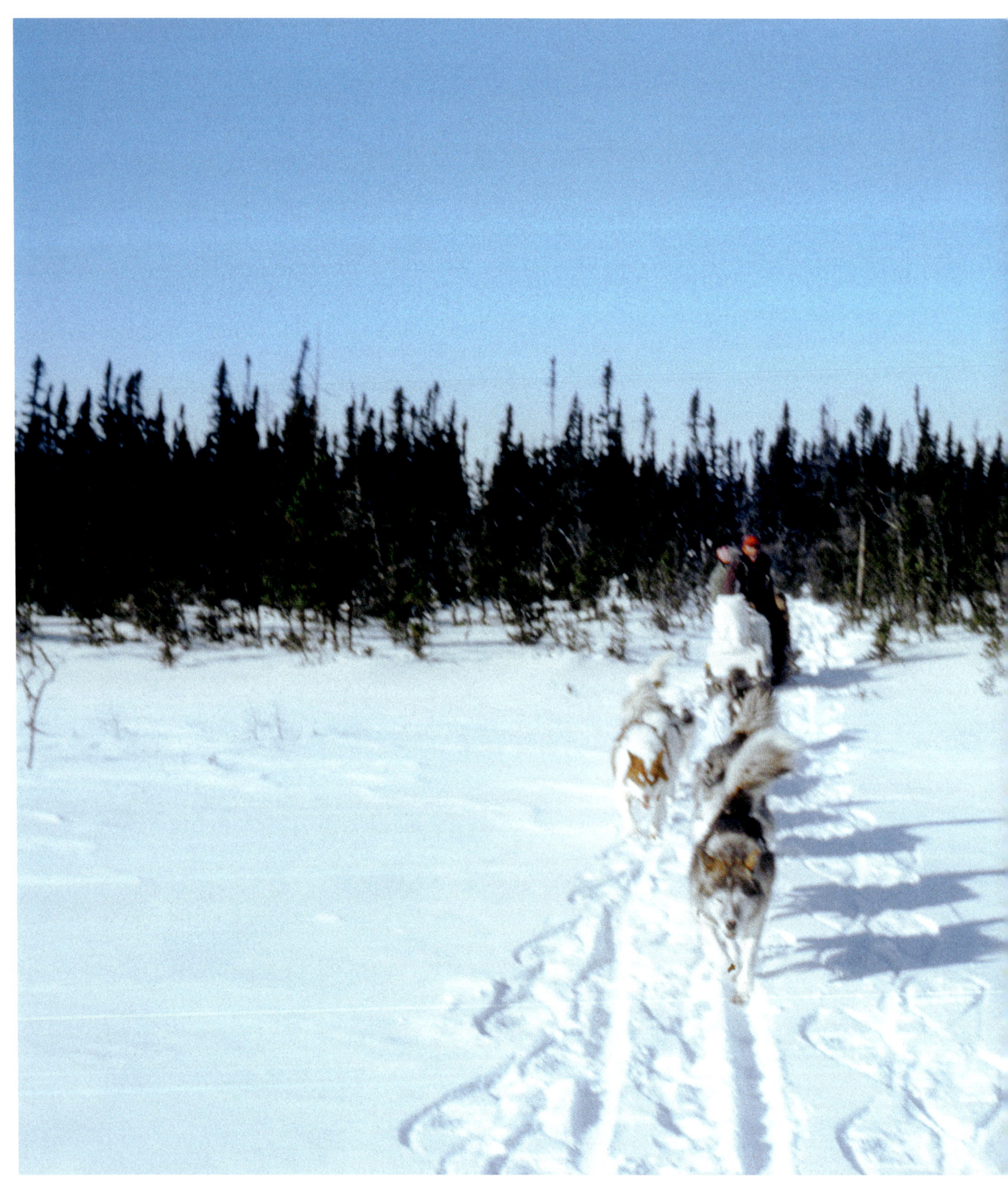

Moses Koostachin and Father Gagnon travelling between Weenusk and Hawley Lake February 1955

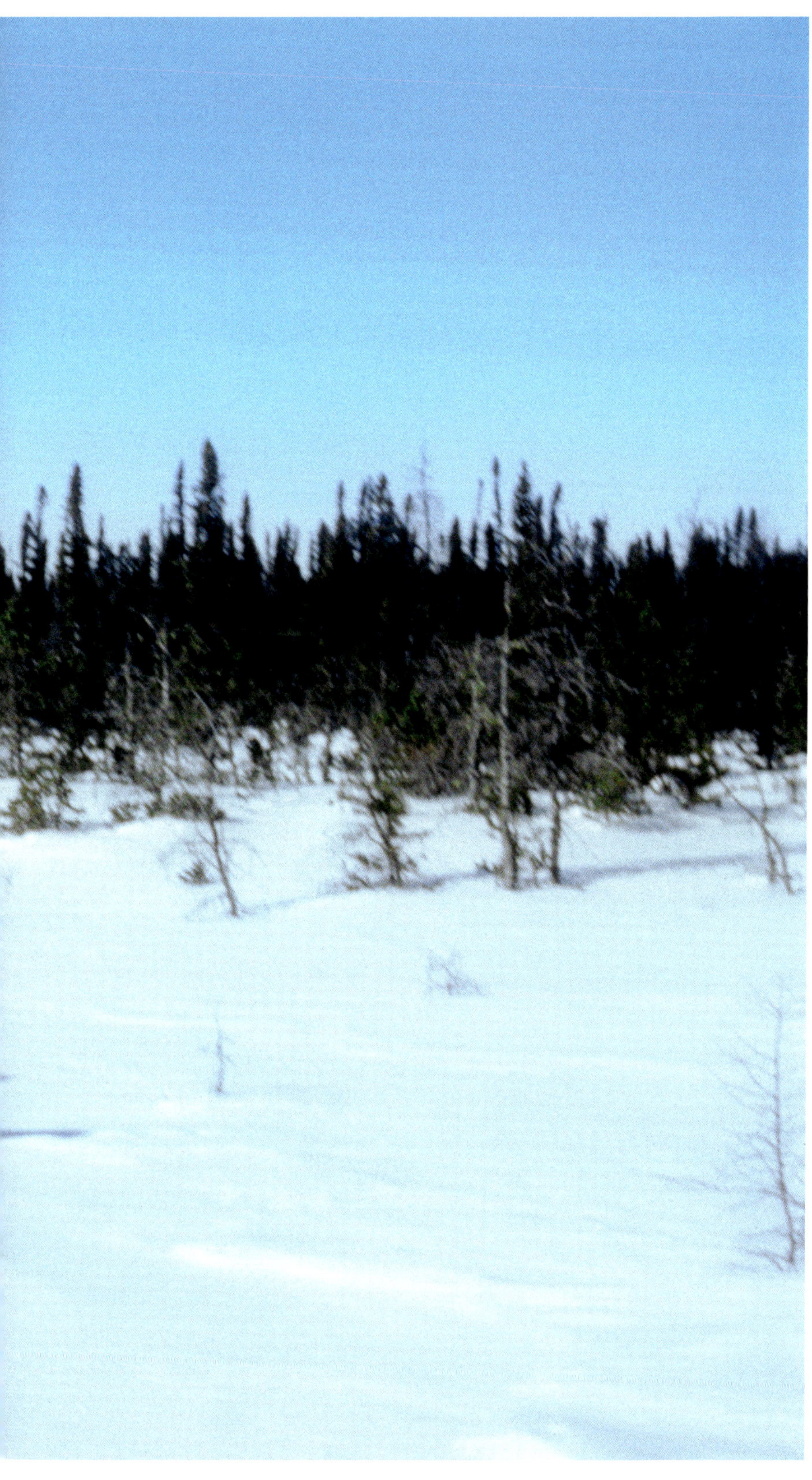

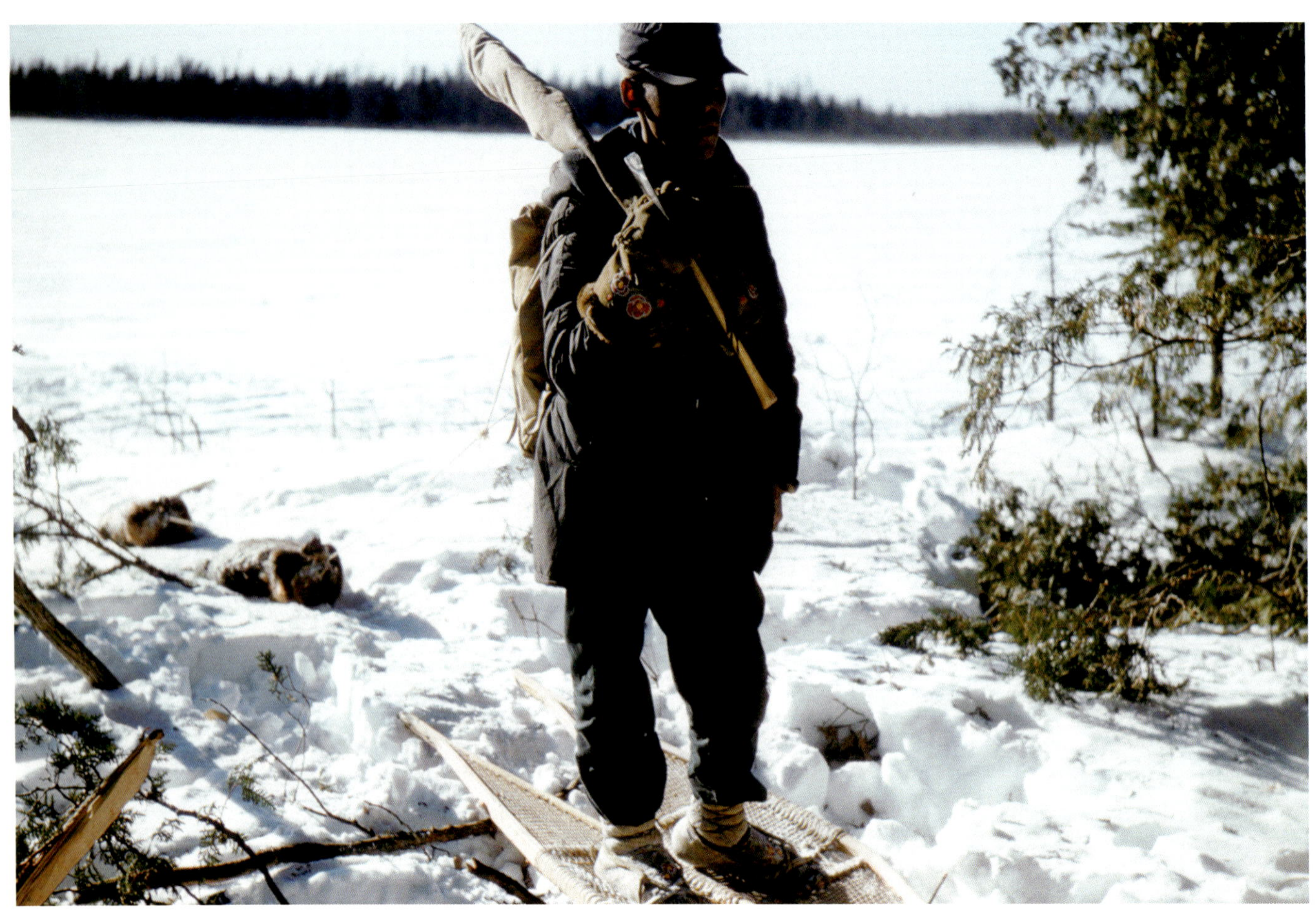

A trapper going hunting in the winter c. 1955

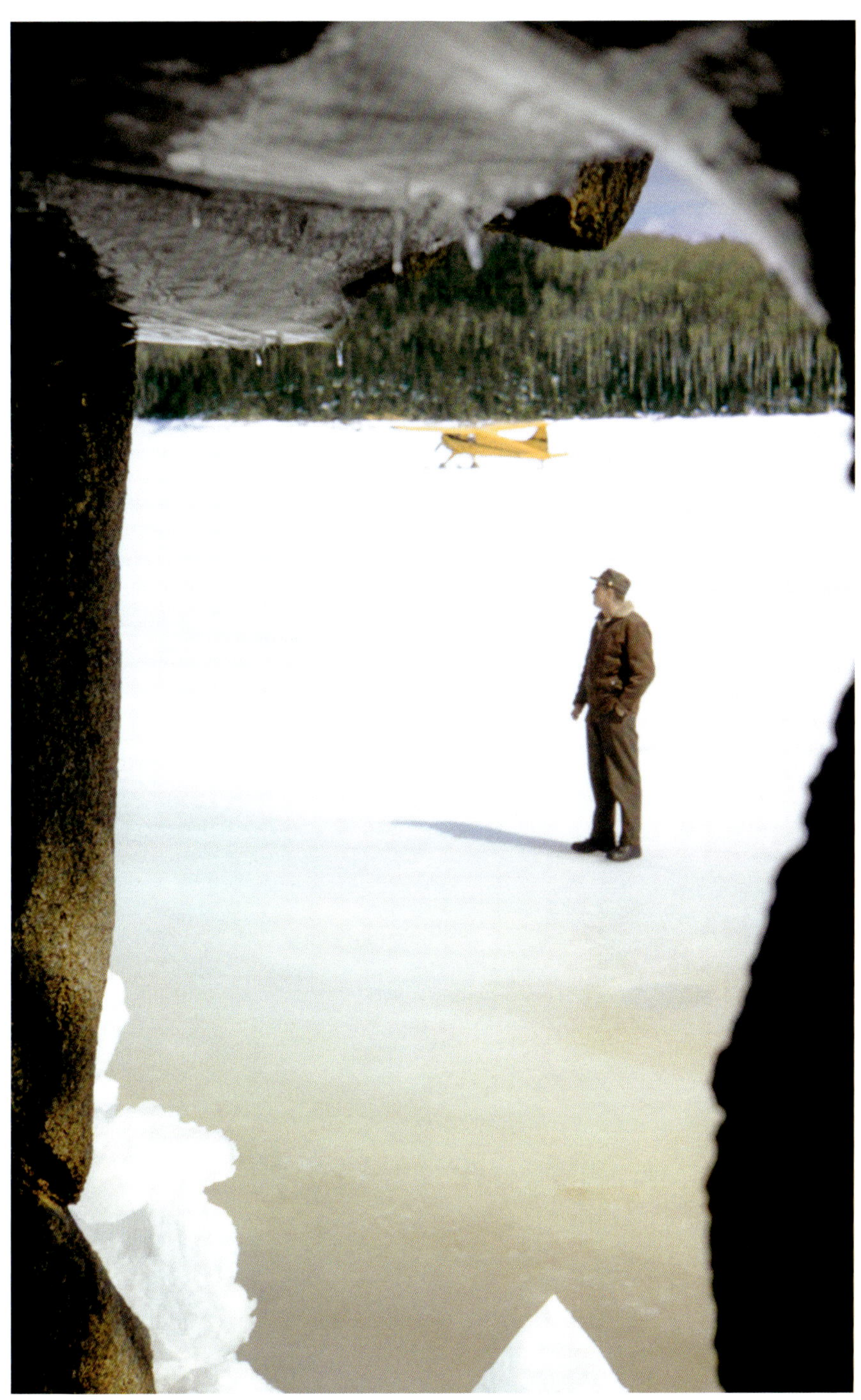

View from inside the mamakwayseeuk (little people) door at Horwood Lake in the Timmins-Cochrane region March 1958

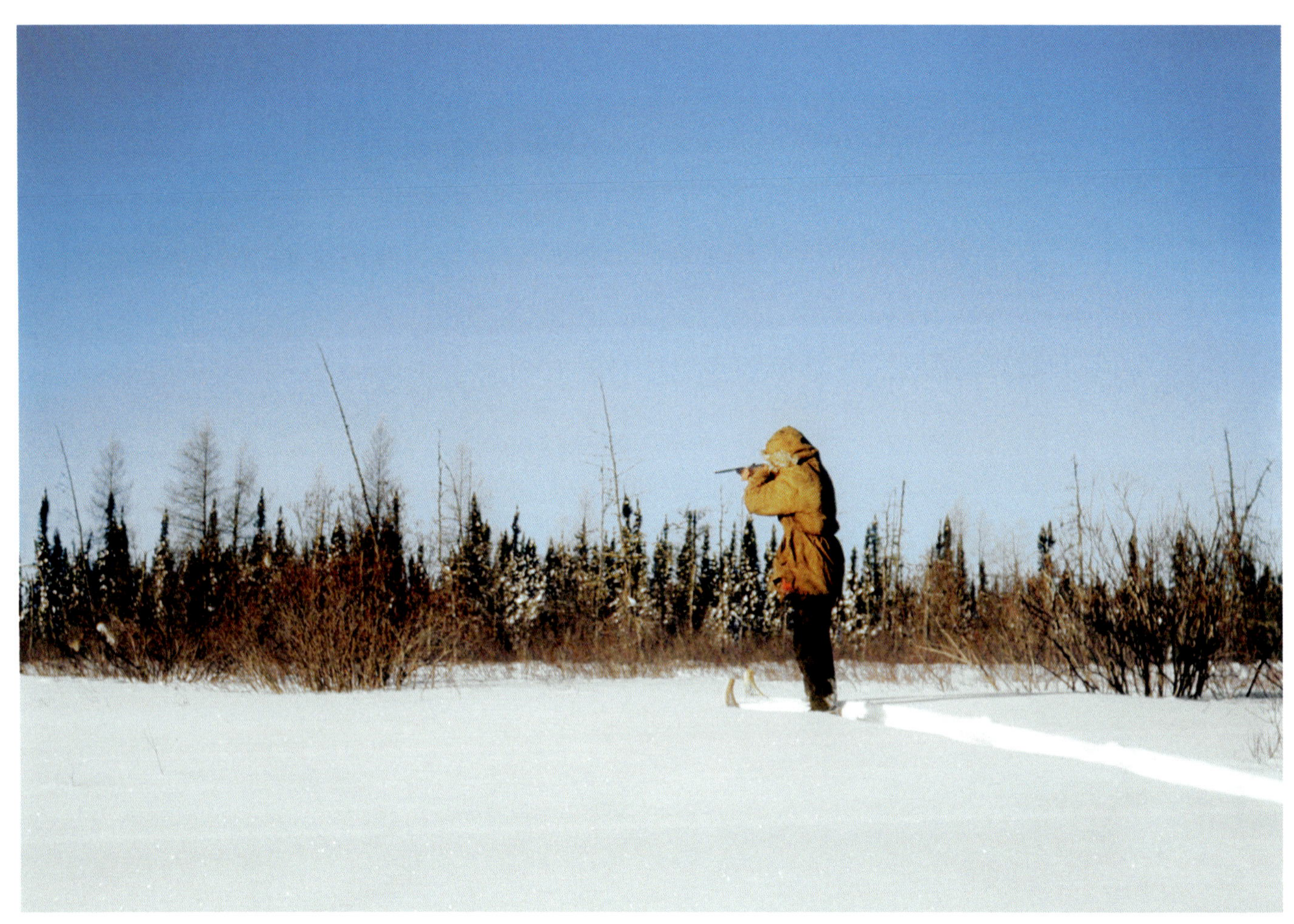

Louis Waswa shooting at sharptail grouse on Pineimuta Lake, Kenora District January 23, 1952

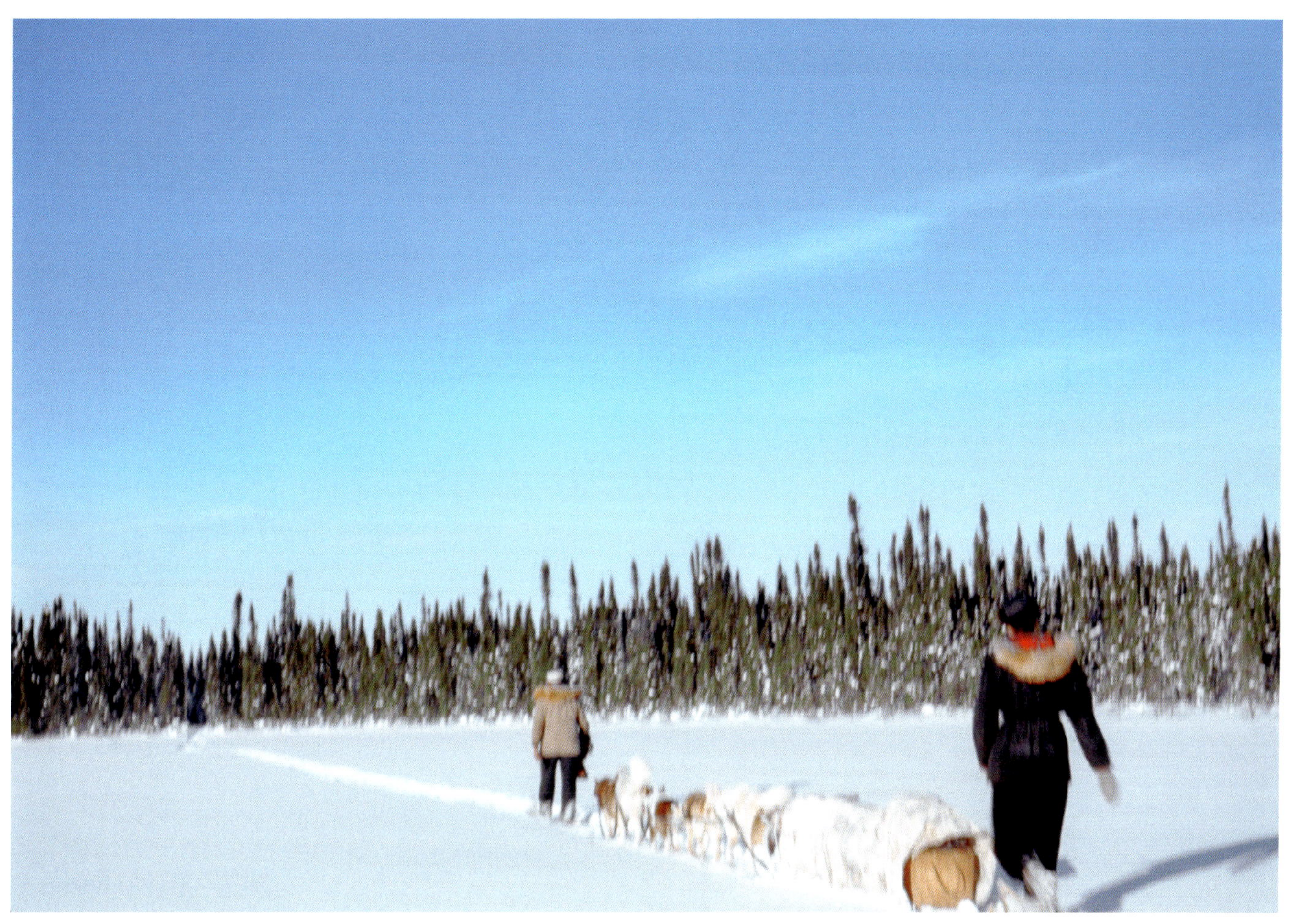

E. Bearox, Alex Fiddler, and a dogsled team on Bearskin Lake, Kenora District north of Sioux Lookout January 1951

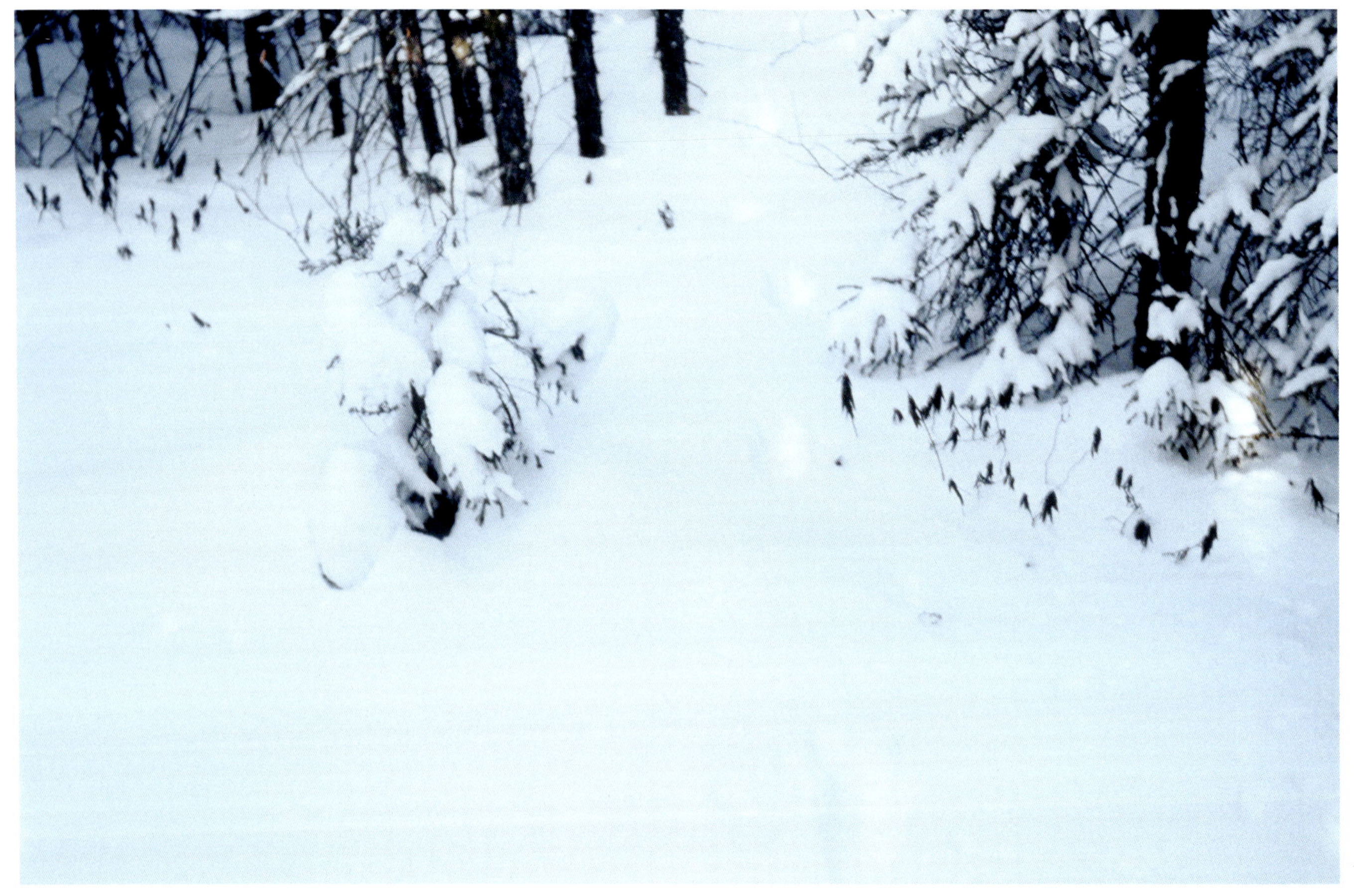

Marten tracks in the snow, Washi Lake on the Albany River December 1951

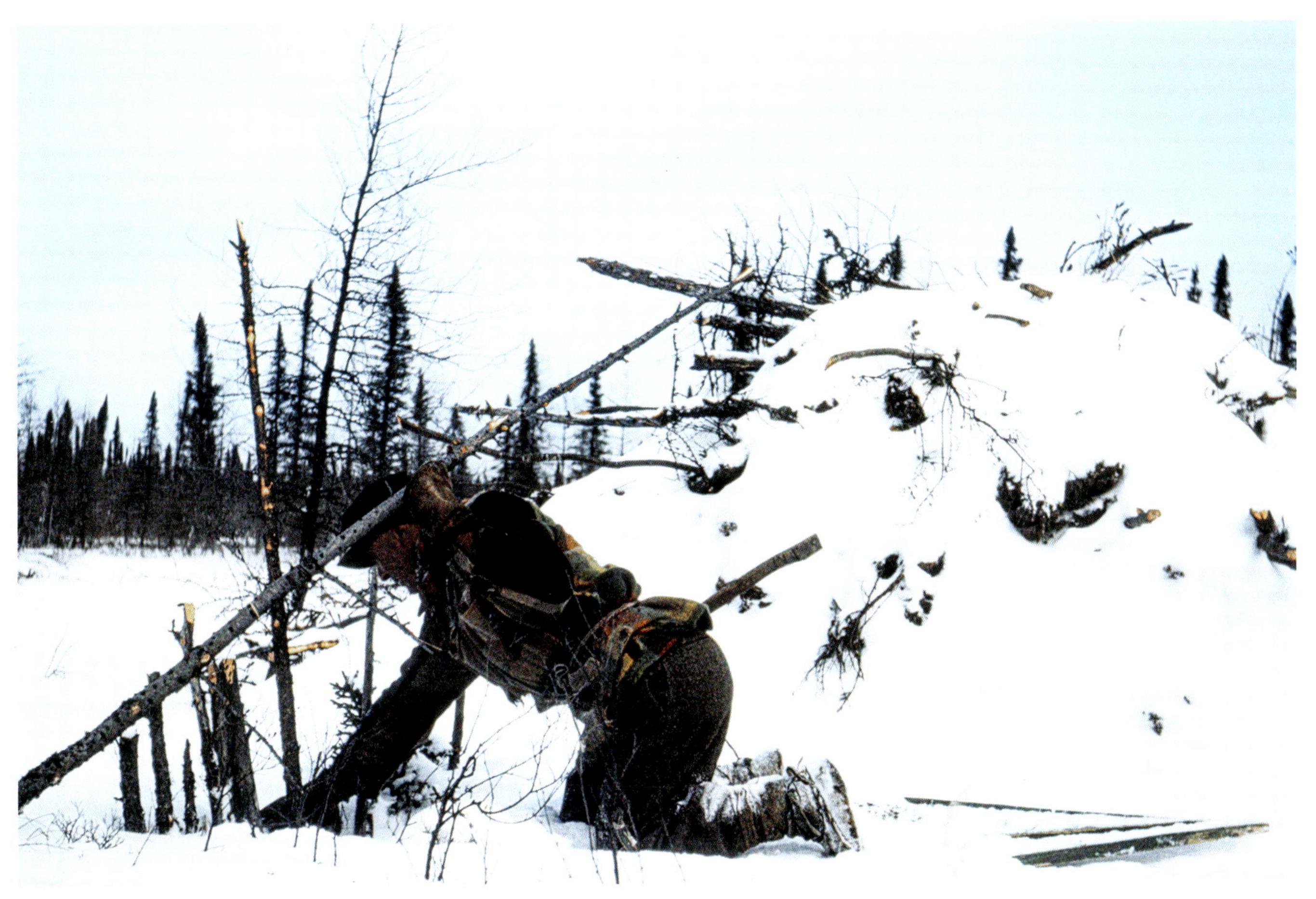

George Baxter checking a snare on his trapline at Washi Lake December 1951

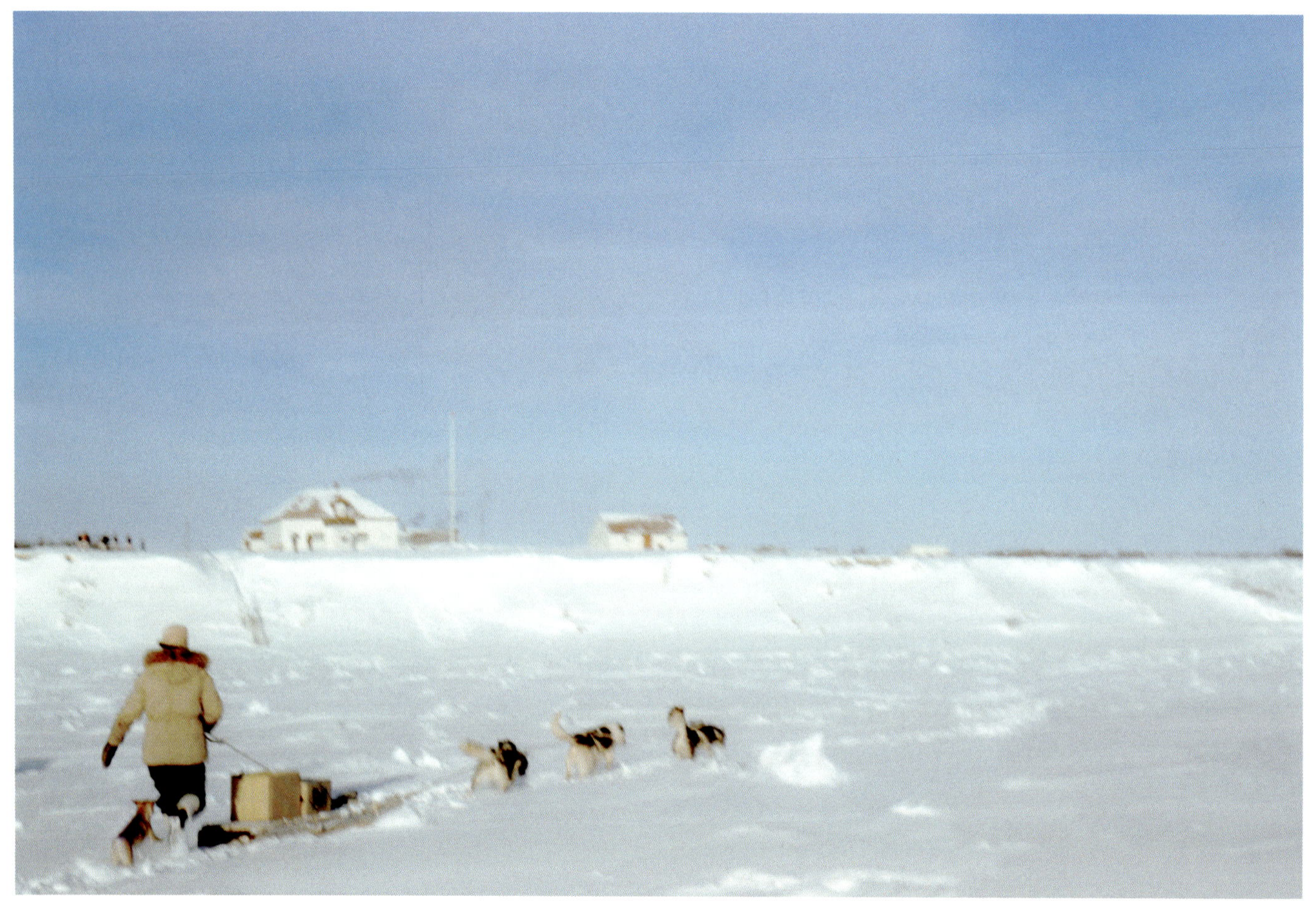

A man and his dog team on the Severn River nearing the Fort Severn Hudson's Bay Company post c. 1953

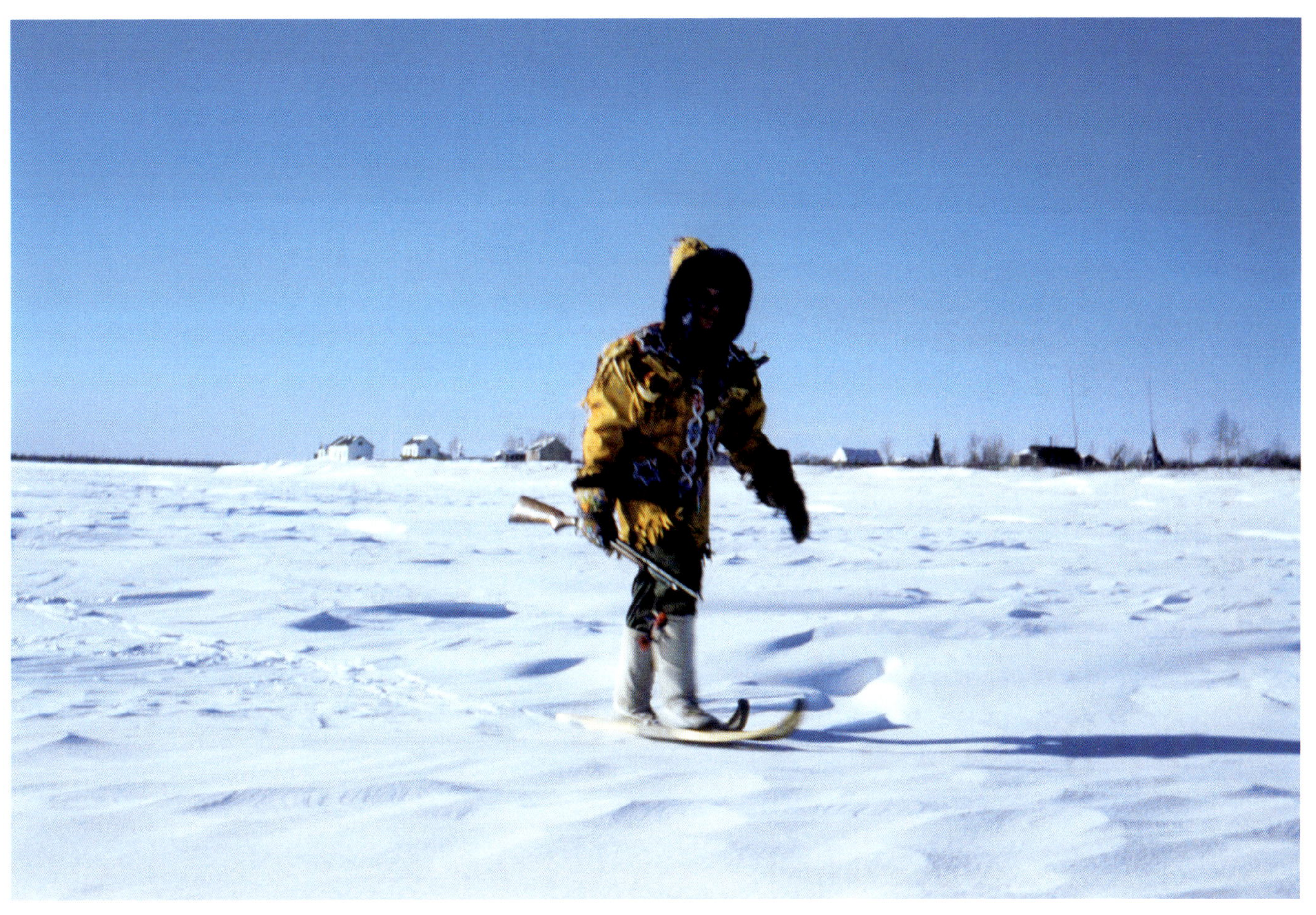

Martin Eva, the Hudson's Bay Company clerk at Weenusk, snowshoeing down the Winisk River to go ptarmigan hunting on the Hudson Bay coastal tundra February 1955

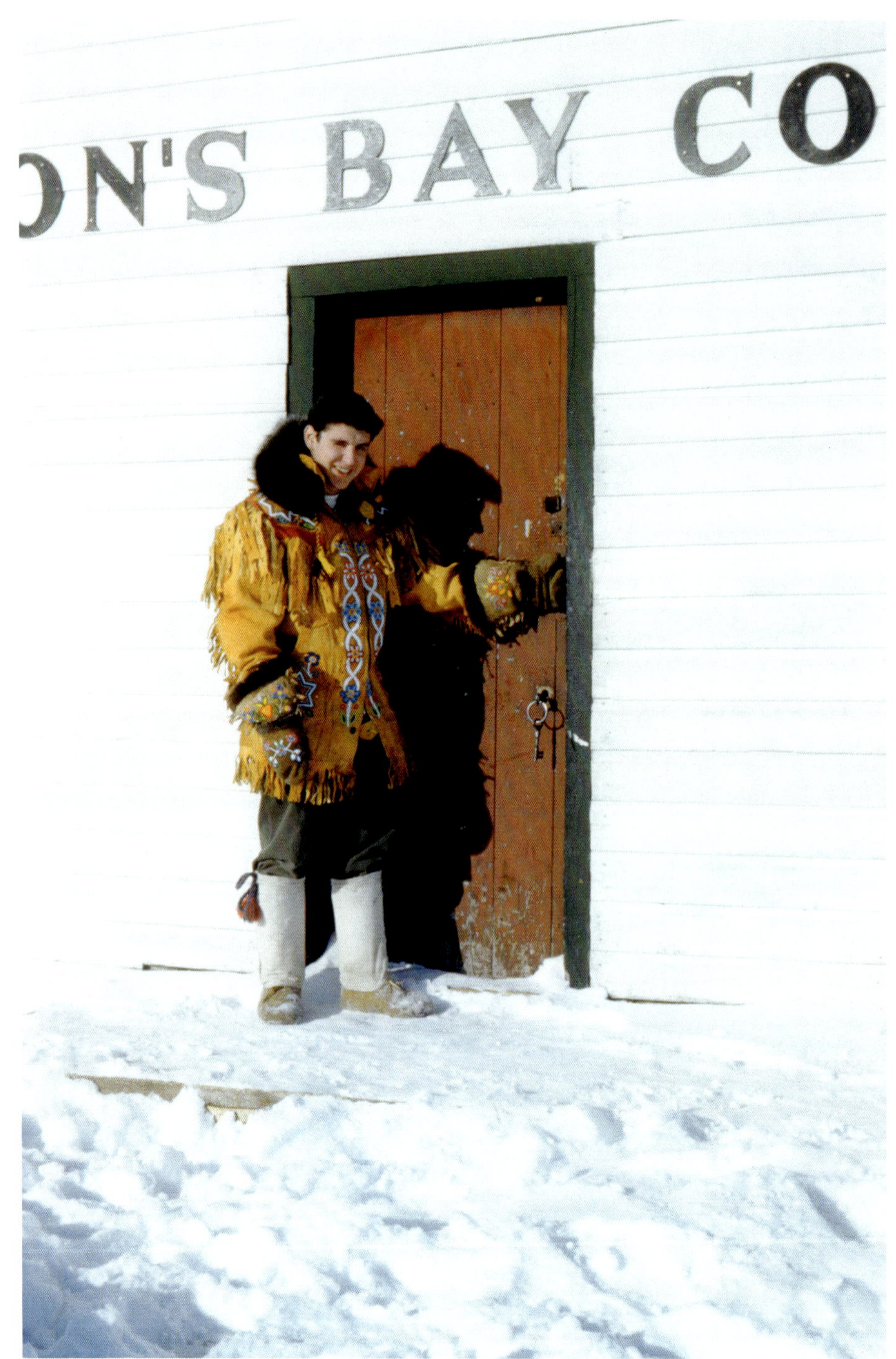

Hudson's Bay Company clerk Martin Eva, at the door of the store at Weenusk February 20, 1955

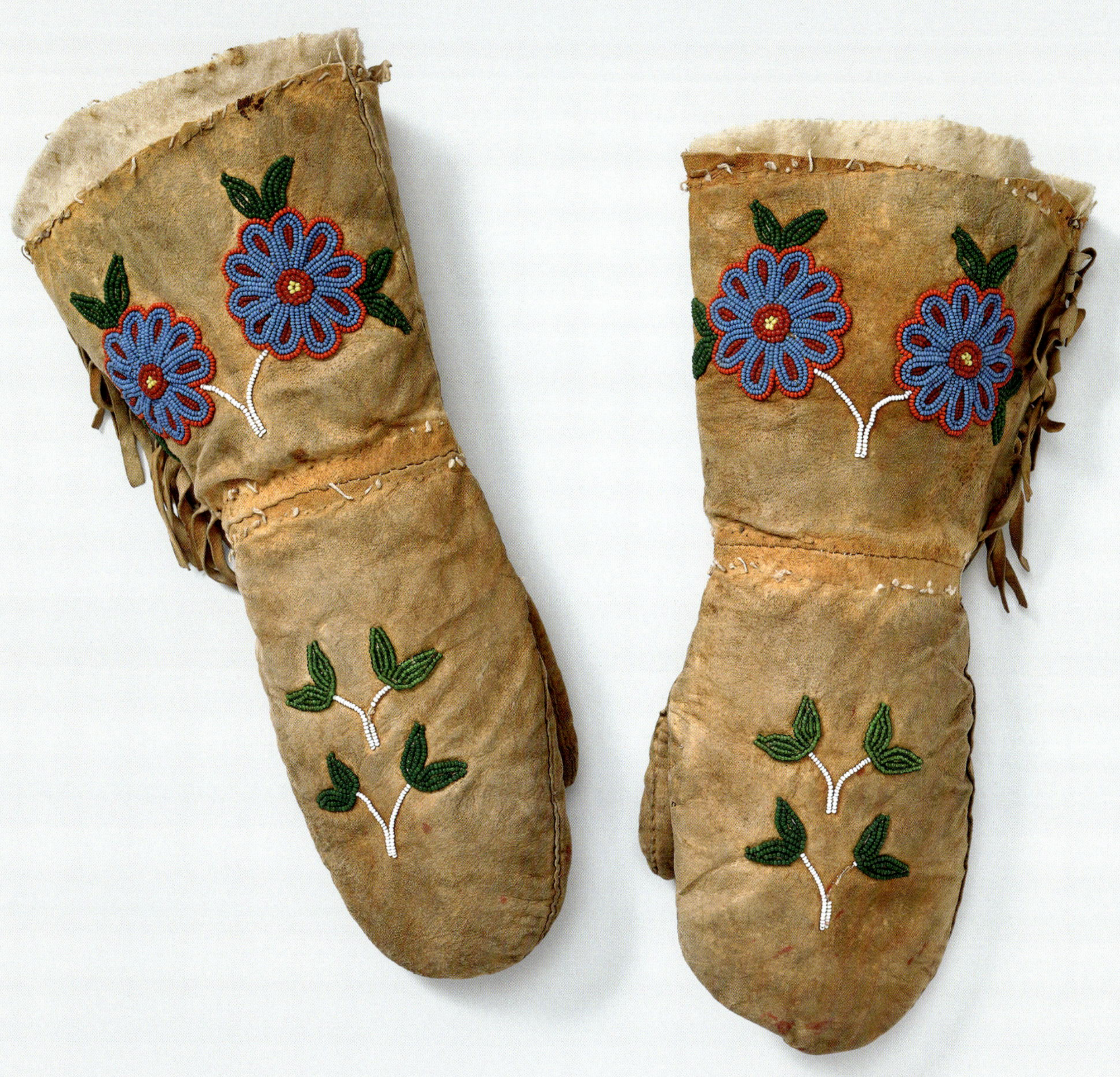

Beaded mitts, collected by John Macfie

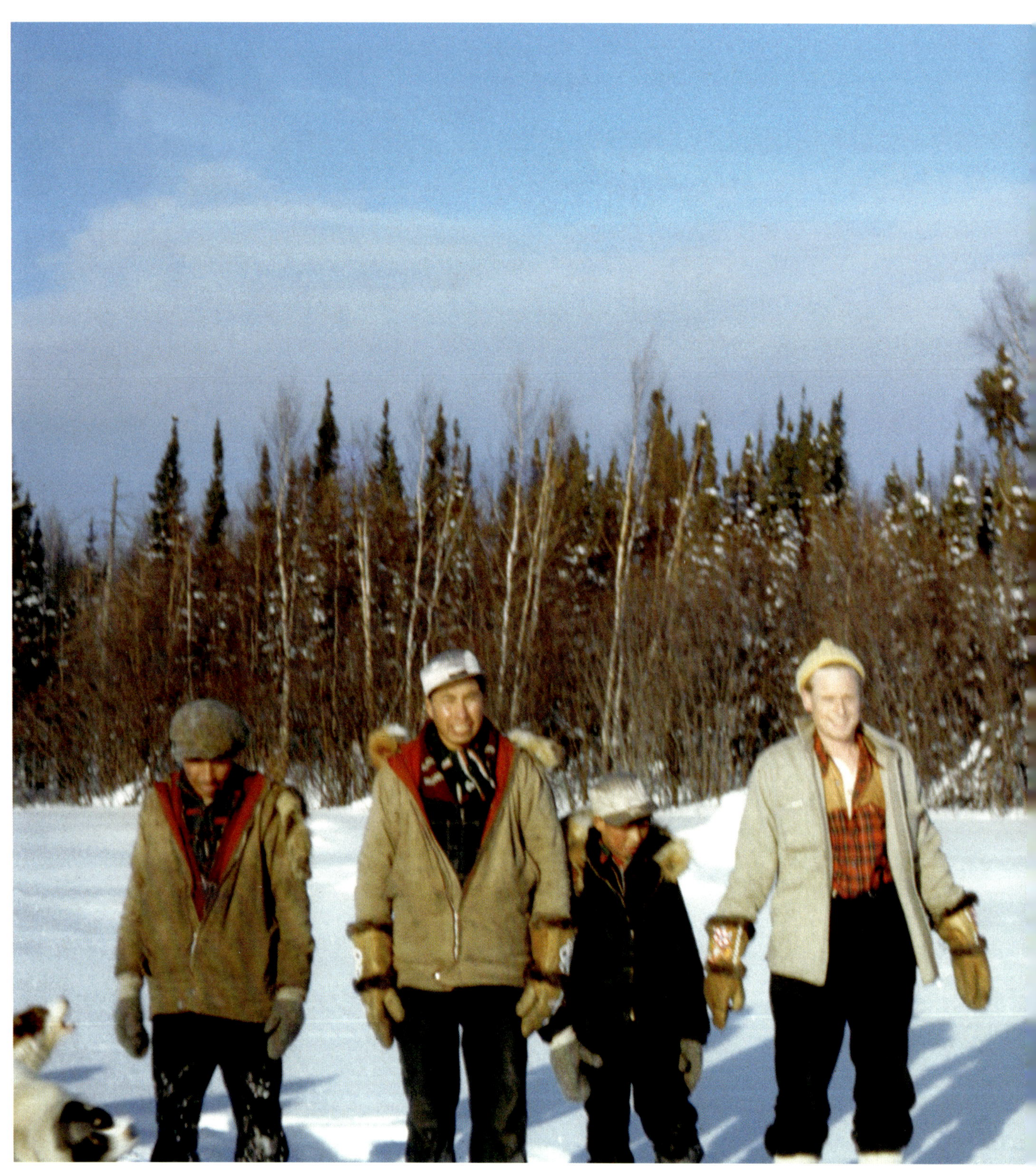

Tommy Fiddler, Elizier Beardy, Edward Fiddler, and John Macfie at Severn River January 1951

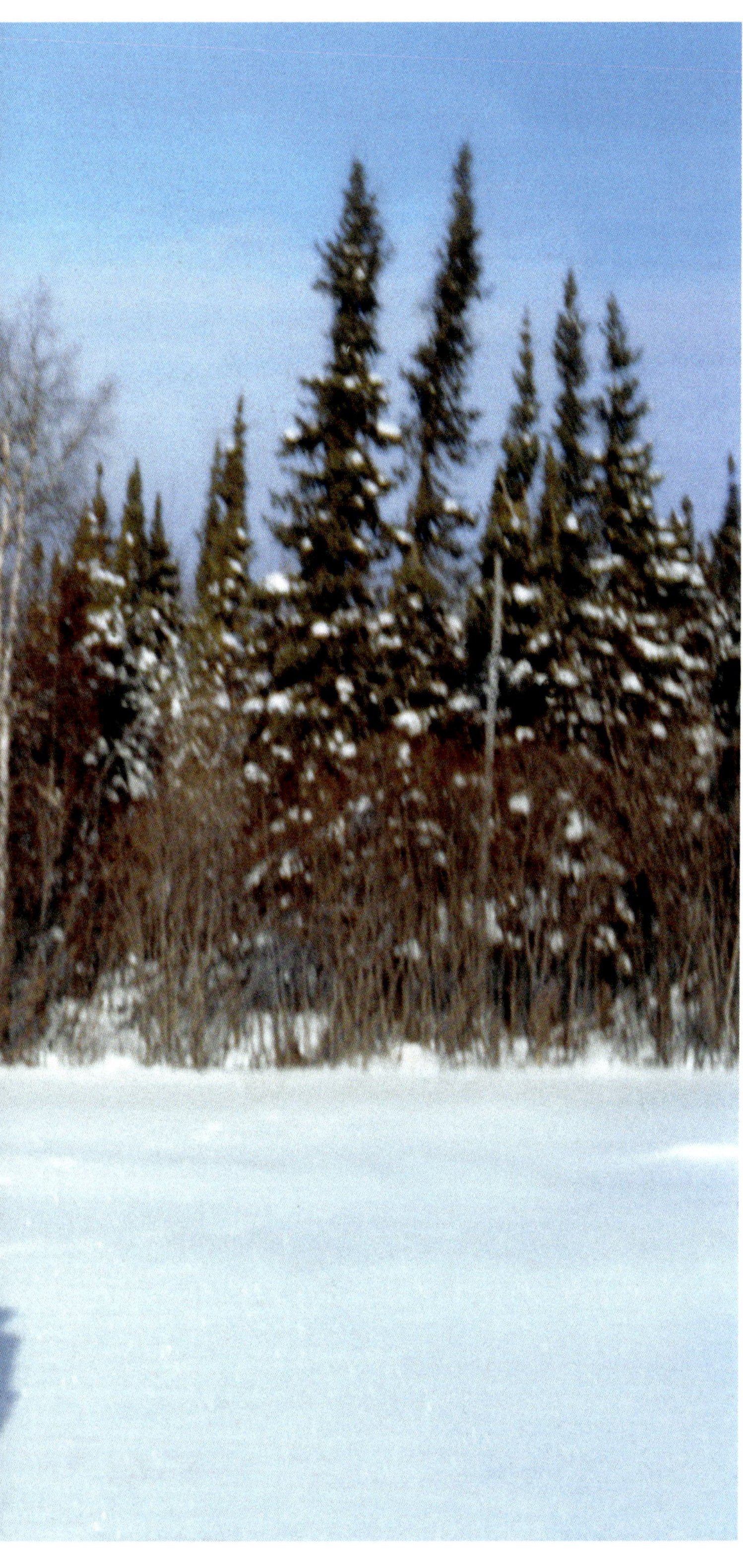

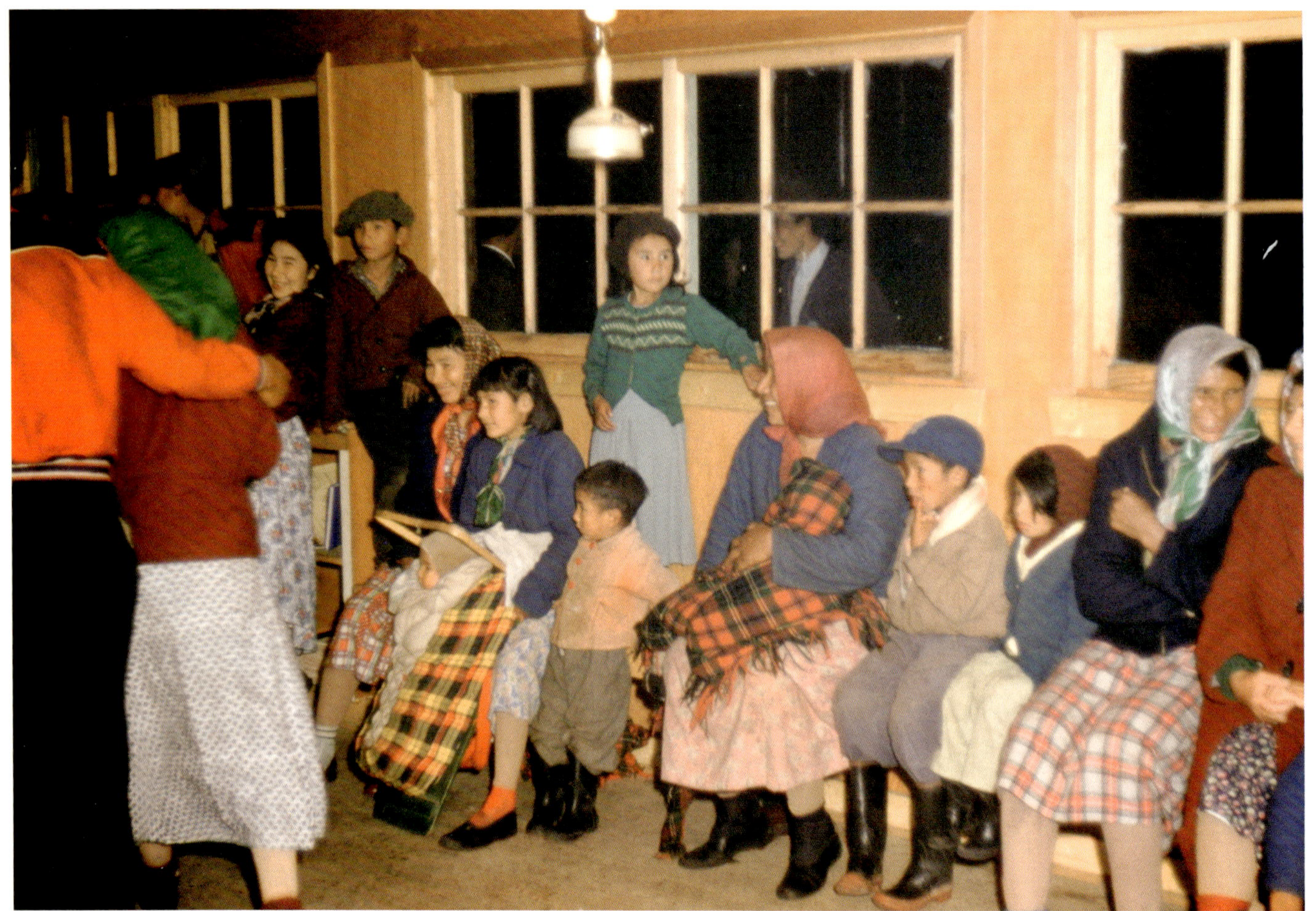

A community dance at Fort Severn c. 1955

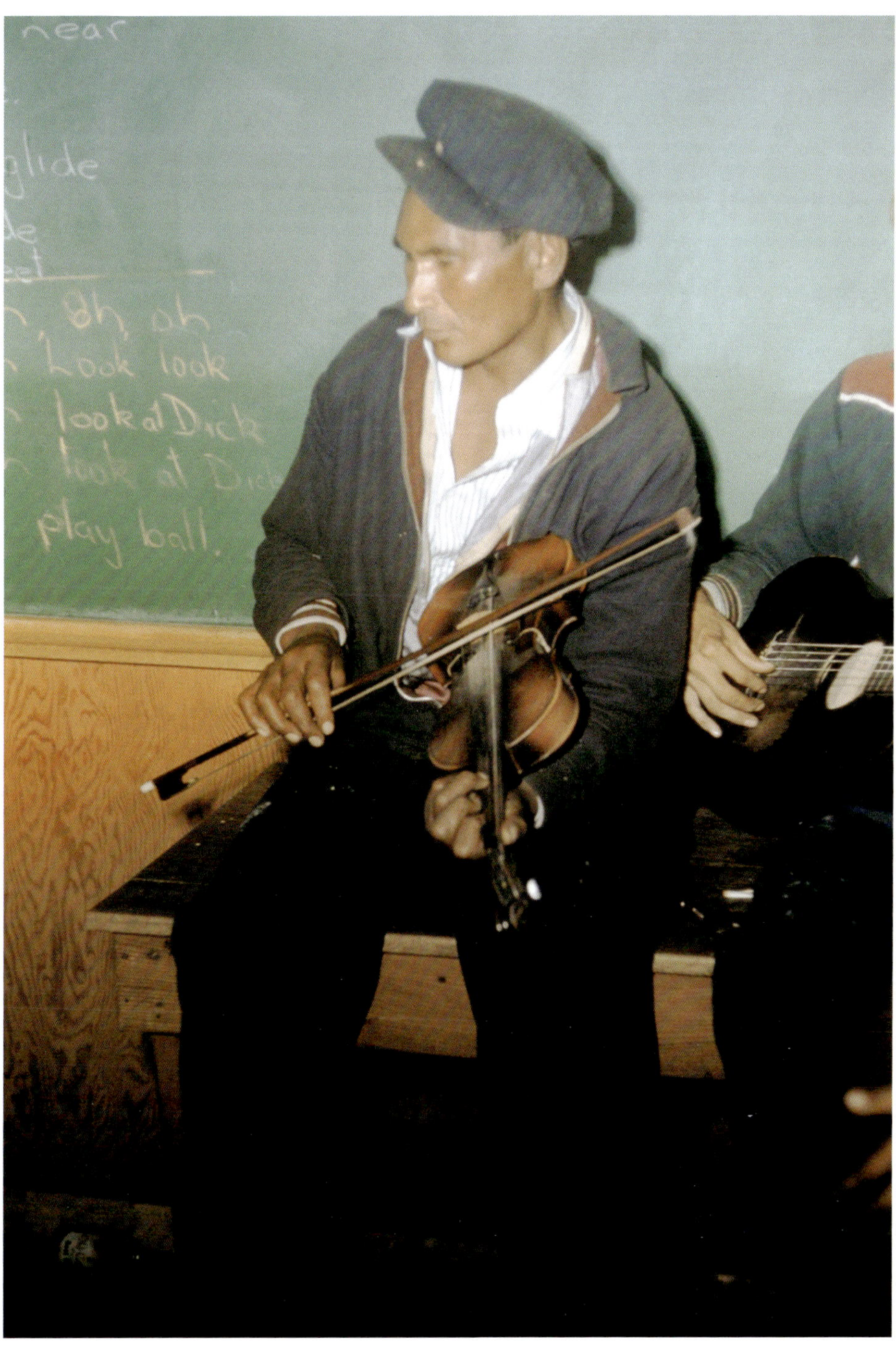

Philip "Swampy" Mathew playing the fiddle at a dance, Fort Severn 1955

A woman at Kasabonika wearing a cap woven from dried strips of untanned snowshoe-hare pelts c. 1953

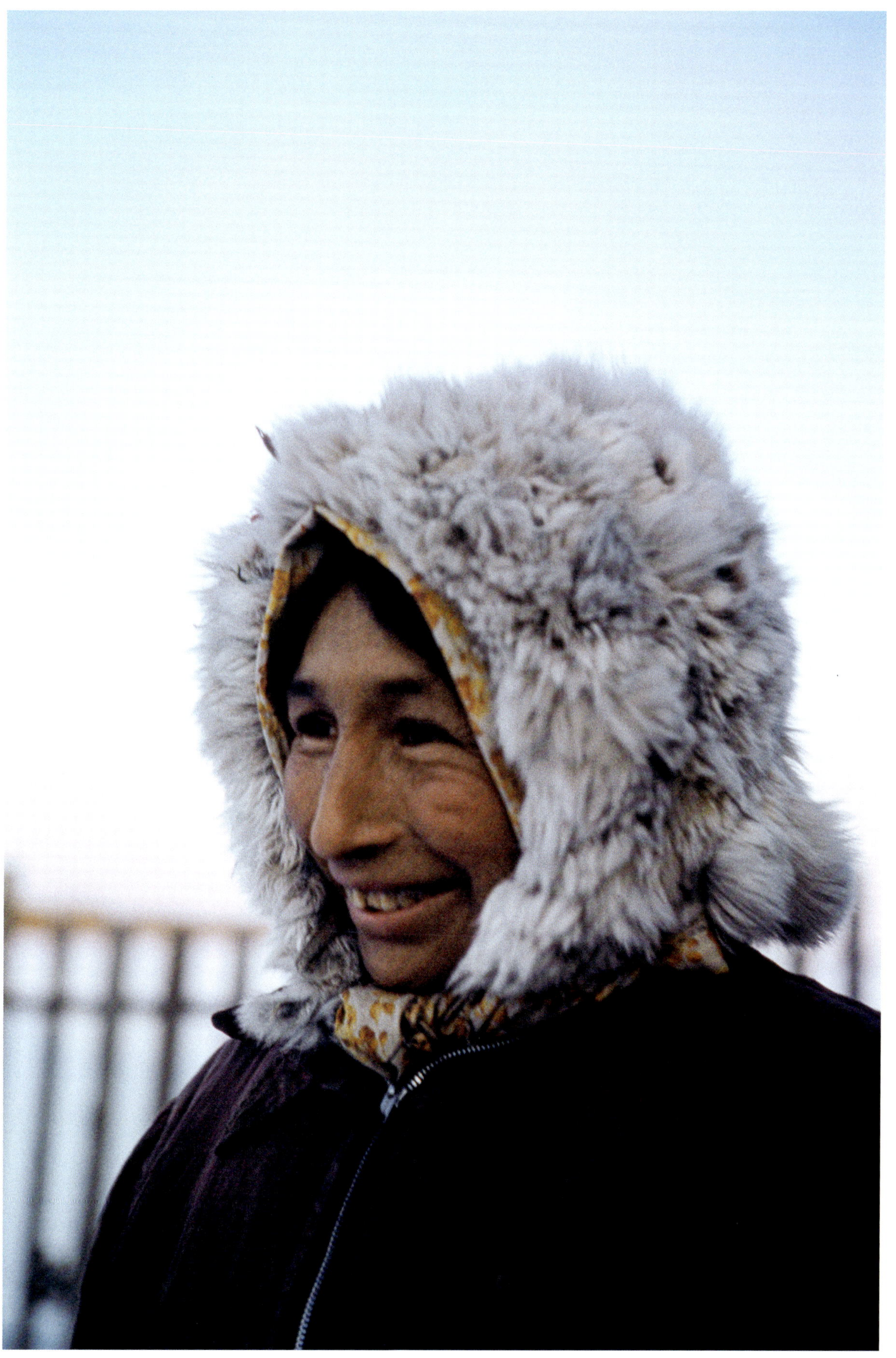

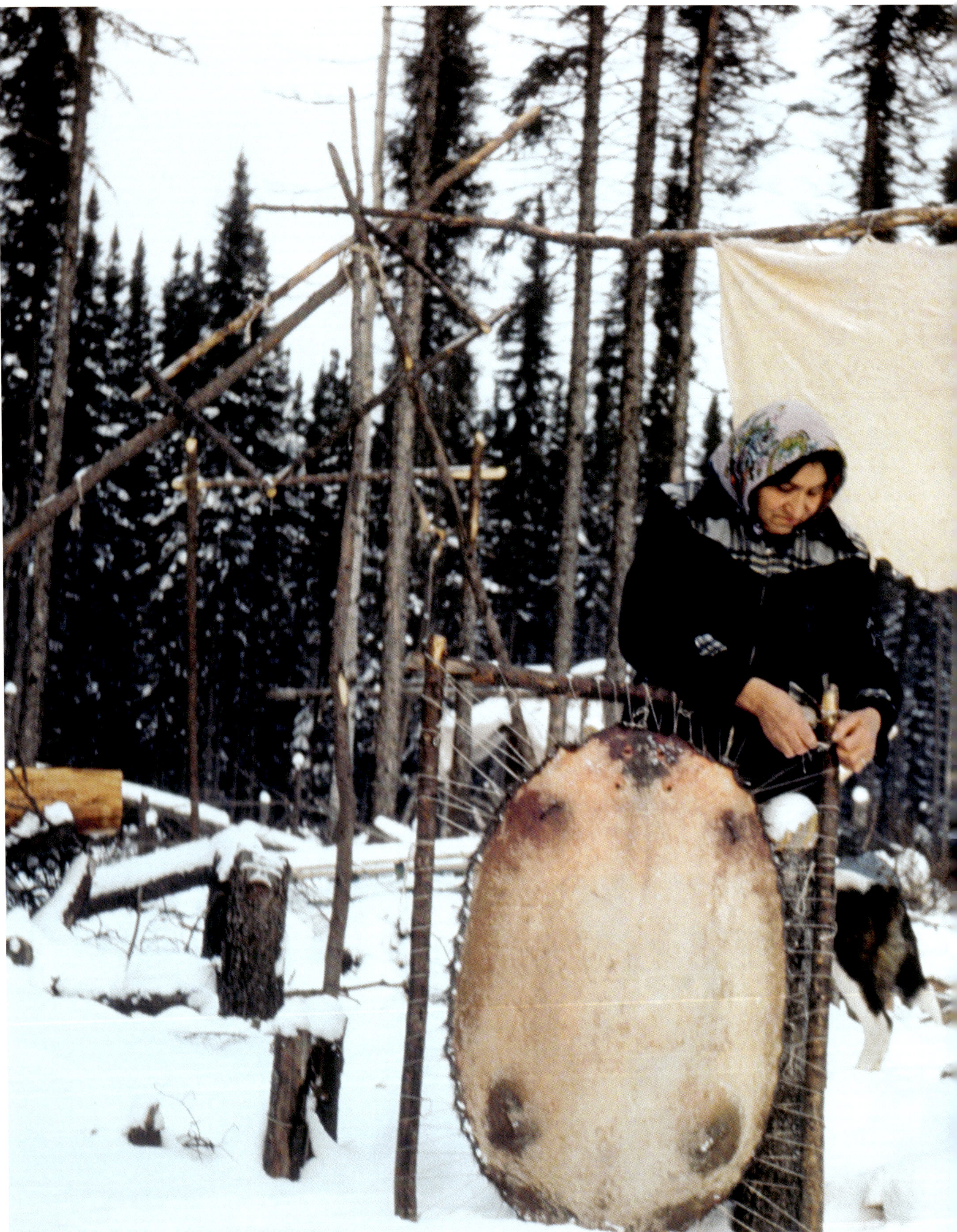

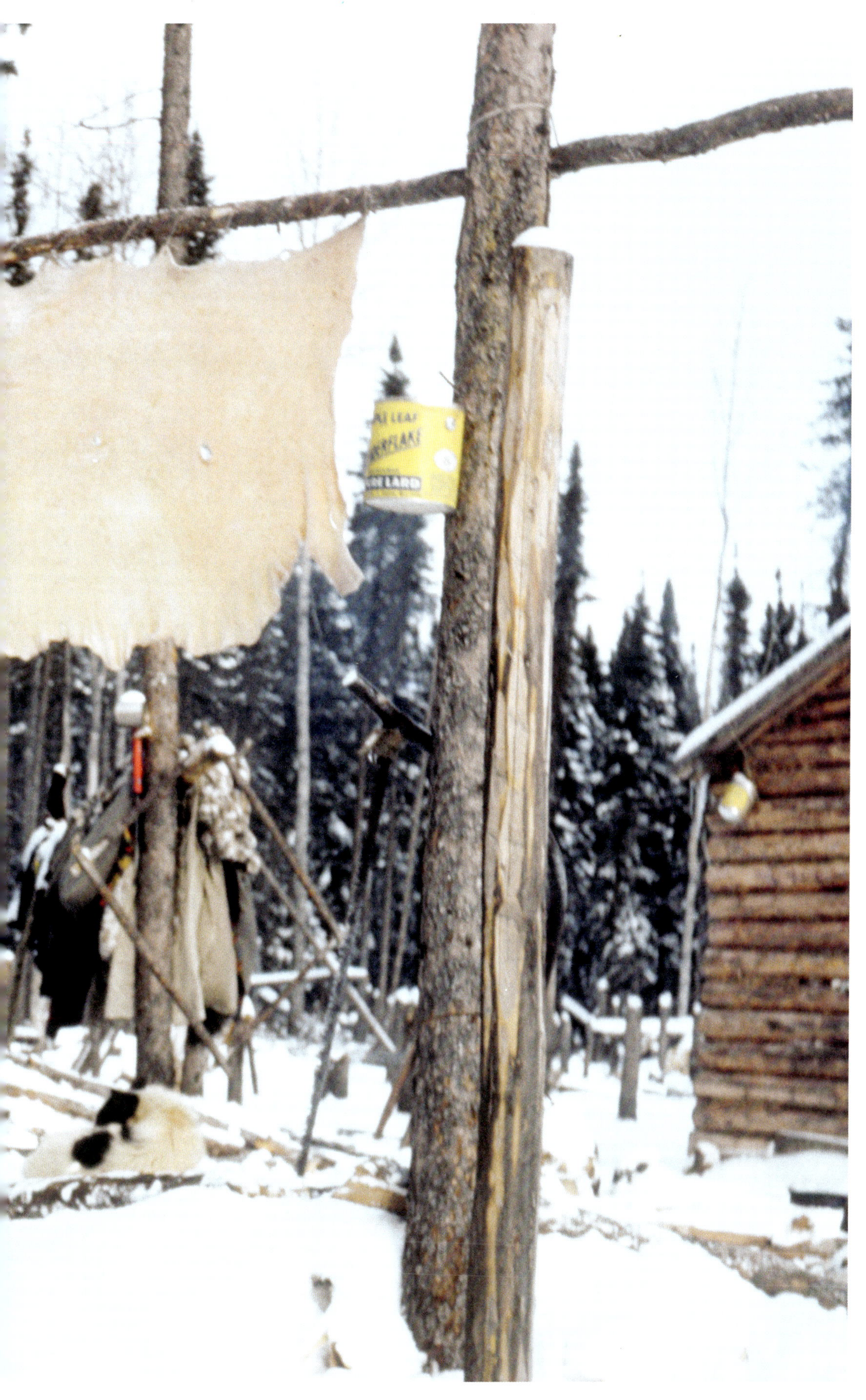

Mrs. George Baxter lacing a beaver pelt into a stretching frame at Washi Lake
December 1951

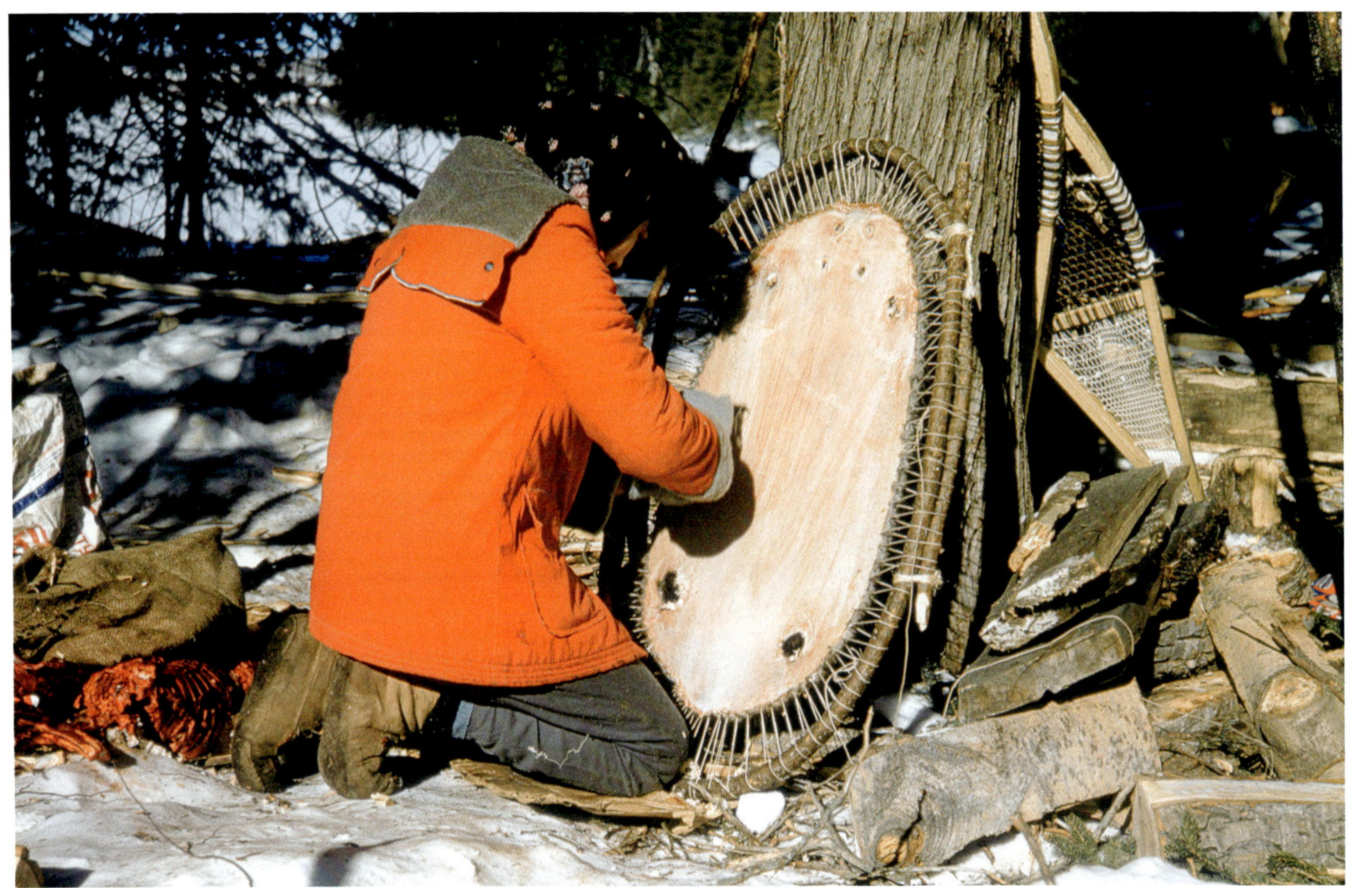

A woman from the Echum family fleshing and scraping a beaver pelt near Gogama 1959

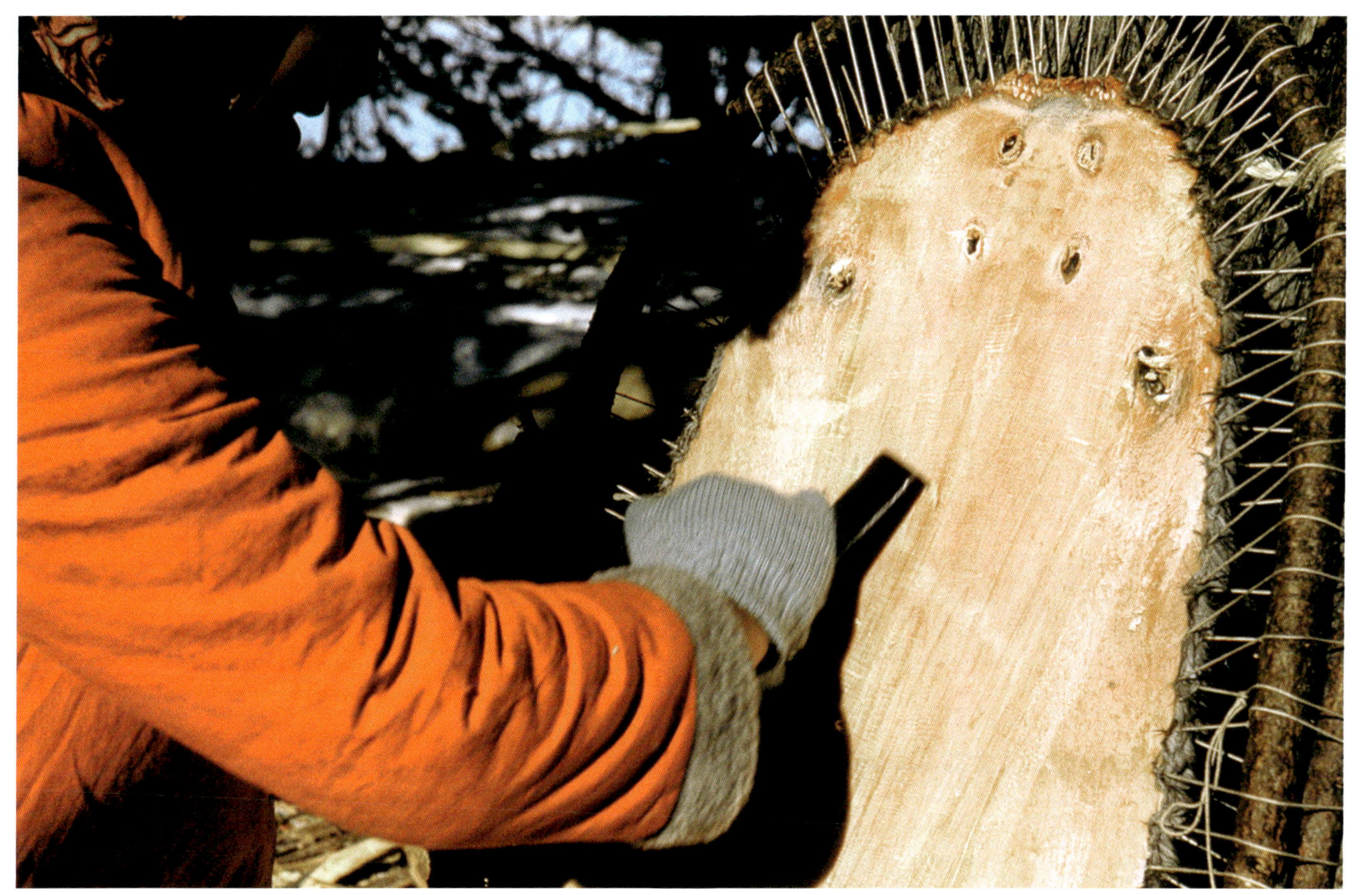

Working the beaver pelt during the frost-drying process 1959

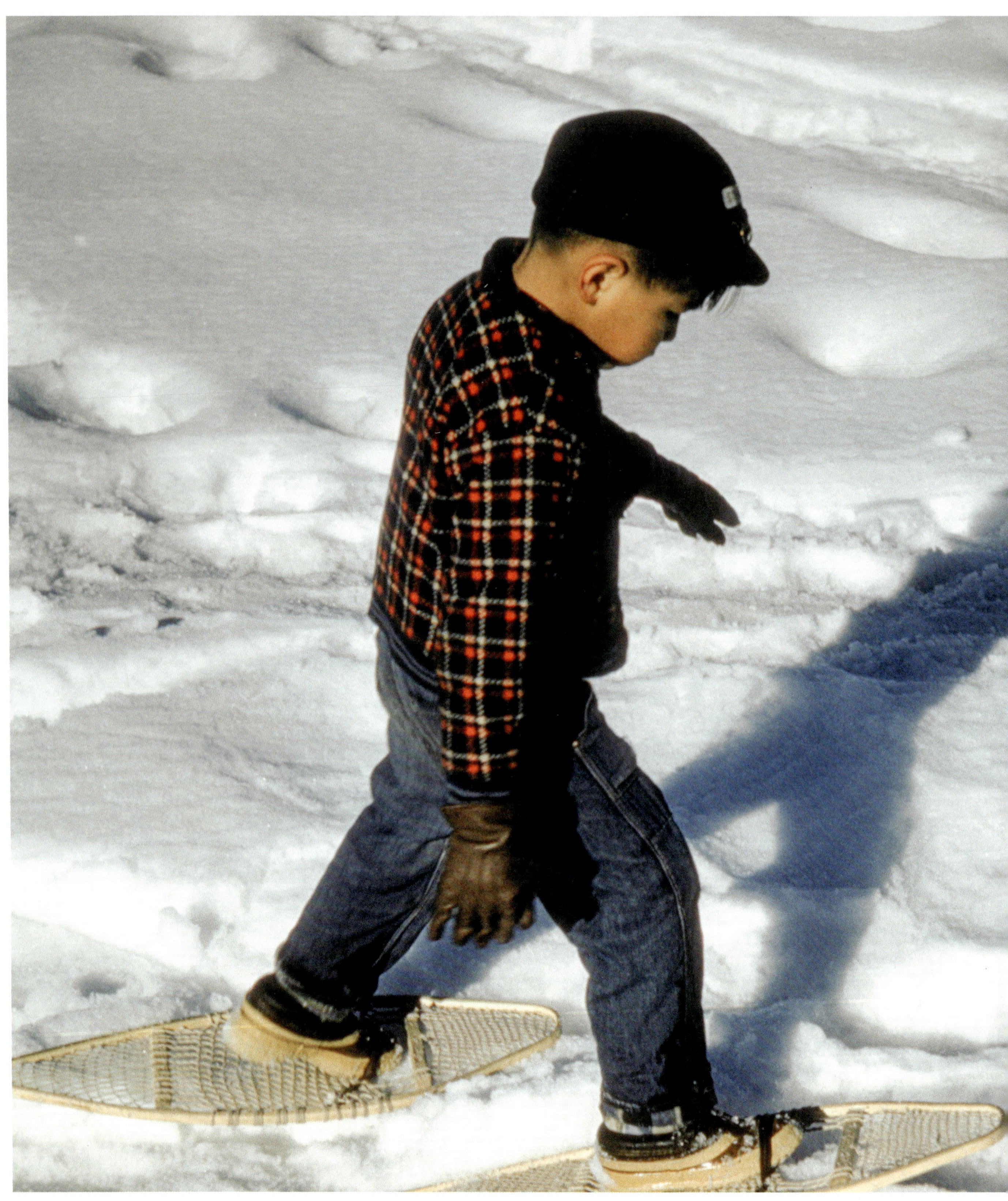

A boy snowshoeing c. 1955

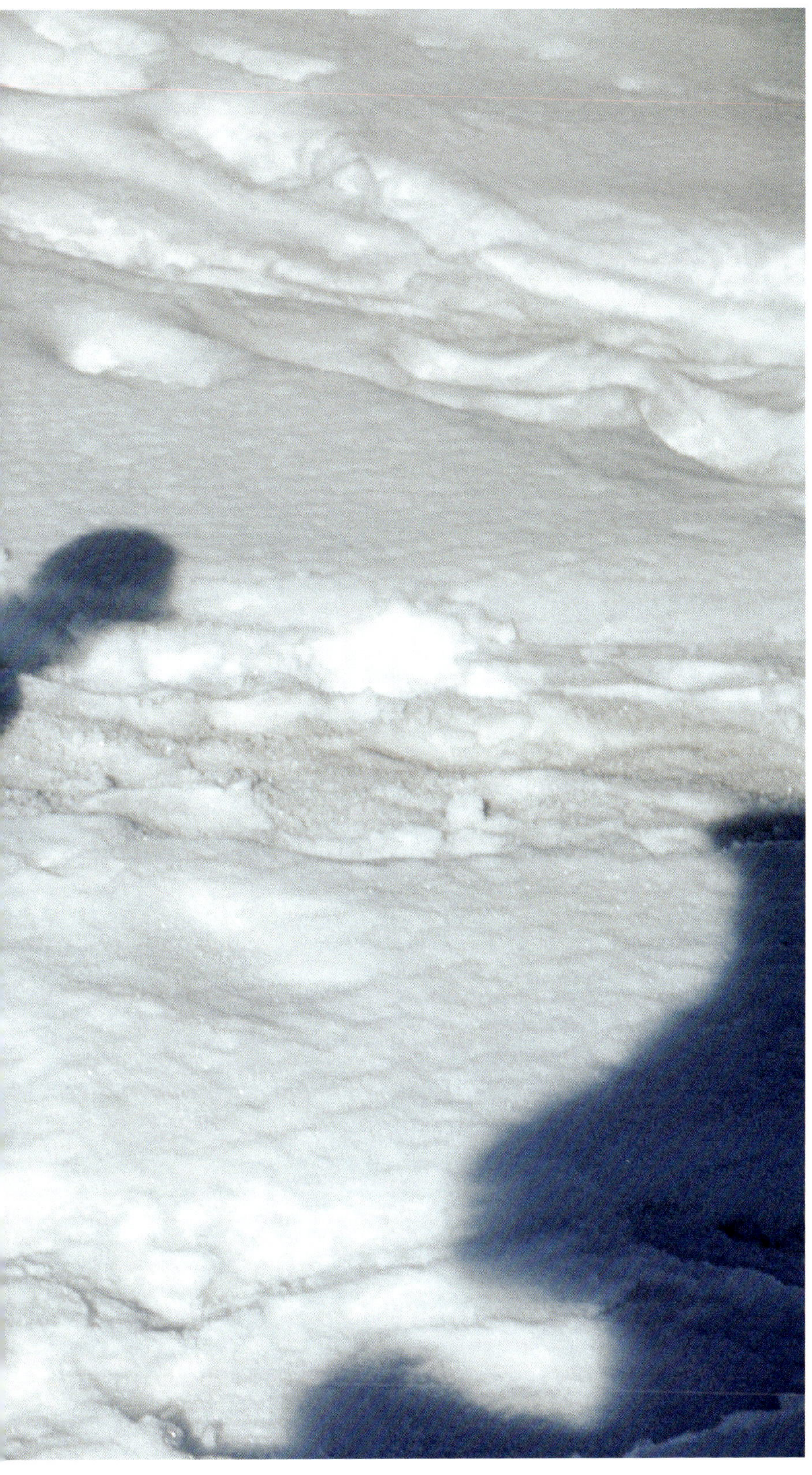

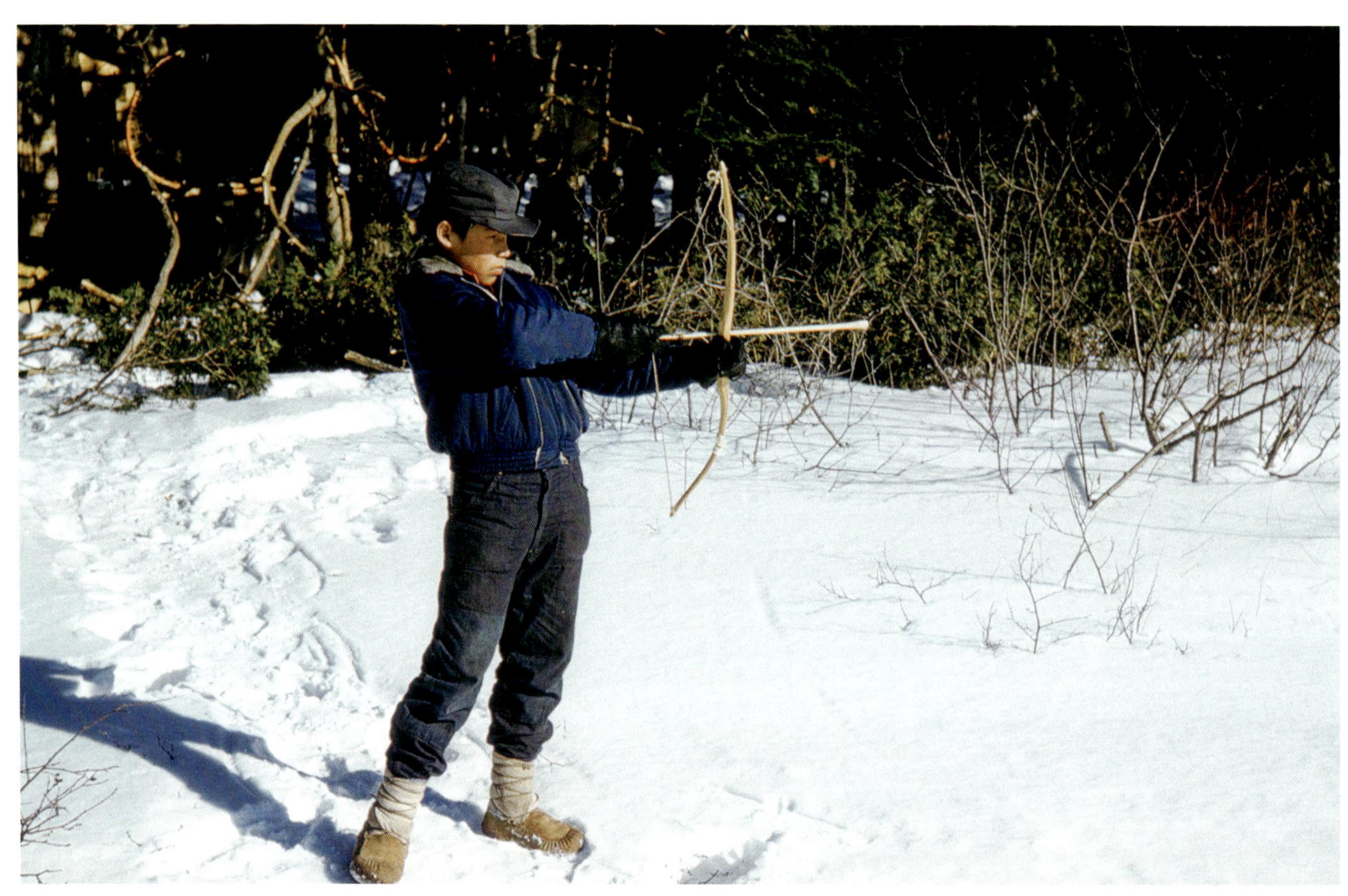

Charlie Echum practising with a toy bow and arrow at Moose Factory, Cochrane District, James Bay 1959

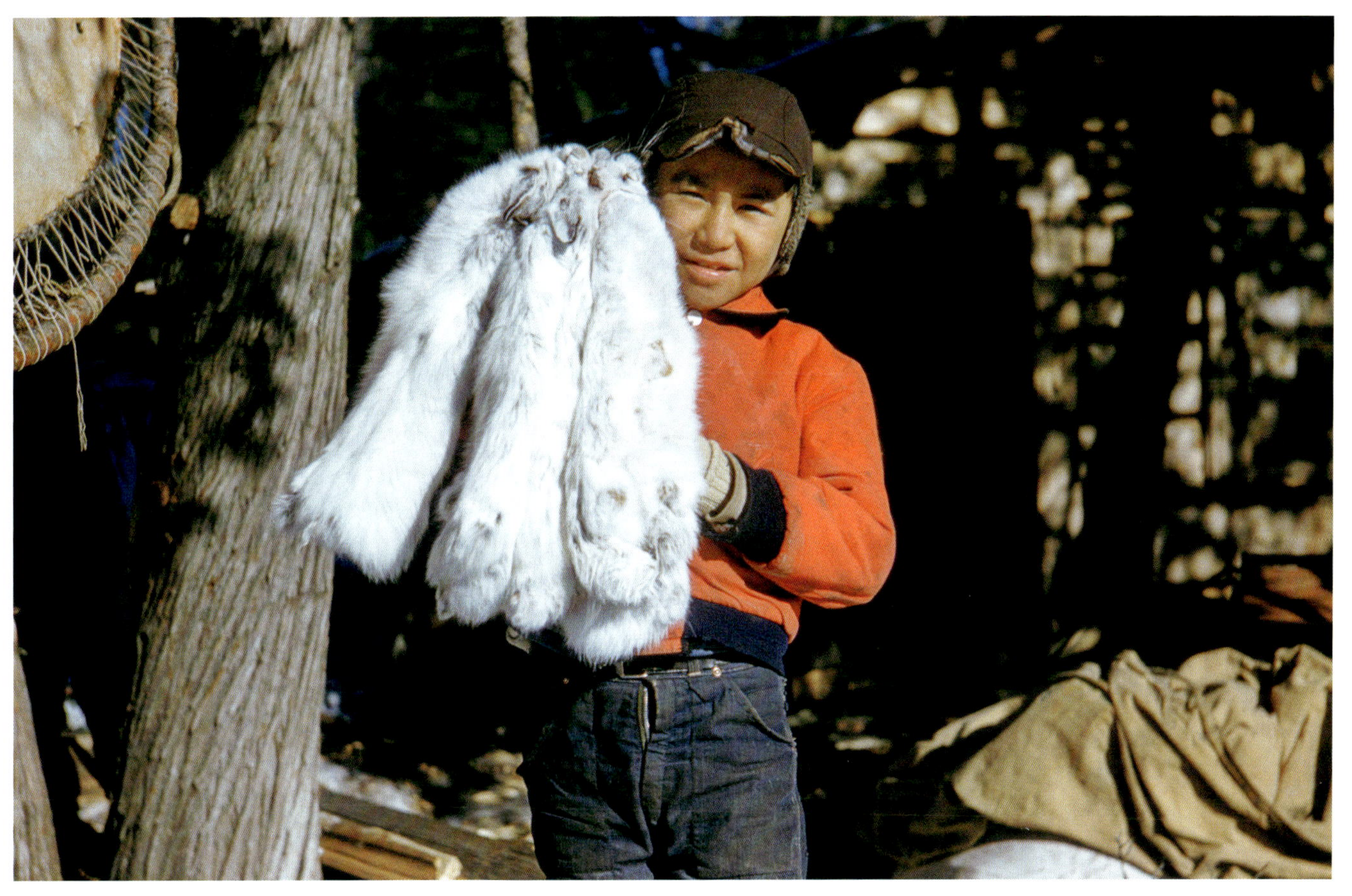

A boy with snowshoe-hare pelts, Moose Factory c. 1963

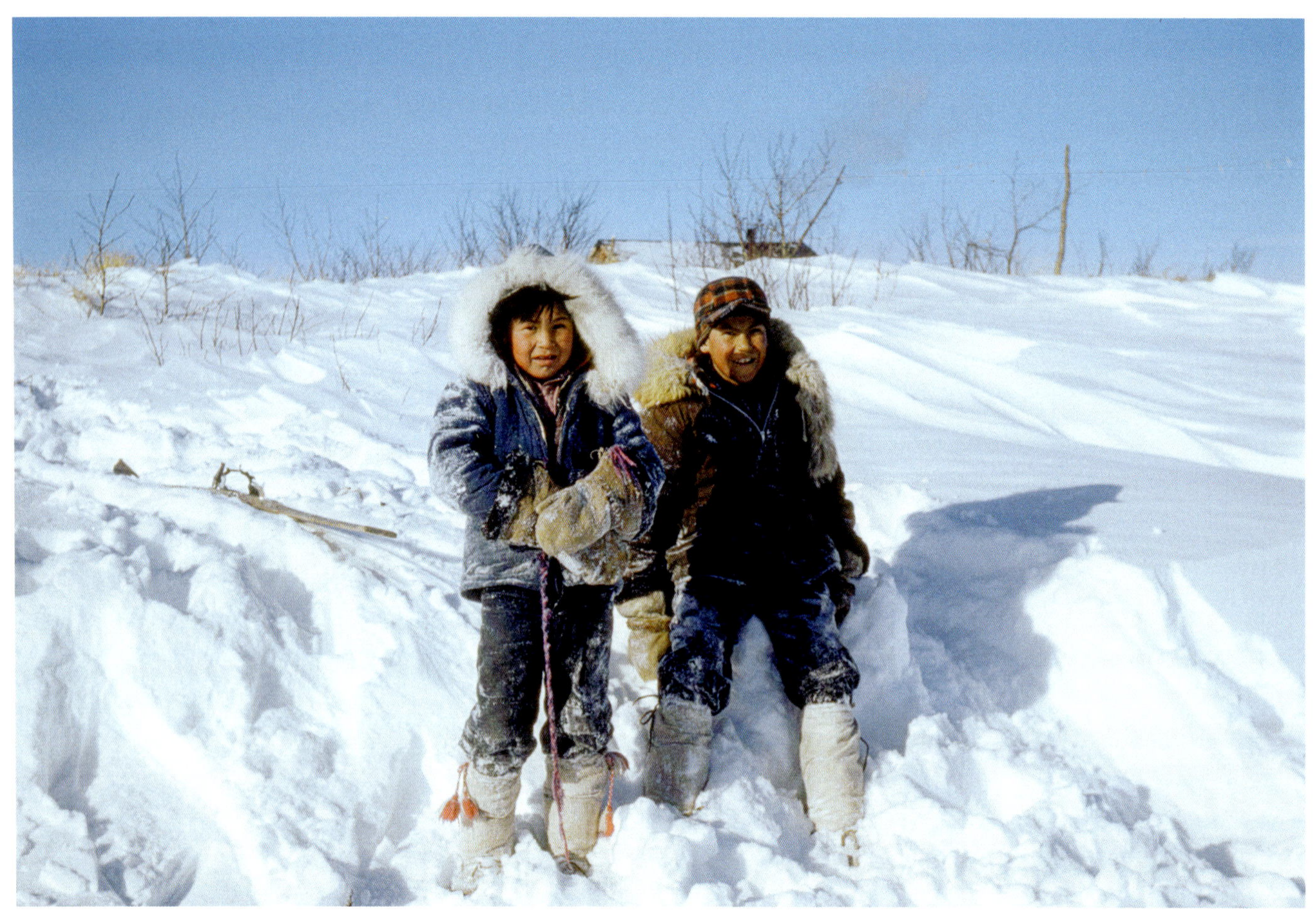

Two boys at Weenusk February 21, 1955

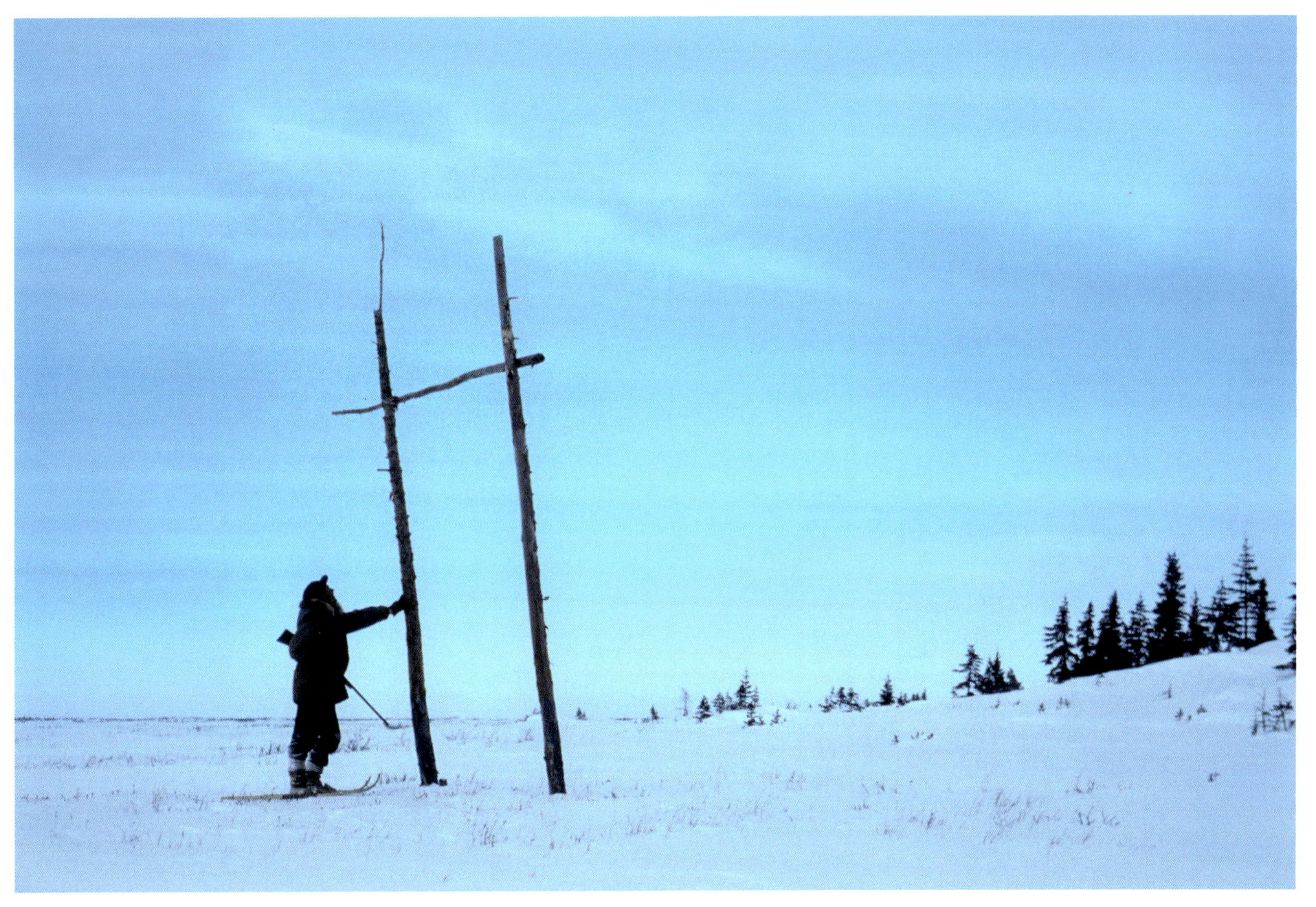

John Macfie hunting ptarmigan at the treeline near the mouth of the Winisk River, Kenora District c. 1955

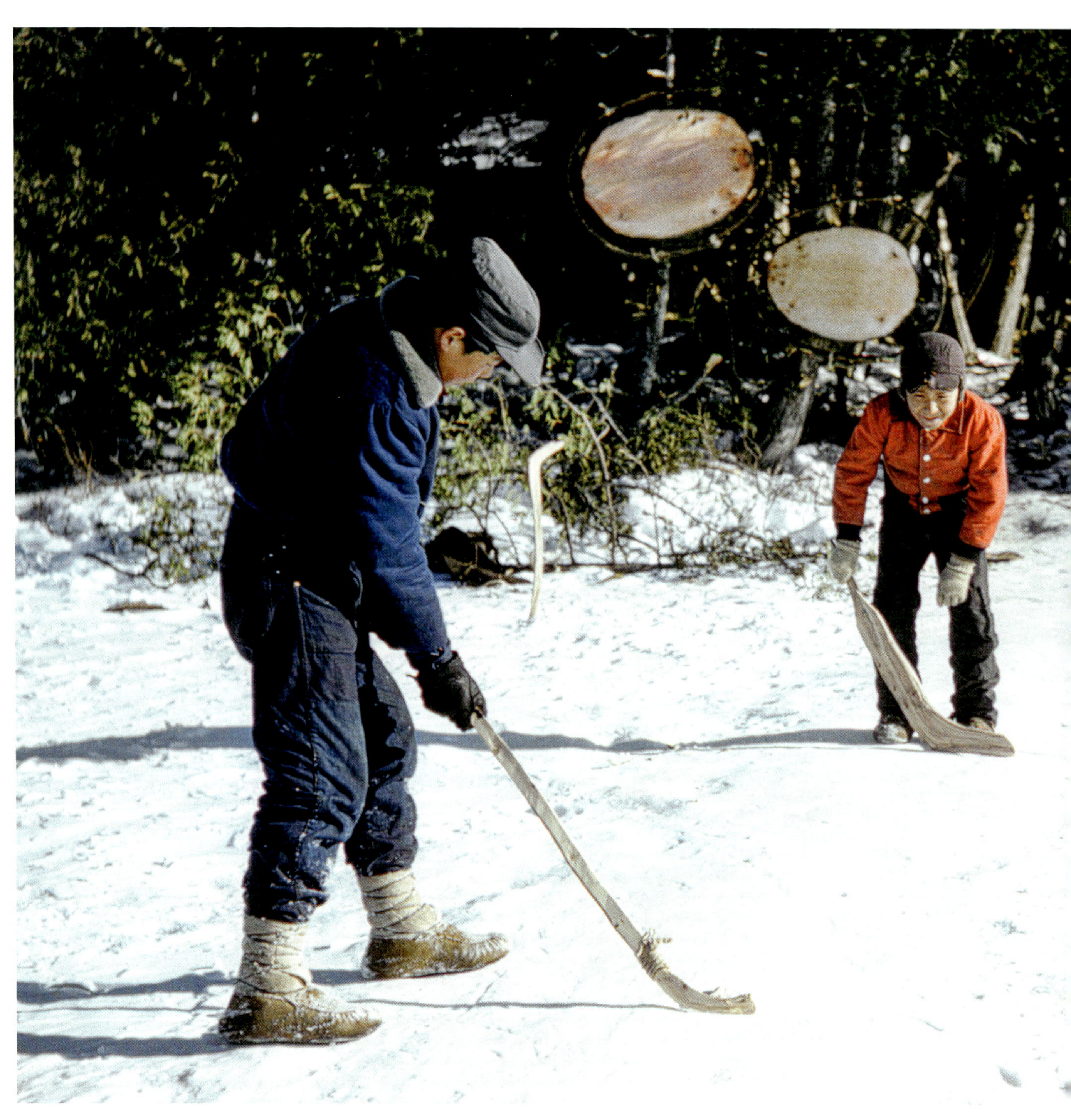

Charlie and Norman Echum from Moose Factory playing hockey with homemade sticks; beaver pelts in the background 1959

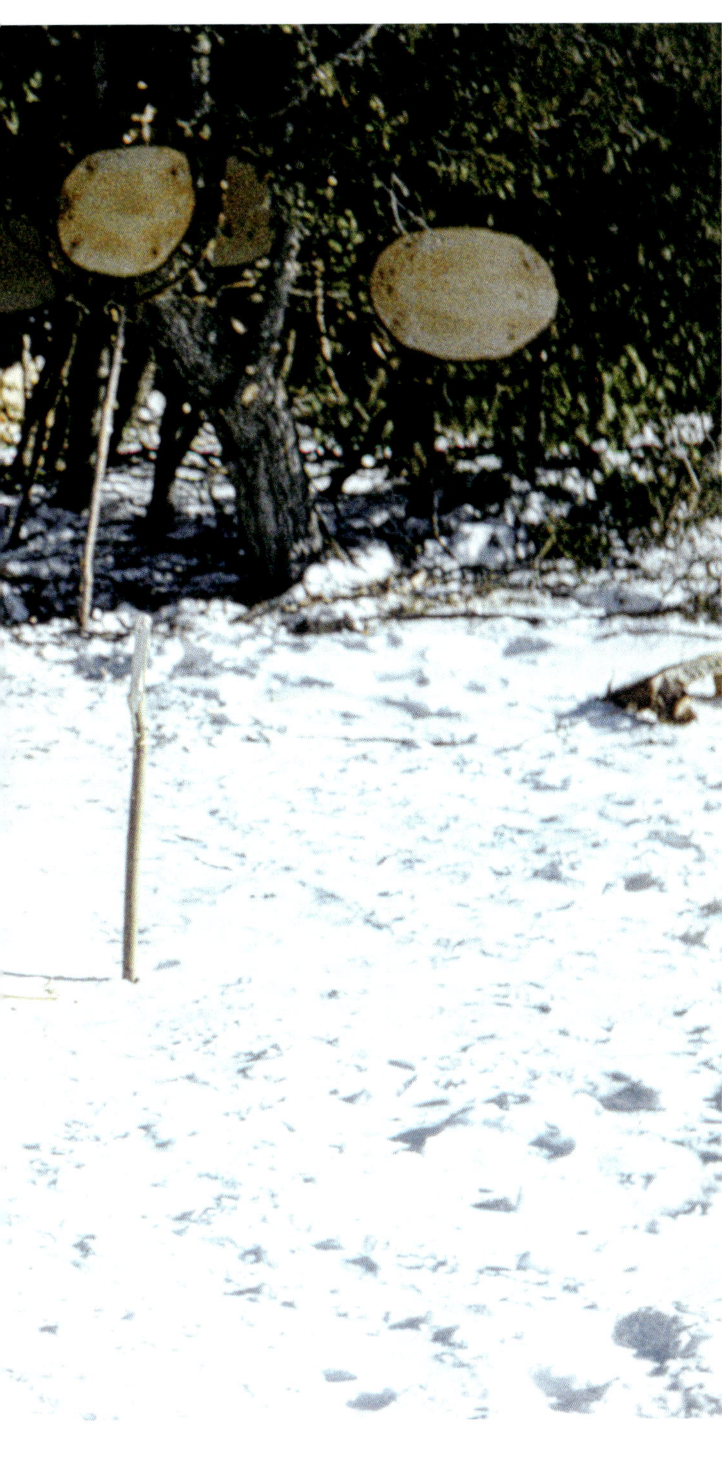

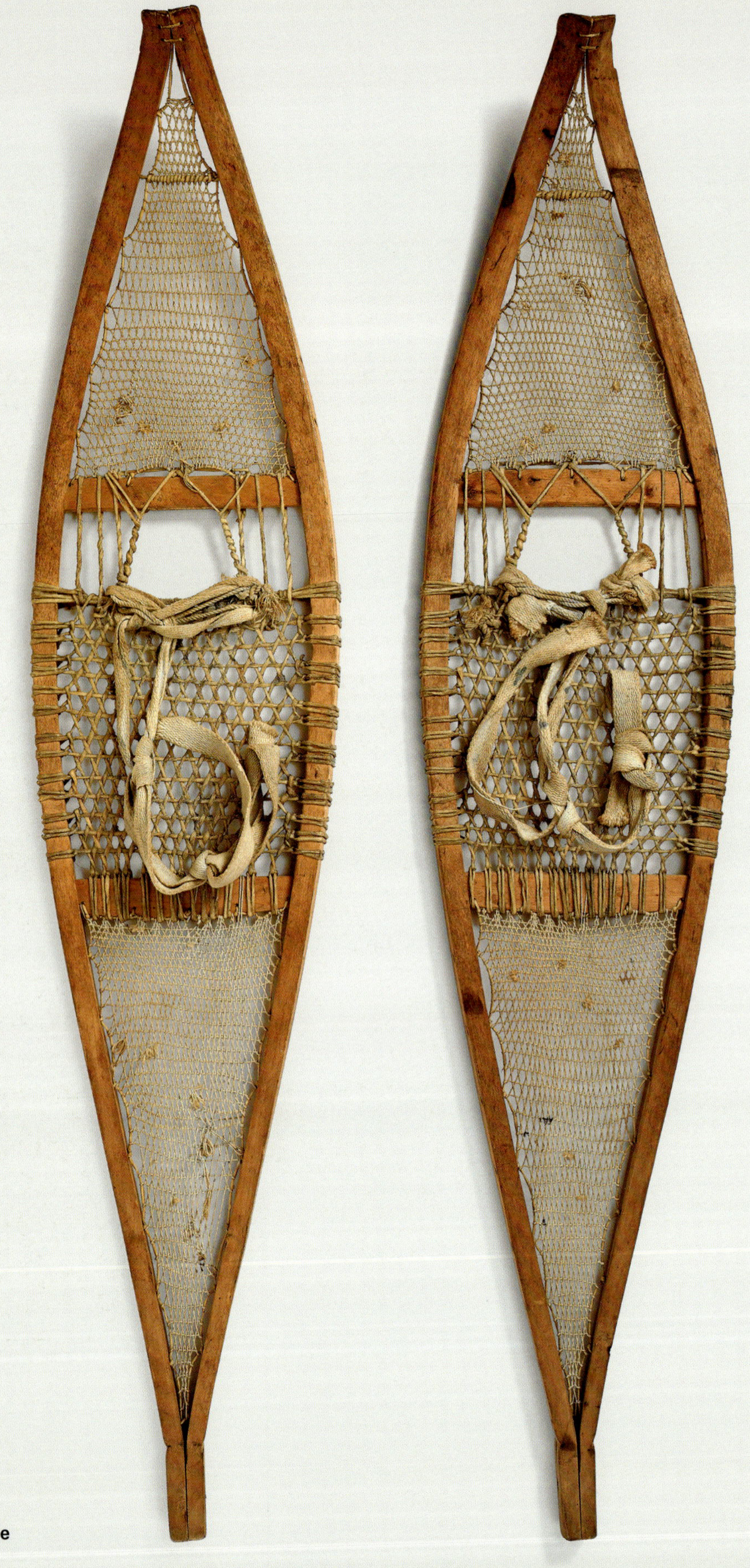

**Snowshoes,
collected by John Macfie**

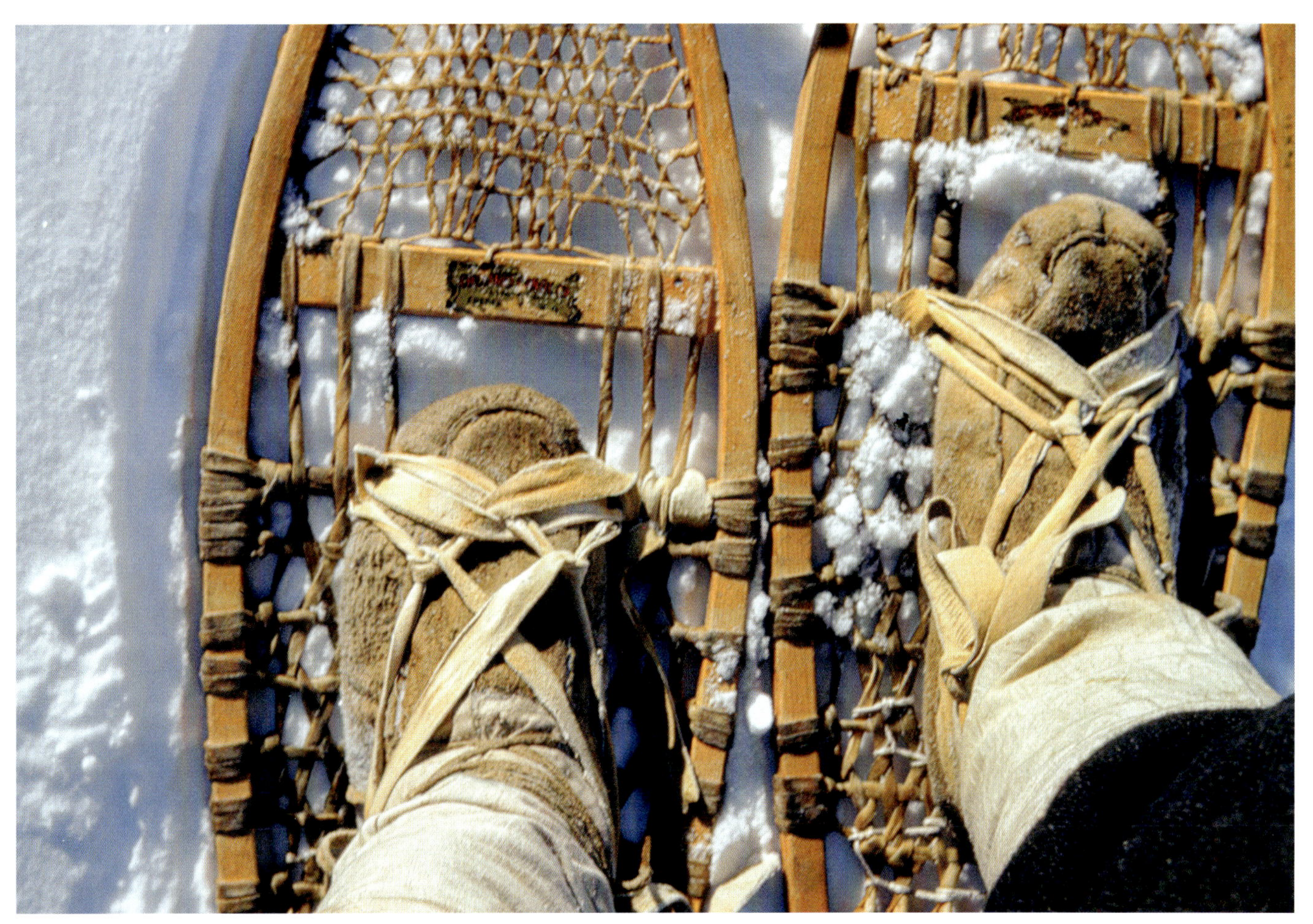

John Macfie wearing lampwick snowshoes bindings on the trail c.1951

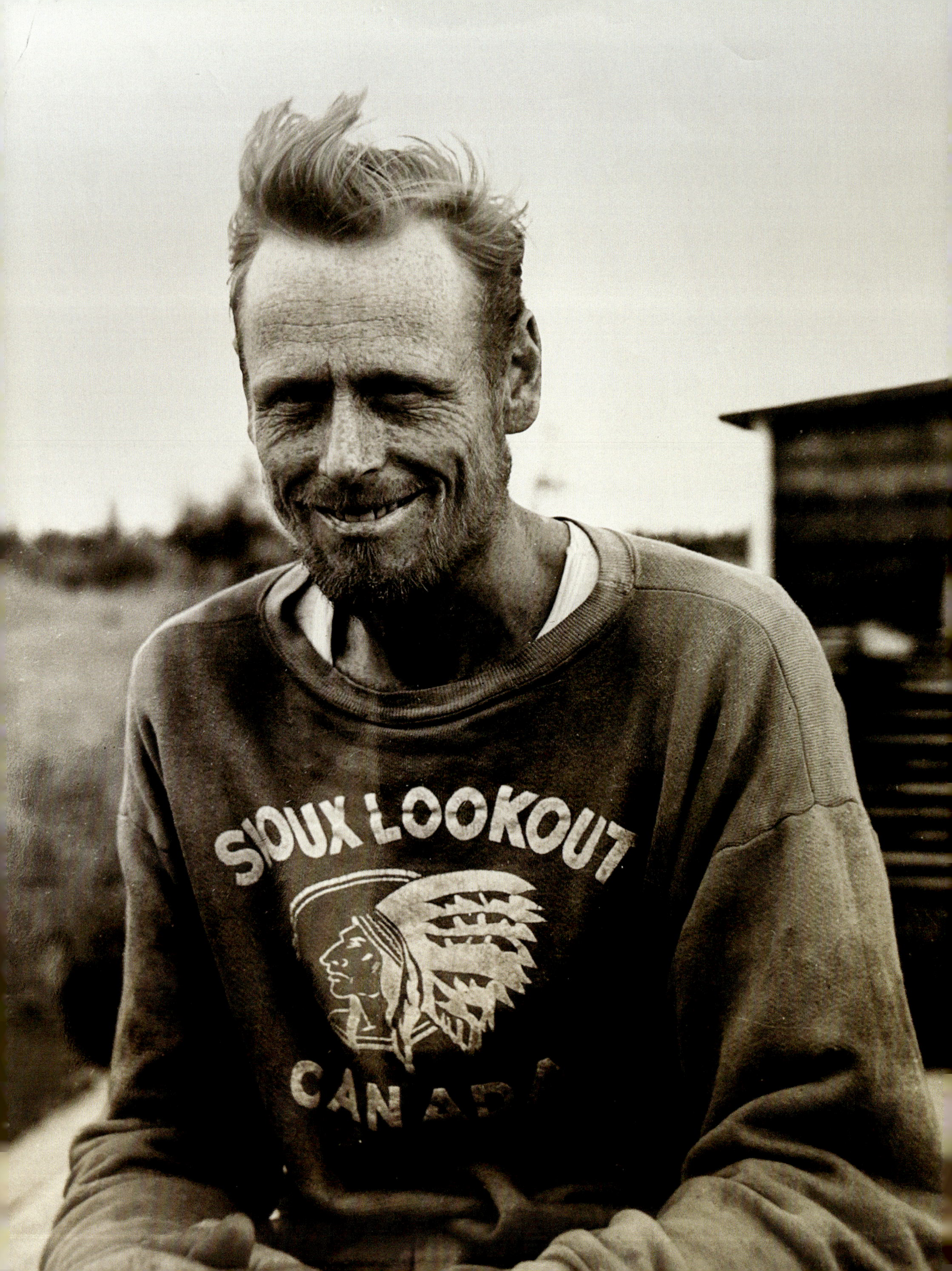
SIOUX LOOKOUT

Macfie's Field Notes on Language

John Macfie on a canoe trip from Big Trout Lake to Fort Severn summer 1952

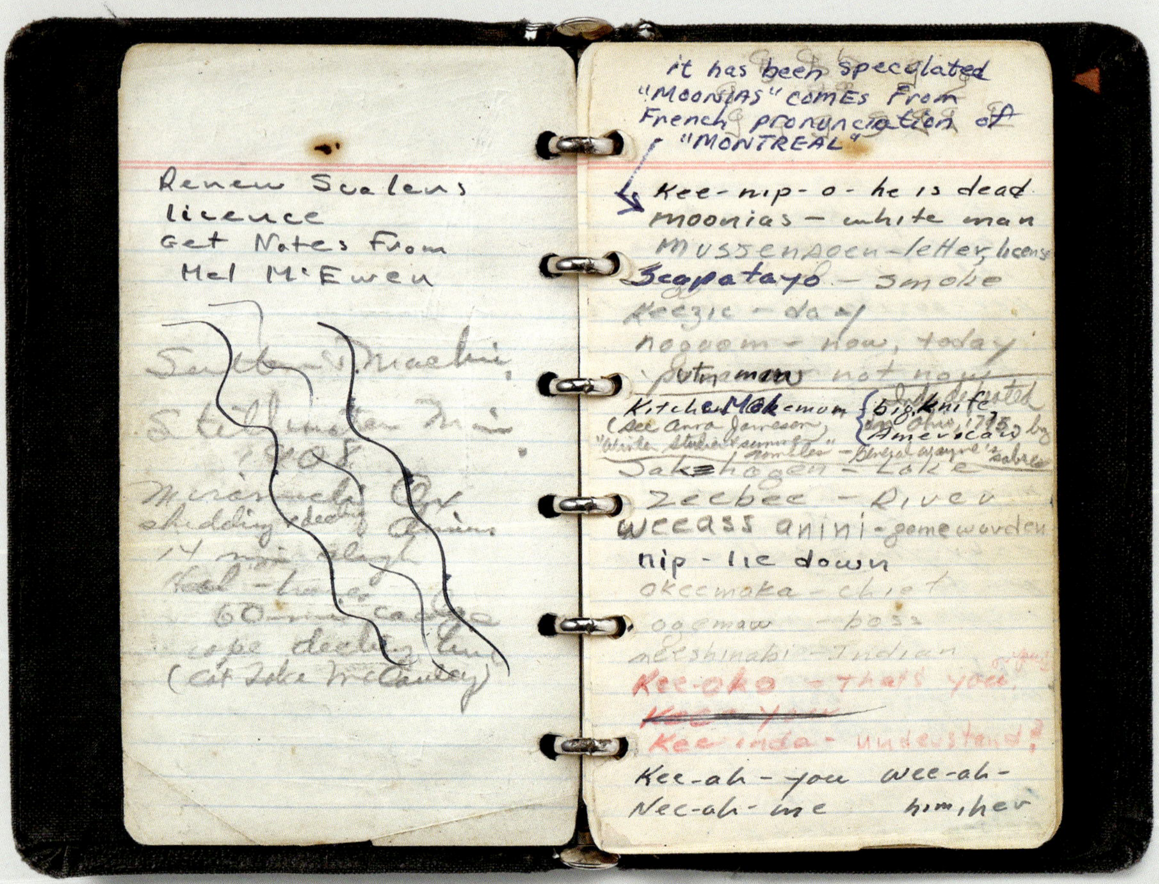

Renew Scalers
licence
Get Notes from
Mel M'Ewen

it has been specqlated
"MOONIAS" COMES From
French pronunciation of
"MONTREAL"

Kee-nip-o - he is dead
moonias - white man
Mussenaoeu - letter, license
Scopatayo - smoke
Keezic - day
noogom - now, today
Kitchemokemon - big knife
Sakahogen - Lake
Zeebee - River
Weeass anini - game warden
nip - lie down
okeemoka - chief
ogemaw - boss
neeshinabi - Indian
Kee-oko - that's you
Kee-inda - understand?
Kee-ah - you
Nee-ah - me
Wee-ah - him, her

Jah-say Kee-oositow - have you already done it, made it out?
Kee-oositow - made it out
Sesay - already
Mish - no
Ah-ha - yes
Mah-scooks - perhaps
megan-tagan - for
esky - map. add musenagen for
megan-tagen musenagen - for return
ahki musinagen - map
Man-napayo boy - Napasis
Woman - iskwayoo girl - iskwaysis
Kamistinow - aircraft
Pagwa - Shallow
Kee-kyoh - deep

Kimowin - rain
weesna - to eat
Wanagee - trap
" musenagen - trap license
Kee Wanagee - are you trapping, etc.
Scooty - fire
Wappo - a liquid form, juice
Scooty-woppo - liquor
Nippy - water
Putaweea - Make a fire
Nistva - friend
Nichis
Musenagen Attik - pencil
Abita - half
" Wabick - half dollar
Abita-Keezic - half day
Payzickwun - the same, alike
Arkiss - he is sick
Kiwi - go home - get out
Annini - person

Animals

Beaver - Ahmik
Muskrat - Wachusk
Mink - Jangwaysee
Otter - Nigkik
Weasel - Seekoosay
Red Fox - Sa-Wagoose (Shona - silver)
Squirrel - Atchitimo
Marten - Wabistan (Wabushesh)
Fisher - Ocheek
Lynx - Pishu
Wolf - Maihegan
Wolverine - Keekwahawgay
Crow - Caw-Cog
Whiskey Jack - Queguish
Mouse - Puksees, Wabagoseese
Bear - Muckwah, Abear - Wabusk
duck - Shee-sheep
goose - whey-whey, Nisko
skunk - Shikak
Grebe - Shingepis
Loon - Mank

cow - Mistoose
white whale - Wab'amik
seal - Ah'kik
FIREFLY - Wah-wah-taysee
(Wahwuh'tay is aurora borealis; "see" is diminutive, so must mean "little Aurora Borealis")
raccoon - ásebon

Nest - Wuchi'stoon
Eagle - Mik'isew
Plate - Wan-ai-gan
Fish - Kin'-amo-shjay
Ptarmigan - Waba-seh
Spruce hen - Chigoubani
Sharp-tail - Agask
White Owl - Wapagáno
Bobcat - Peezcheese
Whitefish - ~~Nemeigo~~ Atikameig
Trout - Nemeigo
Pike - Jawbish (Jackfish?)
Pickerel - Oh'kass
Bedroll - Nip-ah'gan
Shotgun Shells - Seeseep Assini
Raining - Kin'ewin
Snowing - Soap-ah-koon
Lard - Pimitei
Butter - Choo-choo-Shobaw Pimitei
Motor Oil - Apagamin'igam
Lightning - Pah-ginnay
Thunder - Pin-ei-si
Flies, Moskitos - Sug'ah-may
Grass - Muskooshi
Strong - Mus'kowa
Black - Muk'a-tai

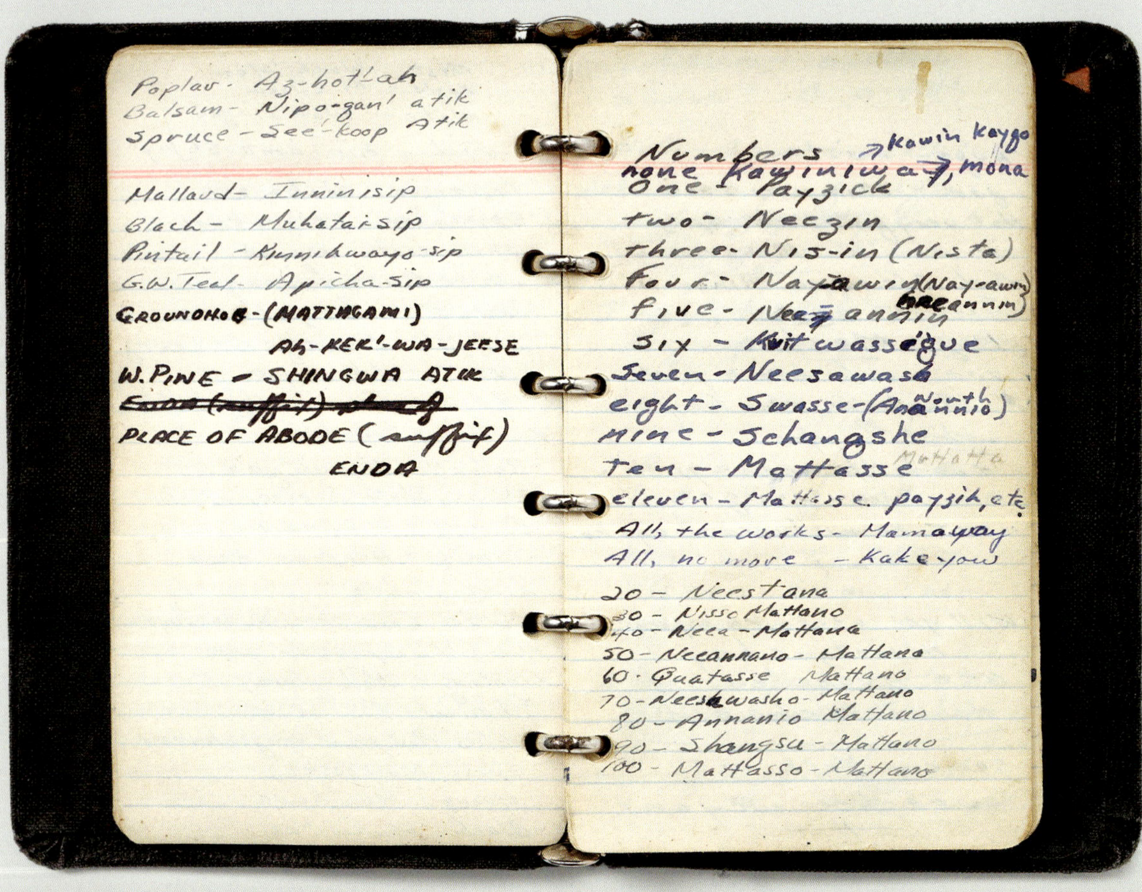

huge - mista
good - Minawssin
Not very good - Kawin Apitz
Minawssin
Bad Nemona Minawssin
Small - ABESHEESE
Big - Mashow
too much money - etc
Sam - mista - hayo
machine ↗ +
too little money, etc
Sam - pungee
out - kamish - na - hayako
+
Will you accompany me.
nemotz - chey
kee - guskentan
ta wee chahin

come & help me.
taweechee weyan
+

where - anday
when - a-nippi
Hello - B'jou - wachi
where are you going?
~~Anday gee shyne~~
(where)
anday - gee - shjyne
+
(see)
I want to talk to you -
Meguap - a - mow ~~keeea~~
#
Where will you see us? -
And-ay - aye - se - noo keeguap - a - ma
#
stove - ta - agamik
Mission - Emmy - how agemik
When are you going? -
(when)
a-nippi - kee - machow
Sam Keeguapamow? - did you see Sam?

kinistota - do you understand?
+
I don't understand Cree
Kawin Neehiow
kinistota

Say again -
Tah-nitwin - Ojibway
+ Koy-gwan Cree
Pungee - a little
+
Kawin Apitz - not much
+
Kawin - no (not definite)
~~Kamish~~ - (not right now)
Putnamow (panama)
A-nippi meenawow
kee tucksin -
when are you coming back.
Kotuck peesim - another month
" kesickow (next day)
" ~~Spyah week~~

another week -
Payzick - emmy - how
kesickow, (one more Sunday)
+
after church -
chistua - emmy - how
+
Kamish nee Kinda -
I don't know
+
Pigeenuck meenawow tucksin - coming back later
Akee muscuagenkee tappahan - did you pay your license
Ahkee muscuagen map

Kee mussenagen andyan
~~whats~~ have you your license

an-dyan - I have some.

Ne guapmau - I want to see it

Kee musenagen sasay? Kee tipahan
have you already paid for your licence

Kamish nee tipahan
I didn't pay.

Nokum kee Tipihan

Will you pay now? (today)

Ah-nay sagassinkee-ah
what is your name?

Kamish, Putnamow
no, not now.
+
Kootuck Aweea
~~Somebody (else)~~ another man
Wee-Wanagee nee miskinow
+
is trapping on my line
+
Kee kinda aweea?
do you know who?
+
Mokatz kee guapamow? -
did you never see him? +
Wee miskinow opukko neguapamow -
I only see his trail

{Antossin T.L.
{tanda-too-keesichan hours.
how many days?

Napayo - man
Chigamow (chigwa)
Sure, that's right.
Seekoop
Asipokop - spruce
Keeshany - crazy
Peezjou - come here
Minawsin - it is good
Ah-koo yasamow -
he speaks English
Puh-pon - winter
Sekwun - spring
Sekwun o'k - last spring
Pashisikun - gun
Katoochikan - musical instrument
Ah-moo Sookah - honey
Kee-mah - canoe
Mee-kum - ice
Keeabich - remaining
horse {Kitche animoos
{Mista-tim

Pa-kwayzikan, - bannock, flour
choo-choo Shabow - milk
Kookoos amisquay - chocolate
amisquay - blood

Mile - Tipahigan
Canoe - Cheemah
Sun - Pesim
Rapids - Pawistik
Night, evening - Tipiskow
Here, this place - Omu
and - Meena, menu
Don't laugh - Kow-ya kee pahpoo
Portage - Nigum
Stove - Squitakan, Keesabu-kisikan
Axe - Wagakwit
Pipe - Pwagin
Cigarette - Semesse
Tobacco - See-mah
Tomorrow - Wabunk
Girl Isquaysis
boy Napaysis
it is cold - Ki-sinna
Have Tea - Minnikwei
Eat a meal - Wees-nah
Food - Mee'jum

Police, soldier –
Shamagannis
Plenty, (Ojibway) Neebiow
Did you kill a moose? –
Moose kee kin'isaw
Fur – Wuh'ty (Cree)
Megan-tagen (Ojibway)
Thats all, complete – Minacey
your child – keegoósis
when { Tanspay
Ah'nippi
How many do you think? –
Tandatoo kee teedatéin
one O'clock –
Poygik Ishisghoyt

NORTH – KEEWAYTINUNG
EAST – WABUNDUNG
SOUTH – SHAWUNUNG
WEST – KAH'-PE-AN-UNG

Dancing Lodge (Sandy L.)
MATAKWAN

Careful – Pay'-gatch
Slow down – Pag-utch
10 gallons – Mettatta
minikwagin
outboard motor:- pim-pan-is-
gikum
Tide receding:- Kee-way'-
chewan
" Coming in:- Key-peechewan

Oatmeal – min-oh'-man
Hill:- wachi
Muskeg:- Paskwa (or shallow
marshy place?)
Clear water – Washagamu

Dog Driving:- Gee – huk
Haw – hayah
Go – hi
Stop – hoa
How old? – antasin pu-pon
Fish – Kenoshi
(also jackfish?)
Sp. Trout – mansemeigos
Shrew – Kay-cheway
(sharp-nosed) Wabegoseese

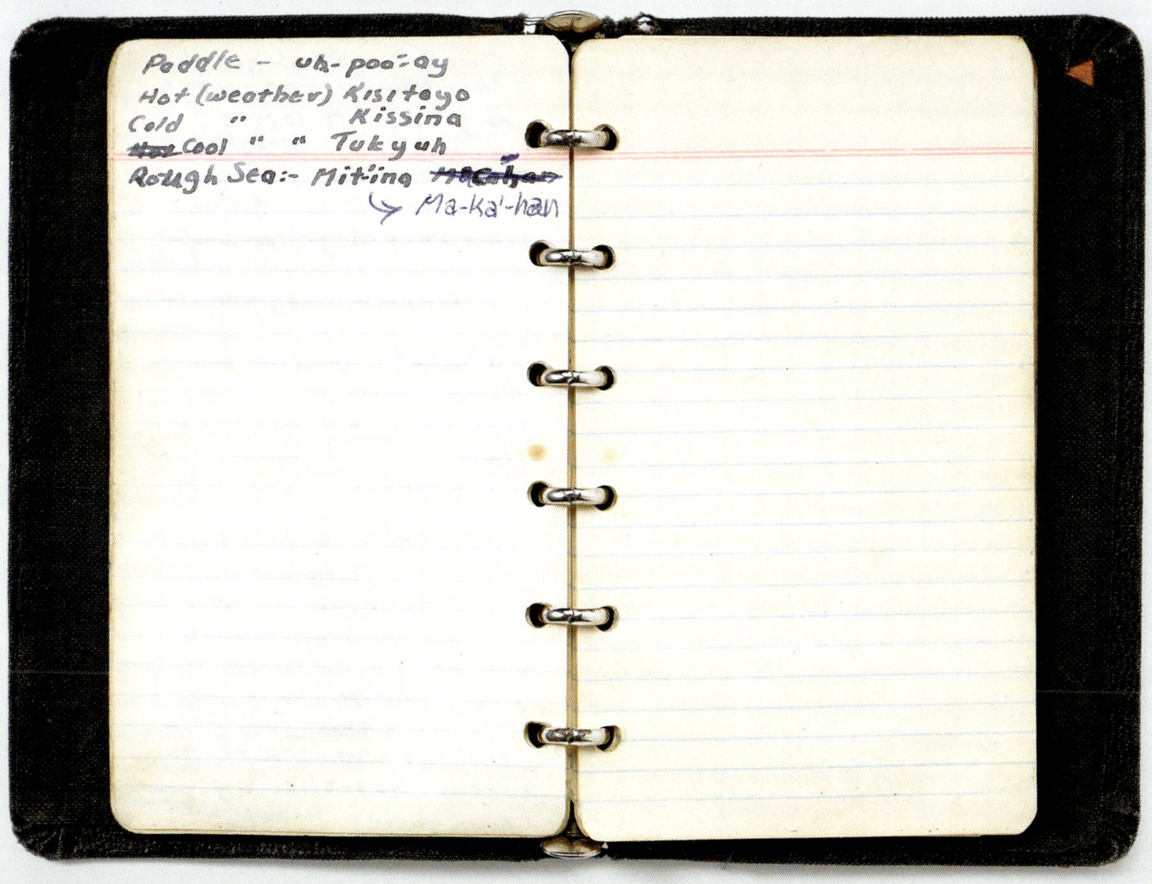

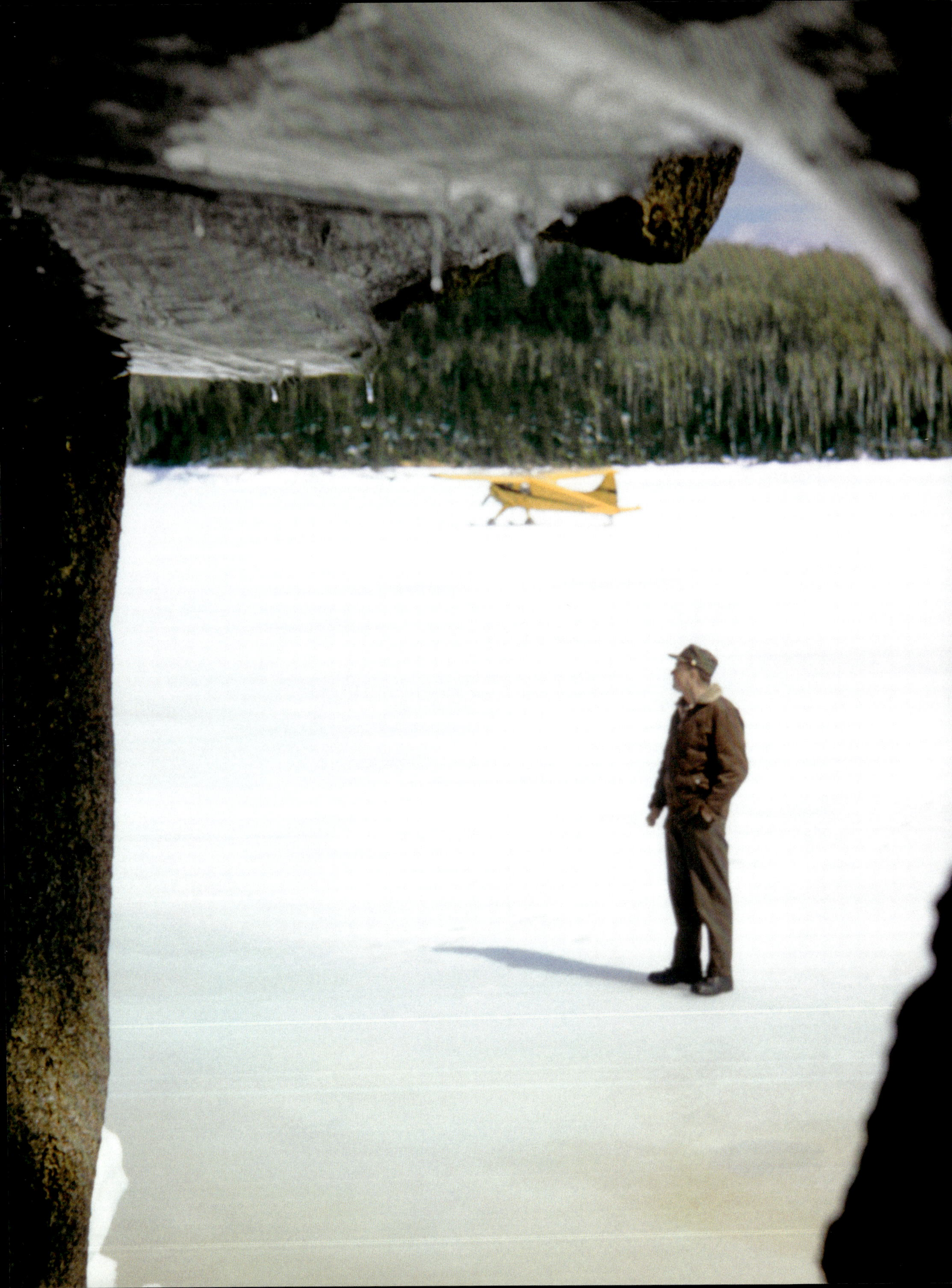

Figures

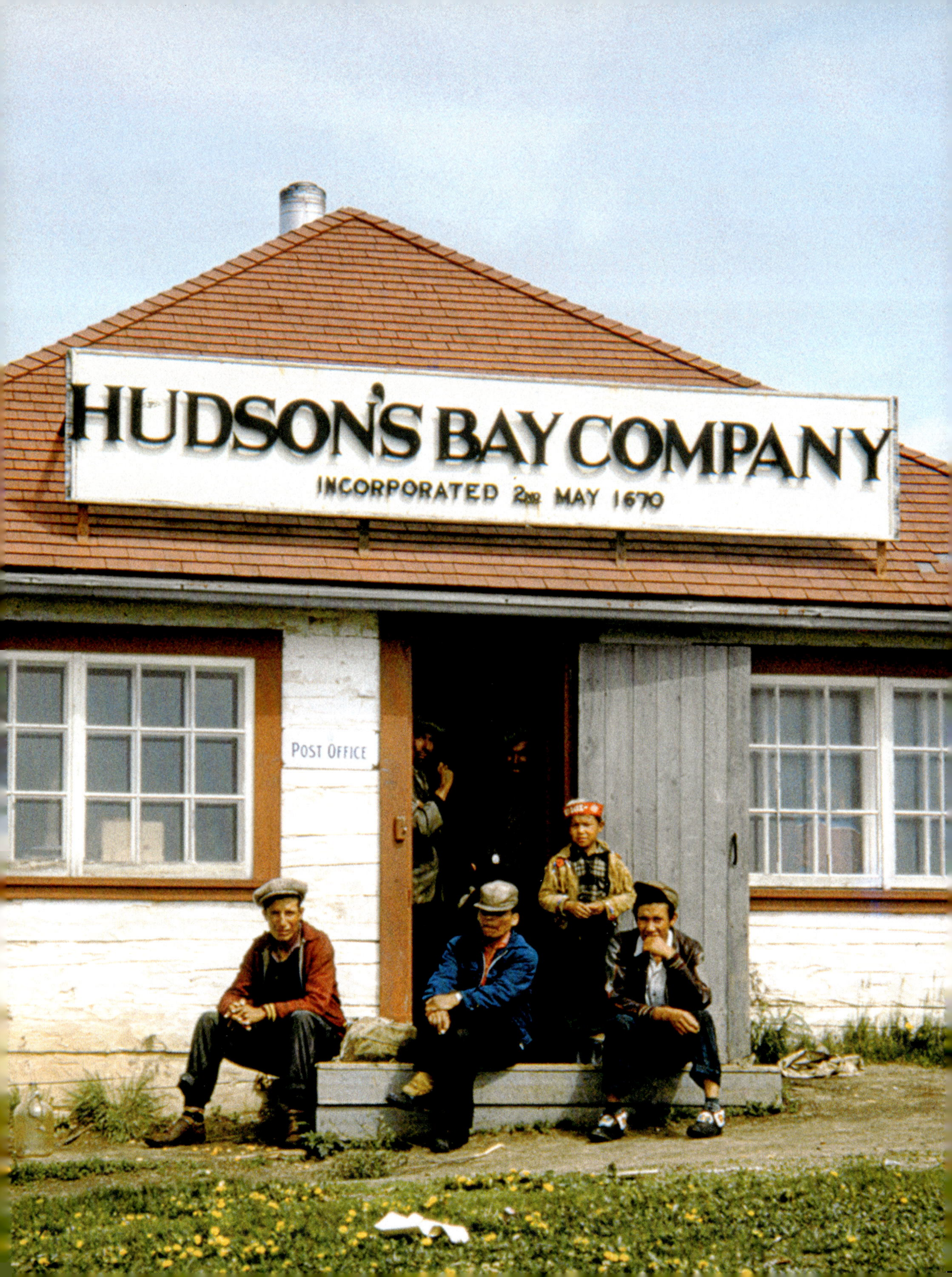
HUDSON'S BAY COMPANY
INCORPORATED 2ND MAY 1670
POST OFFICE

Acknowledgements

This publication honours the work of two great visionaries: the trap manager and photographer John Macfie, who—camera in hand—set out to document the Indigenous way of life and livelihood all across the Hudson Bay watershed during the middle decades of the twentieth century; and Paul Seesequasis, a leading curator and writer who has worked so hard in all his endeavours to honour the humanity of Indigenous people, and their life in community and on the land. We are pleased to support his good work here at the McMichael and thank as well the Macfie family for their support and help at every stage of this project.

So, too, that of our book designer Gilbert Li, who brought his sophisticated touch to this publication, keeping stride with us in solidarity as the book took on ever-greater dimensions. We salute him for his creativity, generosity, and flexibility. Likewise, the splendid gang at Figure 1 Publishing in Vancouver and Toronto (thank you, Chris Labonté and Steve Cameron), staunch allies in our mission to promote Canadian art. Thanks are due also to Doris Cowan, for her astute text editing, and to Paul Jerinkitsch, for his meticulous work on colour correction for the book.

In our own McMichael team, Associate Curator Indigenous Art and Culture Emily Henderson and Associate Curator Collections and Research John Geoghegan have served as invaluable sounding boards for Paul Seesequasis as this exhibition has taken shape, while Exhibitions and Publications Assistant Reid Macfarlane has gone above and beyond the call of duty, readying material from the Archives of Ontario for inclusion here. Our Publications Manager Teija Smith has overseen this book's production with her usual attention to detail, grace, and courtesy, while Curatorial Assistant Shi Qiu and Exhibitions Manager Nicole Dawkins have assisted with many aspects of exhibition preparation, including Shi's heroic cross-country expedition in a snowstorm to Parry Sound to retrieve Macfie's possessions, on display here (beautifully photographed for this publication by Craig Boyko). Meanwhile, the unflappable Eric Pearson continues to exert his masterful hand as we develop the design of our exhibitions, a sage adviser in all our efforts to make the most of our galleries.

Pulling the whole team together is our gifted and beloved Deputy Chief Curator Jennifer Withrow, without whom we would simply not be able to do the things we do. She makes it all possible.

Sarah Milroy
Executive Director and Chief Curator
McMichael Canadian Art Collection

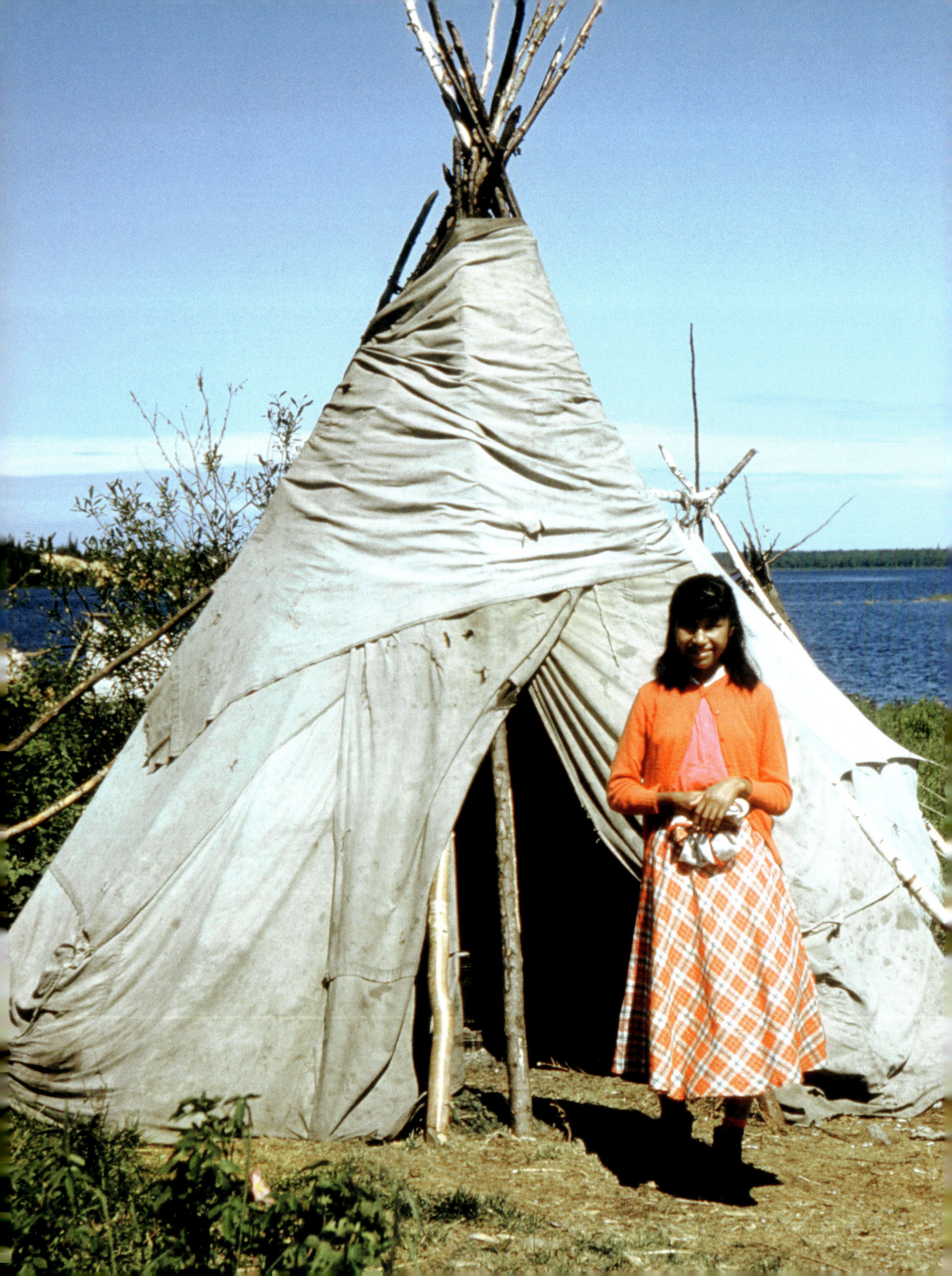

About the Author

Paul Seesequasis is a nîpisîhkopâwiyiniw (Willow Cree) curator and writer in Saskatoon, Saskatchewan. He has been active in the Indigenous arts as an artist and a policymaker since the 1990s, and since 2015 he has curated the Indigenous Archival Photo Project. He is the author of *Blanket Toss Under Midnight Sun: Portraits of Everyday Life in Eight Indigenous Communities* (2019).

About the Artist

John Macfie (1925–2018) was a photographer, local historian, and writer. In the 1950s and 1960s he was a trapline manager with the Department of Lands and Forests in Ontario. He later became a columnist for the Georgian Bay *Beacon* and the Parry Sound *North Star*. This is the first major exhibition of his photography.

Published on the occasion of the exhibition
People of the Watershed: Photographs by John Macfie
McMichael Canadian Art Collection, Kleinburg, Ontario
May 11–November 17, 2024

Curated by Paul Seesequasis

All photographs by John Macfie have been scanned from 35 × 24 mm Kodachrome slides, with the exception of the black-and-white photographs on pp. 8, 17, 52. The McMichael gratefully acknowledges the Archives of Ontario's stewardship of the John Macfie fonds (C 330).

Cataloguing in Publication data available from Library and Archives Canada.

ISBN 978-1-77327-260-3

EXECUTIVE EDITOR
Sarah Milroy

EDITOR
Doris Cowan

PROOFREADER
Alison Reid

PUBLICATION MANAGER
Teija Smith

PUBLICATION ASSISTANT
Reid Macfarlane

DESIGN
The Office of Gilbert Li

COLOUR AND RETOUCHING
Paul Jerinkitsch Imaging

Printed and bound in Canada by Friesens

Distributed internationally by Publishers Group West

Figure 1 Publishing Inc.
Vancouver BC Canada
www.figure1publishing.com

McMichael Canadian Art Collection
Kleinburg ON Canada
www.mcmichael.com

FRONT COVER
A family walking down the boardwalk at Neskantaga First Nation, Kenora District (detail), 1956

BACK COVER
Moses Koostachin and Father Gagnon travelling between Weenusk and Hawley Lake (detail), February 1955

Figure 1 Publishing is located in the traditional, unceded territory of the xʷməθkʷəy̓əm (Musqueam), Sḵwx̱wú7mesh (Squamish), and səlílwətaʔɬ (Tsleil-Waututh) peoples.

The McMichael Canadian Art Collection is located on lands occupied by the Huron-Wendat, the Anishinaabe, the Haudenosaunee, and other Indigenous people. It is uniquely situated along the Carrying Place Trail, which long provided an integral connection for Indigenous people between the north shore of Lake Ontario and the Lake Simcoe–Georgian Bay Region.